UNSETTLED BALANCE

UNSETTLED BALANCE
Ethics, Security, and Canada's International Relations

Edited by Rosalind Warner

UBCPress · Vancouver · Toronto

23 22 21 20 19 18 17 16 15   5 4 3 2 1

Printed in Canada on FSC-certified ancient-forest-free paper (100% post-consumer recycled) that is processed chlorine- and acid-free.

Library and Archives Canada Cataloguing in Publication

Unsettled balance : ethics, security, and Canada's international relations / edited by Rosalind Warner.

Includes bibliographical references and index.
Issued in print and electronic formats.
ISBN 978-0-7748-2865-9 (bound). – ISBN 978-0-7748-2866-6 (pbk.). – ISBN 978-0-7748-2867-3 (pdf). – ISBN 978-0-7748-2868-0 (epub)

   1. Canada – Foreign relations – Moral and ethical aspects.   2. National security – Moral and ethical aspects – Canada.   I. Warner, Rosalind, 1964-, author, editor

FC242.U85 2015   327.71   C2015-900362-8
                                                            C2015-900363-6

Canada

UBC Press gratefully acknowledges the financial support for our publishing program of the Government of Canada (through the Canada Book Fund), the Canada Council for the Arts, and the British Columbia Arts Council.

This book has been published with the help of a grant from the Canadian Federation for the Humanities and Social Sciences, through the Awards to Scholarly Publications Program, using funds provided by the Social Sciences and Humanities Research Council of Canada.

UBC Press
The University of British Columbia
2029 West Mall
Vancouver, BC V6T 1Z2
www.ubcpress.ca

Contents

Acknowledgments

In September 2001, UBC Press published the collected volume *Ethics and Security in Canadian Foreign Policy,* of which I was the editor. That volume had been prompted by the events of the 1990s, including the end of the Cold War, the rise of human security, and the consequent reformulation of Canada's place in the world.

The events of 9/11 accelerated the pace of world events, pushing action ahead of the international community's efforts to advance international humanitarian law, institutions for sustainable and equitable development, and norms for promoting respect for human rights and human dignity. As a result, the need to balance security questions with ethical considerations remains urgent. New security challenges from terrorism to climate change are posing ethical dilemmas that are not fully appreciated in the study of Canada's international relations. Persistent and pervasive injustices and inequalities among social groups, regions, genders, and classes continue to demand attention. Rapidly changing world events, including the wars in Afghanistan and Iraq, the economic meltdown of 2008, and the rising urgency of climate change have, as well, prompted the need for closer consideration of ethics and security.

The context for decision making has become fundamentally different. However, the perennial questions facing Canadian foreign and security policy remain. This book, *Unsettled Balance,* extends the discourse that began in the 1990s and carries it through to the present day. In the process, the book seeks to show that ethical arguments about rights, obligations, norms, and values have played a profound role in Canadian foreign policy and international relations, from debates on the "responsibility to protect" as a norm and a practice to the militarization of humanitarian aid.

I owe many people a debt of thanks for their support in the genesis of this project. I had the great pleasure to work with an outstanding group of contributors who demonstrated their commitment and passion for the project at all the stages of development. This work has also been influenced by great contributions to the field by Lloyd Axworthy, William Bain, Duane Bratt, Andrew Cooper, Ann Denholm Crosby, David Dewitt, Tom Keating, Nelson Michaud, Kim Richard Nossal, Cranford Pratt, Claire Turenne Sjolander, Heather Smith, Denis Stairs, and Wesley Wark.

The book has benefitted immensely from the feedback provided by anonymous reviewers. In addition, J. Marshall Beier, Hevina Dashwood, Chris Kukucha, and Mark Neufeld offered suggestions and ideas that have helped to develop the book. Special thanks to David V.J. Bell and David Leyton-Brown.

My colleagues at Okanagan College have been instrumental in helping to complete this work. In particular, Eve Avis, Linda Elmose, Robert Huxtable, Ayla Kilic, Karen Markle, Craig McLuckie, Eileen Plementos, Mary Staudinger, and the members of OC's Professional Development Committee and Grants-in-Aid committee have been tremendously supportive. In addition, Maria Marsh and Alex Elwood provided research assistance. Thanks go as well to my students, without whom this work would not have been possible.

Among the many people who have enthusiastically contributed to the book's development have been Lesley Erickson, Dallas Harrison, and the always supportive and helpful Emily Andrew. My appreciation and love go out to Paul Warner, Justin Jacob Warner, Michael Irwin, Oscar Irwin, and Sharon and Tony Disanto. This book is dedicated to my mom, Djubaidah Ellen Jean Irwin.

UNSETTLED BALANCE

Ethics and Security
New Issues and Contexts for Decision Making

ROSALIND WARNER

This book was prompted by a wave of international changes over the last few years that have profoundly influenced Canada's international relations. The wars on terror, economic crises, climate change, and humanitarian emergencies have challenged decision makers to think clearly about the ethics of ensuring security. The force of events has pushed decision makers in unexpected, sometimes even unimaginable, directions. This book is an effort to make sense of these changing circumstances by applying the analytical lens of ethics and security to Canada's international relations. It looks back to the debates of the 1990s and carries the discourse forward in entirely new ways suited to the present state of flux.

The literature on Canadian foreign policy often describes a broad opposition between ethics and security. This book takes a somewhat contrary view, arguing that the two are closely linked. Within the literature on Canada's international relations and foreign policy, these concepts have been given a variety of treatments. Ethics have been discussed in terms of values (Geislerova 2001; Lee 2002; Michaud 2011); moral vision (Pratt 2001); norms (Howard and Neufeldt 2011; Knight 2001); and even myths, mirages, or brands (Turenne-Sjolander and Trevenen 2011). Opinions on the role of ethics in foreign policy decision making have been celebratory, critical, and even dismissive. Nevertheless, clear thinking on the ethics-security nexus remains necessary and vital, given its importance. In contradistinction to some views, this book begins with the observation that ethics and security

are intimately linked in processes of decision making. This is because policies are not made in an ethical vacuum; rather, decisions in a democracy
call for elaboration and justification. Human relationships are necessarily
developed within an ethical soup of interpretation, judgment, and expectation. Analysts are tasked with the job of making sense of these contexts.
To this end, the following book presents three general reasons for adopting an ethics-security lens on Canada's international relations: the need for
attention to the scope of ethics, the need for multilevel approaches, and the
necessity of addressing the purposes of decision making.

First, the scope of ethics impinges on decision making. Some analysts
and decision makers, steeped in the academic paradigm of realism, might
argue that only considerations of national interest should be used to determine or study policy, with minimal or no reference to ethics. Others argue
that ethics are unavoidable, and largely implicit, elements of decision making (Smith and Light 2001). Another approach asks not whether there are
"more" or "less" ethics in a given decision but how means, ends, and relationships are determined through the process of decision making. Given
a particular decision, are the ethics coherent and comprehensible? Whose
ethics are represented? In some ways, framing the question as an "either-or"
proposition sheds little light on the matter. Framing the question in more
complex ways recognizes that ethics might be circumscribed by events and
capacities but also takes account of the implicit, interpretive, and constitutive nature of human interactions.[1]

Canada's scope for action is sometimes viewed as circumscribed by its
size and structural position relative to other actors. As analysts have asked,
what capacity does Canada have to effect change, and what ability does it
have to respond effectively to shifts in circumstances (Hawes 1984; Molot
1990, 77; Stairs 1994, 13–15)? At times, Canada has surprised analysts by
expanding its influence, revealing that the country's "range of motion" for
acting in the world has been wider than anticipated. At other times, it has
seemed that ethical action has been heavily limited by international constraints. In addition, there have been times when Canada's stance on human
rights, the environment, equity, and democracy, for example, has been
received more favourably than at other times. There have also been times
when Canada has appeared more circumspect in the face of perceived "crusading" by the United States. Canada has variously been both a decision
maker and a decision *taker*. Ethical considerations are at the heart of expla-
nations for these varying stances. For example, it is difficult to explain how
and why Canada was able to advance the acceptance of the International

Criminal Court without referring to evolving international and domestic norms, the values of human rights, changing notions of impunity, and the principle of the rule of law (Knight 2001 and this volume). A focus on ethics can inform an analysis of how and why Canada has apparently been able to "climb out" of limiting circumstances and move the international community in new, different directions. Canada can take advantage of opportunities where they arise and choose to accept or reject limitations on the scope of ethical behaviour. Ethical arguments and considerations have consequential impacts on Canada's identity, capability, and positioning (see, e.g., Wendt 1992).

A parallel, though less prominent, debate in the literature concerns to what degree policy should (or can) reflect values per se (Lee 2002). In this debate, values are sometimes framed in an instrumental fashion as a kind of *lever* exercised through the use of soft power (Michaud 2011, 435). Following Michaud, one might explore values in terms of their properties: are they elite focused, public, longer term or shorter term, core or peripheral, et cetera? However, such a description of values and their role should be distinguished from an exploration of the *ethics* of decision making. Explaining and labelling the values at work in a given decision can provide a better understanding of the context for decisions. However, the ethical questions that swirl around so-called Canadian values arise not from their explanatory power but from their essential incompatibility. For example, Michaud (2011, 436) suggests that Canadians value human rights and diversity as a goal of foreign policy. They also value, he argues, the rule of law and international consensus over "the rule of power" (437). What is one to make of decisions that put these values in conflict? An ethical analysis requires the scholar to inquire into the essential dilemmas of choosing one priority over another. Evaluating the ethics of decisions is therefore both an empirical process and a normative process. Although there is often a broad conflict between national capabilities and ethical actions (between what *can* be done and what *should* be done), analysts should avoid a kind of essentialism that reduces genuine ethical dilemmas to a predetermined conflict between idealism on the one hand and realism on the other.

Questions of capability are relevant to an ethical analysis. Decision makers must be pragmatic and prudent as well as "good." However, this is not the same as saying that ethics should be excluded from consideration (Smith and Light 2001, 1–2) or that they have no relevance. Describing the relationship between ethics and security as a "balance" suggests that managing the poles of ethics and security involves making trade-offs and confronting "win or lose" dilemmas. This can oversimplify and lead to overgeneralization (see Wark 2006, 1). However, seeing ethics in terms of trade-offs can also reveal much about the dilemmas facing decision makers. The framing of security in one way or another, the identification of one threat or another, activates a particular set of ethical considerations that apply to that circumstance. Security can be defined narrowly and lead to a focus within the field of action on specific concerns and issues. However, this can also bind actors into set patterns of decision making that risk neglecting threats and vulnerabilities that emerge from outside this field of action. Focusing on one set of problems might allow other threats to develop. A lack of imagination can lead to rigidities and inflexibilities in policy that violate the call for prudence. At the same time, pursuing one priority over another can also lead to more ethical questions concerning focus (see Black and Tiessen, this volume). Invoking a wider scope for ethical decision making allows for a more flexible response. Yet a wider scope can mean that priorities are spread too thinly and purposes become muddied, sacrificing ethical coherence. The presuppositions, and their ethical variants, that inform decision making have consequences for the scope of action and the ability to address problems as they arise. In sum, ethical considerations have an important impact on Canada's capabilities, the assessment of values, and the calculation of threats. An analysis of the scope for ethical action involves taking the linkage between ethics and security seriously.

A second important reason for using an ethics-security lens on Canada's international relations is the necessity of managing governance at multiple levels. This remains an enduring analytical, ethical, and practical problem. The borders between domestic and international spheres of governance are porous, with lines of demarcation that are heavily contested. This is apparent in the emergence of new vocal actors, networks of intergovernmental agreements, and shifting international norms. Transnational advocacy networks now operate globally and are increasingly visible, articulating new norms and challenging states to respect established norms and laws (Keck and Sikkink 1998). With the growth of global civil society actors, the number of voices (if not the votes) that confront governments has grown exponentially. The intervention of more actors raises ethical questions about the standing of groups, their legitimacy in representing various populations, and their ability to impact events. These interventions (and sometimes partnerships) invite questions of whom and what interests are legitimately represented in decision making. If civil society actors claim to hold states to "higher" ethical standards than those of the national interest, then it remains to be answered which causes and ethical projects will be taken up (Glasius 2009, 161). People and governments are affected by agenda priorities in various ways. Managing political issues of representation and legitimacy at multiple levels remains an ongoing challenge for decision making, one in which ethics occupy an increasingly prominent place because of the potential for self-defeating actions and cross-purposes.

States find themselves enmeshed in multiple transgovernmental relationships requiring management and monitoring in which the traditional state imperatives and functions are increasingly outmoded. The pursuit of national security means addressing a foundation of cross-cutting international rules, laws, institutions, and norms (Wendt 1992). States are confronted with new vulnerabilities such as fiscal crises and environmental threats, which the infrastructure of defence and national security is ill equipped to solve. Evolving new threats are not well addressed by a conservative, inward-focused, state-based system because these threats often emerge from the networked relationships that states themselves construct. Identifying risks, addressing threats, making priorities, and responding effectively involve a mix of ethical and practical judgments that cuts across the domestic and the international. Addressing these complexities need not mean a diminishment of sovereignty but can mean a realignment of sovereignty (see Knight, Stoett, this volume). The emergence, advocacy, and acceptance of the responsibility to protect (R2P) norm constitute one example of the effort to reconcile new humanitarian intervention norms with state sovereignty norms (see Knight, this volume). The system increasingly involves trade-offs among domestic demands, national imperatives, and evolving and sometimes conflicting norms and ethics of international stability and security.

A third reason for examining ethics and security arises from the need to consider the purposes of policy decision making. A wider scope and more complex layers of decision making can imply greater selectivity among priorities. Selectivity in turn implies some criteria for determining the relative value of different goals and purposes. Even when made up of specific decisions, policies must attract some degree of coherence and "fit." If Canada is to have an impact on the world, then action cannot be purely reactive or reflexive but must involve some degree of rationalization, explanation, and planning for the longer term. What degree of coherence can reasonably be expected is an open question given the nature of world events. Yet by no means is there agreement about how decisions are actually made. Theories that expound the notion of a unified rational actor, organizational or bureaucratic processes, or ideational factors abound (see Allison 1971; Jervis 1968; Waltz 2001). Nevertheless, when the view from inside the country and the view from outside the country are starkly at odds, or when past and present policy stances depart from each other too much, it is more difficult to sustain an effective national purpose. Ethical coherence is important, however, for more than just the sake of appearance. For example, Canada might claim to be *focusing* its development assistance while simultaneously *weakening* its effectiveness (see Black and Tiessen, this volume). If aid becomes less effective rather than more effective, then there can be a loss of support for such efforts and an erosion of confidence among donors and recipients. Ultimately, the original decision to change focus becomes self-defeating. The government might claim to be enforcing strict environmental regulations on companies, but if it ignores violations it risks undermining itself and future efforts to make new environmental laws. Incoherence across many levels increases vulnerability to unexpected shocks or events. Inconsistency across many fields can effectively incapacitate the functional abilities of the state to maintain security, or accomplish other goals, over the long term. In addition to considering the scope for ethics and the implications of multiple layers of governance, then, governments are increasingly called upon to maintain coherence across short-term and long-term purposes.

Clear thinking on the questions of ethics and security is essential to the study of statecraft. The agenda since 2001 has changed in scope, character, and framing. New security challenges, from terrorism to climate change, are posing ethical dilemmas that (despite their importance) are not fully appreciated in the study of Canada's international relations. The context for decision making is fundamentally different. However, there remain perennial questions facing Canadian international and security policy. The chapters in this book address three of these questions. What are the meanings of "ethics" and "security," how are they linked, and how should they be linked? To what extent have considerations of ethics and security changed in the twenty-first century? What are the implications of a shifting historical context for Canada's international relations? *Unsettled Balance* carries the discourse that began in the 1990s through to the present day. It prompts attention to a relatively neglected dimension of Canada's international relations: the relationship between ethical concerns and security concerns. It considers the "practical politics" involved in decision making in a rapidly changing global context. All of the contributors share a concern that improving Canada's relationship with the rest of the world involves consciously and systematically considering the linkage between ethics and security. The contributors develop their work based upon a common premise – that decision making will be shaped as much by ethical arguments about rights, obligations, norms, and values as by national interest. The chapters demonstrate as well that questions of ethics and security are not esoteric intellectual discussions but central considerations in thinking and acting in the world.

The Changing Meanings of Ethics and Security

One of the most enduring philosophical questions of statecraft concerns the sources of ethics. In international relations thinking, positivists claim that the most robust ethical codes emerge from state agreements, treaties, written judicial opinions, international organizations, and an enduring set of national laws and practices. Such codes evolve over time in response to changing circumstances and norms but tend to change slowly and offer relatively conservative options. A competing view (but not necessarily a contradictory one) focuses on the sources of ethics in natural law or human conviction (see Edgar, this volume).[2] In human rights, for example, civil society groups and states often appeal to larger universal notions of "human dignity" to make their arguments. These notions can be described as a kind of natural law to the extent that they draw on and allow for the application of ethical codes outside the system of positive laws and rules buttressed by the historical and foundational norms of state sovereignty. In the event, natural and positive laws are continually intermingled in the processes of decision making.

In a democracy like Canada, governments are expected to pay attention to the prevailing values and priorities of Canadians, including respect for human dignity, environmental sustainability, and equal application of the law. The 1995 *Canada in the World* report identifies "the promotion of Canadian values and culture" as one of its three key objectives (along with prosperity and security) (Canada 1995; Hampson, Oliver, and Molot 1996). The 2005 *International Policy Statement* implicitly referenced values when invoking human rights, democracy, and the rule of law (Canada 2005, 11). Ethical principles can also be found in the common and long-standing practices and norms that inform Canada's international behaviour, such as support for multilateralism. Appeals to conservative institutions and long-standing ways of acting exist alongside calls for change through the continuing efforts of norm entrepreneurs and revolutionaries. Whether derived from an ethics of conviction, an appeal to human dignity or natural law, or an appeal to positive laws such as treaties, decisions inevitably arise from a mixture of ethical considerations.

In a series of academic discussions since the end of the Cold War, theorists and decision makers alike have debated the nature of security as a subject of international law, diplomacy, and national policy. Traditional notions of security that focus on the national interest continue to hold currency and animate discussions on a wide variety of topics, from national economic development to treatment of minorities. Nevertheless, there is growing awareness that national security remains highly contested and that it espouses particular forms of ethical content. A significant body of international law, including the UN Charter, emphasizes self-defence, non-intervention, state sovereignty, and autonomy. A significant group of states, especially those from the developing world, prioritize national sovereignty and national interests and resist intervention. Sovereignty norms, also replicated in diplomatic practices, are confronted by a growing and cross-cutting set of norms around human rights, multilateralism, and development that has emerged within the international community. To various degrees, these sets of laws are constructed by states. Although states often jealously guard their sovereign privileges against challenges from other actors and forces, they have simultaneously confounded these privileges by producing and supporting institutions and laws that work at cross-purposes to national sovereignty.

As a result of the developments discussed above, the effort to invoke national security confronts a measure of incoherence in both the international sphere and the domestic realm. As Chandler (2009, 123) argues, "the demand to forward claims in the terminology of human rights reflects a world in which the international legal order orientated around the constitutive rights of sovereign states is under challenge." Invoking national security means favouring an insular notion of ethics and calling upon a conservative set of norms that is in flux and, arguably, less sustainable in the face of changing circumstances. In addition, a focus on national security potentially narrows the scope for ethical discussion by instrumentalizing other policy goals in the service of security. As a result of states' actions, and despite its persistence in decision-making circles, the idea of national security is now widely questioned in the international community. Few in intellectual or decision-making circles now support without equivocation the unmitigated rights of states to uphold and defend their versions of national security. Those state governments that most strongly insist on unrestricted autonomy find themselves marginalized by the international community, even as they demand privileges and recognition. Such "rogue states" find that the claim to national security can no longer be used to override the demand for democracy, respect for human rights, or the provision of life necessities. These issues, which might have been considered purely domestic matters in the past, are now central questions for international relations as a whole.

Such dilemmas of national security are precisely what push states to broaden the focus of security policy beyond borders and to expand the scope for national action into newer, more innovative, areas. A broader view of national security can be less confining and constraining as well as more flexible. Adopting such a view also means broadening the notion of national interest to incorporate alternative notions of ethics that extend the moral community beyond state borders. As Cranford Pratt (2001, 61) has stated, "ethics intervenes when the motivation is no longer centrally focused on national security and national interests ... [but] when it responds significantly to a concern for the welfare and well-being of foreigners ... in response to sentiments of human solidarity and to an awakening acceptance of obligations towards those beyond its borders." Such an extension is less instrumental than a traditional focus on national interest but is not purely or solely altruistic. An appeal to duties beyond borders necessarily draws on a different, more normative, orientation to ethics but one that, as suggested above, is increasingly accepted by states as a legitimate and robust basis for the conduct of international relations. This acceptance is evidenced by the growth of positive law in the form of international laws, institutions, and procedures for addressing the needs and rights of individuals.[3]

What has driven this shift is the subject of some discussion in the international relations literature. The rise of global civil society, technological changes, and movements for democratization have provoked an "ethical turn" of some consequence for international relations and foreign policy studies. Issues such as climate change, human rights, and gender equality have emerged with much greater force than many anticipated. In addition, a "post-materialist" cultural trend in advanced industrial democracies has made these issue areas more central to public concerns in Western liberal democracies (see Inglehart 1990). Social media and information technology make people all over the globe instantly aware of state transgressions. The future of decision making will likely be shaped in a context of moral arguments about rights, obligations, and values, not only because democratic and deliberative politics demands it, but also because international circumstance demands it.

Canada has been and continues to be affected by these changes. In response to and as part of the changes precipitated by the end of the Cold War, Canada was an early champion of human security as an alternative discourse to that of national security. Canada's prominent minister of foreign affairs, Lloyd Axworthy, picked up on trends within the United Nations to argue that issues such as crime, pollution, drugs, and human rights abuses posed security challenges that implicated multilateral responses to otherwise internal questions (Axworthy 1997; see also Knight, this volume). Working closely with global civil society groups such as the Coalition for the International Criminal Court and the International Campaign to Ban Land-mines, Axworthy followed up with a program of action: material support for the Rome Statute of the International Criminal Court, an Anti-Personnel Mine Convention, action on small arms, and protection of women, children, and refugees.

How Have Things Changed?

The concept of human security tied ethical considerations to security considerations in specific ways. Human security as an idea shifted considerations of ethics from the state to the individual, a focus further extended and given weight by the *Responsibility to Protect* report in 2001 (ICISS 2001). This report set down the responsibilities of states and the international community with respect to a variety of threats to individual security, especially gross and systematic violations such as those encountered in Rwanda and Srebrenica (Kofi Annan, quoted in ICISS 2001, vii). Although they have lost some currency in the time following 9/11, debates over international and human security persist. What follows is a discussion of the intervening years from the height of the discourse of human security in the 1990s up to today. The changes are characterized in terms of three broad shifts. The first shift is a focus on capabilities rather than purposes. The second shift is the deepening association of security with national economic prosperity. The third shift is the move toward a more disaggregated international community, which affects the ability to articulate a coherent ethical stance.

The first shift involves a move toward capabilities and away from purposes. The ethical dimensions of this shift involve a narrowing of the scope for ethical discourse and a retrenchment of focus to national security, together with an expansive application of policy in specific geographies, issue areas, and projects. The roots of this shift toward capabilities lie, among other things, in the claims and criticisms made by early realist critics of the Axworthy doctrine. Some of the most prominent critics of Canada's foreign policy direction during the 1990s sought to redirect the national discussion on ethics away from "human security" and toward a more constrained view of the scope for ethical deliberation in foreign policy. Hampson and Oliver (1998) labelled the Axworthy doctrine "pulpit diplomacy." Bain (1999, 85–86) argued that Canada should avoid "preaching" and "excessive moralism" lest key international norms be upset by a too enthusiastic embrace of alternative views of security. As Hampson and Oliver (1998, 381) stated, Canada had become "a charter member of what we might call the 'moral minority,' that distinguished (and self-styled) group of states and organizations whose 'moral multilateralism' is predicated on their faith that the enunciation of a new set of global norms will lead inexorably to the creation of a just and more equitable international order." At the root of these criticisms were two claims: (1) even if the goals of human security are good ones, Canada is incapable of living up to its commitments because of a constrained and limited foreign policy budget and its relatively small population; (2) Canada's overtly "ethical" approach might distract from more prudential norms and practices that underlie the international system (e.g., national security) and in themselves are valuable and necessary for protecting security and avoiding counterproductive outcomes (Bain 1999).

In retrospect, and recognizing that the "target" of these criticisms was a moving object with many nuances and variations, these criticisms generally embraced an "ethic of responsibility" rather than an "ethic of conviction" (see Edgar, this volume). The attacks on human security as a foreign policy doctrine questioned its outcomes and consequences rather than its underlying purposes. Questions swirled around whether lofty goals can be achieved with insufficient resources. In the 1990s, Hampson and Oliver (1998) emphasized the critical deficiencies in resources that undermined Canada's ability to foster change in the international system, while Nossal (1998, 88) similarly pointed out that "pinchpenny diplomacy" would not succeed without the concerted investment in new capabilities to support it. Peace building, democratization, and some of the other programs of human security (critics argued) might require hard power and military force or simply be beyond our capability to address. The years following 9/11 were characterized by a resounding refrain that Canada was asleep and a country "in decline" (Cohen 2003; Hiller and Molot 2002). Governments responded to these criticisms with new spending on defence and an active and interventionist foreign policy proclaiming a new willingness to contribute, and even to lead, in Afghanistan and other areas of international policy.

As capability and commitment became stand-ins for ethical internationalism and what Nossal (1998) had earlier termed "good international citizenship," some of the original objections to the purposes of human security, which focused on "preaching," faded into the background or took on more limited meanings. The realists' caution against broad mandates was ignored when the Harper government described Canada's goals in Afghanistan in broad terms as a defence of Canadian values and democratic ideals and as an effort to "build a stable, peaceful and self-sustaining democratic country" (Bratt 2011, 318; see also Harper, quoted in Nossal 2013, 25). With a shift in the security discourse toward questions of capability, any ethical questions raised by such an ambitious and expansive agenda were diminished. Canada's mission in Afghanistan moved progressively from a rather narrow support mission to assist NATO and enforce UN resolutions to a wholesale nation-building exercise involving development, diplomacy, and defence (Bratt 2011). Canada's provincial reconstruction teams involved themselves in rebuilding schools and roads, providing jobs, and bolstering education. With the announcement of an additional $5.3 billion in new defence spending by the Harper government in 2006, and with a cost of some $7–10 billion on its military operations in Afghanistan and some $750 million–$1 billion on all other forms of aid and development (Bratt 2011, 530; Moens 2011, 147; Edgar, this volume), Canada's foreign security policy can no longer be accused of being "pinchpenny" or "cheap."

However, together with the Harper government, the critics of Canada's human security doctrine have fallen silent about the ethical implications of these new capabilities and the accompanying willingness to use force to achieve security. Indeed, it is puzzling that the sanctimonious use of hard power to achieve better enforcement of laws "to bring those who are in noncompliance into line" (Hampson and Oliver 1998, 404) is accompanied by such an ethical silence. Having discredited and banished the language of human security, including "soft power" (Nossal 2013, 30), "hard power" is effectively the default language of security. The issue of how to square the use of force with humanitarianism and international law loomed large over the Kosovo action in 1999 but has had little impact on subsequent interventions in Afghanistan and Libya (see Edgar, this volume). With the normative agenda of human security overshadowed by a variety of conflicting and sometimes contradictory sets of policy goals and norms, the lack of explicit attention to ethical considerations is troubling. These developments throw new light onto the statist critics' invocation of the need for prudence and respect for international boundaries. Indeed, the call to end "preaching" now seems to have been selectively targeted only at proponents of soft power approaches. With an increasing willingness and ability to intervene to achieve humanitarian goals, it seems *more* important, not *less*, to subject decisions to ethical and critical scrutiny.

Reflecting on the arguments of the realist critics of human security, one sees that one of their central concerns was the way in which the concept created an assault on traditional statecraft by focusing on public diplomacy and individual rather than state security (Hampson and Oliver 1998, 397; see also Bain 1999). This "assault" would be corrected by governments' foreign policy decisions over the next few years. Axworthy's human security doctrine had identified a variety of threats to security: environmental catastrophe, economic decline, famine, and large-scale human rights violations. The *Responsibility to Protect* report (ICISS 2001) emphasized the principle that states must not threaten their own populations. However, the 2004 *National Security Policy* emphasized a traditional approach, focusing on "risks to the state." It also added the necessity of protecting Canadian values, institutions, and Canadians abroad and not just the physical security of Canada (see Falk, this volume). Similarly, the types of threats identified had subtly shifted by the time of the 2005 *International Policy Statement*. The statement focused on rogue states, failed and fragile states, international criminal syndicates, weapons proliferation, and terrorists (Canada 2005, 3). With a renewed focus on threats to international order and national security, the *International Policy Statement* foreshadowed the marriage of a state-oriented policy stance with a new interventionist approach to ensuring security.

A second trend of the past few years has been the deepening association of security with national economic prosperity. As Michaud (2011, 438) claims, economic and security considerations remain closely linked in discussions of Canadian values, and at times (as when Canada-US trade was affected following 9/11) economic considerations have even driven measures to improve national security. The 1994 *Human Development Report*, instrumental in advancing the notion of human security, argued that security should go beyond civil and political rights to include security of work, income, and food, protection against threats to public health, and protection against environmental degradation, pollution, and disaster (Irwin 2001, 6).

Although generally conservative in policy approach with respect to economic concerns, economic questions were addressed within the Axworthy agenda. Implicit (though not emphasized) within the notion of human security was an awareness that economic globalization and open borders could undermine local economies and create or worsen resource conflicts and repression. For example, Axworthy commented on the disruptive impact of highly valued commodities such as diamonds in Sierra Leone. Globalization also implied a heightened ethical responsibility for states, according to

Axworthy (2001, 20), since "globalization has made individual human suffering an irrevocable universal concern." The Axworthy doctrine included
economic security as a component of human security, but it did not effectively address the ethical dilemmas of prioritizing civil, political, and physical integrity rights over broader economic, social, and cultural rights (Irwin
2001). Critics of both the Axworthy doctrine and the 1995 *Foreign Policy
Statement* have noted that development and economic security issues occupied a less prominent position in discussions of economic threats and vulnerabilities and that economic concerns remained firmly within the narrow
confines of the national interest and the goal of national prosperity (Crosby
Denholm 2003). The further overshadowing of economic and development
questions, already noted by critics of the Axworthy doctrine during the
1990s, is emblematic of this larger shift toward state-based conceptions of
security.

Together with the impact of 9/11, the bursting of the financial bub-
ble in late 2008 and the consequent slowdown and debt crises have had
a complex impact on these discussions. On the one hand, the economic
slowdown transformed the anti-globalization movement that had arisen
to critique free trade, development, and elite forms of multilateralism. In
response to economic crisis, new mass movements against austerity and in
support of human rights and democratization arose abroad in Africa and
Europe. In North America, the Occupy movement followed in 2011, with a
larger agenda of issues that went beyond free trade and cross-cut domestic
and global concerns, including social and economic inequality, financial
accountability, and unemployment. The complexity of these movements
is striking, for they occupy what Rao (2010, 4) has termed a "bifurcated"
position with respect to the state. On the one hand, such movements are
critical of unfettered sovereignty; on the other, they desire a state robust
enough to withstand globalization and neoliberalism. The position of governments in this more complex environment has been contradictory. In
Canada, the government's response to the global economic collapse was
hesitant, lurching, and minimal, considering the economic damage experienced in the manufacturing and retail sectors (McBride 2011). Yet the
uncertain global economic environment has prompted a renewed focus on
national prosperity goals, discursively linked to freer and more open trade
relations. The government's close association of security with economic
prosperity has had more resonance to date with the Canadian public than
the critiques of the protestors, and though it did not initiate this shift the
Harper government in particular has mobilized this global uncertainty to

forward a political agenda oriented toward prioritizing Canadian prosperity and national interests.

There are some ethical dilemmas in conflating national security with economic well-being and national prosperity. First, whether the measures promoted (e.g., free trade and economic growth) will enhance security remains an open question. There is little doubt that Canada remains a country highly vulnerable to changes in the global economy and particularly the American economy. Growth from trade implies interdependence and engagement with the world economy that can actually increase vulnerabilities to external shocks. Second, there remain real differences, as suggested by the Occupy movement and the anti-globalization protests, over the meaning of prosperity and whether it will achieve genuine economic well-being. As Stiglitz and others argue, the meaning of well-being remains highly contested. Well-being is multidimensional and can include health, education, and environmental conditions, among other factors (Stiglitz, Sen, and Fitoussi 2009, 14–15). Third, policy priorities can become distorted in ethically inappropriate ways when national interests are the central concern. As Pratt (2001, 16) has argued, humane internationalism involves the recognition of an obligation *beyond* the state. When understood in this way, humane internationalism is in tension with the idea of national security. Worthwhile programs and goals, such as gender equality or climate adaptation (see Tiessen and Tuckey, and Stoett, this volume), might become instrumentalized and securitized as a result.

The last important shift is really a series of shifts both in policy and in the international order that has impacted the capacities of all states (not just Canada) to articulate effectively coherent stances on a range of international issues. The difficulty of doing so in an increasingly disaggregated international community lacking clear leadership on key questions of human rights, development, trade, and security has intersected with the tendency to vacate the ethical field of contention. The US focus on national security and an accompanying retreat from multilateralism, international law, and human rights norms have left an ethical void. Perhaps surprisingly, then, the sometimes stark contrasts made in the 1990s between individual security and state security have resolved into a patchwork continuum, with variations of sovereignty coexisting with degrees of concern for individual protection. As Chandler (2009, 122–23) argues, the result is an ironic search for values and meaning in a form of humanitarianism that neglects an "ethics of responsibility" in that the welfare of the object of intervention is not the primary focus. Rather, intervention becomes little more than an "act of power without meaning" since responses are necessarily ad hoc and arbitrary. One characteristic of this "light" level of commitment is a low tolerance for ambiguity. This has boosted the premium on short-term action, shallow and deft attitudes to international commitments, and decisive (rather than deliberative) decisions and actions. Prime Minister Harper articulated a profound suspicion of ambiguity, for example, when he recently stated that "moral ambiguity ... [and] moral equivalence are not options, they are dangerous illusions" (quoted in Payton 2011). Nevertheless, ethical ambiguity intervenes in unexpected ways. When decisions respond to domestic and state imperatives, they necessarily impact the effectiveness and legitimacy of efforts to achieve international goals. Neither side of the ethical equation can be definitive. To ask ethical questions is to open a door to critical insights about the motivations, purposes, and consequences of policy decision making.

The events of 9/11 posed a unique set of challenges for conventional notions of national security in that they both undermined and reinforced the traditional national security paradigm. Although the ease and coordination of the attack demonstrated a new vulnerability, the response reinforced a focus on military organization as an appropriate component of national protection. Counterterrorism demanded nimble, technology-based, and intelligence-based approaches to security. At the same time, by invoking a politics of necessity and crisis, it undermined the movement (implicit within the human security discourse) toward a broadening of security threats to include economic, cultural, personal, and environmental threats. The Harper government has continued and deepened this trend to focus on national threats, often invoking the necessity of preventing countries such as Afghanistan from posing a threat to the security of Canadians (Bratt 2011, 319). Furthermore, securitization and instrumentalization have affected other areas of decision making, such as aid, trade, and environmental policies. The prioritization of domestic and state imperatives constitutes a tectonic shift from the 1990s. Whether these trends result in a fully formed and lasting departure from Canada's storied historical commitment to liberal internationalism remains an open question (Smith and Turenne Sjolander 2013, xiv).

The questions tackled by the contributors to this book are informed by an awareness of this changed context and by its ambiguity and complexity. The questions posed here remain perennial in the sense that ethical dilemmas are unavoidable, yet they also provoke new thinking about the changed circumstances in which decision making happens. Although the contributors do not represent a consensus on the meanings of these terms, nevertheless they share recognition that considerations of ethics are inseparable from the actions and words that guide Canada's international relations in the twenty-first century and that ethics lie at the heart of decision making.

The Plan of the Book

Revisiting the three research questions posed in this introduction enables the contributors to extend the conversation begun in 2001 on human security and ethics. The context of decision making has been shifting from broader to narrower notions of security and national interest. The meaning of ethics and its linkage with security have also been changing. Although it is less conscious and conspicuous, considering ethics and security together is no less relevant or important than it was in the 1990s. Indeed, in an age when Canada is raising its profile and adding to its capabilities, an ethical discussion is even more vital. This discussion begins in Part 1, "Freedom from Fear: Humanitarianism and Military Security." The focus is on the international level of action, with Andy Knight, Alistair Edgar, and Chris Hendershot analyzing the pattern of ethics expressed through international norms, laws, and policies. In general, this section offers a complex and nuanced account of the changes in the international environment with respect to security and the normative context impacting humanitarian action in the years since 9/11. These changes can be summed up generally, as described below, as a retreat from the norm of multilateral humanitarian action accompanied by a seemingly contradictory embrace of interventionism in the service of narrower security goals. Part 2, "Security across Borders," looks at the questions raised by anti-terrorism policy and issues of "law and order," both domestic and foreign. The linkage between the domestic and the international occupies centre stage for the contributions in this section, as do the themes of securitization and militarization. Part 3, "Freedom from Want: Development, Gender, and Environment," broadly gathers together chapters within the theme of "freedom from want," using an ethical frame to explore how policies designed to address poverty, gender mainstreaming, and environmental adaptation have evolved over the past decade. Part 4, "Regional Security: Countries and Areas," focuses on Canadian international relations in specific regions and countries, highlighting the unique features of an area or country to explain the interaction between theory and action. By addressing practical questions and cases, the contributors wrestle with the dilemmas of ethics and security, the changing international trends that impact decision making, and the effects of these changes on Canada's international relations. Several broad themes emerge from the chapters and intersect with the above discussion: (1) the scope for ethical decision making, (2) the impact of multilevel governance, and (3) the challenge of ethical coherence.

The above discussion suggests that there is a narrowing of the scope for an explicit discussion of ethics in a rapidly changing world. Andy Knight begins the account with an outline of the historical struggle to strengthen norms of humanitarian protection and achieve their acceptance and enforcement within the international community. Tracing the development and debates that shaped the responsibility to protect doctrine, his narrative explains how changes to the international legal and normative architecture have been advanced by norm entrepreneurs such as Canada, working within the United Nations. Using the ideas of norm development, acceptance, and challenge originally developed by Finnemore and Sikkink (1998), Knight emphasizes that R2P represented a move from "normative clash" to "normative fit" between state sovereignty and human rights protection. He focuses on the modern efforts to strengthen the protection of civilians against genocide, war crimes, ethnic cleansing, and other crimes against humanity, through key international instruments such as the International Criminal Court and the R2P norm. Knight's discussion of the ethical debates and history of protection has implications for humanitarian actions in Libya, Somalia, Syria, and other countries where populations face widespread violations and attacks.

Alistair Edgar continues the discussion with an examination of the more circumscribed scope for humanitarian action. He addresses the ethics of "militarized humanitarianism" and raises questions about the dilemmas of using military means to achieve humanitarian ends. Considering the shift from humanitarian action to war fighting, Edgar argues that the result has been a "shrinking" of humanitarian space. The move toward securitization and militarization had its roots, in his view, in the disillusionment with UN-led peacekeeping in the 1990s but was reinforced by the complexities of the ethical calculations confronting both state and non-state actors post-9/11.

One of the factors contributing to a shrinking scope for humanitarianism was the closer association of private and public actors, a factor also highlighted by Chris Hendershot. Hendershot considers how commercialization of operations and support of the Canadian Forces by commercial military security companies (CMSCs) might contribute to a narrow utilitarian ethic that omits larger considerations (e.g., of equitable distribution). He also confronts the tendency for CMSCs to enclose and limit access to resources by reinforcing liberal and free-market-based "ways of living." The process of enclosure thus has consequences for the scope of ethics as discussions grow around the activities of CMSCs.

Part 2 focuses on the theme of multilevel governance by addressing the various ways in which domestic and international crossover affects considerations of ethics and security. The question of ethical coherence and purposes also resonates through the chapters in Part 2. Barbara Falk explores the intersection of domestic and international law and the ethical incoherence that can result when these areas of law are in conflict. Transnational terrorist groups challenge both bodies of law by operating both inside and outside sovereign boundaries, and states are compelled to address both realms even though they might work at cross-purposes. A process of "verticalization" occurs: events at home have implications for Canadian actions abroad and vice versa. In her survey of recent anti-terrorism legislation and key Charter cases, Falk argues that an inability to address these legal conflicts can have deleterious effects, including a failure to protect security and prevent human rights violations.

In a similar vein, Veronica Kitchen addresses transnational linkages in her analysis of the dilemmas of "mega-event" security decision making. As such events become globalized and states are called upon to formulate security responses, spectacularization and securitization complicate the effort to balance civil liberties with the security needs of dignitaries and demonstrators alike. In particular, such events prompt consideration of how ethics and security are linked through such "exceptional" circumstances and how the lessons learned from mega-events can impact decision making more broadly. A more measured and conscious approach to considering these security dilemmas, Kitchen argues, will help to mitigate the escalation that occurs as a result.

Falk and Kitchen also develop the theme of ethical coherence when they address the "security dilemma." This dilemma occurs when actions designed to ensure security tend to have the opposite effect. For example, as Hendershot argues, Canada's actions in integrating CMSCs can contribute to the very conditions that make humanitarian intervention necessary. He outlines several ways in which intervention exacerbates problems, from exploitative labour relations to inequitable distribution of resources. In addition, as these writers suggest, efforts to advance one form of security can sacrifice other forms. For example, Canada's involvement in extractive industries in Latin America can erode the legitimacy of its moral identity there (Rochlin, this volume). Kitchen argues similarly that mega-events present such a security dilemma by increasing uncertainties and expanding the scope for bureaucracies to define protests as security threats rather than social justice actions.

The chapters in Part 3 engage directly with the scope of ethics. David Black and Rebecca Tiessen examine the impact of an "agenda of aid effectiveness" in Ethiopia. The narrow constraints of this agenda have created ethical problems by making it difficult to engage with a new collaborative politics of aid and food security. As they note, these changes are emblematic of a waning of humane internationalism and the erosion of a core cosmopolitan ethic of assistance for the most needy. Their chapter discusses the evolving context of Canada's aid programs in Ethiopia and uses participant interviews to document the effects of these shifts on Canada's programs in that country. The authors argue that the aid effectiveness agenda and emphasis on "focus" are being driven by domestic considerations, evidenced by a concentration of decision-making power emanating from Ottawa. They note, among other things, that the shifting emphasis on governance priorities and the failure to mainstream gender and environmental factors have made Canadian aid *less* effective in alleviating food insecurity. A restricted agenda for aid, focused on effectiveness, might well leave less scope for the kind of ethical considerations that Black and Tiessen propose, including consideration of the views and experiences of the recipients of aid.

Similarly, Rebecca Tiessen and Sarah Tuckey take on Canada's ostensible commitment to gender equality and argue that there is a shrinking scope for ethics. Canada's willingness to "treat women as targets of Canadian foreign aid and security initiatives" rather than participants in development is emblematic of this narrowing scope. Tiessen and Tuckey note a move away from broader "humane internationalist" discourses and toward a security-focused orientation. They pick up on the tendency of well-meaning but weak efforts at change to create distortions or (worse) ethically incoherent and even self-defeating policies. As they argue, "technical fixes and cookie-cutter formulas" create contradictions in Canada's ethical obligation to gender mainstreaming. A transformational approach to gender mainstreaming holds the promise of achieving a better understanding of the security needs of conflict and post-conflict communities. Such an approach, they argue, will have a better chance of assisting stakeholders in "ensuring that men's and women's needs are understood and addressed" than the present shallow and narrow strategy.

Stoett argues that ethics are inextricably intertwined with the issue of climate change adaptation and raises several questions regarding the scope and coherence of ethics in this policy field. Broadening the understanding of security even slightly, he says, reveals the necessity of addressing not only military or national security issues but also threats to environmental security. Echoing Hendershot's discussion of distributive ethics, Stoett argues that climate change creates dilemmas of distributive obligations with clear ethical implications, and he expands Hendershot's discussion of the colonial enclosure of resources when he raises the critiques of eco-feminists who point to the appropriation of women's work and nature (Isla 2009, cited in Stoett, this volume). Critics of "carbon colonialism" suggest that climate adaptation policies are creating new opportunities for the use of resources and labour in the South to the benefit of the North and that these efforts consequently might be not only environmentally dubious but also counterproductive. A "superficial sense of virtuous accomplishment" might well end up increasing the vulnerability of all to climate change by wasting opportunities and resources on ethically questionable carbon offset projects. Stoett concludes, therefore, that enlightened self-interest would recognize the need for a strong commitment of resources to support the adaptation efforts of the most vulnerable, balanced with a sense of environmental justice and a measure of awareness of our mutual vulnerability and need for security.

As in Part 2, the chapters in Part 4 examine transnational linkages at state and societal levels and their impacts on decision making. Like Falk and Kitchen, James Rochlin, in his chapter on Canada's free-trade agreement with Colombia, illustrates well the ways in which civil society activists play a role in policy making. From the Zapatista rebellion in response to the North American Free Trade Agreement (NAFTA) to the campaign for human rights in the Canada-Colombia Free Trade Agreement (FTA), Rochlin explains how "bottom-up" critical security discourses can have impacts when given higher profiles in trade negotiations. One of the outcomes of this effect has been the groundbreaking HRIA (Human Rights Impact Assessment) agreement, which Rochlin analyzes in light of its effectiveness in improving the human rights situation in Colombia.

In various ways as well, the authors draw attention to the silences and absences in discussions of security. Whether the issue is commercial military and security operations, secrecy surrounding mega-events planning, or gender mainstreaming, a lack of transparency raises ethical issues in a democracy. Civil society has a role to play in revealing and publicizing violations, which can have beneficial effects, as in the case of the Canada-Colombia Free Trade Agreement. Another "absence" noted by the authors is the tendency to overlook the voices and interests of recipients of protection, aid, and trade. The question of "whose ethics" are being considered and represented is therefore crucial.

Edward Akuffo's chapter complements Rochlin's on trade in the Americas by looking at Canada's changing relationship with Africa. Noting that the retreat from a human security discourse coincided with a shift away from the region, Akuffo looks at the "disappearance" of Canada and the consequent decline in support for and engagement with the continent. In addition, he notes, the framing of Canada's moral identity is too closely reliant on particular visions of Africa (as poor and conflict ridden) that confine policy options and tend to create relatively narrow and unidirectional "self-fulfilling prophecies." As shifts in Canada's aid and peacekeeping budget reveal, the continuing paradoxical relationship with Africa can accommodate an interest-based approach when balanced with the goals of protecting human rights, maintaining the rule of law, and supporting poverty alleviation. The broad purpose of policy, therefore, should be to build upon Canada's moral identity in Africa with substantive efforts to enhance mutually beneficial partnerships.

The contributors to this volume examine these questions from a variety of viewpoints and apply their own conceptions of ethics and security to explain the complexity of the world in ethical terms. Although they have not agreed on a set definition of ethics or security, their findings address common themes and issues that point to the necessity of continuing inquiry on these vital questions. Whether it is the examination of mega-events, development assistance, or humanitarian intervention, action is always cloaked in a set of meanings that create and interpret the world in a particular way and so draw on ethical frames either to reproduce or to challenge existing frames. In general, the contributors have chosen to challenge rather than reproduce dominant conceptions of national security. In their critiques of "securitization" and "instrumentalization" processes, they invoke a critical paradigm and seek to reveal the underlying patterns and strategies of decision making. In the process, they show that the notions of security and ethics are inextricably linked, even when balanced, through a fulcrum of theory and action.

NOTES

I am grateful to Alex Elwood for research assistance.

1 International relations researchers operating within the constructivist school have developed these ideas and applied them to a variety of problems and contexts. However, ethics and decision making per se have occupied only part of the focus of constructivists (see, e.g., Finnemore and Sikkink 1998).

2 For an overview of how they relate, see Alderson and Hurrell (2000).
3 The development of laws to protect human rights and facilitate greater international concern over humanitarian violations is documented in Knight's chapter in this volume. The development of the International Criminal Court, the Universal Declaration of Human Rights, and the Convention on Genocide are prominent examples.

References

Alderson, Kai, and Andrew Hurrell. 2000. *Hedley Bull on International Society*. Palgrave MacMillan.

Allison, Graham. 1971. *Essence of Decision: Explaining the Cuban Missile Crisis.* Boston: Little, Brown.

Axworthy, Lloyd. 1997. "Canada and Human Security: The Need for Leadership." *International Journal (Toronto, Ont.)* 52 (2): 183–96. http://dx.doi.org/10.2307/40203196.

Axworthy, Lloyd. 2001. "Human Security and Global Governance: Putting People First." *Global Governance* 19 (7): 19–24.

Bain, William W. 1999. "Against Crusading : The Ethic of Human Security and Canadian Foreign Policy." *Canadian Foreign Policy Journal* 6 (3): 85–98. http://dx.doi.org/10.1080/11926422.1999.9673187.

Bratt, Duane. 2011. "Afghanistan: Why Did We Go? Why Did We Stay? Will We Leave?" In *Readings in Canadian Foreign Policy: Classic Debates and New Ideas,* edited by Duane Bratt and Christopher Kukucha, 316–28. Don Mills, ON: Oxford University Press.

Canada. 1995. *Canada in the World : Government Statement.* Ottawa: Department of Foreign Affairs and International Trade.

Canada. 2005. *Canada's International Policy Statement : A Role of Pride and Influence in the World: Overview.* Ottawa: Department of Foreign Affairs.

Chandler, David. 2009. "Ideological (Mis)Use of Human Rights." In *Human Rights: Politics and Practice,* edited by M. Goodhart, 109–25. Oxford: Oxford University Press.

Cohen, A. 2003. *While Canada Slept: How We Lost Our Place in the World.* Toronto: McClelland and Stewart.

Crosby Denholm, Ann. 2003. "Myths of Canada's Human Security Pursuits : Tales of Tool Boxes, Toy Chests, and Tickle Trunks." In *Feminist Perspectives on Canadian Foreign Policy,* edited by Claire Turenne Sjolander, Heather A. Smith, and Deborah Stienstra, 90–107. Oxford: Oxford University Press.

Finnemore, Martha, and Kathryn Sikkink. 1998. "International Norm Dynamics and Political Change." *International Organization* 52 (4): 887–917. http://dx.doi.org/10.1162/002081898550789.

Geislerova, Marketa. 2001. Canadian Centre for Foreign Policy Development. *Report from the 3rd Annual Academic Roundtable Canadian Foreign Policy: Interests and Values.* Toronto. http://publications.gc.ca/collections/Collection/E2-431-2001E.pdf.

Glasius, Marlies. 2009. "Global Civil Society and Human Rights." In *Human Rights: Politics and Practice,* edited by Michael Goodhart, 147–63. Oxford: Oxford University Press.

Hampson, Fen O., and Dean F. Oliver. 1998. "Pulpit Diplomacy: A Critical Assessment of the Axworthy Doctrine." *International Journal (Toronto, Ont.)* 53 (3): 379–406. http://dx.doi.org/10.2307/40203320.

Hampson, Fen O., Dean F. Oliver, and Maureen Appel Molot. 1996. "Being Heard and the Role of Leadership." In *Canada among Nations 1996: Big Enough to Be Heard,* edited by F.O. Hampson and M.A. Molot, 3–20. Ottawa: Carleton University Press.

Hawes, Michael K. 1984. *Principal Power, Middle Power, or Satellite? Competing Perspectives in the Study of Canadian Foreign Policy.* Toronto: Research Programme in Strategic Studies, York University.

Hiller, N., and M.A. Molot. 2002. *Canada among Nations 2002: A Fading Power.* Oxford: Oxford University Press.

Howard, P., and R. Neufeldt. 2011. "Canada's Constructivist Foreign Policy: Building Norms for Peace." *Canadian Foreign Policy Journal* 8 (1): 11–38. http://dx.doi.org /10.1080/11926422.2000.9673233.

ICISS (International Commission on Intervention and State Sovereignty). 2001. *The Responsibility to Protect: Report of the International Commission on Intervention and State Sovereignty.* Ottawa: International Development Research Centre.

Inglehart, R. 1990. *Culture Shift in Advanced Industrial Society.* Princeton, NJ: Princeton University Press.

Irwin, Rosalind. 2001. "Linking Ethics and Security in Canadian Foreign Policy." In *Ethics and Security in Canadian Foreign Policy,* edited by Rosalind Irwin, 3–13. Vancouver: UBC Press.

Isla, Ana. 2009. "Who Pays for the Kyoto Protocol? Selling Oxygen and Selling Sex in Costa Rica." In *Eco-Sufficiency and Global Justice: Women Write Political Ecology,* edited by Ariel Salleh, 199–217. London: Pluto.

Jervis, Robert. 1968. "Hypotheses on Misperception." *World Politics* 20 (3): 454–79. http://dx.doi.org/10.2307/2009777.

Keck, Margaret E., and Kathryn Sikkink. 1998. *Activists beyond Borders : Advocacy Networks.* Ithaca, NY: Cornell University Press.

Knight, Andy. 2001. "Soft Power, Moral Suasion, and Establishing the International Criminal Court: Canadian Contributions." In *Ethics and Security in Canadian Foreign Policy,* ed. Rosalind Irwin, 113–37. Vancouver: UBC Press.

Lee, Steve. 2002. "Canadian Values in Canadian Foreign Policy." *Canadian Foreign Policy Journal* 10 (1): 1–9. http://dx.doi.org/10.1080/11926422.2002.9673303.

McBride, Stephen. 2011. "Canada and the Global Economic Crisis." In *Readings in Canadian Foreign Policy: Classic Debates and New Ideas,* edited by Duane Bratt and C.J. Kukucha, 390–405. Toronto: Oxford University Press.

Michaud, N. 2011. "Values and Canadian Foreign Policy-Making: Inspiration or Hindrance." In *Readings in Canadian Foreign Policy: Classic Debates and New Ideas,* edited by Duane Bratt and C.J. Kukucha, 433–51. Toronto: Oxford University Press.

Moens, Alex. 2011. "NATO and the EU: Canada's Security Interests." In *Europe and Beyond: Canada's National Security in the Post-9/11 World: Strategy, Interests, and Threats,* edited by D.S. McDonough, 141–59. Toronto: University of Toronto Press.

Molot, M.A. 1990. "Where Do We, Should We, or Can We Sit? A Review of Canadian Foreign Policy Literature." *International Journal of Canadian Studies* 1 (2): 77–96.

Nossal, Kim Richard. 1998. "Pinchpenny Diplomacy: The Decline of 'Good International Citizenship' in Canadian Foreign Policy." *International Journal (Toronto, Ont.)* 54 (1): 88–105. http://dx.doi.org/10.2307/40203357.

Nossal, Kim Richard. 2013. "The Liberal Past in the Conservative Present: Internationalism in the Harper Era." In *Canada in the World: Internationalism in Canadian Foreign Policy*, edited by Heather A. Smith and Claire Turenne Sjolander, 21–35. Don Mills, ON: Oxford University Press.

Payton, Laura. 2011. "Harper Speech Fires Up Convention Crowd." *CBC.* http://www.cbc.ca/news/politics/harper-speech-fires-up-convention-crowd-1.976268.

Pratt, Cranford. 2001. "Moral Vision and Foreign Policy: The Case of Canadian Development Assistance." In *Ethics and Security in Canadian Foreign Policy*, edited by Rosalind Irwin, 59–76. Vancouver: UBC Press.

Rao, Rahul. 2010. *Third World Protest : Between Home and the World.* Oxford: Oxford University Press. http://dx.doi.org/10.1093/acprof:oso/9780199560370.001.0001.

Smith, Heather A., and Claire Turenne Sjolander. 2013. "Introduction: Conversations without Consensus – Internationalism under the Harper Government." In *Canada in the World: Internationalism in Canadian Foreign Policy*, edited by Heather A. Smith and Claire Turenne Sjolander, i–xxviii. Don Mills, ON: Oxford University Press.

Smith, K.E., and M. Light. 2001. "Introduction" in *Ethics and Foreign Policy*, edited by K.E. Smith and M. Light, 1–14. Cambridge: Cambridge University Press. http://dx.doi.org/10.1017/CBO9780511491696.

Stairs, Denis. 1994. "Will and Circumstance and the Postwar Study of Canada's Foreign Policy." *International Journal (Toronto, Ont.)* 50 (1): 9–39. http://dx.doi.org/10.2307/40202995.

Stiglitz, J.E., A. Sen, and J.P. Fitoussi. 2009. *Report of the Commission on the Measurement of Economic Performance and Social Progress (CMEPSP).* http://www.stiglitz-sen-fitoussi.fr/en/documents.htm.

Turenne Sjolander, Claire, and Kathryn Trevenen. 2011. "Constructing Canadian Foreign Policy: Myths of Good International Citizens, Protectors, and the War in Aghanistan." In *Readings in Canadian Foreign Policy: Classic Debates and New Ideas*, edited by Duane Bratt and C.J. Kukucha, 96–108. Toronto: Oxford University Press.

Waltz, Kenneth. 2001. *Man, the State, and War: A Theoretical Analysis.* 2nd ed. New York: Columbia University Press.

Wark, Wesley K. 2006. *National Security and Human Rights Concerns in Canada: A Survey of Eight Critical Issues in the Post-9/11 Environment.* Ottawa: Canadian Human Rights Commission. http://www.chrc-ccdp.ca/sites/default/files/ns_sn_en_1.pdf.

Wendt, Alexander. 1992. "Anarchy Is What States Make of It: The Social Construction of Power Politics." *International Organization* 46 (2): 391–425. http://dx.doi.org/10.1017/S0020818300027764.

PART 1

FREEDOM FROM FEAR: HUMANITARIANISM AND MILITARY SECURITY

The Responsibility to Protect
From Evolving Norm to Practice

W. ANDY KNIGHT

The Canadian government, under Prime Minister Martin, can be credited with being a norm entrepreneur when it comes to advocating the cause of humanitarian intervention to protect people at risk of extermination by governments that are supposed to protect them or by groups within countries plagued by civil conflicts. What guided the Canadian government's decision to lead the way, as a middle power, in introducing the norm of the responsibility to protect during the 1990s was the history of the mentality that causes seemingly sane humans to slaughter other humans deliberately en masse.

The systematic and bureaucratic elimination of 6 million European Jews during the Second World War is an example of this genocidal mentality. German National Socialists under Hitler exterminated not only Jews but also Roma, Soviets, ethnic Poles, some Slavic people, gays, disabled people, and Jehovah's Witnesses. The total number of deaths from that mass killing reached close to 17 million.[1]

The "international community" said "never again" after the Holocaust, yet other horrific slaughters of innocent people continued in the twentieth century (in places such as Burundi, Cambodia, the Democratic Republic of Congo, East Timor, Haiti, Kosovo, Liberia, Rwanda, Sierra Leone, Somalia, Sudan, and the former Yugoslavia).

Canada played a role in the Kosovo War of 1999, which ended in Serbia's retreat from Kosovo and the defeat of President Slobodan Milosevic.

Canadian troops, weapons, and war planes were involved in this NATO humanitarian intervention, which resulted in bombing campaigns (in 1995 and 1999) and what one can call a war-fighting strategy designed to end the atrocities in the former Yugoslavia. Some Canadian academics, such as Michael Ignatieff, made the moral case for Western intervention to prevent the further loss of lives in that civil conflict. Canada's role in supporting the emergence of this new norm of civilian protection was made even more explicit by the minister of foreign affairs at the time, Lloyd Axworthy, who publicly (rhetorically and materially) supported Canada's commitment to this NATO intervention and called it a peace support operation that put people first when it comes to human security (Axworthy 1999).

Canada also supported the establishment of the ad hoc International Criminal Tribunal for the Former Yugoslavia. For instance, the Canadian government provided support to the tribunal in a number of ways: offering a financial assistance package; contributing to the witness protection program, including the resettlement of witnesses and their families; financially assisting the construction of a new courtroom; supporting the program of mass grave exhumations to uncover corroborating evidence used in court cases; and providing gratis expert personnel to the Office of the Prosecutor.[2] The tribunal indicted Dragan Nikolic, the Bosnian Serb concentration camp commander, as well as twenty-one other Bosnian Serbs charged with the crime of committing atrocities against Muslim and Croat civilian prisoners. In 1995–96, the tribunal issued ten public indictments against thirty-three individuals from the former Yugoslavia alleged to have been involved in crimes against humanity and ethnic cleansing. These charges were brought against Radovan Karadzic and Ratko Mladic, along with Milosevic, who died before his trial was concluded. This demonstrated that Canada's norm entrepreneurship was not limited to the protection of innocent civilians during civil conflicts but included the ending of impunity in conscience-shocking atrocities.

Axworthy's contribution led Canada to advance the contentious matter of humanitarian intervention. In his capacity as co-president of the UN Security Council, Axworthy proposed a UN commission to examine the legality of humanitarian intervention in cases of genocide and other mass atrocities. Supported by the public advocacy of influential figures such as the former Australian minister of foreign affairs, Gareth Evans, Axworthy's norm entrepreneurship led the United Nations to adopt the "responsibility to protect" (R2P) doctrine in 2005, which contained provisions for the Security Council to authorize the use of force to prevent or punish acts such as those committed in Bosnia and Kosovo.

Despite Canada's and Axworthy's efforts, conscience-shocking atrocities spilled over into the twenty-first century (e.g., in Chechnya, Darfur, Iraq, Libya, Kenya, Myanmar, and Syria). But the ethical question that continues to haunt us is whether we can continue to turn a blind eye to this malignancy and stand idly by in the face of mounting deaths and the suffering of populations at risk, in places such as Syria, where there have been over 130,000 deaths since March 2011 because of sectarian violence. Do we not have a moral responsibility to put an end, once and for all, to this carnage?

This chapter examines and explains the development of R2P in the context of its place in emerging and evolving normative patterns within global society and the interstate system and the prospect of transforming this norm from "promise into practice, words into deeds" – to echo the words of UN Secretary General Ban Ki-moon (United Nations 2008). This innovative norm of international relations, R2P, emerged out of an evolving narrative[3] that has raised the level of consciousness among peoples and their leaders about the need to see and treat all people on our planet – regardless of race, ethnicity, religion, or social standing – with human dignity and to focus on people-centred security. R2P takes that narrative further by using it as the foundation upon which to build a new normative architecture designed to foster the belief that sovereignty should no longer be used as a fig leaf to cover up the most egregious crimes committed against innocent people. Canada was one of the architects of this new norm. However, it is unfortunate that the country, under the hyper-partisan Harper administration, has distanced itself from the role that the previous Liberal government played in nurturing this fledgling norm (Nossal 2013).

The Evolving Narrative

The evolving narrative referred to above began with the promotion of a legally binding Convention on the Prevention and Punishment of the Crime of Genocide, adopted by the UN General Assembly in December 1948 and entered into force in January 1951.[4] The Genocide Convention owes its genesis to norm entrepreneur Raphael Lemkin (1944, especially 79–95), the Polish Jewish lawyer who, in response to the Holocaust, coined the term "genocide" in 1943 after campaigning vigorously at a conference hosted by the Legal Council of the League of Nations in 1933 (and in state capitals) to have acts of barbarity outlawed. The convention acknowledges that genocide, whether committed in time of peace or war, is a punishable crime under international law and requires states to take domestic measures to

secure its punishment.[5] The definition of genocide includes a range of deliberate acts "committed with the intent of destroying, in whole or in part,
an entire national, ethnical, racial, or religious group."[6] Although several
states have lodged reservations regarding parts of this convention,[7] the pro-
hibitions found in it are considered customary international law that binds
non-state parties to this treaty (Totten and Bartrop 2009, 145). The intent of
the convention was to prevent and punish genocide if not all mass atrocity
crimes.

As time progressed, the narrative was extended in several stages. In
December 1948, the UN General Assembly adopted the Universal Declaration of Human Rights, a document drafted by Canadian legal scholar John
Humphrey. Twenty years later, in May 1968, a proclamation was adopted at
the International Conference on Human Rights in Tehran reaffirming the
principles embodied in the Universal Declaration of Human Rights and urging all peoples and governments "to redouble their efforts to provide for all
human beings, a life consonant with freedom and dignity and conducive
to physical, mental, social and spiritual welfare."[8] In 1966, two covenants –
the International Covenant on Civil and Political Rights and the International Covenant on Economic, Social, and Cultural Rights – codified the key
provisions of the non-binding declaration into two legally binding treaties,
which both came into force in 1976.

The narrative was further amplified in November 1968 when the
UN General Assembly adopted Resolution 2391 (XXIII) – the Convention on the Non-Applicability of Statutory Limitations to War Crimes
and Crimes against Humanity,[9] which recognized that war crimes and
crimes against humanity were among the gravest of crimes in international law and that those who commit such crimes should be punished.[10]
This was followed in December 1973 by General Assembly Resolution
3074 (XXVIII), which proclaimed the basic principles of international
cooperation in the detection, arrest, extradition, and punishment of persons guilty of war crimes and crimes against humanity.[11] In September
1981, another milestone was reached with the affirmation of the Universal Islamic Declaration of Human Rights, a declaration based upon the
Qur'an and the Sunnah.[12]

The Right of Humanitarian Intervention
In the decade after the end of the Cold War, the UN Security Council built
upon the foundation of this evolving narrative by authorizing direct coercive and non-coercive interventions, at times against the wishes of the

governments of the target states involved or without the consent of those governments, to stop mass killings and associated crimes committed against humanity.[13] In almost all cases, this required the invocation of Chapter VII of the UN Charter to sidestep the embedded Charter principles of sovereignty and non-intervention. Chapter VII is a recognized exception, in the interest of maintaining international peace and security, to the sovereignty and non-intervention principles. Thus, by using this existing exception, the Security Council was able to extend the narrative referred to above, thus opening up discussion and debate on the proper use of "humanitarian interventions" to stop mass atrocities. Such interventions are usually defined as "coercive action by one or more states involving the use of armed force in another state without the consent of its authorities, and with the purpose of preventing widespread suffering or death among the inhabitants" (Roberts 2001, 5). The humanitarian nature of these interventions varied, including attempts to prevent large-scale loss of life (genocide or mass killing), massive forced migration and ethnic cleansing, and widespread or systematic abuse of human rights.

Although, in almost every case of humanitarian intervention, the international community – as represented by the UN Security Council – was responding to seriously at-risk populations, some observers were uncomfortable with the concept of interference in the internal affairs of states (see Weiss 1995). Ramesh Thakur (2006, 251) encapsulates the unease this way:

> The phrase "humanitarian intervention" is used to trump sovereignty with intervention at the outset of the debate: it loads the dice in favour of intervention before the argument has even begun, by labelling and delegitimizing dissent as anti-humanitarian. It is a mobilizing device to mask commercial and geopolitical motives in the call to arms for rallying citizens to the cause of unnecessary war.

As shown later, this particular line of argument has buoyed resistance to the R2P norm, particularly since the illegal intervention in Iraq by the United States. It has also been used by states such as Russia and China to prevent intervention in civil conflicts such as that in Syria. A related concern with humanitarian intervention, shared by a number of scholars, has been that, even when justification for such intervention is less objectionable, there is a sense that the paternalistic nature of the intervention tends to undermine "the credibility of the enterprise" (International Commission on Intervention and State Sovereignty 2001, 17).

The Sanctions Regime

For those concerned with this rather negative perspective on the coercive military nature of humanitarian intervention, perhaps the widespread use of international economic and political sanctions, as well as arms embargoes, during the 1990s seemed less objectionable as a strategy and as a continuation of the narrative used to address mass slaughter, crimes against humanity, and other atrocities (see Cortright and Lopez 2000; Farrall 2007; Knight 2004). Many observers have labelled the 1990s as the "sanctions decade" because the UN Security Council imposed more sanctions during that period than in the previous forty years combined. But the sanctions regime quickly became discredited because of the concomitant humanitarian suffering that it caused in many civilian populations (Weiss et al. 1997). We have learned from the comprehensive use of UN sanctions, for instance in Iraq, that they can be rather blunt instruments. They are punitive in intent (Clawson 1993), and one recurrent problem has been unintended collateral damage to innocent individuals or groups within the target state, to those in neighbouring states, and to people in proximate states locked into interdependent relationships with the target state (Christiansen and Powers 1993; Damrosch 1993). As well, arms embargoes are undermined, in many cases, by the underground trade in small arms and light weapons to many of the countries in which humanitarian atrocities are carried out and by some states' incapacity to regulate and control the activities of black marketeers, war lords, armed gangs, and even some permanent members of the UN Security Council. Smart sanctions, or targeted sanctions, were intended to improve the sanctions regime by reducing the suffering caused by the more comprehensively imposed sanctions. However, operational problems in implementing these types of sanctions remain a daunting challenge (Brzoska 2001, 2003).

"Core" Crimes and International Criminal Law

Another aspect of the evolving narrative leading to the construction of R2P can be seen in the important work done by the International Law Commission on codifying laws, such as the Draft Code of Crimes against the Peace and Security of Mankind, related to serious international criminal activity and intervention for humanitarian purposes (Knight 1997).[14] A momentous foreshadowing event, also related to this narrative, was the establishment of two ad hoc International Criminal Tribunals to prosecute individuals who committed mass atrocity crimes in the former Yugoslavia (referred to earlier) and Rwanda.

The Draft Code of Crimes, and developments before the Yugoslav and Rwandan tribunals, fed into deliberations at the 1998 Conference of Plenipotentiaries that created the International Criminal Court. Canada was a driving force for the establishment of this court. It chaired the coalition of states – the "Like-Minded Group" – that helped to motivate the international community to adopt the Rome Statute; it generated support for an independent and effective International Criminal Court through public statement and extensive lobbying; it contributed to a UN Trust Fund to enable less developed countries to participate in the International Criminal Court negotiations; it helped with the funding of NGOs from developing states so that they could participate in the discussions leading up to the establishment of the court; and Phillippe Kirsch, a senior Canadian diplomat, was voted unanimously as the chairman of the Committee of the Whole at the Conference of Plenipotentiaries in Rome that negotiated the text of the Rome Statute.[15]

Indeed, the Rome Statute of the International Criminal Court consolidated much of the existing international humanitarian and international criminal law previously agreed to by states, including the conceptualization of what constitutes international "core" crimes (mainly genocide, crimes against humanity, and war crimes).[16] According to the Rome Statute, the International Criminal Court would be given competence over those core crimes (Article 5), and it was widely agreed that the legal principles of *nullum crimen sine lege* ("no crime without law") and *nulla poena sine lege* ("no penalty without law") should be followed strictly by the court (Articles 22 and 23). On 17 July 2002, the International Criminal Court began operations when the sixtieth state party ratified the Rome Statute. The narrative of the establishment of the International Criminal Court contributed to the foundational material used in the construction of the responsibility to protect architecture by explicitly detailing, in the Rome Statute, what was meant by "core" crimes (see Robinson 1999).

R2P and the New Normative Architecture

When one looks back at the last decade of the past century, one realizes the extent to which conscience-shocking atrocities occupied the international agenda. During that decade, it also became clear that the international community, as symbolized by the United Nations, failed miserably in its attempt to live up to the promise of "never again," allowing the barbarity of genocide, mass slaughter, and other crimes against humanity to prevail in various areas of the globe. In speaking of the atrocities of the 1990s, Thakur

(2006, 26) put it starkly: "We generally failed to rise to the challenge, and the price of our failure was paid by large numbers of innocent men, women and children." This sentiment holds for the situation today in Syria, where, since March 2011, over 100,000 people have been slaughtered and the UN Security Council has failed to invoke R2P provisions. This situation has led some observers to conclude that "the R2P is the emperor's new clothes, unable to cover up the nakedness of an international system unable to deal with mass atrocities" (Strauss 2012).

One reason for this institutional malfunction has been the obvious lack of consensus among states over how the evolving narrative of protecting human rights can be woven into a new normative framework for ending the most egregious crimes against humanity while preserving and protecting a state's right to be sovereign. Yet, despite the lack of consensus, the UN Security Council has been able to authorize Chapter VII coercive multilateral interventions in some states where people have been subject to the most heinous cases of "man's inhumanity to man." The council was able to justify its decisions to intervene in those cases by labelling these humanitarian crises "threats to international peace and security," including regional peace and security. Even when the Security Council was stymied in its actions by the prospect of a Russian veto, in the case of Kosovo, an alliance of NATO countries thought it necessary to band together in a plurilateral arrangement[17] to halt the massacre of Albanians in Kosovo by the Milosevic Serbian regime (Evans and Walker 1998).

But some of these cases also revealed a growing skepticism about the use of military force on humanitarian grounds. Of particular concern was the notion of subcontracting responsibility for enforcing human rights to regional bodies or "coalitions of the willing" because it has raised serious concerns about the use of UN Security Council authority as a legitimizing cover for the foreign policy objectives of powerful states, such as the United States.[18] For example, at the July 2009 UN General Assembly's thematic dialogue on R2P, the president of the General Assembly, Miguel d'Escoto Brockmann (a former Sandinista priest), commented that "recent and painful memories related to the legacy of colonialism ... give developing countries strong reasons to fear that laudable motives can end-up being misused, once more, to justify arbitrary and selective interventions against the weakest states."[19]

At the beginning of the new millennium, with the gap growing between the evolving narrative of humanitarian intervention and the norm of sovereignty and non-intervention (enshrined in the UN Charter in 1945 but with exceptions regarding human rights violations and threats to international peace and security), there was a sense among some state leaders that something had to be done to address these competing visions. Canada, through the financial support of its International Development Research Centre, facilitated the discussion, which eventually led to a shift from the twentieth-century narrative of humanitarian intervention to the conceptualization and evolution of the R2P norm.[20]

Few scholars have written more persuasively and authoritatively about the normative development of the responsibility to protect than Thomas Weiss. He notes that, though the normative architecture of R2P was built essentially by the International Commission on Intervention and State Sovereignty (ICISS) (a Canadian government initiative), the "new thinking" and conceptual foundation for this normative architecture were provided, first, by the work of Francis Deng and Roberta Cohen and, later, by the public statements and arguments of the former UN secretary general, Kofi Annan (2007a, 88–118).

Because of the changing nature of warfare throughout the 1990s, Deng became concerned with the dramatic rise in the number of refugees and internally displaced persons worldwide. His book *Protecting the Dispossessed: A Challenge for the International Community* (1993) was a testament to his growing unease with the immense human suffering faced by millions of innocent people driven from their homes because of civil war. Deng and Cohen combined their efforts to document the plight of refugees and internationally displaced persons and to challenge state authorities that seemed to use state sovereignty as a carte blanche for treating their citizens any way that they pleased. The analytical efforts of Deng and Cohen broke new ground essentially by reframing sovereignty as responsibility, consequently plugging it into the new narrative, discussed above, trumpeting the notion that the international community has a responsibility to promote respect for human rights and humanitarian standards inside the boundaries of failed or failing states (Cohen and Deng 1998a, 1998b).

Canada, and these early R2P norm entrepreneurs, joined other human rights advocates, such as Annan, in highlighting the fact that ensuring sovereignty and protecting people at risk are not mutually exclusive concepts. For this growing body of individuals, sovereignty was not absolute but contingent; it entailed that a government was accountable not only to the population within the territorial boundaries of the sovereign state but also to the community of legitimate sovereign states that can give to or withhold from that government recognition of sovereignty. Put this way, each sovereign state has the principal responsibility to ensure the security of its people, and the international community of states can exercise a residual responsibility to ensure the security of those people if the non-compliant state in question proves unable or unwilling to offer that guarantee. From this standpoint, the sovereignty of a state is conditional on how the governors of a state treat the governed. Indeed, Annan (1999, 49–50) was explicit and convincing on this point when he stated that states are really instruments "at the service of their people, and not vice versa," and that a close reading of the UN Charter today should make us ever more conscious that this constitutive treaty aims "to protect individual human beings, not to protect those who abuse them." This attempt by norm entrepreneurs to reconcile the need for human rights protection with the principle of state sovereignty lay at the heart of the campaign to convince state leaders, who jealously guard their right to sovereignty, to buy in to the argument that human security should take precedence over state security (Axworthy 2001).

This was not an easy sell for the norm entrepreneurs. Despite the difficulties, a case was made vociferously and convincingly by a coalition of norm like-minded individuals in the Human Security Network and the Canadian government's Department of Foreign Affairs and International Trade.[21] Axworthy, then the minister of foreign affairs for Canada, and just after his remarkable success in coalition building that resulted in the drafting, signing, ratification, and implementation of the treaty to ban anti-personnel landmines by 1999,[22] put together a formidable and independent international commission of twelve high-profile individuals representing the global North and global South to lay down the normative markers for this emerging R2P norm, following global consultations.[23]

Some of the primary normative markers along the evolutionary path of the R2P norm included the linkage between national sovereignty and responsibility and the responsibility of the international community to assist states in their quest to protect their own people, to prevent the human-made crises that generally result in populations being put at risk, to react swiftly and decisively if preventive measures are unsuccessful, and to rebuild target states after outside military intervention has taken place. This logical continuum of responsibility was designed to allay fears normally associated with the "cruder" concept of humanitarian intervention or, more bluntly, "military humanitarianism." This holistic conceptualization and shift in language gave priority to prevention and restricted the use of coercive military measures to "last resort." This move proved exceedingly important in getting certain humanitarian actors on board – particularly those concerned that R2P might be used as an excuse by the strong to impose their will on the weak – a concern that re-emerged in the summer of 2009 in New York City at the thematic dialogue on R2P facilitated by the president of the UN General Assembly. But the "responsibility continuum" also had the unintended effect of muddying the waters when it came to deciding how R2P might be implemented.

For instance, in reality there are no clear-cut or tidy divisions among the policy instruments of prevention, reaction, and rebuilding. How do we know which instruments of prevention to use when there is little consensus on the root causes of conflicts (see Newman 2006)? How do we know that the money and resources spent on prevention will actually stop an atrocity from occurring? Can the United Nations' underresourced prevention mechanism (under the auspices of the special adviser to the UN secretary general) be expected to take a lead role in this area? In light of the need for a coordinated and central R2P early warning mechanism in the United Nations, will UN member governments allow the world body to be involved in this type of intelligence gathering?[24] When exactly should the move be made from prevention to reaction in a dynamic conflict? What exactly is the "R2P trigger" that would alert the international community to contemplate a military response? Will military intervention be determined by who has the means to intervene? What precisely does rebuilding involve? Will it take into consideration tackling the structural or root causes of violence? If so, would R2P not simply overlap with UN specialized agencies tasked with that mandate? Will intervening actors assume responsibility for damage caused during reaction to a crisis?

Weiss (2007a, 104) had this to say about the attempt of the ICISS to give priority in the R2P policy continuum to prevention:

> Most of the mumbling and stammering about prevention is a superficially attractive but highly unrealistic way to try and pretend that we can finesse the hard issues of what essentially amounts to humanitarian intervention. The ICISS's discourse about prevention is a helpful clarification, but it nonetheless obscures the essence of the most urgent part of the spectrum of responsibility, to protect those caught in the crosshairs of war.

Clearly, the R2P policy continuum – from "responsibility to prevent" to "responsibility to react" to "responsibility to rebuild" – seems logical, but there are definitely conceptual uncertainties and ambiguities in each phase and at the transitional points between phases.

Two other important normative markers, laid down by the ICISS, became necessary for holding together the normative architecture of R2P as well as allaying the fears of state actors, particularly from the global South. The first was the threshold to be set for R2P interventions, and the second was the justification to be used for R2P interventions. Both markers aimed to assuage concerns about the possibility of using coercive R2P unwisely and illegitimately. As Gareth Evans (2005, 10) put it, the members of the ICISS recognized the importance of avoiding "cowboy diplomacy."

In the first instance, the ICISS thought that the use of coercion under the guise of R2P would have to be exceedingly exceptional. This was why the commission reached back to embrace a deontological set of moral guidelines – grounded in the just war *(justum bellum)* tradition of the early medieval period – for justifying when and how to use force during R2P interventions. That position held that, as far as R2P was concerned, there ought to be clearly laid-out criteria, in advance, for justifying the use of force and deciding how such coercion should be carried out. In just war terminology, these two elements are known as *jus ad bellum* and *jus in bello* respectively. The list of criteria for the resort to force in any R2P intervention consists of (1) right authority, (2) just cause, (3) right intentions, (4) last resort, (5) proportionality, and (6) reasonable likelihood of success.[25]

With respect to the first criterion, the right authority, the commission thought that, if a state fails to protect people under its jurisdiction who are at risk, there is only one body that has the legitimate authority to decide to intervene militarily on behalf of those people – that body, according to the ICISS, is the UN Security Council. The United Nations is the only universal governing body on our planet and therefore represents the so-called international community of states. This community outlawed the use of force, via the UN Charter, except for cases involving individual and collective security (including cases involving Chapter VII decisions made by the Security Council), and based upon that fact, as ICISS correctly asserted, under the UN Charter, the Security Council is the primary body for authorizing the use of force to settle international disputes and override national authority.[26] Although there is a long list of concerns over the Security Council's legitimacy, efficiency, effectiveness, and credibility (see Knight 2000; Weiss 2009, 55–60), Thakur and other members of the ICISS still argued that "there is no better nor more appropriate body than the UNSC [UN Security Council] to authorize military intervention for humanitarian purposes. The task therefore is not to find alternatives to the UNSC as a source of authority but to make it work better" (Thakur 2006, 259). I would add that, given the often sluggish track record of the Security Council, and the possibility that it could be inundated in the future with requests to authorize various types of R2P interventions, perhaps the time has come for the UN system to embrace the principle of subsidiarity as a means of delegating some of the "operational" tasks of R2P to regional, transregional, and subregional bodies and agencies. Doing so would relieve the Security Council of certain burdens without denying its authoritative status. This could give the council breathing room to undergo necessary reforms that will help it to adapt to twenty-first-century tasks and concerns (e.g., protecting people at risk).

For the commission, the second criterion – just cause – had to be modified from its traditional conception to deal with contemporary scenarios. Traditionally, just cause referred strictly to a state's right to defend itself from external attack. However, during the contemporary period, in which intrastate conflicts are predominant spectacles internationally, the just cause criterion has been reformulated to respond to what were referred to above as "core crimes." R2P intervention would only be justified, according to the commission, when there is an actual or a predicted large-scale loss of life, such as mass killing or genocide, because of the deliberate actions of a state, its negligence, or its inability to act to prevent such slaughter. Just cause could also be invoked in response to such atrocities when a country fails to function as a state. Another modification of the just cause criterion was made to address the actual or apprehended crime of large-scale ethnic cleansing, whether carried out by murder, forced expulsion, acts of terror, or mass rape. Conscience-shocking war crimes and crimes against humanity were also included in the ICISS report as just causes for the invocation of R2P-type interventions. Ultimately, the international community chose to limit just cause to the core "mass atrocity" crimes of genocide, war crimes, ethnic cleansing, and crimes against humanity, implying that R2P interventions would be reserved for cases involving potential or actual large-scale loss of life and human suffering. As such, the bar is set intentionally high to weed out other types of unconscionable actions that could be dealt with using other tools available to the international community. But it is still unclear which elements of the core crimes would be jettisoned, or deemed not conscience shocking enough, when contemplating an R2P intervention. One can argue that all the core crimes are conscience shocking by their very definitions.

The criterion of right intentions was included by the commission to emphasize that the motivation behind any R2P intervention ought to be about preserving innocent lives at risk and averting human suffering rather than about the preservation of narrow national self-interest or aggrandizement. Presumably, this means that R2P should not be appropriated or used as an excuse to invade countries for the purpose of overthrowing regimes, going after terrorists, imposing a preferred political system, or securing coveted natural resources. Yet some of those acts may be required to save people at risk or alleviate their suffering. So the subjective nature of this criterion could result in the misapplication of R2P or the failure to use this norm when it is absolutely needed.

The criterion of last resort was introduced by the commission to recognize that the international community has many diplomatic paraphernalia in its toolkit to deal with threats to international peace and security. Chapter VI of the UN Charter, for instance, lists a number of non-coercive tools in the diplomatic arsenal of the United Nations, such as negotiation, enquiry, mediation, conciliation, arbitration, judicial settlement, resort to regional agencies or arrangements, and other means of pacific settlement. Essentially, the idea of last resort seems to imply that all of the non-coercive tools should be exhausted before any contemplation of coercive military intervention to deal with potential or actual genocide, war crimes, ethnic cleansing, and crimes against humanity. This is congruent with the Charter's structure of using Chapter VI mechanisms before those of Chapter VII are contemplated. If the use of peaceful measures does not bring about the desired result, then the option of coercive intervention (including economic pressure and sanctions) or military intervention, as a last resort, would be considered. But at least one of the ICISS commissioners argued that this particular "guideline was not intended to mean that every non-military option must literally have been tried and failed. Given that there will often be simply no time for that process to work itself out, what is necessary is that there be reasonable grounds for believing, in all the circumstances, that these other measures would not have worked" (Evans 2009, 144).

The criterion of proportionality refers to the need to ensure that any coercive action taken to avert suffering and death of people at risk must be commensurate with the ends and in line with the magnitude of the threat to those individuals. Put another way, the minimum amount of force necessary to bring the situation under control should be the amount used – no more, no less. But, of course, the application of proportionality is not an exact science, so it should not come as a surprise if in an R2P operation overwhelming (or underwhelming) force is used simply because of an inaccurate assessment of the threat.

This brings us to the final criterion – reasonable likelihood of success. Clearly, this criterion is based upon prior assessment of the prospect of averting suffering and loss of life. But it also implies that the policy makers implementing an R2P intervention will assess the "balance of consequences" before the military option is chosen. Would the costs of action be higher than the costs of inaction? Would the logistical difficulties make the costs of military action prohibitive? Is the intervening military force stronger or weaker than the military force of the target country? Can the intervening force be summoned quickly enough, after the decision to use coercion is made, to avoid putting the aggrieved population at further risk?

In building this normative architecture, using the pillars of sound and established ethical principles, the members of the ICISS hoped to demonstrate that R2P could in fact be a carefully circumscribed and logically "phased" approach to humanitarian intervention, and clearly they hoped to convince member states of the international community, as well as populations within those states, that by adopting this new norm the world would never again have to say "never again" when faced with conscience-shocking atrocities like those that transpired in Rwanda.

Advocacy, Tipping Points, and Diffusion of the R2P Norm

In developing the normative architecture for R2P, the ICISS engaged with representatives of governments, intergovernmental organizations, non-governmental organizations, civil society groups, and universities in a series of roundtable discussions in various capitals around the world. The purpose of these meetings was not only to gather a range of opinions on the issue of humanitarian intervention but also to advocate on behalf of the new norm of the responsibility to protect. The groundbreaking ICISS report is testament to the range of debate, the coalition building, and the North-South compromises reached to construct this new norm.

The advocacy strategy developed by the ICISS was simple. The commissioners used broad consultations to enlist an increasing number of like-minded actors to the R2P cause. They then used this growing alliance to build momentum for the diffusion and eventual acceptance of the new norm among other, perhaps less convinced, actors.[27] These norm entrepreneurs all had a good sense of how international organizations (both governmental and non-governmental) operate and of the nature of the caucuses operating within them. It also helped that they were familiar with the process of getting R2P placed on the international agenda, in various bodies and processes (at the United Nations, in peacekeeping operations,[28] in post-conflict peacebuilding and Demilitarization, Demobilization, and Reintegration programs (see Knight 2008), in regional organizations), and with the procedures through which the new norm could gain support – both informal (through corridor and backroom diplomacy with state representatives and representatives of civil society) and formal (with the tabling of resolutions or motions).

Based upon the earlier discussion on the stages in the development of a norm, we know that to achieve a cascading or tipping effect norm entrepreneurs and like-minded actors have to convince international, regional, and national institutions to incorporate the norm into their modus operandi and perhaps even in their rules, laws, and constitutional documents. Note that the Africa Union is the only intergovernmental body, so far, to have the R2P concept entrenched in its founding charter. According to the Constitutive Act of the African Union, the union has the right to intervene in the internal affairs of African states when the people of target states are at risk of war crimes, crimes against humanity, and genocide.[29]

The cascading effect of the norm is generally aided by the emergence of pressing issues and crises within the environment that call attention to the need for the norm. So, for instance, the genocide in Rwanda and the ethnic cleansing in Bosnia caused many within the international community to call for the establishment of a norm that would prevent such occurrences in the future. Similarly, the rapid deterioration of the Somali state and the internecine clan violence that accompanied its descent into statelessness caused many within the international community to cry out for a norm that would support non-consensual military and humanitarian intervention in that case and possibly R2P in the future. Linked to the above example are conflict-ridden states in which the government is unable to govern for whatever reason. In such cases, the international community has supported the idea of the establishment of an interim outside authority until elections can be held and the local people are ready to govern themselves (e.g., East Timor) (see Wilde 2008). This could be considered a precursor to the preventive and rebuilding elements of the current R2P norm. This kind of scenario helped to initiate a tipping effect that eventually led to the embrace of R2P as a critical mass of actors became increasingly convinced that a new norm was in fact needed.

In 2002–03, there were numerous instances when issues of protection were placed squarely into the policies and decision-making processes of UN member states and the UN system at large. For instance, UN entities operating in Afghanistan, Burundi, and Iraq used the *aide-mémoire* formulated by the president of the UN Security Council[30] to assemble an active collaborative framework for the protection of civilians. This resulted in a more coherent interagency response to humanitarian crises. During the same period, human rights officers deployed with the Office of the Humanitarian Coordinator for Iraq developed a policy framework on human rights protection together with UN humanitarian bodies and other international organizations to guide humanitarian assistance in that country. UN human rights advisers led interagency technical working groups on protection-related issues in Côte d'Ivoire and Iraq, and certain UN peacekeeping missions, as well as those of regional and subregional organizations and some states, began to include principles of protection in their mandates (e.g., the UN Mission in the Democratic Republic of the Congo, the Economic Community of West African States, and French forces in Côte d'Ivoire). Today there are sixteen UN peace operations in the field, and thirteen of them have mandates for civilian protection.

In October 2002, a series of regional workshops was launched to tackle issues pertaining to the protection of civilians in armed conflict. Since that time, workshops have been held in East Asia and the Pacific, Europe, the South Pacific, southern Africa, western Africa, Latin America, and South Asia. These workshops have examined the nature of humanitarian challenges during complex emergencies within each of the above regions and explored possible means of addressing such challenges from a regional perspective.[31]

Another tipping point with respect to the R2P norm came in 2004 with the report of the High-Level Panel on Threats, Challenges, and Change. The responsibility to protect norm received renewed emphasis in this report, titled *A More Secure World: Our Shared Responsibility.* The UN secretary general at the time, Kofi Annan, had established the panel and asked it to identify major threats facing the international community in the broad field of peace and security and to generate new ideas about the policies and institutions that could be used to prevent and/or confront those challenges. After deliberating for a year, the High-Level Panel issued its findings, which included an endorsement of the "emerging norm" of R2P. The panel noted that there was growing recognition of every state's responsibility to protect when it comes to people suffering from avoidable catastrophes such as "mass murder and rape, ethnic cleansing by forcible expulsion and terror, and deliberate starvation and exposure to disease" (United Nations 2004).[32] It went on to state that there is "a growing acceptance that while sovereign Governments have the primary responsibility to protect their own citizens from such catastrophes, when they are unable or unwilling to do so that responsibility should be taken up by the wider international community" using "a continuum involving prevention, response to violence, if necessary, and rebuilding shattered societies." The panelists concluded by endorsing the emergence of a norm calling for "a collective international responsibility to protect, exercisable by the Security Council authorizing military intervention as a last resort, in the event of genocide and other large scale killing, ethnic cleansing or serious violations of international humanitarian law which sovereign Governments have proved powerless or unwilling to prevent."[33]

But perhaps the most high-profile and celebrated tipping point, which had the greatest cascading effect for the R2P norm, came in the fall of 2005 during the World Summit at UN headquarters in New York City to celebrate the sixtieth anniversary of the founding of the world body. At that summit, world leaders and representatives from 191 countries discussed and agreed to take action on a range of issues, such as the development and achievement of the Millennium Development Goals by 2015; strategies to fight terrorism; the creation of a peacebuilding commission, a new standing police capacity for UN peacekeeping, and the strengthening of the UN secretary general's mediation and good offices; the responsibility to protect norm; the establishment of a Human Rights Council and improvements to democratization processes and the rule of law; UN management reform; the serious challenge posed by climate change and ways to meet that challenge; responses to pandemics and infectious diseases; improvements in humanitarian assistance; and reforms to the UN Charter. The outcome document that resulted from this summit made particular mention of the R2P norm in paragraphs 138 and 139:

138. Each individual state has the responsibility to protect its populations from genocide, war crimes, ethnic cleansing and crimes against humanity. This responsibility entails the prevention of such crimes, including their incitement, through appropriate and necessary means. We accept that responsibility and will act in accordance with it. The international community should, as appropriate, encourage and help States to exercise this responsibility and support the United Nations in establishing an early warning capability.

139. The international community, through the United Nations, also has the responsibility to use appropriate diplomatic, humanitarian and other peaceful means, in accordance with Chapters VI and VIII of the Charter of the United Nations, to help protect populations from war crimes, ethnic

cleansing and crimes against humanity. In this context, we are prepared to take collective action, in a timely and decisive manner, through the Security Council, in accordance with the Charter, including Chapter VII, on a case-by-case basis and in cooperation with relevant regional organizations as appropriate, should peaceful means be inadequate and national authorities are manifestly failing to protect their populations from genocide, war crimes, ethnic cleansing and crimes against humanity. We stress the need for the General Assembly to continue consideration of the responsibility to protect populations from genocide, war crimes, ethnic cleansing and crimes against humanity and its implications, bearing in mind the principles of the Charter and international law. We also intend to commit ourselves, as necessary and appropriate, to helping States build capacity to protect their populations from genocide, war crimes, ethnic cleansing and crimes against humanity and to assisting those which are under stress before crises and conflicts break out.[34]

One cannot help but note the resounding absence in these paragraphs of the responsibility to prevent, the guidance and criteria for the use of force, and any language reflecting the responsibility to rebuild. Also missing is any of the ICISS language indicating that natural disasters might be a trigger for an R2P intervention. For some, this version of the norm in the 2005 outcome document was considered "R2P lite" (Weiss 2007b). But the fact that these paragraphs were adopted unanimously by the General Assembly, as with the rest of the outcome document, was truly remarkable, given that some state leaders in the developing world, especially in the Non-Aligned Movement (NAM), thought that the new norm was already tainted by its association with the 2003 US intervention in Iraq.

We have already begun to see signs of internalization of the R2P norm within the UN system. In 2006, a new Human Rights Council was established. This was followed by the creation of the long-awaited Peace Building Commission – an intergovernmental advisory body set up by the Security Council and the General Assembly to focus on the transition of war-torn states from conflict to sustainable and lasting peace (see Keating and Knight 2004). According to Security Council Resolution 1645, adopted in 2005, the main purposes of the Peace Building Commission are

(a) To bring together all relevant actors to marshal resources and to advise on and propose integrated strategies for post-conflict peacebuilding and recovery;

(b) To focus attention on the reconstruction and institution-building efforts necessary for recovery from conflict and to support the development of integrated strategies in order to lay the foundation for sustainable development; [and]

(c) To provide recommendations and information that would improve the coordination of all relevant actors within and outside the United Nations, to develop best practices, to help to ensure predictable financing for early recovery activities and to extend the period of attention given by the international community to post-conflict recovery.[35]

Although the Peace Building Commission is not an operational body and does not have an enforcement mechanism, it acts as a coordinating instrument for peacebuilding activities across the UN system as well as an advisory body for the Security Council, the Economic and Social Council, and all other actors involved in the peacebuilding process.

Also, building on the momentum of the World Summit endorsement, the UN Security Council included an express affirmation of the R2P concept, as espoused in the outcome document, in Resolution 1674, adopted on 28 April 2006, concerning the protection of civilians in armed conflict.[36] On 31 August 2006, the Security Council again recognized the importance of R2P in Resolution 1706, which called for the establishment of a peacekeeping mission to Darfur.[37] Since April 2006, the Security Council has entertained debates on the Protection of Civilians in Armed Conflict, at roughly six-month intervals. After each debate, a presidential statement has been issued reaffirming paragraphs 138 and 139 of the World Summit outcome document.

Added to this, in May 2007, UN Secretary General Ban Ki-moon appointed Francis Deng as his new special adviser on the prevention of genocide.[38] On 17 July 2012, the secretary general appointed Adama Dieng of Senegal after Deng completed his assignment. In February 2008, after much controversy, Ban Ki-moon also appointed American Edward Luck his special adviser on proposals on responsibility to protect.[39] On 12 July 2013, Canadian Jennifer Welsh succeeded Luck and has been working under the guidance of Dieng "to further the conceptual, political, institutional and operational development of the responsibility to protect concept" (UN News Centre 2013). In February 2008, a new Global Centre for the Responsibility to Protect was officially opened in New York City at the Ralph Bunche Institute for International Studies, City University. This centre supports the international community's efforts to ensure that R2P moves from normative concept to reality and serves as an information clearing house and resource for governments, intergovernmental institutions, and non-governmental organizations leading the fight against mass atrocities. Associated R2P centres are being established across the globe with similar goals in mind.

Conclusion

Clearly, the responsibility to protect norm has evolved considerably from its aspirational beginnings. It emerged at a propitious moment in history when changes in the international political and security environment began to support other compatible norms, such as the human rights norm and the democratic or popular sovereignty norm. Consensus seemed to be building since the end of the Cold War period around the notion that sovereignty really lies in the hands of citizens and that state leaders are merely custodians of that sovereignty. Using this logic, sovereignty should not be used by state leaders as an entitlement to treat their citizens as they please. Basically, this indicated that the days of absolutism were coming to an end and that the so-called incompatibility of human rights and sovereignty could somehow be bridged.

This chapter provides a glimpse of the evolving narrative that preceded the adoption of responsibility to protect as a new norm in international relations. This narrative was reflected in a number of the conventions, declarations, proclamations, and UN General Assembly resolutions. It was a narrative that called states and other actors to action on protecting human rights and putting people first when it comes to security – the mantra of Canadian Lloyd Axworthy. It also provided the incentive for using multilateral and plurilateral configurations for humanitarian intervention (both consensual and non-consensual), sanctions, and arms embargoes in a number of countries where the outbreak of atrocities threatened the lives of people and forced them from their homes. However, when conscience-shocking atrocities, such as the genocide in Rwanda and the ethnic cleansing in the former Yugoslavia, were allowed to erupt in the final decade of the past century, people everywhere began to wonder if "never again" – after the Holocaust – really meant "never again."

The Canadian government must be given credit for taking the lead in pushing for the development of a norm that seeks to avert genocide, mass slaughter, and ethnic cleansing. It was this government that established the independent International Commission on Intervention and State Sovereignty, which did an outstanding job in bridging the seemingly incompatible principles of sovereignty and humanitarian intervention. Instead of a "normative clash" between existing norms of sovereignty and non-intervention and the emerging R2P norm, what has been shown in the above discussion is an attempt to develop a "normative fit." This fit was described in the following manner by the co-chairs of the ICISS:

> The Commission believes that "responsibility to protect" resides first and foremost with the state whose people are directly affected. This fact reflects not only international law and the modern state system, but also the practical realities of who is best placed to make a positive difference. The domestic authority is best placed to take action to prevent problems from turning into potential conflicts ... When solutions are needed, it is the citizens of a particular state who have the greatest interest and the largest stake in the success of those solutions, in ensuring the domestic authorities are fully accountable for their actions or inactions. (ICISS 2001, 17)

The members of the ICISS, along with key individuals within the Canadian government, such as Minister of Foreign Affairs Lloyd Axworthy, and a number of leaders within the NGO community, acted as norm entrepreneurs once the normative architecture for R2P was designed. They advocated on behalf of the new norm and developed a process of global consultations to ensure the diffusion of the normative ideas undergirding R2P. They also managed skilfully to inject the R2P idea into discussions, resolutions, and actions of intergovernmental bodies. The norm diffusion reached a tipping point at the 2005 World Summit at the United Nations in New York City, with the path-breaking adoption, by consensus, of the responsibility to protect concept in that summit's outcome document, though some have argued that this "R2P lite" version is a step back from that of the ICISS. However, since that momentous achievement in 2005, and despite the successes of its use in the cases of Kenya and Libya, there has been some backsliding by states such as China, South Africa, Egypt, Malaysia, Sri Lanka, and Cuba. This buyer's remorse seems to have dampened, temporarily, the enthusiasm among some of the advocates of this norm, and one gets the sense that the norm has begun to lose some traction. Indeed, the fact that it is not being triggered by the crimes against humanity and war crimes in Syria today makes one question whether the R2P norm is now weakened to the point where it can be challenged by other norms.

Perhaps this is why UN Secretary General Ban Ki-moon has taken it upon himself to get the norm back on track.[40] To some extent, he has taken a risk. Opening up debate on this subject could have the effect of opening up Pandora's box. The delicate balance negotiated between the global North and the global South that led to the unanimous endorsement of R2P in the 2005 outcome document could become partially or completely undone in this debate, and the level of support that the norm has received up to this point could be severely weakened. But, if the UN secretary general's special advisers on genocide and R2P can develop the type of state–civil society coalition that produced the successful ban on anti-personnel landmines, there is hope that a new and even broader-based consensus (involving not just state leaders but also the ordinary citizens for whom R2P was envisaged) can be reached on this evolving norm. But for this to happen, the UN secretary general has to get backsliders from the norm, such as the current Canadian government, back on board.

NOTES

1 Other well-known crimes against humanity include the Assyrian mass slaughter at the end of the First World War, the Armenian killings and forced displacement by the Ottoman Empire in 1915, and the Simele massacre in Iraq in 1933.

2 The full name of this tribunal is the International Tribunal for the Prosecution of Persons Responsible for Serious Violations of International Humanitarian Law Committed in the Territory of the Former Yugoslavia since 1991. See http://www.icty.org/sid/7424.

3 I use "narrative" here to mean an account of a sequence of events that connects those events in a coherent manner – that is, similar to the recounting of a story that has a specific plot – and shapes the meaning and texture of the story being told. An "evolving narrative" is therefore one that reveals, over time, basic layers of connected, and sometimes seemingly disconnected, elements that eventually expose the underlying "plot" of the story being told. In the case of R2P, the evolving narrative can be considered an aspiration (i.e., short of a "norm"), but it lays the foundation upon which the normative architecture of R2P is built.

4 Adopted 9 December 1948, 78 UNTS 277 (entered into force on 12 January 1951).

5 Genocide Convention, Articles 1, 5, and 6.

6 See the Genocide Convention, Article 2.

7 See, further, https://treaties.un.org/Publication/MTDSG/Volume%20I/Chapter%20IV/IV-1.en.pdf.

8 Tehran Proclamation on Human Rights, published in the Final Act of the International Conference on Human Rights, Tehran, 22 April–13 May 1968, UN Doc. A/CONF.32/41 at paragraph 2.

9 Adopted 26 November 1968, 754 UNTS 73 (entered into force 11 November 1970).

10 Note that this convention emphasized that there shall be no statutory limitations placed on such crimes, regardless of when they were carried out.

11 Within this resolution, the UN General Assembly also proclaimed agreement with its 1967 Declaration on Territorial Asylum and the principle of denying asylum to anyone suspected of committing crimes against peace, war crimes, or crimes against humanity. See GA Res. 3074 (XXVIII) at paragraph 7.

12 See http://www.alhewar.com/ISLAMDECL.html.

13 These cases include Liberia (1990–97), northern Iraq (1991), the former Yugoslavia (1992–95), Somalia (1992–93), Rwanda (1994–96), eastern Zaire (1994–96), Haiti (1994–97), Sierra Leone (1997–2002), Kosovo (1999), and East Timor (1999). Note that all of these cases are well documented in the report by the International Commission on Intervention and State Sovereignty 2001, Chapter 5.

14 The document can be found at http://legal.un.org/ilc/texts/instruments/english/draft%20articles/7_4_1996.pdf.

15 Later Kirsch was elected as a judge of the International Criminal Court and as the president of the court.

16 Note that, since states could not agree on including terrorism and drug trafficking on that list of core crimes, and since they could not agree on a definition of aggression, these issues were left for a review conference held in Kampala, Uganda, from 31 May to 11 June 2010.

17 On plurilateralism, see Knight (2005).

18 See, for example, the press reports concerning comments by the former president of UNGA (Father Miguel d'Escoto Brockmann of Nicaragua, a Sandinista priest) at the R2P "thematic dialogue" hosted by UNGA in July 2009: http://www0.un.org/ga/president/63/interactive/responsibilitytoprotect.shtml and http://www.ais.org/~jrh/acn/ACn19-1.pdf.

19 See http://www.un.org/ga/president/63/statements/openingr2p230709.shtml and http://www.un.org/ga/president/63/interactive/responsibilitytoprotect.shtml.

20 Excellent accounts of this evolution are provided by Bellamy (2009); Evans (2009).

21 The Human Security Network included participants from Austria, Canada, Chile, Ireland, Jordan, The Netherlands, Norway, Slovenia, Switzerland, and Thailand.

22 Convention on the Prohibition of the Use, Stockpiling, Production and Transfer of Anti-Personnel Mines and on Their Destruction, adopted 18 September 1997, 2056 UNTS 241 (entered into force 1 March 1999).

23 That group consisted of the following: Gareth Evans (former foreign minister of Australia) and Mohamed Sahnoun (an Algerian diplomat and former special representative of the UN secretary general) as co-chairs; Ramesh Thakur (India); Cyril Ramaphosa (South Africa); Fidel Ramos (Philippines); Eduardo Stein (Guatemala); Vladimir Lukin (Russia); Lee Hamilton (USA); Michael Ignatieff (Canada); Klaus Naumann (Germany); Cornelio Sommaruga (Switzerland); and Gisèle Côté-Harper (Canada). Note that much of the research for this team was compiled and coordinated by Thomas Weiss (director of the Ralph Bunche Institute for International Studies at City University, New York), Stanlake Samkange (Zimbabwe), and Don Hubert (DFAIT, Canada). Administrative support for the commission was provided by a secretariat housed in the Department of Foreign Affairs and International Trade, Canada (Ottawa), staff members at Canadian embassies around the globe, and the International Development Research Centre of Canada. Funding for the work of the commission was provided by Canada, Switzerland, and the United Kingdom, as well as by the Carnegie Corporation of New York, the William and Flora Hewlett Foundation, the John D. and Catherine T. MacArthur Foundation, the Rockefeller Foundation, and the Simons Foundation.

24 Note that the last attempt was the Office of Research and Collection of Information (ORCI), which did not fare well. See Knight and Yamashita (1993).
25 See section 4.1.6 of the ICISS report at http://www.iciss.ca/pdf/Commission-Report. pdf.
26 There have been instances when the Security Council was stymied in its actions because of excessive use of the veto by one or more of the permanent five members of this body. In such cases, as the ICISS noted, the General Assembly can be authorized to take action, using the precedent of the Uniting for Peace Resolution.
27 For examples of a similar strategy, see Franceschet and Knight (2001).
28 See UN Security Council Resolution 1706 (2006), UN Doc. S/RES/1706/2006.
29 Constitutive Act of the African Union, 11 July 2000, 2158 UNTS 3 (entered into force 26 May 2001), paragraph 4(b).
30 UN Doc. S/PRST/2002/6, annex.
31 Report of the SG on the work of the organization, UN Doc. A/62/1 (2002), 21–22.
32 The outcome document does not propose that deliberate starvation and exposure to disease be used as a trigger to activate R2P.
33 See United Nations (2004), especially paragraphs 201 and 203.
34 "2005 World Summit Outcome," General Assembly Resolution 60/1 of 16 September 2005, UN Doc. A/Res/60/1 (2005).
35 UN Doc. S/RES/1645 (2005) at paragraph 2.
36 UN Doc. S/RES/1674 (2006) at paragraph 4.
37 UN Doc. S/RES/1706 (2006), preamble, paragraph 2.
38 UN Doc. SG/A/1070 (29 May 2007); see http://www.un.org/News/Press/docs//2007/ sga1070.doc.htm.
39 UN Doc. SG/A/1120 (21 February 2008); see http://www.un.org/News/Press/docs// 2008/sga1120.doc.htm.
40 United Nations, General Assembly, A/63/677 (12 January 2009).

References

Annan, Kofi. 1999. "Two Concepts of Sovereignty." *The Economist*, 18 September, 49–50.
Axworthy, Lloyd. 1999. "NATO's New Security Vocation." *NATO Review* 47 (4): 8–11.
Axworthy, Lloyd. 2001. "Human Security and Global Governance: Putting People First." *Global Governance* 7 (1): 19–23.
Bellamy, Alex. 2009. *A Responsibility to Protect: The Global Effort to End Mass Atrocities.* Cambridge: Polity Press.
Brzoska, Michael. 2001. *Design and Implementation of Arms Embargoes and Travel and Aviation Related Sanctions: Results of the Bonn-Berlin Process.* Bonn: Bonn International Centre for Conversion.
Brzoska, Michael. 2003. "From Dumb to Smart? Recent Reforms of UN Sanctions." *Global Governance* 9 (4): 519–35.
Christiansen, Drew, and Gerard F. Powers. 1993. "Sanctions: Unintended Consequences." *Bulletin of the Atomic Scientists* 49 (9): 41–45.

Clawson, Patrick. 1993. "Sanctions as Punishment, Enforcement, and Prelude to Further Action." *Ethics and International Affairs* 7: 17–37. http://dx.doi.org/10.1111/j.1747-7093.1993.tb00141.x.

Cohen, Roberta, and Francis M. Deng. 1998a. *Masses in Flight: The Global Crisis of Internal Displacement.* Washington, DC: Brookings Institution.

Cohen, Roberta, and Francis M. Deng, eds. 1998b. *The Forsaken People: Case Studies of the Internally Displaced.* Washington, DC: Brookings Institution.

Cortright, David, and George A. Lopez. 2000. *The Sanctions Decade: Assessing UN Strategies in the 1990s.* Boulder, CO: Lynne Rienner.

Damrosch, Lori. 1993. "The Civilian Impact of Economic Sanctions." In *Enforcing Restraint: Collective Intervention in International Conflicts,* edited by Lori Damrosch, 274–315. New York: Council on Foreign Relations.

Deng, Francis M. 1993. *Protecting the Dispossessed: A Challenge for the International Community.* Washington, DC: Brookings Institution.

Evans, Gareth. 2005. "The Responsibility to Protect: Evolution and Implementation." *International Crisis Group,* 1 July, 10.

Evans, Gareth. 2008. *The Responsibility to Protect: Ending Mass Atrocity Crimes Once and for All.* Baltimore: Brookings Institution Press.

Evans, Gareth. 2009. "The Responsibility to Protect and the Use of Military Force." International Crisis Group. http://www.crisisgroup.org/en/publication-type/speeches/2007/evans-the-responsibility-to-protect-and-the-use-of-military-force.aspx.

Evans, Michael, and Tom Walker. 1998. "NATO Bombers on Alert for Order to Hit Serbs." *Times,* 12 October.

Farrall, Jeremy. 2007. *United Nations Sanctions and the Rule of Law.* Cambridge: Cambridge University Press. http://dx.doi.org/10.1017/CBO9780511494352.

Franceschet, Antonio, and W. Andy Knight. 2001. "International(ist) Citizenship: Canada and the International Criminal Court." *Canadian Foreign Policy Journal* 8 (2): 51–74. http://dx.doi.org/10.1080/11926422.2001.9673245.

International Commission on Intervention and State Sovereignty. 2001. *The Responsibility to Protect: Research, Bibliography, Background.* Ottawa: International Development Research Centre.

Keating, Tom, and W. Andy Knight, eds. 2004. *Building Sustainable Peace.* Tokyo: United Nations University Press; Edmonton: University of Alberta Press.

Knight, W. Andy. 1997. "Legal Issues." In *A Global Agenda: Issues before the 52nd General Assembly of the United Nations,* edited by John Tessitore and Susan Woolfson, 267–98. New York: Rowman and Littlefield.

Knight, W. Andy. 2000. *A Changing United Nations: Multilateral Evolution and the Quest for Global Governance.* New York: Palgrave Macmillan. http://dx.doi.org/10.1057/9780333984420.

Knight, W. Andy. 2004. "Improving the Effectiveness of UN Arms Embargoes." In *The United Nations and Global Security,* edited by Richard Price and Mark Zacher, 39–55. New York: Palgrave Macmillan.

Knight, W. Andy. 2005. "Plurilateral Multilateralism: Canada's Emerging International Policy?" In *Canada among Nations 2005: Split Images,* edited by Andrew F. Cooper and Dane Rowlands, 93–114. Montreal/Kingston: McGill-Queen's University Press.

Knight, W. Andy. 2008. "Disarmament, Demobilization, and Reintegration and Post-Conflict Peacebuilding in Africa: An Overview." *African Security* 1 (1): 24–52. http://dx.doi.org/10.1080/19362200802285757.

Knight, W. Andy, and Mari Yamashita. 1993. "The United Nations Contribution to International Peace and Security." In *Building a New Global Order: Emerging Trends in International Security,* edited by David Dewitt, David Haglund, and John Kirton, 284–312. Oxford: Oxford University Press.

Lemkin, Raphael. 1944. *Axis Rule in Occupied Europe: Analysis, Proposals for Redress.* Washington, DC: Carnegie Endowment for International Peace.

Newman, Edward. 2006. "Exploring the 'Root Causes' of Terrorism." *Studies in Conflict and Terrorism* 29 (8): 749–72. http://dx.doi.org/10.1080/10576100600704069.

Nossal, Kim Richard. 2013. "The Use – and Misuse – of R2P: The Case of Canada." In *Libya: The Responsibility to Protect and the Future of Humanitarian Intervention,* edited by Aidan Hehir and Robert Murray, 110–29. Houndmills, UK: Palgrave Macmillan.

Roberts, Adam. 2001. "The So-Called 'Right' of Humanitarian Intervention." In *Yearbook of International Humanitarian Law* 3: 3–51. The Hague: T.M.C. Asser.

Robinson, Darryl. 1999. "Defining Crimes against Humanity at the Rome Conference." *American Journal of International Law* 93 (1): 43–57. http://dx.doi.org/10.2307/2997955.

Strauss, Ekkehard. 2012. "From Idea to Experience: Syria and the Responsibility to Protect." 28 February. http://www.iss.europa.eu/publications/detail/article/from-idea-to-experience-syria-and-the-responsibility-to-protect/.

Thakur, Ramesh. 2006. *The United Nations, Peace, and Security: From Collective Security to the Responsibility to Protect.* Cambridge: Cambridge University Press. http://dx.doi.org/10.1017/CBO9780511755996.

Totten, Samuel, and Paul R. Bartrop. 2009. "The History of Genocide: An Overview." In *The Genocide Studies Reader,* edited by Samuel Totten and Paul Bartrop. New York: Routledge. 135–57

United Nations. Secretary General's Office. 2004. *A More Secure World: Our Shared Responsibility: Report of the High-Level Panel on Threats, Challenges, and Change.* UN Doc. A/59/565, 2 December. http://www1.umn.edu/humanrts/instree/report.pdf.

United Nations. Secretary General's Office. 2008. "Secretary-General Defends, Clarifies 'Responsibility to Protect' at Berlin Event on 'Responsible Sovereignty: International Cooperation for a Changed World." SG/SM/11701, 15 July. New York: UN Department of Public Information, News and Media Division.

UN News Centre. 2013. "Secretary-General Appoints Special Adviser to Focus on Responsibility to Protect." 12 July. http://www.un.org/apps/news/story.asp?NewsID=45398#.UgjwjV_D_oY.

Weiss, Thomas. 1995. "Military-Civilian Humanitarians: The Age of Innocence Is Over." *International Peacekeeping* 2 (2): 157–74. http://dx.doi.org/10.1080/13533319508413549.

Weiss, Thomas. 2007a. *Humanitarian Intervention: Ideas in Action.* Cambridge: Polity Press.

Weiss, Thomas. 2007b. "R2P after 9/11 and the World Summit." *Wisconsin International Law Journal* 24 (3): 741–60.

Weiss, Thomas. 2009. *What's Wrong with the United Nations and How to Fix It.* Cambridge: Polity Press.

Weiss, Thomas, David Cortright, George A. Lopez, and Larry Minear. 1997. *Political Gain and Civilian Pain: Humanitarian Impacts of Economic Sanctions.* Lanham, MD: Rowman and Littlefield.

Wilde, Ralph. 2008. *International Territorial Administration.* Oxford: Oxford University Press. http://dx.doi.org/10.1093/acprof:oso/9780199274321.001.0001.

2 War-Fighting and the Decline of Humanitarian Space in Canadian Security Policy

ALISTAIR EDGAR

Humanitarianism takes many forms and is understood in many different – not always complementary or even compatible – ways by individuals, groups, governments, and international organizations. Here, I use the term primarily in direct reference to the notion of humanitarian intervention that emerged in Canadian foreign and security policy discussions during the 1990s within the then-new framework of human security, espoused and championed by the Liberal minister of foreign affairs, Lloyd Axworthy, and that eventually was expressed in the December 2001 report, *The Responsibility to Protect*,[1] issued by the Canadian-government-sponsored International Commission on Intervention and State Sovereignty. Secondarily, and in more generic terms, though still closely connected in practice to this first usage, I refer to humanitarianism as meaning a focus on the needs of people facing imminent crises that threaten their physical safety; as will be indicated, this is the narrower Canadian understanding (freedom from fear) rather than the alternative preferred by states such as Japan that add broader economic and social development components (freedom from want as well as freedom from fear).[2] Finally, "humanitarian space" refers here both to the (declining) attention paid to such considerations *within* the policy-making process in Ottawa and to what many humanitarian NGOs and individual commentators report or have experienced as the problematic operational and in-theatre effects of the increasing militarization of international humanitarian interventions.[3]

The 9/11 attacks finally and tragically brought onto American soil and into the forefront of (North) Americans' contemporary lived experience the violence and destruction from terrorism and war that have plagued so many other states and societies and the daily lives of millions of innocent individuals elsewhere in the world. Since September 2001, Canadians for their part have witnessed, but not always or clearly recognized, their country shift from being a globally acknowledged and respected supporter of multilateralism to being regarded as US and NATO (and pro-Israeli) focused, explicitly and loudly critical of global norms that do not match Harper government views and values.[4] At the same time, the Canadian Forces have changed from being considered as highly professional contributors to UN peacekeeping and peace enforcement to being viewed (in Ottawa and other capitals around the world) and used increasingly as warfighters in support of Washington's causes. Although this is the government's choice to make – and indeed has had strong support within the Canadian Forces from groups who have become disillusioned by the inevitable politics of UN missions – it has come at a heavy price both in casualties and in costs in an American- and NATO-led Afghan mission whose outcome in 2013–14 is at least as uncertain, unsatisfactory, and messy as any complex UN operation.

Canadian security policy during this period, but also (as will be argued here) beginning in the 1990s, has become much more militarized both in its goals and in its instruments, just as Canadian foreign policy generally (including its overseas development assistance policy, now folded within Foreign Affairs) has become increasingly "securitized" in its public rhetoric, policy planning, and policy practice. Security defined, and hence resourced, in instrumental terms – military and economic in nature, narrowly self-interested in focus – has taken centre stage in Ottawa and, as Rosalind Warner notes in the introduction to this volume, consequently and deliberately (indeed, I would argue, belligerently) has pushed alternative views and broader understandings of humane internationalism to the sidelines. In place of human security and informed consideration of divergent ideas has come what Warner describes aptly in the introduction as "the sanctimonious use of hard power."[5]

Engagement in the so-called Long War in Afghanistan certainly has been both an important source and a consequence of this militarization and securitization of Canadian foreign and security policy. However, Canada's increasingly deep engagement in that war from 2001 to 2011, prior to the decision to reposition the Canadian Forces from their combat mission in

Kandahar to a much smaller training mission based in or around Kabul, was not the only or always the most important direct influence on these shifts in the content and framework of foreign and security policy. As noted in the next section, on addressing human security and intervention in the 1990s, there were other domestic, continental, and international agents (governmental and non-governmental), as well as related events and policy debates, that at times had significant roles and effects as drivers of change in Canadian policy.

It should be clear from these introductory comments that the analysis presented here – or the narrative told primarily in qualitative form – moves across and between domestic and international/global levels of analysis and traverses the artificial but at times heuristically useful boundaries among social, economic, political, and security issues. It will also become apparent that in this analysis or narrative, dissenting somewhat from the title of the volume, "ethics" is not considered as something that has to be, or that can be, balanced or measured *against* "security" in Canadian foreign policy – such a view implies that the two terms refer to distinct entities or goals that might be mutually exclusive (e.g., more ethics mean less security, while an emphasis on security means that a policy is less ethical or possibly even unethical?). Instead, I take security itself to be an essentially contested concept: the debates over its content include differing views on what and whose values, standards, and codes of behaviour, as well as material interests, are to be protected and/or promoted; how, where, and when they are to be pursued; and hence the set(s) of rules or justifications deployed for doing so. These are debates over the ethical form and content *of* security rather than debates over the balance *between* ethics and security.

Descriptions of differing understandings of security in this sense include the realist state-centred definition focusing on state (sometimes confused with "national") security interests and emphasizing hard power military resources; a liberal perspective that mixes state- and people-centred interests and values and recognizes the utility of soft power as well as military power; and a cosmopolitan interpretation that focuses on individuals and recognizes issues of structural inequality and insecurity that are economic, social, and cultural and can be addressed only through systemic change.[6] Proponents of each might describe themselves as being ethical – where ethics are understood to mean a set of rules or standards of behaviour in practice, usually within the wider context of a moral understanding of "right" and "wrong" or "good" and "bad." Here too, when dealing with humanitarian intervention, I add the debate between proponents of an "ethics of principled conviction," in which a good or right intent is the critical consideration by which to evaluate subsequent actions, and an "ethics of responsibility," which argues that the possible (especially the actual) negative consequences and outcomes of decisions or actions (and of refusals to act) must be considered rather than simply set aside or justified by reference to good intentions (see Wheeler 2002).

Finally, without seeking to impose any particular trajectory on the chronological narrative as having been causally inevitable, the story line of Canada and humanitarian intervention since the early 1990s has been marked – and in many ways shaped – by a number of milestone events or experiences that are highlighted in the following sections. At the time of writing the initial draft of this chapter, I argued that this story line was expressed, ironically, in the engagement of the Canadian government under Conservative Prime Minister Stephen Harper in enforcing the UN Security Council–sanctioned and NATO-led mission to impose a no-fly zone in Libya. Reviewing and revising the chapter several months later, I see no reason to change that initial characterization. Dubbed Operation Unified Protector, the mission was justified by its sponsors in the UN Security Council as protecting the Libyan civilian population from the threat of massive violence, while also directly supporting the forces of the rebel National Transitional Council in their ground war against troops loyal to deposed Libyan leader Moammar Gadhafi.

The Harper government – supported by the senior leadership of the Canadian Forces – had moved deliberately since 2006 to reject all requests from the UN secretary general in New York City to join what Ottawa saw as open-ended and ill-fated UN peacekeeping operations and to distance itself at home and abroad from the policy initiatives of its Liberal government predecessors. However, the Conservatives sought out and chose in 2011 to take on a new multilateral (though strongly urged by Washington and its NATO allies) military engagement in Africa, with no clearly established end date – only an end state, meaning the "victory" of the National Transitional Council. So long as the United States backed the mission, it did not seem to be a concern in Ottawa that the intervention was being justified globally by reference to the humanitarian intervention principles of the United Nations as expressed in *The Responsibility to Protect,* a new norm-cum-doctrine of humanitarian intervention recently approved by member states of the United Nations at the 2005 UN World Summit that, as Andy Knight's detailed analysis of R2P (as it became known) describes, was developed at the initiative and with the strong support of previous Liberal governments.

Human Security and Humanitarian Intervention in the 1990s

UN Failures in Peacekeeping: No Peace to Keep

The experiences of the early and mid-1990s were almost uniformly negative for Canadian security policy makers. The engagement of the Canadian Airborne Regiment Battle Group as part of UNOSOM I in Somalia, in 1992–93, ended in scandal and disgrace despite its participation in many otherwise successful civil-military cooperation projects. Although neither Canada nor the Canadian Airborne Regiment Battle Group was involved thereafter in the US-led UNITAF operation or UNOSOM II, the ill-fated end of the US military in the so-called Battle of Mogadishu on 3 October 1993, which led to US withdrawal from Somalia and UNOSOM II, played an important part in shaping deeply negative views in Western capitals – including Ottawa – of making military commitments to UN-led operations in African or other regional intrastate conflicts.[7] While the repercussions of the Canadian engagement in Somalia under UNOSOM I played out at home, another conflict much closer to Europe reinforced negative views of the capacity of the UN Security Council to take firm action and provide capable leadership for military interventions in civil wars and humanitarian crises. The disintegration of the Federal Republic of Yugoslavia led to a short war between Serbian and Croatian militaries and most notably to the outbreak of a brutal civil war in Bosnia-Herzegovina. The UN Protection Force, UNPROFOR, including the Canadian Forces, was provided neither with the Security Council mandate nor with the equipment and manpower to respond effectively. The culmination of this disgrace took place in mid-1995 with the massacre by Bosnian Serb forces of several thousand Muslim men and boys at the UN-designated "safe area" of Srebrenica, the worst mass killing of civilians in Europe since 1945.

If these two experiences were not sufficient by themselves to overdetermine a deeply negative view in Ottawa and especially within the Department of National Defence of the existing forms of UN-led peacekeeping operations, they were reinforced profoundly by the horrendous spectacle in 1994 of genocide being committed in Rwanda while the members of the UN Security Council stood aside and pretended not to know and of Canadian UNAMIR Force Commander Lieutenant General Romeo Dallaire desperately requesting 2,000 additional troops to halt the anticipated mass killings – but effectively and infamously being ignored by UN headquarters in New York City.[8]

Human Security: From Soft Power Idealism to Hard Power Realism?

This was the recent historical background and experience of deep disillusionment and tragic failure that influenced many practitioners' as well as scholars' opinions about Canadian foreign and defence policy – especially about undertaking overseas military commitments within a UN peacekeeping framework – in Ottawa when Lloyd Axworthy became the minister of foreign affairs in January 1996, taking over the office from André Ouellet. Axworthy strongly championed the view that a new (liberal though not necessarily Liberal[9]) notion of people-centred "human security" had to be adopted and should supplement the traditional (realist) focus on state-centric national security. With his energetic leadership, and backed by Canadian Ministry of Foreign Affairs resources, remarkably rapid – and, for many observers, unexpected – progress was accomplished by a shifting alliance of small- and middle-power "like-minded" states and a plethora of dedicated civil society actors. Despite criticism from, and at times active opposition by, the US administration, the Anti-Personnel Mines Ban Convention of December 1997 and the Rome Statute of July 1998 establishing a permanent International Criminal Court were the fruits of what was widely termed the "Ottawa process." Other initiatives aimed at outlawing child soldiers, and setting up a global compact to monitor and restrict the trade in small arms and light weapons, met with less success but still drew widespread public attention to these people-centred human security issues.

Each of these human security policy initiatives can be seen as cases best described by a liberal or even a cosmopolitan understanding of the ethics of security. They engaged and involved the efforts of not only government bodies but also many different non-governmental actors. Their subject matter was related clearly to protecting or promoting the physical security of individual people in situations of violent conflict, but the means or instruments employed were those of soft power – political, diplomatic, legal, technical, and public activism via social media dissemination and the monitoring of information before, during, and after the agreements were (or were not) signed. The landmines ban and International Criminal Court agreements themselves were signed by state parties, and the commitment by Axworthy of state funding and his provision of Canadian diplomatic support (and that of other like-minded states) were important, but a wealth of critical expertise and popular impetus were also provided by civil society groups and individuals. There undoubtedly existed an ethics of principled conviction among those individuals and groups seeking to advance the human security agenda, but there was also an ethics of responsibility visibly engaged, as the initiatives were aimed at deterring or otherwise minimizing possible future as well as present harm to civilian populations through peaceful and cooperative multilateral measures.

As much as these diplomatic-political-social accomplishments were celebrated, however, the human security agenda faced a different challenge with the eruption of violence in the restive southern Serbian (former Federal Republic of Yugoslavia) province of Kosovo in 1998–99. In the case of the Kosovo crisis, a commitment to the human security agenda in Ottawa (and in the British Labour government of Prime Minister Tony Blair) meshed with the purported lessons learned in Washington, London, and Ottawa from the ineffectual or non-existent interventions to protect civilians in Rwanda and Bosnia. There nevertheless took place, and still remains, intense debate regarding the official justification for the eventual NATO-led bombing campaign of March–July 1999 in which the Canadian Forces took a leading combat role. Leaders such as Blair called it a "war for values" and a "moral war," even "the first post modern war," fought for humanitarian rather than geopolitical reasons.[10] Liberal and left-leaning civil society groups in Canada, the United States, and Europe found themselves in the unexpected position of supporting a large-scale military campaign conducted by NATO to prevent what they believed was an imminent campaign of ethnic cleansing or worse against the Kosovo Albanian population. Western critics of intervention came from the right side of the political spectrum and opposed what they argued was a premature and illegal intervention in the internal affairs of a sovereign state (Dashwood 2000).

At NATO headquarters, one motivation among several was the strategic consideration to demonstrate that the Atlantic alliance remained a credible, capable, and relevant organization for ensuring European security in the post-Cold War era. There might have been some satisfaction as well in Western capitals at the opportunity to act against the Serbian leader who had frustrated and humiliated Western governments during the Bosnian Civil War of 1992–95.[11] A detailed evaluation of the merits of these positions – and of the opposition and criticism that came from Serbian ally Russia – would go far beyond the analytical scope of the review here. Important to the current story is that, in this case, the pursuit and exercise of the new human security agenda involved both governments and civil society groups engaging actively in the securitization and militarization of that agenda.

Principled conviction among many of the advocates of intervention justified – in their view – the bombing of targets and the killing of people (military and paramilitary forces) in Kosovo and elsewhere in Serbia to prevent something that they believed was about to happen. That, of course, is also the dilemma of preventive and pre-emptive action in such circumstances – by definition, its success means that the feared action or activity constituting a mass and systematic abuse does not take place, and this can leave ground for significant disagreement over end results in the absence of any clear and convincing evidence that the action was imminent. The ethics of responsibility, at the same time, are a difficult case to make in such circumstances. In the case of Kosovo, the mass displacement of civilians occurred mainly after the start of the NATO bombing rather than before it, and Serbian as well as Kosovo Albanian civilians were killed by errant bombing strikes or because they happened to be in the vicinity of military targets. The campaign took far longer than originally anticipated before President Milosevic announced the withdrawal of Serbian military units from Kosovo, and those units appeared to have been largely unscathed despite the bombing campaign. When the Milosevic regime was toppled finally, it came about through the efforts of internal Serbian opposition movements after a disputed presidential election in September 2000 rather than as a result of Western campaigning.[12]

The bombing of Kosovo was a deeply controversial issue in Canada in foreign and security policy. It demonstrated that the narrower definition of human security adopted by Canada – with its focus on "freedom from fear," meaning the physical security of people from threats or acts of mass violence – at times and in some circumstances could itself require the credible threat or use of force. If an advantage of the narrower definition was that it thus became more focused and manageable, a disadvantage was that, when challenged by external circumstances requiring action, that action quickly took on a military character at least in part for lack of any alternatives. Broader or longer-term global structural inequalities of economic, social, and cultural forms ("freedom from want") that might be the underlying sources of conflict between groups in fragile states and societies fell, in this approach, to the remit of overseas development assistance rather than human security.

Advocates of the action among Western governments and non-governmental organizations described the Kosovo intervention as having been

legitimate but illegal.[13] In the absence of a prior UN Security Council resolution authorizing the use of force against Serbia as a sovereign state, and
aware that any proposed resolution would face a Russian veto, the leaders of
NATO states chose to act outside the UN framework as an "alliance of the
willing." Following this experience, which also caused great disillusionment
and disaffection among some of the domestic civil society supporters of
Axworthy, Canada again took a lead role in supporting efforts to rethink the
framework of human security and humanitarian intervention. Working on
the realistic (and realist) assumption that international interventions would
take place or be called for again in the future, the goal was to develop a better framework and set of commonly accepted global standards by which the
legality and legitimacy of such interventions might be recognized in a timely
manner, preferably within but if necessary outside the Security Council.
Thus, in September 2000, at the opening of the UN General Assembly in
New York City, and one month before Axworthy would be replaced as minister of foreign affairs by John Manley, Canada announced its support for
the establishment of the International Commission on Intervention and
State Sovereignty.[14]

Human Security and Humanitarian Intervention since 2001

The New Interventionism and Shrinking Humanitarian Space

Humanitarian intervention as an emerging global norm took shape as a
direct result of the analysis and recommendations of the International
Commission on Intervention and State Sovereignty expressed in its December 2001 report. The "lessons learned" from Somalia, Bosnia, Rwanda, and
most recently Kosovo played a role in informing the thinking of the commissioners, as did dozens of special regional consultations and submissions.
Public attention to the presentation of the final report, *The Responsibility
to Protect*, understandably was lost in the immediate aftermath of the 9/11
terrorist attacks and the beginning of the US-led military campaign to oust
al-Qaeda and the Taliban regime from Afghanistan. Still, the rapid defeat
of the Taliban regime and the widely accepted right of the United States
to respond militarily against the organization behind the attacks initially
left ample intellectual and political space for discussion and dissemination
of the R2P framework of prevention, protection, and rebuilding. However,
both R2P and the Afghan campaign were overshadowed soon by the subsequent manoeuvring of the Bush administration during 2002–03 in search
of excuses to justify its illegal and illegitimate invasion of Iraq – an elective

war pushed through by a political clique in Washington for a mixture of narrowly self-interested motives rather than an act of national self-defence.

The invasion of Iraq divided American society almost as much as it divided global opinion and destroyed the sympathy for America that the 9/11 attacks had created. As Andy Knight's study of the emergence, diffusion, and institutionalization – and arguably diminishment and decline – of R2P indicates, it had the additional consequence of reinforcing the existing suspicions of developing world leaders that the R2P norm could and would be abused by the United States or the former European colonial powers to justify military interventions that those powers wanted to pursue for their own geopolitical and commercial interests. Despite this skeptical and even hostile political climate, Prime Minister Paul Martin placed his own and Canada's reputations behind R2P in advance of the 2005 World Summit in New York City marking the sixtieth anniversary of the founding of the United Nations. Although high-profile proposals for UN Security Council reform faltered and then failed in the face of deeply divided state interests, Martin personally called upon other world leaders by telephone and in person and promoted the new humanitarian intervention norm as a genuinely significant advance in global governance and the prevention of mass violence against innocent civilian populations.[15] With his direct support, at the September 2005 World Summit, the UN General Assembly accepted and adopted wording in favour of R2P as a new global principle or norm of human security and as a new doctrine of national and global responsibility.[16]

Although Martin's arguments in favour of R2P appeared to have proven sufficiently persuasive among more hesitant world leaders in 2005, the United Nations had experienced by then the increasingly troubling effects of the perceived and real decline of "humanitarian space" – the space, both figurative and literal, that humanitarian agencies had enjoyed for conducting their activities as neutral and impartial actors focused on relieving the suffering of all individuals caught in zones of conflict. In mid-August 2003, a suicide bomber struck the UN compound in Baghdad, killing twenty-two UN and other staff, including Special Representative Sergio Vieira de Mello, and injuring over 100 others. Assuming that it would be safe because its focus was on delivering humanitarian assistance to ordinary Iraqis, and perhaps because the UN Security Council and even the secretary general had voiced their opposition to the US-instigated invasion of Iraq, the compound was relatively weakly protected and thus an easy target.[17] A second attack in September against UN offices led to the withdrawal of the 600 UN civilian staff from Iraq.

The attack on the UN compound was a tragic lesson that, in a conflict with such a strong religious or ideological element, any activity that might be seen as providing support for the goals and objectives of one party can be targeted deliberately by another party to the conflict. If the United Nations performed its humanitarian tasks well in Iraq, then its success would make the US-led invasion easier for Washington to justify as being beneficial for the Iraqi population; however, if the UN operations were stopped, then the burden of providing such support – and the popular blame for its failure – would be pushed onto US shoulders. This practical calculation, among others, by al-Qaeda and other opposition groups in Iraq made the United Nations and any other humanitarian relief agency operating there ready-made and easy targets for kidnapping and murder.

The lesson was slowly learned, and the reluctance of humanitarian groups to accept it led to several notable attacks, kidnappings, and beheadings of foreign aid workers and others by militant opponents of the US occupation (as noted in Power 2008, 504–08; Weiss 2007a, 71–72). In Iraq, and soon elsewhere, the result was that humanitarian NGO aid workers and organizations, faced with an increasingly hostile and dangerous operating environment, decided that they needed to be protected by private security companies or, increasingly, by operating in a more integrated manner with the US or other Western military forces.[18] However, this only reinforced the perception that humanitarian aid had become part of the operational capacity (and the arsenal) of these militaries – and thus a legitimate target for opponents. Humanitarian space declined precipitously, and the militarization of aid delivery rose equally steeply.

Canada in Afghanistan and the Militarization of Humanitarian (Policy) Space

Canada's military engagement in Afghanistan came about in several stages beginning with the deployment of Joint Task Force 2 forces in support of the initial US-led assault in December 2001. The internal story of this incrementally increasing and often poorly understood commitment has been carefully detailed elsewhere (see Stein and Lang 2007) and thus need not be repeated here. However, some elements of the story do require emphasis because they shed light on the nature of that engagement and hence, centrally for this analysis, on the decisions about the importance of humanitarian calculations and objectives as part of Canadian security policy regarding Afghanistan.[19] Here we see both the external and the internal sources or causes of the militarization of that security policy and of the securitization and militarization of its civilian, humanitarian component.

It needs to be understood and acknowledged clearly that Canada did not become involved in Afghanistan based upon any broad national and altruistic concern for promoting the human rights of Afghan citizens, or because of any interest in ensuring their physical safety from violence or their democratic political freedoms, or to advance the rights of Afghan women and girls. All of these rights and freedoms and personal securities had been denied, threatened, or abused for several years before 2001 under Taliban rule and during the years of brutal civil war that had preceded the Taliban takeover. After the Soviet withdrawal from Afghanistan in February 1989, Canadian attention, like that of the West in general, shifted elsewhere, and Afghans faced more than a decade of isolation. Ottawa, Washington, and the political elites in other capitals (as well as public opinion in those countries) looked to the political transitions taking place in the states of the former Soviet Union but virtually forgot about Afghanistan until the terrorist attacks of 9/11 focused their attention once again. Indeed, from 1995 to 1997, the US State Department even had described the Taliban as "useful allies" in pacifying unrest in Afghanistan and in eliminating poppy production (Griffiths 2001, 236). Another way of looking at this is to ask a counterfactual question: if the 9/11 attacks had not taken place, or perhaps even if the Taliban after 9/11 either had expelled Osama bin Laden and his al-Qaeda group from Afghanistan or had agreed to hand him over to US forces (perhaps via Pakistan), would the United States and NATO have invaded Afghanistan simply to oust the obscure and otherwise non-threatening Taliban regime from that country, when the West had shown no interest in doing anything there since 1989?[20]

The point here is that the central consideration behind US, Canadian, and NATO policy regarding Afghanistan has not been a humanitarian concern with human rights, women's rights, social or economic development, or democratic freedoms. Saudi Arabia – one of the few countries to recognize the Taliban as the government of Afghanistan in the 1990s – practised (and still practises) severe restrictions on women's rights and human rights generally and engages in punishments that include amputations, stonings, and public executions by beheading, firing squad, and even crucifixion, yet the oil-rich monarchy remains a friend and ally of the West and a major market for Western military equipment sales (Taylor 2013). Rather, the central concern in the West has been about American, Canadian, and other NATO states' national security, and the instrument for protecting that security has been the "forward deployment" of military force. And, in the case of Canada, Ottawa's chief consideration in the immediate aftermath of

9/11 had nothing to do with ordinary Afghans or Afghanistan itself – it was to ensure that Canada was not seen as a source of vulnerability or a weak link by either the White House or, equally importantly, Congress. First and foremost, and perhaps reasonably, Ottawa sought to ensure that any new perimeter security measure from Washington did not disrupt Canadian manufacturers' access to the US market, which accounted for almost 80 percent of Canada's exports and imports. The first set of calculations shaping Canadian policy was continental and bilateral in scope and economic in nature and certainly not driven by – or even shaped by – any altruistic or idealistic interest in human rights and humanitarian conditions in Afghanistan (Waisová 2010).[21]

Three further considerations played important parts in shaping subsequent decision making in Ottawa on what became Canada's military mission in Afghanistan. First, in 2002–03, as President Bush and the White House searched for reasons to invade Iraq and to oust the regime of Saddam Hussein, Ottawa wavered on joining this elective war. Canadian diplomats and public opinion alike were unconvinced by the constantly changing arguments for war advanced by the White House, and Prime Minister Jean Chrétien finally announced his decision on 17 March 2003 not to participate in any invasion of Iraq without a UN Security Council resolution authorizing such action (see Freeman 2013). At the time, it was clear that neither Russia nor France (and probably China) would accept such a resolution in the Security Council. Instead, by boosting Canada's military commitment to the ongoing campaign in Afghanistan, Ottawa could argue reasonably convincingly that its troop commitment there left it with little or no additional capacity to engage in another mission elsewhere and that this increased Canadian commitment freed up US troops to be moved to the Iraq mission.[22] Thus, Ottawa could demonstrate to the White House and a protectionist Congress that Canada remained a firm US ally in its newly minted "War on Terror."

A second issue that played at least some role in prompting or influencing Ottawa's decisions on engagement in Afghanistan, and that again had no direct bearing on any Canadian concerns with humanitarian or other policy goals for Afghans, was the domestic debate in 2004 over the NORAD agreement renewal. The White House sought a Canadian commitment to participate in its new Ballistic Missile Defence program as part of the NORAD renewal agreement negotiations, but Prime Minister Martin was aware that Canadian public opinion, Parliament, and the Liberal caucus all opposed any such commitment. Inside the Ottawa bureaucracy, the Department of

National Defence leadership argued that rejecting this American request to participate might have adverse effects on bilateral military cooperation. Since the prime minister nonetheless chose to decline the request for domestic political reasons, the Department of National Defence made the case that boosting the commitment of the Canadian Forces to operations in Afghanistan could help to alleviate any adverse impact on bilateral cooperation.[23]

A third impetus behind accepting a greater military role, in the form of a combat mission in Kandahar, similarly was related more to internal bureaucratic interests in Ottawa. During the late 1980s and 1990s, the Department of National Defence and Canadian Forces had suffered considerably under successive and deep budget cuts by Liberal governments. These cuts, and the constant uncertainty that accompanied them in all aspects of defence policy, greatly eroded critical CF capabilities, and did much harm to military morale, even while the same Liberal governments made new commitments to UN peacekeeping operations such as Rwanda and Bosnia (and Kosovo under NATO with belated UN endorsement) and asked the military to maintain its roles in national and continental defence and within NATO. For the Canadian Forces, this was what Chief of the Defence Staff General Rick Hillier provocatively called the "decade of darkness" of Liberal government neglect (*Ottawa Citizen* 2007). Now a fully fledged combat mission in Afghanistan offered the Canadian Forces solid ground for fast-tracking equipment procurement and increasing training budgets, greatly improved troop morale through a return to its raison d'être of war-fighting and away from the ill-starred UN-led peace operations, and much more political influence within the Ottawa bureaucracy. Department of National Defence leaders really cannot be faulted for seeing this as an opportunity to regain lost material capabilities and political-bureaucratic authority. It is thus not a criticism of the Department of National Defence to argue here that an important component of its focus on and interest in promoting deeper Canadian military engagement, and a greater emphasis on the combat role, in Afghanistan was its overriding bureaucratic or organizational objective of addressing the budgetary and materiel (and material) shortfalls caused by two decades of federal government neglect – but again this objective had no relationship with ensuring humanitarian support for the Afghan population.

The net effects of these disparate motivations behind the evolving Canadian engagement in Afghanistan – from Joint Task Force 2, to the Canadian Battle Group, to CF leadership of the NATO International Security Assistance Force mission in Kabul, to the Canadian Provincial Reconstruction

Team and combat mission command in Kandahar, and to the draw down to a training mission based in Kabul prior to a planned withdrawal in 2014 – have been that, while the policy rhetoric emanating from Ottawa has talked about building civilian capabilities and assisting ordinary Afghans to build support for the Karzai government, the money trail has told a very different story. In Ottawa, the policy community was organized with some public fanfare into a "three-D" approach – defence, diplomacy, and development operating together in mutually reinforcing programs and priorities – and this became broadened as a "whole-of-government" approach. In budgetary terms, however, between 2001 and 2007, Ottawa spent approximately $7–10 billion on its military operations in Afghanistan and some $750 million to $1 billion on all other forms of aid and development (including basic services, humanitarian assistance, national institutions and democratic development, political reconciliation, and management of the Afghan-Pakistan border).[24] The CF commitment of 2,500 troops and staff was supplemented by fewer than fifty civilian government employees (on the basis that security conditions did not permit their safe duty assignment). Ottawa was not alone in this enormous differential emphasis in resource commitments: for NATO states, the total expenditure on military operations in Afghanistan was approximately US$82.5 billion, and on all forms of development and reconstruction assistance it was US$7.3 billion. For Canada as for NATO, military spending outran all other forms of assistance in Afghanistan by a 10:1 ratio.[25] If this reflected the three-D or whole-of-government approach, then it was clear where the priority lay politically, bureaucratically, and financially.

To make the above points is not to say that the reported Canadian military expenditures were unnecessary or excessive for the mission; given the previous years of Liberal government defence budget cuts, there was much to make up for, and much more was needed at short notice to protect and enable Canadian troops serving in high-intensity combat operations in Afghanistan. And it is not to argue that the Canadian Forces did not conduct activities at a high level of professionalism and effectiveness, which I witnessed first-hand in Kandahar. Rather, it might be the case that Ottawa's (and NATO's) civilian-oriented and humanitarian expenditures were far too low in comparison and that much greater effort should have been made to fund, support, and sustain Afghan civilians' capacities, rights, and opportunities despite the difficult and often dangerous security environment. Some important programs were supported, and at least short-term gains were achieved, for example in child education, access to education for girls, child immunization, and basic health-care access. A stable currency, a functioning central bank, and an elected parliament emerged.

However, the overwhelming emphasis on the military dimension left the delivery of civilian goods and services far behind, to the frustration of many Afghan as well as Western NGO observers, who saw Western military interests taking precedence over Afghan needs and priorities. This relative neglect was complicated further as the threat of a resurgent Taliban meant that international NGO workers often had to be protected by Western military forces, further reinforcing the perception (indeed the reality) that civilian, humanitarian programs and projects had become part of the broader array of policy instruments – part of the arsenal – of US, Canadian, and other NATO forces. And, the more that this perception and reality have taken hold, the more that such civilian projects, programs, and staff become viewed as important, and relatively "soft" or easy, targets of Taliban and other opposition groups' attacks throughout Afghanistan (Paddon and Owen 2012, 274–77). Humanitarian space has declined on the ground in Afghanistan, just as it declined in Ottawa's prioritization, planning, resourcing, and implementation in its policy regarding Afghanistan – if it existed in the first place.

Conclusion: "Military Humanitarianism" in Canadian Security Policy and Implementing R2P in Libya

Discussing the approach of the International Committee of the Red Cross to the problematic preservation of "humanitarian space" in the context of counterinsurgency operations, Michael Khambatta (2012, 241) observed that debate within the humanitarian community over whether parties to a conflict – for instance, the US military, NATO, and the Canadian Forces – should engage in civilian- or humanitarian-oriented activities "is now largely beside the point. Stability operations are here to stay and humanitarian actors will need to adapt to them." The preceding analysis has identified, traced, and attempted to shed some critical light on the process as well as the critical dilemmas emerging from the securitization – and especially the militarization – of humanitarian space in Canadian security policy. They included the narrowing of security concerns in Ottawa, driven primarily by the perceived need to manage political and economic ties with (and dependence on) Washington and the complex, often unhappy, relationship between "principled conviction" and responsibility for outcomes both positive and negative. Both could be recognized especially in Canadian and NATO policies in Afghanistan after 2001. The subsequent expression of both this narrowing of focus and the uncomfortable relationship between convictions and responsibilities, in the security policies of the current government in Canada (and other governments, including that of the United Kingdom), could be seen in the hollow-ringing espousal by Ottawa of a form of R2P regarding the Libya "crisis" in 2011 that focused on military instruments and a declared need to demonstrate immediate material benefits to Canada from any international "humanitarian" intervention.

After entering office as a new minority government in 2006, the Harper-led Conservatives sought systematically to distance themselves from the policy initiatives of their Liberal predecessors. One expression of this effort was that any public discussion by Foreign Affairs officials on the idea or norm of the responsibility to protect – specifically the idea and the document supported and promoted by Minister of Foreign Affairs Axworthy and then by Prime Minister Martin – was rejected. The term itself would not be used except in direct reference to the report – and then only with considerable reluctance. Support for printing and distributing new copies of the report by Foreign Affairs also halted. In Ottawa, as the military effort in Afghanistan was ramped up, the Department of National Defence focused on its new and welcome war-fighting role, which brought the Canadian Forces much-needed political attention and budgetary resources. For reasons of its own, Foreign Affairs was opposed to Canada taking on any other military commitments – especially the sort of open-ended and presumably UN-led missions in fragile and failed (and mainly African) states that might be a result of following the R2P norm. Requests made to Ottawa from the UN secretary general asking for Canadian military leadership in African peacekeeping missions – particularly leadership of the difficult mission in the Democratic Republic of the Congo – were declined (Clark 2010).

Since Somalia, Bosnia, and Rwanda in the early 1990s, many in the Department of National Defence were deeply skeptical of any such ill-defined and unpredictable complex peace mission; even the narrow definition of human security that had led to military intervention in Kosovo was unsatisfactory to the extent that the intervention had been bogged down in UN Security Council politics. As the combat mission for the Canadian Forces in Afghanistan was being drawn down under domestic political pressure, however, another NATO-led military intervention gave the Department of National Defence the opportunity to demonstrate its continued value as an instrument of Canadian foreign policy and the government the chance to demonstrate its willingness and ability to cooperate with its US ally and other NATO allies. Ironically, this mission also was authorized by the UN Security Council and justified publicly by its advocates as a critical demonstration by the international community of its willingness to support the emerging norm of R2P.

Moammar Gadhafi had been "normalized" for several years and treated as an accepted and recognized – or at least tolerated and, when advantageous, courted – head of state by Canadian and other governments. However, in February 2011, his bellicose threats and initial acts of mass violence against domestic political opposition groups and populations, energized by the successful "Arab Spring" revolts in Tunisia against the government of Zine El Abidine Ben Ali and in Egypt against the ruling regime of Hosni Mubarak, were taken as sufficient grounds to mobilize international military intervention. Libya was already suspended as a member by the Arab League, and its call for an international intervention in Libya led to the UN Security Council passing Resolution 1973 authorizing "all necessary measures to protect civilians under threat" (Isaac 2012, 121–23). President Obama was careful not to press for action until other regional states – notably the four Arab countries Qatar, Jordan, Morocco, and United Arab Emirates – and bodies had agreed to do so and until the UN Security Council had passed its resolution authorizing the establishment of a no-fly zone, the use of force to protect civilian populations from imminent harm, the enforcement of an arms embargo, and the freezing of Libyan government assets.

Thus equipped politically, diplomatically, and legally, a US- and NATO-led military mission, Operation Unified Protector, was established to enforce Resolution 1973 – which also, in practice if not initial intention, meant actively taking the side of the rebel National Transitional Council as the legitimate alternative political leadership of Libya against the forces and civilian population still loyal to Gadhafi. Thus, though never saying so explicitly as an objective, the Western military-led intervention to protect the civilian population of Libya from the threat of harm also meant using Western military capabilities and assets to support regime change in Libya – an ambitious and open-ended political and social-economic as well as military commitment.[26] Humanitarian intervention took the form of bombing by Western aircraft, including the active participation by Canadian jets, as in 1999 in the secessionist Serbian province of Kosovo – where deep political divisions and social unrest continue to be expressed more than a decade later.

This is not the place to debate the merits of, or the possible motives behind, such a rapid and willing Western, NATO-led intervention in oil-rich Libya while at the same time (in 2011) simply issuing diplomatic condemnations of the violent repression of opposition populations and groups in Syria and of violence in Yemen and Bahrain and continuing actively to support and sell weapons to the politically and socially repressive government of Saudi Arabia. National interest, *realpolitik*, and perhaps – but not widely reported if they did exist – careful assessments of what could be done with a reasonable chance of success and proportionate use of force all played roles in the calculations of Western and other nations' policy makers (Isaac 2012, 122). Of note in the context of this examination of Canadian policy is that the Harper government and Department of National Defence leadership in Ottawa were willing and eager to demonstrate their commitment to the US-led position in favour of a rapid military intervention in a sovereign state – an intervention at least notionally based upon the norm of R2P.

Seeking to avoid the appearance of a US-dominated mission, both Washington and its European NATO allies found Canadian Lieutenant General Charles Bouchard, deputy commander of the NATO Allied Joint Force Command in Naples and familiar to them through NORAD, to be a highly experienced candidate to lead the UN-sanctioned no-fly-zone mission. Ottawa committed the Canadian Forces to provide six CF-18 jets, two refuelling tankers, and two CP-140 Aurora reconnaissance aircraft to the aerial mission as well as one frigate to its naval component. By late 2011, with Gadhafi's forces defeated in the field and the deposed leader killed in disputed circumstances shortly following his capture by rebel troops, the cost of the Canadian military-humanitarian commitment in Libya was approximately $100 million.

During these months, any discussion in Ottawa on the needs of or demands for non-military support for the Libyan population, and the provision of assistance for critical state-building processes under the new National Transitional Council government, was framed narrowly and instrumentally in terms of identifying and exploiting commercial economic opportunities and seeking "a return on our engagement and investment" by ensuring that existing contracts signed by Canadian businesses with the deposed Gadhafi regime were honoured and looking to the incoming regime for new commercial opportunities (Berthiume 2013). Any assertion of "principled conviction" would ring hollow when viewed against such an emphasis on maximizing national economic benefits; again, as Andy Knight's examination of R2P noted, such public statements would reinforce the perception of skeptics that Western states use or abuse the norm and doctrine of R2P when and where it suits their narrow geopolitical and commercial interests. At the same time, efforts by observers to offer evaluations of NATO's – or,

in our current context, Canada's – commitment to an "ethics of responsibility" for the development of post-intervention Libya must balance the inevitable instability and associated violence of a post-revolutionary regime and
state with the rapid disengagement from Libya by Western military forces.
The US and other NATO/Western governments sought, perhaps in this
instance with strategic wisdom, to emphasize the centrality of "homegrown"
Libyan leadership and avoid falling into another costly and ultimately destruc-
tive Afghanistan- or Iraq-style long-term military entanglement (Sadiki 2013).[27]

As noted at the beginning of this discussion, ethics and security are not
seen here as separate and/or opposed concepts. They are not inevitably
competitive or mutually exclusive domains; more ethics does not necessarily mean less security and vice versa. That makes sense – after all, long traditions of ethical thinking about warfare deal with the notion of "just war,"
and the Geneva Conventions explicitly address the expectation for "just"
or ethical conduct during war. Contravening these expectations can lead
to charges of committing war crimes, or of launching a war of aggression,
though the latter remains a political rather than legal judgment, rendered by
the UN Security Council and not (yet) by the International Criminal Court
since it is not currently a defined crime under international law. Instead, in
the analysis presented above, security itself is understood to be a contested
concept and the fertile ground for many reasonable and reasoned disagree-
ments over its content – specific assumptions, goals, objectives, interests,
and methods, even its referent objects (states, groups, individuals, ideas,
and values). Realist, liberal, and cosmopolitan perspectives do differ from
each other across several of these criteria, but each nonetheless would lay
claim to being based upon an ethical framework.

Highlighted in examining the issue of humanitarian space and the securitization and militarization of humanitarian intervention is that practical
experience indicates a potentially negative outcome of mixing narrow, state-
defined (in this case primarily Western states) concepts and instruments
of security with broader, societal-defined notions of humanitarianism supported by non-governmental actors as instruments. In Iraq and Afghanistan,
the adoption and/or leadership of humanitarian tasks by Western militaries
also engaged in combat operations, which have been seen and explicitly referenced by those militaries as valuable "force multipliers" in their military
campaigns, instead has transformed any such project into a legitimate target
of militant opponents and likewise made independent humanitarian NGO
staff and their own projects into targets. This situation has forced NGOs to
take on increased security, in turn reinforcing their appearance as being part

of the (Western) military or militarized operations. The narrowly self-defined "right intent" of these Western governments and their military instruments of policy has led to negative consequences, which also undermine the long-term achievement of the intent. Neutral humanitarian space is squeezed out, and the local population suffers while the conflict continues.

NOTES

1 See ICISS (2001). A useful overview and sometimes critical reflection on Canadian foreign policy ideas and practices during this period is Hampson, Hillmer, and Molot (2001).

2 A review of Canadian, Norwegian, and Japanese approaches, set within the context of a broader study of the concept, is provided in Alkire (2003). More recently, a useful examination of how the notion of human security as expressed by the responsibility to protect doctrine is viewed elsewhere is provided by Mani and Weiss (2011).

3 A valuable and insightful recent collection of works examining this subject is Perrin (2012). A more dated, but still useful and highly readable, self-critical account of a personal shift from supporting interventionism to being deeply concerned over its effects on humanitarianism in practice is provided by Rieff (2002). Another critical – or perhaps ideologically skeptical – analysis of the promotion by Western governments (and Western-defined human rights organizations) of a purported human rights-based interventionism is Chandler (2002).

4 On the former, see Keating (2002).

5 In addition to the excellent contributions to Irwin (2001), more recent expositions of the trend toward militarization and securitization are found in a number of the contributions in Beier and Wylie (2010); Hynek and Bosold (2010).

6 For helpful discussions of cosmopolitanism and earlier perspectives, see Ramsbotham, Woodhouse, and Mial (2005); Sinclair (2012). Daniel Madar (2000) offers a dated but still useful introductory application of realist, liberal, constructivist, and critical theories of international/global relations to an understanding of Canadian examples.

7 Rutherford (2008) offers a detailed analysis of the American- and UN-led interventions and the repercussions of the experiences there in subsequent US views toward "armed interventionism" and "armed nation building." Also helpful is Jan (2001). For a thoughtful Canadian perspective, see Bush (1998).

8 Two of the best-known Canadian publications on these ill-fated missions must be Major General Lewis MacKenzie's *Peacekeeper: The Road to Sarajevo* (1993) and Lieutenant General Romeo Dallaire's *Shake Hands with the Devil* (2003). Although written and published before the events in Srebrenica in 1995, MacKenzie's book offers an inside look at the problematic nature of the UN mandate compared with the reality of the situation on the ground in the former Yugoslavia. Dallaire's book vividly recounts the problems that Dallaire faced as the force commander of UNAMIR, the UN mission in Rwanda at the time of the genocide.

9 The Mulroney government had been supportive of humanitarian intervention under UN authority both in Yugoslavia and in Somalia; see Dashwood (2000, 278–80).

10 See, for example, IICK (2000).

11 Rieff (2002, 197–203) addresses these considerations in his chapter on intervention in Kosovo.

12 As well as Rieff, Chandler, and the Independent International Commission on Kosovo, a critical perspective by an informed analyst who worked inside Serbia and observed events first-hand is provided by Scott Taylor in two studies (2000, 2002).

13 On the matter of legality and legitimacy, see IICK (2000, 163–98).

14 A careful and insightful critique of Axworthy's human security agenda is Hillmer and Chapnick (2001, 67–88).

15 Martin personally called the leaders of South Africa, Algeria, Pakistan, Jamaica, and Chile, all opponents of R2P, and persuaded them to support or at least cease their opposition to the proposed new norm. See Johnston (2013).

16 For Martin's statement to the UN General Assembly, see Martin (2005).

17 A detailed account of the attack and its aftermath can be found in Power (2008).

18 On the need for, and the problems created by, humanitarian organizations' use of private security contractors, see respectively Bearpark (2012, 157–67); Williamson (2012, 168–80).

19 A particularly helpful review of the application of integrated military and humanitarian operations by Canada in Afghanistan is given in Paddon and Owen (2012, 266–84).

20 Of course, such a handover would have been very difficult for the Taliban to make as the hosts of bin Laden; see Griffiths (2001, 229).

21 An insightful, and deeply critical, consideration of the manipulation of narratives explaining Canadian engagement in Afghanistan is Turenne Sjolander and Trevenen (2010, 44–57).

22 Not generally publicly recognized, but acknowledged by Paul Cellucci, the US ambassador at the time, was the fact that Canada did contribute more to the Iraq War than most of the declared US coalition partners, including four Canadian warships (with 1,300 crew members) that were part of Task Force 151; thirty Canadian Forces members who served at US Central Command in Qatar; approximately 150 troops serving on exchanges with US and UK forces; several Canadian Forces officers who held senior command roles in the coalition; and Canadian Air Force pilots stationed with NORAD who flew combat missions with the US Air Force E-3 Sentry AWACS aircraft, providing surveillance, command, and control services to US combat aircraft, or flew Boeing C-17s into Iraq and Canadian C-130s in supply roles (see Sanders 2008).

23 This debate is covered well in Stein and Lang (2007, 152–77).

24 "The Fiscal Impact of the Canadian Mission in Afghanistan" (2008). Page's report, of course, was controversial since it suggested that the costs of the Canadian mission had been dramatically understated by the Department of National Defence and government of Canada; his report estimated that the cost of Canada's Afghan mission through to 2011–12 could be as high as $18 billion.

25 Government of Canada reports acknowledged that military spending accounted for 80 percent of all Canadian spending in Afghanistan, though its figures excluded estimates for CF veterans' disability and health-care costs, which Page's report included (see Page 2008). See also Bell (2010, 61).

26 President Barack Obama, Prime Minister David Cameron, and President Nicolas Sarkozy co-signed a public letter in which they wrote that "our duty and our mandate under UN Security Council Resolution 1973 is to protect civilians ... It is not to remove Gaddafi by force." At the same time, though, they noted that "it is unthinkable that ... (the Libyan leader) ... can play a part in their future government." More explicitly yet, they argued that, "for that transition to succeed, Colonel Gaddafi must go, and go for good." See BBC News Africa (2011).
27 A more critical perspective on the consequences of the intervention is Lobe (2013).

References
Alkire, Sabine. 2003. "A Conceptual Framework for Human Security." CRISE Working Paper 2, Queen Elizabeth House, University of Oxford.
BBC News Africa. 2011. "Libya Letter by Obama, Cameron, and Sarkozy: Full Text." BBC News Africa, 15 April. http://www.bbc.co.uk/news/world-africa-13090646.
Bearpark, Andrew. 2012. "The Case for Humanitarian Organizations to Use Private Security Contractors." In *Modern Warfare: Armed Groups, Private Militaries, Humanitarian Organizations, and the Law*, edited by Benjamin Perrin, 157–67. Vancouver: UBC Press.
Beier, J. Marshall, and Lana Wylie, eds. 2010. *Canadian Foreign Policy in Critical Perspective*. Oxford: Oxford University Press.
Bell, Colleen. 2010. "Fighting the War and Winning the Peace: Three Critiques of the War in Afghanistan." In *Canadian Foreign Policy in Critical Perspective*, edited by Marshall J. Beier and Lana Wylie, 58–71. Oxford: Oxford University Press.
Berthiume, Lee. 2013. "Files Say Canada Protected Bottom Line in Libya" *Star Phoenix*, 19 March.
Bush, Kenneth D. 1998. "Somalia: When Two Anarchies Meet." In *Canada and Missions for Peace: Lessons from Nicaragua, Cambodia, and Somalia*, edited by Gregory Wirick and Robert Miller, 79–109. Ottawa: International Development Research Centre.
Chandler, David. 2002. *From Kosovo to Kabul (and Beyond): Human Rights and International Intervention*. London: Pluto Press.
Clark, Campbell. 2010. "Canada Rejects UN Request to Lead Congo Mission." *Globe and Mail*, 30 April. http://www.theglobeandmail.com/news/politics/canada-rejects-un-request-to-lead-congo-mission/article1386861/.
Dallaire, Romeo. 2003. *Shake Hands with the Devi: The Failure of Humanity in Rwanda*. Toronto: Random House.
Dashwood, Hevina S. 2000. "Canada's Participation in the NATO-Led Intervention in Kosovo." In *Canada among Nations 2000: Vanishing Borders*, edited by Maureen Appel Molot and Fen Osler Hampson, 275–302. Don Mills, ON: Oxford University Press.
Freeman, Sunny. 2013. "Canada's 'No' to Iraq War a Defining Moment for Prime Minister, Even 10 Years Later." *Huffington Post*, 19 March. http://www.huffingtonpost.ca/2013/03/19/canada-iraq-war_n_2902305.html.
Griffiths, John C. 2001. *Afghanistan: A History of Conflict*. London: Carlton Books.
Hampson, Fen Osler, Norman Hillmer, and Maureen Appel Molot, eds. 2001. *Canada among Nations 2001: The Axworthy Legacy*. Don Mills, ON: Oxford University Press.

Hillmer, Norman, and Adam Chapnick. 2001. "The Axworthy Revolution." In *Canada among Nations 2001: The Axworthy Legacy,* edited by Fen Osler Hampson, Norman Hillmer, and Maureen Appel Molot, 67–88. Don Mills, ON: Oxford University Press.

Hynek, Nik, and David Bosold, eds. 2010. *Canada's Foreign and Security Policy: Soft and Hard Strategies of a Middle Power.* Oxford: Oxford University Press.

ICISS. 2001. *The Responsibility to Protect: Report of the International Commission on Intervention and State Sovereignty.* Ottawa: International Development Research Centre.

IICK (Independent International Commission on Kosovo). 2000. *Kosovo Report: Conflict, International Response, Lessons Learned.* Oxford: Oxford University Press.

Irwin, Rosalind, ed. 2001. *Ethics and Security in Canadian Foreign Policy.* Vancouver: UBC Press.

Isaac, Sally Khalifa. 2012. "NATO's Intervention in Libya: Assessment and Implications." In *IEMed Mediterranean Yearbook 2012,* 121–23. Barcelona: European Institute of the Mediterranean. http://www.iemed.org/observatori-en/arees-danalisi/arxius-adjunts/anuari/med.2012/Khalifa_en.pdf.

Jan, Ameen. 2001. "Somalia: Building Sovereignty or Restoring Peace?" In *Peacebuilding as Politics: Cultivating Peace in Fragile Societies,* edited by Elizabeth M. Cousens and Chetan Kumar, 53–88. Boulder, CO: Lynne Rienner Publishers.

Johnston, Geoffrey. 2013. "R2P: Canada Finds Hope in Darkness." *Kingston Whig-Standard,* 8 February. http://www.thewhig.com/2013/02/08/r2p-canada-finds-hope-in-the-darkness.

Keating, Tom. 2002. *Canada and World Order: The Multilateralist Tradition in Canadian Foreign Policy.* 2nd ed. Oxford: Oxford University Press.

Khambatta, Michael. 2012. "Humanitarian Space and Stability Operations." In *Modern Warfare: Armed Groups, Private Militaries, Humanitarian Organizations, and the Law,* edited by Benjamin Perrin, 235–45. Vancouver: UBC Press.

Lobe, Jim. 2013. "Libya in the Rear View Mirror: How NATO Intervention Unleashed Militias and Destabilized Mali." *AlterNet,* 5 April. http://www.alternet.org/print/world/libya-rear-view-mirror-how-nato-intervention-unleashed-militias-and-destabilized-mali.

MacKenzie, Lewis. 1993. *Peacekeeper: The Road to Sarajevo.* Vancouver: Douglas and McIntyre.

Madar, Daniel. 2000. *Canadian International Relations.* Scarborough, ON: Prentice Hall Allyn and Bacon Canada.

Mani, Rama, and Thomas G. Weiss, eds. 2011. *Responsibility to Protect: Cultural Perspectives in the Global South.* London: Routledge.

Martin, Paul. 2005. "Statement by the Right Honourable Paul Martin, Prime Minister of Canada, to the High-Level Meeting of the Sixtieth Session of the United Nations General Assembly." 16 September. Ottawa: Office of the Prime Minister.

Ottawa Citizen. 2007. "Top General Calls Liberal Rule 'Decade of Darkness.'" *Ottawa Citizen,* 17 February. http://www.canada.com/ottawacitizen/news/story.html?id=d569d0fb-d9cf-4119-84cb-39dd89571625.

Paddon, Emily, and Taylor Owen. 2012. "Whither Humanitarian Space? The Costs of Integrated Peacebuilding in Afghanistan." In *Modern Warfare: Armed Groups, Private Militaries, Humanitarian Organizations, and the Law,* edited by Benjamin Perrin, 266–84. Vancouver: UBC Press.

Page, Kevin. 2008. "Fiscal Impact of the Canadian Mission in Afghanistan." Office of the Parliamentary Budget Officer, Ottawa, 9 October.

Perrin, Benjamin, ed. 2012. *Modern Warfare: Armed Groups, Private Militaries, Humanitarian Organizations, and the Law.* Vancouver: UBC Press.

Power, Samantha. 2008. *Chasing the Flame: Sergio Vieira de Mello and the Fight to Save the World.* New York: Penguin .

Ramsbotham, Oliver, Tom Woodhouse, and Hugh Mial. 2005. *Contemporary Conflict Resolution.* 2nd ed. Cambridge: Polity Press.

Rieff, David. 2002. *A Bed for the Night: Humanitarianism in Crisis.* New York: Simon and Schuster.

Rutherford, Kenneth R. 2008. *Humanitarianism under Fire: The US and UN Intervention in Somalia.* Sterling, VA: Kumarian Press.

Sadiki, Larbi. 2013. "Libya Two Years On: Revolution and Devolution." *Aljazeera,* 17 February. http://www.aljazeera.com/indepth/opinion/2013/02/20132178950966868.html.

Sanders, Richard. 2008. "Canada's Secret War in Iraq." *Common Ground,* February. http://commonground.ca/OLD/iss/199/cg199_iraq.shtml.

Sinclair, Timothy J. 2012. *Global Governance.* Cambridge: Polity Press.

Stein, Janice Gross, and Eugene Lang. 2007. *The Unexpected War: Canada in Kandahar.* Toronto: Viking Canada.

Taylor, Jerome. 2013. "As the Smoke Clears after Saudi Arabia's Latest Mass Execution by Firing Squad ... Charles and Camilla Fly In" *The Independent,* 13 March. http://www.independent.co.uk/news/world/middle-east/as-the-smoke-clears-after-saudi-arabias-latest-mass-execution-by-firing-squad-charles-and-camilla-fly-in-8533382.html.

Taylor, Scott. 2000. *INAT: Images of Serbia and the Kosovo Conflict.* Ottawa: Esprit de Corps Books.

Taylor, Scott. 2002. *Diary of an Uncivil War: The Violent Aftermath of the Kosovo Conflict.* Ottawa: Esprit de Corps Books.

Turenne Sjolander, Claire, and Kathryn Trevenen. 2010. "Constructing Canadian Foreign Policy: Myths of Good International Citizens, Protectors, and the War in Afghanistan." In *Canadian Foreign Policy in Critical Perspective,* edited by J. Marshall Beier and Lana Wylie, 44–57. Oxford: Oxford University Press.

Waisová, Sárka. 2010. "The Transformation of Canada's Development Policy through the Security-Development Approach." In *Canada's Foreign and Security Policy: Soft and Hard Strategies of a Middle Power,* edited by Nik Hynek and David Bosold, 81–100. Oxford: Oxford University Press.

Wheeler, Nicholas J. 2002. *Saving Strangers: Humanitarian Intervention in International Society.* Oxford: Oxford University Press. http://dx.doi.org/10.1093/0199253102.001.0001.

Williamson, Jamie. 2012. "The Use of Armed Security Escorts: A Challenge to Independent and Neutral Humanitarian Action." In *Modern Warfare: Armed Groups, Private Militaries, Humanitarian Organizations, and the Law,* edited by Benjamin Perrin, 168–80. Vancouver: UBC Press.

3

The Commercial Military and Security Services Industry
A Canadian Consideration?

CHRIS HENDERSHOT

Since the launch of the global "War on Terror" on 20 September 2001, the commercial military and security services industry has become an intimate aspect of global security relations. By training, consulting, guarding, surveilling, repairing, transporting, feeding, healing, and building in (post-)conflict zones, commercial[1] military and security companies (CMSCs)[2] have increasingly shouldered the burden of services once predominantly provided by entities of states. Reasons for this rise of CMSCs include, but are not limited to, the wars in Afghanistan and Iraq, public policy preferences for efficient/cost-effective solutions, resource extraction from unstable/conflict-riven regions, piracy in the Gulf of Aden, and increasing one-upmanship of staging large-scale events such as the Olympics and World Cup. Arguably, with the rebellions/insurgencies/wars in Iraq, Libya, Somalia, Syria, and the Islamic Maghreb, the opportunities for CMSCs to ply their services will only continue to grow (see Abrahamsen and Williams 2011; Rosèn 2008).

Despite the long and varied list of services currently undertaken by CMSCs in (post-) conflict zones, proposals that CMSCs be solely responsible for conducting humanitarian interventions, such as those historically conducted by the Blue Helmets of the United Nations, remain relatively contentious (Spearin 2011). Accordingly, this chapter considers the ethical dilemmas raised by the promotion of the idea that CMSCs should be playing more prominent roles in not only supporting but also conducting armed humanitarian interventions (Brooks and Chorev 2008; Fitzsimmons

2006; Pavel 2010). As proponents of greater participation by CMSCs contend, the United Nations is no longer an effective institution through which meaningful interventions can be coordinated and conducted. Governments from the global North are also increasingly resistant to committing their militaries to humanitarian operations not in their geopolitical/political-economic interests. However, something must be done, for millions of people continue to suffer from the ravages of war. This is where CMSCs can step in to rectify the operational gap and thus "save lives" (Brooks and Chorev 2008). Further sweetening the pot, proponents maintain that CMSCs can conduct effective and efficient interventions, thus keeping costs as low as possible.

Although no Canadian government official has publicly supported a move to further integrate or solely rely on the services of CMSCs, the idea that they should feature more prominently raises important ethical concerns about the steps that Canada can and should be taking to alleviate humanitarian crises. As Alistair Edgar's chapter in this volume demonstrates, Canada's approach to the conduct of humanitarian interventions has increasingly shifted toward militarized considerations, thereby reducing "humanitarian space" to a series of practices focusing on the short-term, technical, and tactical necessities required to alleviate crises. Building upon his concerns, and using insights from poststructuralist and historical materialist theories, this chapter pursues an analysis that demonstrates how the commercialization of humanitarian intervention will privilege crisis management imperatives, which (driven primarily by financial logics) will undoubtedly fail to redress issues not of an immediate physically violent character (e.g., the inequitable distribution of space, resources, and influence).

This chapter also pursues an analysis that questions humanitarian discourse more generally or, as David Campbell (1998, 506) contends, practices that produce "people as victims, incapable of acting without intervention." Three issues are of particular concern: (1) that CMSCs might do more to exacerbate a humanitarian crisis than to alleviate it, (2) the supposed antithetical relationship between CMSCs and the altruistic, impartial, and neutral principles of liberal humanitarianism, and (3) that CMSCs represent a further enclosure of the spaces by and through which people can live their lives without the need to be saved. Through this analysis, it will become clear that the problems of a CMSC-led humanitarian intervention are not that such interventions will violate the rhetorical precepts of (liberal) humanitarianism but that such interventions will further entrench liberalized preferences for free markets, private property, and individualism.

Prior to undertaking this analysis, I outline the relationships between Canada's foreign policy apparatus and the commercial military and security services industry. A sketch of the relationship between Canada and CMSCs makes clear that the latter play an intimate role in the articulation and actualization of Canadian foreign policy. It is noteworthy that the integration of commercial actors into the actualization of Canadian foreign policy began in earnest in the 1990s following significant cuts to the defence budget. Canada's turn toward the commercial sector was further sharpened with the launch of the Canadian Forces Contractor Augmentation Program in December 2002, and Canadian operations in Afghanistan from 2002 to 2012 solidified Canadian reliance on CMSCs. Whether or not a CMSC-led humanitarian intervention actually occurs, it is important to recognize that Canadian efforts to "get more bang for our buck" have contributed to the emergence of the commercial sector as a key player in global security relations. Moreover, in privileging an ethics of security driven by financial logics, Canada's international relations must be recognized as contributing to the need for humanitarian interventions rather than to the alleviation of such crises.

Canada and the Commercial Military and Security Services Industry

Discussion of the commercial military and security services industry has not captured sustained popular attention in Canada – even though some of the most respected analysts of the industry hold Canadian passports. More disconcerting is the deficiency of meaningful debate by and among parliamentarians and bureaucrats over which roles CMSCs ought to be performing in the service of Canada's foreign policy apparatus. This lack of popular and governmental debate is attributable to a host of factors, including a low social profile for Canadian-based companies, the reluctance of government agencies to share information about their contracts with CMSCs, and the fact that no Canadian-based or Canadian-contracted CMSC has been involved in any of the spectacular controversies that have made Blackwater, KBR, Tim Spicer, and Executive Outcomes household names in the United States, the United Kingdom, and South Africa. A low social profile aside, the Department of National Defence and the Department of Foreign Affairs, Trade and Development (DFATD) have increasingly relied on the services of CMSCs since the turn of the twenty-first century. Likewise, Canadian-based CMSCs and CMSC employees holding Canadian passports are fixtures of contemporary (post-)conflict zones.

Services provided by CMSCs to the Department of National Defence and DFATD include armed security for persons, places, and things, logistical support for the Canadian Armed Forces operations, specialized training for Canadian Armed Forces personnel, and materiel maintenance. More specifically, CMSC personnel have been and currently are guarding Canadian embassies and diplomats around the globe. CMSC personnel have been responsible for the planning, setting up, maintaining, and disassembling of Canadian Armed Forces bases in Afghanistan as well as providing food for all the people[3] working on those bases. CMSC personnel were also responsible for ensuring perimeter security of Canadian Armed Forces bases and convoy security for materiel lines of supply in Afghanistan. Canadian Armed Forces personnel have also received specialized counterinsurgency training[4] from CMSCs, and CMSC personnel assist the Canadian Armed Forces with operating and maintaining its fleet of drones. Some of the non-Canadian-based CMSCs that the Department of National Defence and DFATD have contracted include Saladin, Hart, Blue Hackle Group, ArmorGroup, and the company formerly known as Blackwater. Although obtaining reliable numbers for the value of Department of National Defence and DFATD contracts with CMSCs is notoriously difficult, it is estimated that from 2002 to 2007 $1.34 billion was spent on contracts for logistical services by the Department of National Defence through the Canadian Forces Contractor Augmentation Program (Mayeda and Blanchfield 2007). For personal and site security services in Afghanistan, the value of Department of National Defence contracts was an estimated $7.78 million in 2008–09 (Galloway 2009) and $9 million in 2009–10 (Montpetit 2010). The DFATD is believed to have spent in 2006 the majority of its $35.2 million budget on protective services on contracts with CMSCs (CanWest News Service 2007a).

Beyond contracts and financials, public and government officials, particularly representatives of the Canadian Armed Forces, are clear in their support for the roles that CMSCs have played and can play in the achievement of Canada's foreign policy goals. Lieutenant Colonel Michael Rostek and Dr. Peter Gizewski of the Directorate of Land Concepts and Design contend that the increasing significance of CMSCs "increases incentives for governments and their militaries to adopt proactive approaches capable of maximizing the benefits they offer while minimizing – if not eliminating – the problems they can create" (Rostek and Gizewski 2009). Major Shane Gifford (2008) maintains that, as long as CMSCs are contracted to conduct primarily defensive tasks (i.e., no combat roles), then these companies can increase the operational capabilities of the Canadian Armed Forces. Accordingly, contracting CMSCs to provide logistics, training, transport, and security services allows the Canadian Armed Forces to address better and adapt to the stresses of increasingly complex (post-) conflict environments and thus better defend Canadian interests. Speaking on the relationship between the Canadian Armed Forces and CMSCs in Afghanistan, Brigadier General Denis Thompson (quoted in Fitzsimmons 2009) echoes Major Gifford's assessment: "Without [commercial] security firms, it would be impossible to achieve what we're achieving here." Major Mike Blanchette (quoted in Montpetit 2010) adds that "a lot of these companies fulfil an important need that does contribute to the good guys cause" by acting as force multipliers for overstretched NATO forces. In short, Canada can no longer actualize its foreign policy goals without the assistance of CMSCs.

On the industry side, Canada is home to a relatively small, yet globally active, number of CMSCs. For instance, SNC-Lavalin PAE, a joint venture between the Montreal-based engineering firm SNC-Lavalin and PAE Government Services, based in Arlington, Virginia, was the sole-source provider for the Canadian Forces Contractor Augmentation Program. During its decade-long contract with the Canadian Armed Forces, SNC-Lavalin PAE provided logistical support for operations in Bosnia and Afghanistan. Other notable Canadian-based CMSCs include Skylink Aviation, which provides charter flights and aircraft maintenance, and ING Engineering, which provides maintenance, operation, and training for the operation of unmanned aerial vehicles.

Canada is also home to a number of CMSCs that provide armed security services. GardaWorld is a Montreal-based company that bills itself on its website as "the largest privately owned business security solutions and security services provider in the world," employs 45,000 people globally, is listed on the Toronto Stock Exchange, and has been contracted by the DFATD and the British Foreign and Commonwealth Office to provide security services for embassies in Haiti and Baghdad. Tundra Group and Global Risk International are two other globally active, Canadian-based CMSCs. According to their respective websites, Tundra Group employs over 1,300 people, has operated in fifteen countries, and has served over 200 clients, while Global Risk has operated in Africa, Central and South America, and Asia. Although the exact number is unknown, numerous individuals holding Canadian passports, typically former Canadian Armed Forces personnel, have also taken up employment as armed security contractors for a variety of clients (Pugliese 2005). Department of National Defence officials have also expressed concerns about poaching from the ranks of the Canadian Armed Forces, especially the specially trained operators from Joint Task Force 2. Concern that Joint Task Force 2 personnel were fleeing the ranks of the

Canadian Armed Forces for the lucrative salaries paid by CMSCs prompted the Canadian Armed Forces to raise its salaries and benefits package in 2006 (*National Post* 2006).

Similar to Canada's contractual and industrial relations, its regulatory relationship with CMSCs (i.e., its commitment to govern the actions of CMSCs) is relatively limited. Domestically, there are no specific legal mechanisms that govern either individuals seeking employment with a CMSC or that govern the operations of CMSCs based in Canada. Provisions under the Foreign Enlistment Act can be applied to prevent individuals from being employed by a foreign-based CMSC, and the Export and Import Permits Act or the Special Economic Measures Act can be used to limit the use and export of restricted materiel and technology by CMSCs (Antonyshyn et al. 2009). That the Foreign Enlistment Act failed to prevent 1,200 Canadians from travelling to Spain to fight against the forces of General Franco portends the difficulty of bringing the operations of CMSCs under a regulatory framework that is not specifically designed to govern the activities of CMSCs (Spearin 2004). Internationally, the one convention – the International Convention against the Recruitment, Use, Financing, and Training of Mercenaries – that could be used to regulate the activities of CMSCs globally "has already been termed inappropriate and anachronistic when assessed in terms of contemporary state craft and the nature of the [CMSC] marketplace" (ibid., 6). As such, at present there are no binding conventions or customary practices that specifically govern the activities of CMSCs.

Yet Canada and Canadian-based CMSCs are party to a number of nonbinding (i.e., non-enforceable) regulatory conventions and codes of conduct. The first is the Montreux Document, which "reaffirms the obligation on States to ensure that [commercial] military and security companies operating in armed conflicts comply with international humanitarian and human rights law" (ICRC 2008). Signed by seventeen states, including Canada, in 2008, the Montreux Document commits signatories to a series of non-binding good practices regarding the management and oversight of CMSCs. On the industry side, the International Stability Operations Association is an industry advocacy group that represents fifty-two companies. To continue to be a member of the association, CMSCs must abide by a code of conduct that seeks to develop "consistent ethical standards for [members] operating in complex environments so that they may contribute their valuable services for the benefit of international peace and human security" (ISOA 2013). As signatories of the association's code of donduct, member companies also commit themselves to abide by all major human rights, weapons, and security conventions such as the Geneva Conventions, the Chemical Weapons Convention, and the Montreux Document. Gardaworld and Hart are members of the association. In addition to the International Stability Operations Association, the International Code of Conduct for Private Security Providers counts an ever growing list of CMSCs as signatories. As of August 2011, 166 CMSCs had signed the code of conduct, including Saladin, Hart, Blue Hackle Group, GardaWorld, and Tundra Strategies. Like the Montreux Document, the code of conduct is the outcome of a 2005 initiative by the Swiss Federal Department of Foreign Affairs to encourage compliance with international humanitarian law and human rights conventions by CMSCs operating in (post-)conflict zones.

As one of Canada's foremost experts on the commercial military and security services industry, Christopher Spearin (2005, 70) provides a succinct assessment of Canada's relationship with CMSCs: "Canada is not yet equipped to deal with the [CMSC] issue." Spearin cites poor regulation, limited monitoring mechanisms, the potential for human rights violations, and CMSCs poaching the best trained and most experienced members of the Canadian Armed Forces as the reasons for his assessment. He is not alone in his concern. As Benjamin Perrin (2008, 5) writes, "we need to take a hard look at what roles these [commercial] firms are taking on, in order to protect [Canada's] reputation and interests in Afghanistan and elsewhere, and whether sufficient safeguards are in place to ensure proper conduct." Although applicable to the general issue of the emergence of CMSCs as significant global actors, the concerns of Spearin and Perrin are magnified when applied to the question of whether CMSCs should play a more significant role in supporting or conducting humanitarian interventions. With a track record of unethical, immoral, and illicit activities in Iraq and Afghanistan, concerns that CMSCs might do more harm than good now become paramount.

To Minimize Harm?

Perhaps the single most difficult issue facing proponents seeking to expand the role of CMSCs in humanitarian interventions is the recent history of improper conduct by CMSCs and their personnel operating in Iraq and Afghanistan. Canadian-based CMSCs and companies contracted by the Canadian Armed Forces or DFATD have not been implicated in the more egregious activities; however, some concerns have been raised that the Canadian Armed Forces has contracted CMSCs that have connections with former Afghan warlords. The same cannot be said about American-based CMSCs and/or those contracted by American government agencies. Unfortunately, notable instances from Iraq include (1) allegations of the torture of prisoners in Abu Ghraib by Titan and CACI contractors, (2) accusations that shoddy electrical work by KBR contractors was responsible for the electrocution deaths of twelve enlisted US personnel, (3) the shooting and killing of seventeen Iraqi civilians by Blackwater contractors in 2007, (4) allegations that numerous CMSCs equipped their contractors with offensive weapons (e.g., fragmentation grenades and rocket-propelled grenade launchers) and that numerous CMSCs procured their weapons through illicit channels, and (5) the alleged cover-up of the rape of a female KBR employee by a male KBR employee and a US soldier. In Afghanistan, local contractors and not expatriate contractors are alleged to have committed serious ethical and legal offences. In one instance, a US Senate investigation revealed that in 2007 ArmorGroup employed Afghan contractors involved in kidnapping, bribery, and anti-coalition activities (Canadian Press 2011). Critics prone to hyperbole have used these instances to paint the commercial military and security services industry as populated by cowboys, thieves, and deviants. The retort from industry advocates is that these incidents have been caused by a few bad apples or, in the parlance of the industry, "tier bubba" contractors. More measured and disinterested commentators, such as Spearin and Perrin, have focused on a lack of oversight and poor management of contracts by government agencies. From this perspective, CMSCs and their personnel are no more or no less prone to committing unethical or immoral acts than other actors involved in alleviating a crisis. As a 2007 report reveals, "between January 2004 and the end of November 2006, the UN probed allegations of sexual exploitation and abuse involving 319 peacekeeping personnel 'in all missions,' from East Timor, the Middle East and Africa to Kosovo and Haiti" (CTV.ca 2007). Accordingly, the most effective way to prevent improper conduct is to move toward tighter control over who is being contracted to do what. Some examples of and suggestions for tighter control include ensuring (1) that contractors are held legally accountable for their actions, (2) that contracting agencies set out clear rules of engagement, (3) that clear lines of command (i.e., who is the final arbiter for on-the-ground decisions) are created, and (4) that companies or contractors accused of committing an ethical or legal offence are no longer eligible for contracts.

Given the spectacular character of many of the allegations against CMSCs operating in Iraq and Afghanistan, it is not all that surprising that these instances should come to the forefront when discussing an expansion of CMSCs into humanitarian interventions. However, if the decision to contract one CMSC or a number of CMSCs to conduct an intervention in Sudan, as Fitzsimmons (2006) asserts, focuses exclusively on preventing imminent heinous behavior, then a series of more mundane actions and decisions that all intervening forces must take and make go unquestioned. Of specific concern, one that has caused humanitarian NGOs much consternation, is the "idea that the provision of assistance often fuels the very conflicts it is supposed to ameliorate" (Campbell 1998, 499). The operations of CMSCs are not immune to this concern. For example, anecdotal evidence from Iraq reveals that many CMSCs employed the services of fixers, local Iraqi men who helped CMSCs to procure food, weapons, bases of operations, and recruits. One of the biggest problems encountered with local fixers is that they regularly relied on favouritism and nepotism to fulfill the demands of CMSCs. These methods allowed the social, economic, or ethnic strata to which the fixers belonged to secure better access to funds, weapons, and jobs provided by CMSCs than those groups not related or connected to the fixers. Just as troubling, if the fixers were not criminals themselves, they often relied on criminal or illicit networks to procure provisions for CMSCs.

The exacerbation of tensions among economic, social, and ethnic strata and the (inadvertent) support of criminal elements are certainly not new problems facing intervening forces or actors. Far from resolving these issues, a CMSC intervention force might actually exacerbate them inasmuch as one of the key "benefits" of contracting a CMSC is cost effectiveness. Purportedly, Canada could contract a CMSC to conduct an intervention at a much reduced cost compared with the cost of mounting an operation using the Canadian Armed Forces. Pressure to keep costs low can drive CMSCs to seek opportunities to reduce the costs of labour and material. Less speculatively, that CMSCs operate as for-profit organizations and are intimately linked to global financial markets means that any external pressure by a client to keep costs low is redundant. In other words, external pressure to keep costs low is unnecessary since keeping labour and material costs as low as possible is a driving feature of the business operations of CMSCs. Moreover, because the vast majority of contractors employed in (post-)conflict zones are from the global South, any move to increase the humanitarian responsibilities of CMSCs will subsequently increase the circumstances in which exploitative labour conditions can flourish.

One of the more glaring examples of exploitative labour conditions is the wage differential between contractors from the United States, England, South Africa, and Canada versus those from the global South. Reportedly, contractors from the former countries have made up to ten times the monthly salaries of contractors from the global South (Spearin 2011, 199). Despite the relative financial windfall for security contractors from Uganda (see Mmali 2009), for instance, the absolute financial differentials between contractors from the North and South reinforce broader financial structures that situate the global South as a reservoir of cheap labour. Higate (2012) also notes that CMSCs often hire contractors from the global South because of gendered and racialized beliefs that certain nationalities or ethnic groups are better suited for the rigours of security work. With this said, another potential problem of employing local contractors is that in Afghanistan, for instance, local employees of CMSCs earn substantially more than the nascent security forces of the Afghan National Police and Afghan National Army. Afghans working for CMSCs can earn double the monthly salaries of those working for the national police (Spearin 2008b, 9). The conclusion made by many observers, including former Afghan President Hamid Karzai, is that CMSCs are inhibiting the development of the Afghan National Police since Afghans are choosing the more lucrative, and typically better armed, positions offered by CMSCs (see Spearin 2011). Therefore, labour force competition is creating a situation in which public forces are not only struggling to attract employees but also competing with CMSCs to be viewed as legitimate security authorities.

Competition with public forces aside, the high rate of pay relative to other occupations in Afghanistan and Iraq is offset by the extreme daily dangers faced by contractors. Contracted to provide mobile security or be truck drivers for convoys transporting food, ammunition, and fuel for NATO forces, Afghan employees face the constant danger of improvised explosive devices and small-arms fire all without the protection of armoured vehicles or body armour. Reporting for the *National Post* in 2008, Tom Blackwell noted that Afghan security contractors are typically untrained men as young as eighteen whose only "protection" from ambush is an AK-47. Mohammed Salim, a representative of Commando Security, a CMSC based in Afghanistan, is aware of the deaths of about 500 fellow Afghan contractors in the five years that he has been working as a security guard (ibid.). The situation in Iraq is similar to that in Afghanistan: anecdotal evidence suggests that Iraqi contractors are more readily exposed to the dangers of working in a hostile environment.

Moving from day-to-day issues, with no benefits packages, no ability to unionize, and in many cases working for subcontractors of subcontractors, contractors are subject to arbitrary termination, get no compensation if they are injured on the job, and have little room for advancement. These work conditions are certainly not limited to employment with a CMSC, nor are CMSCs primary agents of perpetuating poor work conditions in the global South. However, any move to have CMSCs figure more prominently in the conduct of humanitarian interventions must be not only cognizant of the recent history of poor work conditions for contractors but also prepared to implement oversight and accountability mechanisms not limited to managing the tactical aspects of an intervention. Of course, this would also require broader changes to the management of labour globally, and for many politicians, academics, activists, and industry advocates such changes are beyond the scope of humanitarianism – they are political, and humanitarianism must be apolitical.

Principled Intervention?
Writing for Rabble.ca, Jerry West (2007) is adamant that Canada needs to become a global leader in a movement to prohibit "the commercialization of force." This concern is common among commentators who view the existence of CMSCs as a violation of the foundational myth of the modern nation-state that the preparation for and application of physical violence can only be undertaken by people (i.e., enlisted/conscripted soldiers and police officers) and organizations (i.e., national militaries and police forces) motivated by patriotism and not personal or organizational gain (i.e., profit). It is beyond the scope of this chapter to delve further into the (il)legitimacy of the moral soldier–immoral mercenary dichotomy. Nevertheless, concern that the for-profit/market orientation of CMSCs violates the founding precepts of humanitarianism certainly requires closer consideration, if only because "many NGOs themselves are stretching the meaning of 'humanitarian,'" and thus it is difficult to "dictate what is and is not humanitarian and what entities are appropriate deliverers of assistance" (Spearin 2008a, 377).

Accepting that humanitarianism is founded upon principles of altruism, impartiality, neutrality, and universality, it is not difficult to understand why any penetration by for-profit entities such as CMSCs into "humanitarian space" is met with much disdain. Indeed, the above concerns that CMSCs might perpetuate conditions that necessitate intervention do not even have to come into play to disqualify CMSCs as legitimate humanitarian actors. As for-profit entities, CMSCs and their personnel violate the notion that humanitarianism is and must be motivated by altruistic concern. Likewise, as (subsidiaries of) publicly traded or financial management firms (e.g., Dyncorp is a subsidiary of the private investment firm Cerberus Capital

Management, LP), CMSCs are intimately connected to global financial structures and are thereby in violation of the principles of neutrality and impartiality.

Regarding contrasting motivations, Pattison (quoted in Pavel 2010, 329) insists that "having the proper motivation is offset by more substantial concerns such as 'responding to a just cause, using force proportionally, following *jus in bello*, and having a reasonable chance of success.'" Pattison is correct in noting that possessing "selfish" motivations or being organizationally oriented toward profit does not immediately preclude an actor from conducting "just" operations or following "just" codes of conduct. Therefore, whether CMSCs can be legitimate humanitarian actors should be judged on their ability to abide by international humanitarian law, the laws of war, and/or the local statutes in the region of intervention. As mentioned above, however, the ability of CMSCs to abide by humanitarian as well as other legal statutes is too limited a condition to justify an expanded role for them. Indeed, limiting the requirement of CMSCs to abiding by humanitarian, military, and legal precepts, as Pattison does, perpetuates ignorance of the political-economic dimensions that should figure more prominently in determinations of whether CMSCs are legitimate humanitarian actors.

Impartiality and neutrality have long been upheld as necessary conditions for humanitarian actors to alleviate suffering. Having no vested interest in a region of intervention other than helping the victims of a crisis, and not choosing sides, humanitarian NGOs, such as the International Committee of the Red Cross and Médicins sans Frontières, argue that they are not only able to gain access to the suffering but also able to ensure their own safety because belligerents do not view humanitarians as shifting a conflict in any particular direction. However, many observers, including Edgar in this volume, point to numerous incidents of humanitarian actors being targeted by belligerents in Afghanistan, Iraq, and Somalia. In response to the harassment, kidnapping, and killing of humanitarians, NGOs turned to both state and commercial forces for protection. Although the International Committee of the Red Cross and Médicins sans Frontières remain ardent supporters of impartiality and neutrality, it is no longer, if it ever was, practically and conceptually tenable to uphold humanitarianism as the exclusive preserve of impartial and neutral actors.

This acknowledgment does not automatically clear the way for greater CMSC involvement in humanitarian operations. That CMSCs are intimately connected to global financial structures remains an issue of significant concern. Rather than simply perpetuating poor employment conditions in the global South, CMSCs occupy a troublingly close position to the structures and actors that uphold the inequitable distribution of global resources – for example, capital, space, food, and political influence. Troubling is not that any single CMSC might factor profit margin into a decision about conducting an intervention or into tactical or on-the-ground decisions; rather, troubling is that any single CMSC is unlikely to make a decision or take an action that might challenge the extraction of profit period. Drawing inspiration from Pugh's (2004) contention that UN peacekeeping missions are little more than "riot control" exercises, it is difficult to see how a CMSC-conducted humanitarian intervention can succeed in promoting anything more than a temporary cessation of the conditions causing the most immediate physical suffering. Hence, concerns that CMSCs will prolong a crisis or refuse to intervene in an unprofitable crisis are relatively minor, considering that CMSCs are bound not to contest a key structural condition, such as the inequitable distribution of resources around the globe, that precipitates a humanitarian crisis. A better redressing of global inequity is not a panacea for humanitarian crisis. Rather, a more equitable distribution of resources, be they financial, political, medical, or edible, will curb the need to conduct humanitarian interventions since the so-called victims of crisis will not be overly dependent on resources from altruistic/selfish, impartial/biased, or universal/selective actors.

Saving Lives?

Assertions that the continued underutilization of CMSCs "costs lives" are common in advancing the role for CMSCs in humanitarian interventions. The imperative to protect human life rings particularly loudly in Canada as the legacies of peacekeeping, the treaty to ban landmines, and the human security agenda remain relevant. Even with the current prime minister's view that international terrorism represents the gravest threat to Canada's national security, protecting human lives remains at the core of Canada's foreign policy. There is little doubt that CMSCs assist with the preservation of human life: intelligence gathering and specialized training services are readily assisting with anti-terror operations and mine clearing, water purification, medical provision, and personnel and materiel transport services are readily assisting with humanitarian operations. What should be doubted is that human life or, more appropriately, the category of human being, is apolitical and universal (Campbell 1998). Put more contentiously, it is with astonishing conceit that proponents of increasing the responsibilities of CMSCs claim that CMSC-led interventions can "save lives" (Brooks and Chorev 2008). As Dillon and Reid (2009, 127) contend, "all living is, of course, a practice and not a brute fact." In other words, the life of a human being is not an objective condition, for ways of being human are regularly promoted/denied and supported/left to die by the socio-political, economic, and onto-epistemic manoeuvrings of other ways of being human (ibid.). Despite insistence to the contrary, humanitarianism and the interventions launched in its name are not immune to these manoeuvrings. Saving, securing, and protecting human lives are never so simple.

Humanitarian practices should be interpreted cautiously as not simply practices that preserve life but also practices that affect the conditions by and through which humans can go about living their/those lives. As noted at the start of this chapter and periodically throughout it, a significant deficiency of humanitarian ethics and their practice is the inability or unwillingness of humanitarianism to better redress the inequitable distribution of resources globally. This is not because humanitarians are not altruistic and impartial enough (i.e., preventing CMSCs from assuming larger roles in interventions does not get at the core issue of humanitarianism). The core issue is that humanitarianism, in its liberal variations at least, cannot divorce itself from liberal ways of living. The problem with this is that liberal preferences for individualism, rationalism, universalism, equality, free markets, private property, and representative democracy are not necessarily benign or progressive ways of living. Put polemically, private property requires the demarcation of an enclosed (i.e., exclusive) preserve of people, places, and things, which subsequently requires submission to violent enforcement of the enclosure. Free markets require capital and a system of inequitable extraction and distribution, which subsequently requires submission to a hierarchy of access. Democracy requires representation, which cannot be effective as long as the distribution of local, regional, and global space, wealth, and knowledge remains inequitable.

The greater inclusion of CMSCs in humanitarian interventions by no means addresses these concerns. The very existence, and continued growth, of the commercial military and security services industry rely on the continued existence of private property and the growth of free markets. Although many CMSCs currently provide services to non-security or non-military clients to secure market access in hostile environments, such immediate connections to the global distribution of material resources need not be the sole reason to connect CMSCs to the pernicious aspects of liberal ways of living. Specifically, CMSCs are agents or proxies of profit extraction and poor labour conditions, but more generally they are also a more recent iteration of humans organizing and maintaining exclusionary and inequitable ways of living. CMSCs might be able to save lives, but this life saving rests on a discursive-material economy of living that assisted in both opening the political and economic space for CMSCs to emerge as significant global actors and (further) enclosing the political, economic, and geographic space in which humans can live their lives without those lives needing to be saved. In other words, as long as humanitarianism and/or humanitarian interventions remain focused on preserving life and not contesting how certain ways of living require life to be saved, and I say this derisively, it only seems logical that CMSCs should be the primary agents to conduct these life-saving operations.

Conclusion

As laid bare in the previous three sections, the issue with allowing CMSCs to have a greater role in supporting and/or conducting humanitarian interventions is not that the operations of CMSCs are antithetical to humanitarian practices but that drawing CMSCs into "humanitarian space" only furthers the need for humanitarian intervention in the first place. Turning to the commercial sector will only exacerbate the narrowing of humanitarian practices to those that focus on addressing the short-term, technical, and tactical necessities of a crisis. Indeed, the commercialization of humanitarian interventions ensures that they are little more than crisis management operations, and, as long as global relations continue to be dominated by exclusionary and hierarchical distributions of space, resources, and influence, there will be no shortage of crises to manage. This is a particularly significant assentation to make given Canada's narrowing focus on the alleviation of threats due to terrorism and violent persecution motivated by ethnicity, religion, gender, or political allegiance. With solutions to terrorism and violent persecution regularly cast as a need to eradicate the bad guys, to confront evil, and/or to stand up for those who cannot, a subsequent narrowing of humanitarian space to the need to save lives as efficiently and cost effectively as possible leaves little room for ethical considerations not rooted in militarized and commercialized logics. Accordingly, if Canada's foreign policy decision makers move to increase the participation of CMSCs, it will be very difficult for Canadian foreign policy to achieve any meaningful semblance of "stability, good governance, and orderly international relations" (Spearin 2005, 70). Indeed, if stability, good governance, and orderly international relations are ever going to be achieved, then a concerted effort (i.e., an ethical commitment) needs to be made to redress global inequity better.

NOTES

1 Although I am loath to add another acronym to the long list of acronyms used to describe companies that provide military and/or security services, it is time that the lexicon moves away from prefacing military and security companies with the word *private*. It is time to replace that word with the word *commercial* because it better signals the market/profit orientation of these companies and circumvents the ideational impact of the public/private dichotomy that prevents a more nuanced and thorough understanding of how the operations and ideologies of commercial, governmental, and civil society entities interact with and through each other in the twenty-first century.

2 Because the organizational size, ownership structure, country of origin, services provided, and primary employee pool vary greatly among companies that provide military or security-oriented services to the military, diplomatic, development, and intelligence apparatuses of governmental and non-governmental entities, this chapter considers only issues relevant to companies that can provide logistical support and/or armed personnel for interventions to relieve some of the planet's worst humanitarian crises. For some critiques to refer to these companies as CMSCs is a euphemistic cover for the more appropriate designation of these companies as mercenary outfits. There is little room in this chapter to consider the conceptual, legal, moral, practical, and popular histories that produce the "mercenary" as one of the most vilified characters of global military practice. Nonetheless, it is important to recognize that CMSCs are not the same as the companies of soldiers of fortune commanded by Mike Hoare or Bob Denard during the 1960s in sub-Saharan Africa.

3 By virtue of the operation of a coffee and doughnut outlet at the Kandahar airfield from 2006 to 2011, Tim Hortons can be considered a CMSC.

4 At its North Carolina facilities, Blackwater/Xe/Academi operates a "Mirror Image" training course that focuses on preparing trainees, typically enlisted personnel, to understand "the mindset and culture of insurgents" (Scahill 2010).

References

Abrahamsen, R., and M.C. Williams. 2011. *Security beyond the State: Private Security in International Politics*. Cambridge: Cambridge University Press.

Antonyshyn, D., J. Grofe, and D. Hubert. 2009. "Beyond the Law? The Regulation of Canadian Private Military and Security Companies Operating Abroad, PRIV-WAR Report – Canada." *PRIV-WAR*, 12 February.

Blackwell, T. 2008. "Private Security Personnel Easy Targets in Afghanistan." *National Post*, 20 October. http://afghanistan.nationalpost.com/private-security-personnel-easy-targets-in-afghanistan/.

Brooks, D., and M. Chorev. 2008. "Ruthless Humanitarianism: Why Marginalizing Private Peacekeeping Kills People." In *Private Military and Security Companies: Ethics, Policies, and Civil-Military Relations*, edited by A. Alexandra, D.P. Baker, and M. Caparini, 116–30. New York: Routledge.

Campbell, D. 1998. "Why Fight? Humanitarianism, Principles, and Post-Structuralism." *Millennium* 27 (3): 497–521. http://dx.doi.org/10.1177/03058298980270031001.

Canadian Press. 2011. "Canada's Hired Guns Slammed in U.S. Report." *Metro,* 7 February.

CanWestNewsService.2007a."CanadianForcesHireControversialSecurityFirm."Canada. com. http://www.canada.com/topics/news/national/story.html?id=7b297175-8b15-4414-81ea-b274d18bbcd7.

CTV.ca. 2007. "UN Investigated Over 300 for Alleged Sex Offences." CTV.ca. http:// www.ctv.ca/servlet/ArticleNews/story/CTVNews/20070106/un_offences_07010 6/20070106?hub=TopStories.

Dillon, M., and J. Reid. 2009. *The Liberal Way of War: Killing to Make Life Live.* New York: Routledge.

Fitzsimmons, S. 2006. "A Private Solution to a Humanitarian Catastrophe." *Vanguard,* 1 September. http://vanguardcanada.com/a-private-solution-to-a-humanitarian-catastrophe/.

Fitzsimmons, S. 2009. "Shadow Warriors: Shedding Light on Private Security Contractors in Afghanistan." *Vanguard,* 1 April. http://vanguardcanada.com/shadow-warriors-shedding-light-on-private-security-contractors-in-afghanistan/.

Galloway, G. 2009. "$8-Million, No Oversight: Forces Given Rein to Hire Private Guards in Kandahar." *Globe and Mail,* 18 November.

Gifford, S. 2008. "The Armed Private Military Company and the Canadian Forces: The Next Step in Contractor Support?" *Canadian Army Journal* 11 (1): 76–97.

Higate, P. 2012. "Martial Races and Enforcement Masculinities of the Global South: Weaponizing Fijian, Chilean, and Salvadoran Postcoloniality in the Mercenary Sector." *Globalizations* 9 (1): 35–52.

ICRC (International Committee of the Red Cross). 2008. "The Montreux Document on Private Military and Security Companies." ICRC. http://www.icrc.org/eng/ resources/documents/misc/montreux-document-170908.htm.

International Stability Operations Association. 2013. "ISOA Code of Conduct." ISOA. http://www.stability-operations.org/?page=Code.

Mayeda, A. and M. Blanchfield. 2007. "Military Should Shed More Light on Private Contractors to Afghan Mission." *CanWest News Service,* 20 November. http://www2.canada.com/shareit/voices/story.html?id=2c4e93d3-253d-422a-86a8-71ebe7d04d71&k=69915.

Mmali, J. 2009. "Why Ugandans Want to Work in Iraq." *BBC News,* 6 November. http://bbc.in/27J9Hh.

Montpetit, J. 2010. "Canadian Military Using Private Afghan Security Despite Pending Ban." *Toronto Star,* 25 October. http://www.thestar.com/news/canada/ 2010/10/25/canadian_military_using_private_afghan_security_despite_pending_ ban.html.

National Post. 2006. "Special Forces Get Pay Raise." *Canada.com,* 26 August. http:// www.canada.com/story.html?id=1109da57-944c-45a4-962d-9f89d591341a.

Pavel, C.E. 2010. "Alternative Agents for Humanitarian Intervention." *Journal of Global Ethics* 6 (3): 323–38. http://dx.doi.org/10.1080/17449626.2010.524803.

Perrin, B. 2008. "Guns for Hire – With Canadian Taxpayer Dollars." *Human Security Bulletin* 6 (3): 5–6.

Pugh, M. 2004. "Peacekeeping and Critical Theory." *International Peacekeeping* 11 (1): 39–58. http://dx.doi.org/10.1080/1353331042000228445.

Pugliese, D. 2005. "Soldiers of Fortune," Ottawa Citizen, 12 November.

Rosén, F. 2008. "Commercial Security: Conditions of Growth." *Security Dialogue* 39 (1): 77–97.

Rostek, M., and P. Gizewski. 2009. "PMCs and the Comprehensive Approach." *Vanguard*, 1 June. http://vanguardcanada.com/pmcs-and-the-comprehensive-approach/.

Scahill, J. 2010. "Blackwater's Black Ops." *The Nation*, 4 October. http://www.the-nation.com/article/154739/blackwaters-black-ops?page=full.

Spearin, C. 2004. "International Private Security Companies and Canadian Policy: Possibilities and Pitfalls on the Road to Regulation." *Canadian Foreign Policy* 11 (2): 1–15. http://dx.doi.org/10.1080/11926422.2004.9673363.

Spearin, C. 2005. "Canada and International Private Security Companies: Issues and Challenges for Special Operations Capabilities." In *Choice of Force: Special Operations for Canada,* edited by D. Last and B. Horn, 69–84. Montreal/Kingston: McGill-Queen's University Press.

Spearin, C. 2008a. "Private, Armed, and Humanitarian? States, NGOs, International Private Security Companies, and Shifting Humanitarianism." *Security Dialogue* 39 (4): 363–82. http://dx.doi.org/10.1177/0967010608094034.

Spearin, C. 2008b. "What Manley Missed: The Human Security Implications of Private Security in Afghanistan." *Human Security Bulletin* 6 (3): 8–11.

Spearin, C. 2011. "UN Peacekeeping and the International Private Military and Security Industry." *International Peacekeeping* 18 (2): 196–209.

West, J. 2007. "Canada's Turn to Stand Up to Mercenaries." *Rabble.ca,* 4 October. http://rabble.ca/columnists/canadas-turn-stand-up-mercenaries.

PART 2

SECURITY ACROSS BORDERS

4

Charter Values and Post-9/11 Security and Terrorism Law and Policy
Comparing Canada's "Home" and "Away" Games

BARBARA J. FALK

Less than ten days after the al-Qaeda attacks of 9/11, President George W. Bush portrayed the conflict against a transnational terrorist network as a war rather than a law enforcement effort, and his remarks signalled not so much a paradigm shift as an additional layer of law and policy for both the United States and allies such as Canada.[1] The response morphed into a global "War on Terror," whereas previous domestic and international counterterrorism and anti-terrorism efforts had been addressed by law enforcement agencies, even when militaries had been engaged, as with British forces in Northern Ireland in the 1970s.[2] Indeed, the international organization responsible for the thirteen universal legal instruments relating to both the prevention and the suppression of terrorism is the United Nations Office on Drugs and Crime, located in Vienna. Nonetheless, post-9/11 military efforts, particularly by NATO states such as Canada, did not seek to replace or duplicate legal efforts but *add* to those efforts – thus, it would be both misleading and incorrect to suggest that a pre-existing legal paradigm was supplanted by a military paradigm. Nevertheless, a robust military response – against either specific groups or states that harbour them – runs into difficulty in meeting the demands of international humanitarian and human rights law and at times runs directly against both.

The challenge, conceptually and practically, is that both approaches are governed by different bodies of law responding to different ethical requirements and can operate at cross-purposes with one another. Moreover, the bodies of law involved (internationally, humanitarian law, the law of armed conflict, and human rights law; domestically, criminal law, immigration law, and constitutional law) do not always cohere, exist for different purposes, and are subject to varying levels of norm adoption, adherence, and enforcement. None fully address the challenge of transnational terrorists who do not claim to represent any state and whose activities, in terms of intent and effect, transcend state boundaries. Moreover, the legal and ethical coherence of the domestic criminal sanction that prohibits murder in all cases runs counter to the legal use of force against legitimate targets and the principle of combatant immunity found in international humanitarian law. Domestic criminal law is reactive, highly regulated in the use of controlled force, and limited in terms of prevention, whereas the law of armed conflict is more proactive, more permissive in terms of the use of force, and, especially after 9/11, seen at least partially through the lens of fighting a conflict overseas as a means to deter and contain the threat both at home and abroad. Nevertheless, post-9/11 foreign, security, and defence law and policy were hardly devoid of ethical dimensions or quandaries.

As with most democratic states rushing to comply with UN Security Council Resolution 1373 after the 9/11 attacks in the United States, Canada sought to balance liberty concerns with security dilemmas. This translated into a calculated – and not always successful – strategy of balancing the values and ethics inherent in the Charter of Rights and Freedoms and security law and policy, both at home and abroad. Moreover, this largely reactive rather than proactive approach responded to shifting security risks – both "homegrown" and "transnational." Although there has been divisive debate regarding the appropriate law and policy mix to address this "brave new world" of counter- and anti-terrorism and globally networked or homegrown threats, there has been an uneasy political consensus that a "whole-of-government" approach is required, meaning that all the instruments of state power are deployed, both at home and abroad, including the RCMP, the Canadian Security Intelligence Service, Communications Security Eestablishment Canada, the Canadian Forces, and the Department of Foreign Affairs, Trade and Development (DFATD). At the same time, national security law and policy are increasingly globalized: actions taken in deployments abroad have generated considerable political, legal, and ethical costs at home. In particular, the detention or prosecution of individuals suspected as security risks at home, or of Canadian citizens abroad, starkly illustrates how the "home" and "away" games cannot be kept separate and have profound consequences beyond our borders. The boundary between domestic and international governance is porous and contested, and this is increasingly the case in security law and policy.

This chapter considers the evolution of post-9/11 security and terrorism law and policy through a number of controversial and illustrative cases that, taken together, amply demonstrate the security and intelligence concerns at stake, the real and potential violation of human rights, and the difficult yet necessary struggle to keep our foreign and domestic responses consistent not only with the Charter narrowly but also with Charter values and ethics more broadly. In so doing, key pieces of legislation and policy documents are examined, such as the 2001 Anti-Terrorism Act and the 2004 National Security Policy, as well as key cases, such as those of Maher Arar, Omar Khadr, Momin Khawaja, and the so-called Toronto 18, and the use of security certificates under the Immigration Refugee Protection Act. Finally, the extraterritorial application of the Charter to those detained by serving members of the Canadian Forces overseas and the internationalization of terrorist-related prosecutions are addressed.[3]

Ethics, Security, and Terrorism: Definitions in Law and Policy

Despite vigorous debates in international relations theory regarding definitions of ethics and security and the assumptions embedded therein, this chapter focuses on more concrete definitions: how these terms have been *actually* defined and followed in law and policy since 9/11 and the implications that these definitions have for Canadian foreign and security policy at home and abroad.

Ethics is not defined specifically in Canadian law or public policy but arguably is embedded in various documents and judicial decisions that focus on Canadian values. If ethics can be defined as focusing on procedure and behaviour, values are the norms that those procedures are designed to express and fulfill, and in Canada these values are primarily codified in the Charter. Indeed, the impact of the Charter over the past thirty years illustrates how a constitutional bill of rights philosophically rooted in natural law and the "principles of fundamental justice" has been substantively interpreted, considers community norms and values, and does not ignore competing ethics or beliefs. In addition, the *Secession Reference*, which laid out the ground rules for Quebec's possible secession from Canada, also outlined five interrelated and equally important principles as "fundamental" to the Constitution and, by extension, Canada's "way of life": federalism, democracy, constitutionalism, the rule of law, and the protection of minorities.[4]

Together the Charter and the *Secession Reference* constitute a normative and legal basis for a discussion of ethics in Canada.

Post-9/11, and consistent with Charter values writ large, the 2004 National Security Policy outlined the core values of openness, diversity, and respect for civil liberties that must be balanced with Canada's core interests. Moreover, the Supreme Court of Canada has sought to incorporate these values into its decisions: this has been clearly evident in the evolution of security law and policy since 9/11, in which the court has aimed for consistency in Canada's actions at home and abroad. Nationally, we use the language of the Charter and civil liberties. Internationally, we use the language of human rights yet increasingly attach the Charter to our assessment of Canada's actions abroad by officers of the Canadian Forces or members of our security and intelligence agencies.

The Supreme Court weighed in early on the definition of security in the 2002 immigration case *Suresh v. Canada*, involving a member of the Liberation Tigers of Tamil Ealam. Significantly, the court did not rule out prohibited deportation to a state given a substantial risk of torture (and has not since even though Canada is a signatory to the Convention against Torture). Also at issue was the phrase "danger to the security of Canada" in the Immigration Act (now the Immigration Refugee Protection Act). The Supreme Court acknowledged that security is difficult to define, as "highly fact-based and political in the general sense," but nevertheless concluded that (a) the threat can be direct or indirect; (b) must be serious (i.e., there must be an objective reasonable suspicion based on evidence); and (c) must be substantial – the threatened harm must be significant and non-negligible. Nothing in the *Suresh* decision limits internal or external "threats" to states or state-based actors; indeed, it was written in the shadow of 9/11 with the non-state threat posed by terrorism clearly in mind.

Two years after *Suresh*, the state and human security debates of the 1990s were implicitly referenced in the 2004 National Security Policy, with the government of Canada defining security in an all-hazards manner that included protecting not just *Canada* but also *Canadians both at home and abroad* and not only the physical security of Canadians but also our values and key institutions. Moreover, because of the timing of the process, the 2003 SARS epidemic that hit Vancouver and Toronto was also influential on policy makers, dramatically illustrating how threats can be no less severe if viral rather than political. The policy also responded to a more traditional vision of security emphasizing risk to the state. While recognizing the transnationality of threats and the realities of globalization, the policy incorporated two broad responsibilities: to ensure that Canada is not a base for threats to our allies and to contribute to international security. Because so much of the evolution of security law and policy has been in response to terrorism, in particular the attacks of 9/11, that is the focus here.

In the 2004 policy, ethical deliberation was directly suggested with the requirement that the "interests" outlined must be implemented or measured against the core values of liberty, diversity, and respect for civil liberties. However, the policy is soft, unlike law, which necessitates the balancing approach embedded in the "*Oakes* test," which requires governments and courts to consider Charter violations only when enshrined in law with a pressing and substantial objective that can be defended as a "reasonable limit" in a "free and democratic society."[5] In practice, given the paucity of evidence on decision making because of security restrictions on access to information, it is not easy to tease out considerations of ethics and Charter values from security concerns at the policy level. However, this has not stopped the courts from applying the Charter to ethically troubling cases, such as those of Adil Charkaoui and Omar Khadr. After all, and well before 9/11, critical Charter rights and values engaged questions relevant to international security and human rights, such as the section 7 protection of "the right to life, liberty, and security of the person"; the section 8 guarantee "against unreasonable search or seizure"; the section 9 right against arbitrary detention; and, upon arrest or detention, the section 10 right to counsel and the ability to question the validity of the detention via *habeas corpus*.

Still, the functional requirements of law and political exigencies in upholding order and minimizing risk can collide with ethics – and with high stakes given topics as serious as security and terrorism. Threats are often discussed in the media in highly charged and emotional language, designed to prey on public fear, an intended goal of terrorist attacks in the first place. On the political side, there is a sense of urgency and a high risk of non-action. The various tools and techniques that a state can employ involve extraordinary power – whether of police investigation, law enforcement, intelligence surveillance, or deployment of the military – and risk encroaching on important domestic and international rights and freedoms in the process and promoting unethical behaviour in the name of security. At the same time, there is a high probability of what Alan Dershowitz calls "false positives": drastic actions that seemed necessary at the time when, in hindsight, authorities were misinformed about the situations or contributed to the injustices. (Dershowitz 2006, 16–17). Acting pre-emptively can come at a high price to a mistakenly targeted individual, as occurred with Arar.

Before 9/11, terrorism was not defined in Canadian criminal law – despite Canada's experiences with the Front de Libération du Québec, Prime Minister Pierre Trudeau's invocation of the War Measures Act in 1970, and the Air India bombings of 1985. Bill C-36 was introduced within weeks of 9/11 and added new offences to the Criminal Code of Canada relating not only to terrorist activity but also to the provision of money, property, and other forms of assistance to terrorist groups, participation in the activities of a terrorist group, and instruction of the carrying out of activities of terrorist groups (Roach 2005, 514).[6] Perhaps mindful of section 2d (freedom of association) and section 27 (Canada's multicultural heritage) of the Charter, the resulting Anti-Terrorism Act did not criminalize membership in a terrorist organization. Still, the law applies extraterritorially – that is, to crimes committed inside or outside Canada, similar to war crimes and genocide provisions – yet requires guilt beyond a reasonable doubt and prohibits secret evidence. To "Charter-proof" the legislation additionally, drafters were careful not to include any reverse onus provisions and required high levels of subjective fault, such as knowledge or purpose (Roach 2011, 381). The Anti-Terrorism Act does not define terrorism per se, exempting lawmakers from addressing the thorny issue of whether or not terrorism is an ideology or simply a set of tactics to be employed by various domestic and international actors. However, "terrorist activity" is defined in two ways: first, in reference to UN counterterrorism conventions and protocols; second, as an omission or act committed "for a political, religious, or ideological purpose" and "with the intention of intimidating the public, or segment of the public, with regard to its security, including its economic security," that intentionally causes death or bodily harm using violence or endangers a person's life, causes substantial private or public property damage, or interferes with or disrupts an essential service other than through advocacy, protest, dissent, or work stoppage.[7] Conspiracy offences are included, as well as attempts, threats, and being an accessory after the fact. However, the law carefully excludes acts committed during armed conflict or by military forces in exercising their official duties – excluding the possibility of state terrorism under Canadian law if the agents of state action are the armed forces of that state.

The Anti-Terrorism Act also included a new procedure under section 38 of the Canada Evidence Act allowing for the prohibition of disclosure of information if its release would be"injurious to international relations or national security." In "regular" domestic criminal law, all relevant information must be fully disclosed to the accused.[8] Canada's signals intelligence agency, Communications Security Establishment Canada, was publicly acknowledged and given a statutory framework (Roach 2011, 376, 389–90). In response to UN Resolutions 1373 and 1267, terrorism financing offences were included, allowing for the ministers of public safety and national revenue to strip charities of their tax status, and a listing regime was implemented to designate groups and even specific individuals as terrorists, yet provided for judicial review. Controversially, the legislation permitted seventy-two-hour preventive arrests upon ministerial and judicial authorization, and investigative hearings allowing compelled testimony, though such testimony cannot be subsequently used in criminal proceedings. The latter process was judicially upheld in 2008 but has been used only once, during the Air India trial.[9] Preventive arrests never occurred, and although both provisions expired in 2007, they were reinstated for five years via the Combatting Terrorism Act, which came into effect in May 2013.

During the C-36 debate – both publicly and in Parliament – concerns were voiced regarding the uncertainty of the new law as either "cosmetic or overbroad" (Roach 2005, 515). If new offences merely duplicated existing provisions in the Criminal Code regarding inchoate crimes and participatory acts, then they were unnecessary and confusing; if they went beyond existing provisions, then there was the possibility of guilt by association and crimes based upon status (Roach 2003, 2005). The definition of "terrorist activity" criminalized motive for the first time, distinguishing terrorist activity from other forms of crime, a restrictive provision requiring police and prosecutors to investigate and bring forward at trial evidence regarding motive. Indeed, terrorist prosecutions in the past decade have borne the fruit of these initial misgivings.

Yet in *Suresh*, the Supreme Court effectively ignored the definition of terrorist activity available in the Anti-Terrorism Act and, for immigration law, borrowed from existing UN protocols, defining terrorism as any

> act intended to cause death or serious injury to a civilian, or to any person
> not taking part in the hostilities of a situation of armed conflict, when the
> purpose of such an act by its nature or context is to intimidate a population
> or to compel a government or an international organization to do or abstain
> from doing any act.[10]

The court's initial post-9/11 pattern of national security deference continued with a reference case on the controversial investigative hearing provisions of the Anti-Terrorism Act, in which the court famously expressed the dilemma of balancing counterterrorism initiatives while respecting the rule of law: "Although terrorism necessarily changes the context in which the rule of law must operate, it does not call for the abdication of law. Yet at the same time, while respect for the rule of law must be maintained in the response to terrorism, the Constitution is not a suicide pact."[11]

With *Suresh*, the Supreme Court asserted its independent prerogative to provide its own definitions of security and terrorism. Nevertheless, the definition of security recognized threats that must be serious and substantial and in no way pre-empted or limited the language of the 2004 policy. And the court specifically noted that the rule of law cannot be ignored or perforce be an ethical yoke that inhibits legislative or prosecutorial action.

The Post-9/11 "Home" Game

The events of 9/11 were obviously a critical juncture in the evolution of law and policy with respect to ethics and security. However, *within* Canada, two pre-9/11 events were effectively reframed in public and political consciousness because of the World Trade Center and Pentagon attacks. The 1985 bombing of Air India Flight 182, which exploded en route from Montreal to London, carrying luggage loaded in Vancouver and killing all 329 on board, was slowly embraced by Canadians as a homegrown tragedy, for most of the victims were Canadian citizens.[12] To this day, it remains the most deadly terrorist attack involving Canadians and unfortunately a high-water mark in terms of ineffective response. After an investigation of more than twenty years, and much-criticized bungling, lack of coordination, and rivalry between the then relatively new and inexperienced CSIS (Canadian Security Intelligence Service) and the RCMP, three prosecutions resulted, and two separate inquiries were conducted, each with its own report and recommendations.[13] Similarly, the case of Ahmed Ressam, the so-called Millennium Bomber, cast an ominous shadow over Canada-US relations, given his apprehension at the Canada-US border. Ressam was a member of an al-Qaeda cell, had been trained in Afghanistan, and used a Canadian passport obtained with false identity papers. Although he was under surveillance by both CSIS and the RCMP, Ressam left Canada undetected with the intention to blow up the Los Angeles International Airport on New Year's Eve 1999, earning him a media moniker while stoking American fears of lax Canadian border and security policies and a too liberal refugee policy. His case was a key source of the much-repeated myth that at least some of the 9/11 terrorists had entered Canada, a myth that has been repeatedly filtered through popular and political culture.[14]

The inherent transnationality of most post-9/11 terrorist cases argued in domestic courts raises sensitive issues such as interstate intelligence sharing and the use of undisclosed evidence against terrorist suspects, rendering any clear separation between the domestic and the international nigh impossible. The standard of reasonable doubt as the threshold beyond which the prosecution must prove guilt is the strictest possible – one that even the International Committee of the Red Cross has recognized might make domestic prosecution difficult (see ICRC 2004). Nevertheless, the reasonable doubt standard is necessary given the nature of the criminal sanction, especially for offences with stiff sentences and significant social stigma.[15] The BC Supreme Court reaffirmed this principle in its reasoning accompanying its acquittal in *R. v. Malik* – better known to the Canadian public as the Air India bombing trial of Ripudaman Singh Malik and Ajaib Singh Bagri in 2005 – when the judge described "the horrific nature of these cruel acts of terrorism" and then noted that "justice is not achieved, however, if persons are convicted on anything less than the requisite standard of proof beyond a reasonable doubt."[16]

Initially, there was little prosecutorial action under the Anti-Terrorism Act – the preferred approach was the use of immigration law, with political and legal reasons for taking this route. Politically, in American eyes, Canada's allegedly lax and generous immigration and refugee laws and policies, combined with the ease of traversing the historically "undefended" border, suggested a potentially vulnerable and unreliable ally. Immigration law is legally but less ethically attractive in allowing for procedural shortcuts, greater secrecy, significant ministerial discretion, and a lower standard of proof in responding to individuals deemed security risks. Indeed, section 34 of the Immigration Refugee Protection Act allows for the inadmissibility of non-citizens for reasons of security on the basis of membership in a listed organization or if there are reasonable grounds to believe that a person engages, has engaged, or will engage in terrorism.

Most controversial has been the government's use of security certificates to detain non-citizens. Although security certificates had existed in law since 1978, they came under increasing public and judicial scrutiny after 9/11. Authorized via ministerial discretion, they can be used to detain and remove non-Canadians seeking entry into Canada if deemed a risk to national security. Those detained can challenge their detention – but via hearings conducted *in camera*, on the basis of limited disclosure. Public concern about the use of secret evidence and potential deportation to states known for practising torture (an eventuality not ruled out in *Suresh*) came to a head with the 2007 case of Adil Charkaoui, an Algerian suspected of terrorist activity. Charkaoui challenged the reasonableness of the certificate process, claiming that review procedures violated the Charter, including his section 7 right to liberty and security of the person. Alarmed at the absence of adversarial challenge to secret evidence, a less deferential Supreme Court unanimously found that the Immigration Refugee Protection Act's procedure violated sections 7, 9, and 10 of the Charter and declared a one-year suspension of invalidity, allowing Parliament to design a new process.[17] Parliament responded with the appointment of specially trained and security-cleared advocates to protect the interests of those subject to security certificates in hearings held *in camera*.[18] The special advocate process is supposed to allow for enough disclosure to permit adversarial challenge of the evidence, a crucial norm in our legal history and process.[19] Still, intelligence officials have been less content with having to retain and disclose intelligence never originally intended to serve as evidence. In 2008, the Supreme Court ruled again on Charkaoui's case, on the duty of CSIS to preserve raw intelligence and disclose investigation notes, which the court likened to requirements regarding disclosure of police officers' notes.[20]

Meanwhile, the case of Mohamed Harkat, an alleged al-Qaeda sleeper agent held on a security certificate since 2002, tested the constitutionality of the security certificate regime established after *Charkaoui*. Harkat's case has bounced between the Federal Court of Canada, which upheld the government's assertion that Harkat continued to pose a security threat, setting the stage for his deportation to his native Algeria, and the Federal Court of Appeal, which ruled in 2012 that trial fairness had been compromised by the destruction of wiretap recordings.[21] In a majority judgment penned by Chief Justice Beverley McLachlin released in May 2014, the Supeme Court upheld the constitutionality of the reformed IPRA security certificate regime, paving the way for Harkat's removal from Canada. However, in the same case, the court rejected the extension of any class privilege for CSIS human sources.[22]

Despite the judicial-parliamentary dialogue on the issue of security certificates and the court's ruling on *Harkat*, it seems politically unlikely at present for the Canadian government to engage in any further widespread use of these certificates. They are failures in terms of both policy and ethics: intelligence officials do not like disclosure and legal challenge, and the public does not like the use of secret evidence in proceedings that fall far short of criminal trials in terms of process or determination of guilt. Long-term detention is expensive, while deportation is legally difficult and ethically fraught. Covert investigation is likely as effective in terms of tracking risks, requires no disclosure or restrictive control orders, and is thus far less costly politically. Given the success of recent terrorist prosecutions, the default route will likely be arrest and prosecution, depending on admissible evidence available.

More egregious has been the case of Maher Arar, an engineer living in Ottawa who became a "person of interest" in an RCMP investigation (Project AO Canada) regarding a plot to blow up Parliament Hill. Although in his royal commission report Justice Dennis O'Connor found no evidence that Canadians participated in or acquiesced to the American decision to "rendition" Arar to his birth place, Syria, where he was held captive for ten months and tortured, the United States "very likely" relied on RCMP information that portrayed Arar in an inaccurate and unfair manner (see Canada 2006). O'Connor's report exonerated Arar and made detailed recommendations to avoid Canadian complicity in torture and other human rights abuses. Arar's case was kept in the media spotlight by his very sympathetic and media-savvy spouse, Monia Mazigh (2008). His return to Canada, along with his harrowing description of suffering endured at the hands of his Syrian interrogators, was moving and unforgettable. Eventually, Arar settled all legal claims with the Canadian government and received a public apology from the prime minister as well as a settlement of $10.5 million.[23] His case demonstrated the costly nature of "false positives" – all the more so given Canada's sensitivity to wrongful convictions and miscarriages of justice in cases such as those of Donald Marshall, David Milgaard, Guy Paul Morin, and Stephen Truscott. An additional judicial inquiry conducted by Justice Frank Iacobucci examined three similar rendition cases: Abdullah Almalki, Ahmad Elmaati, and Muayyed Nureddin. All three were tortured while detained in Syria or Egypt yet were innocent of terrorist affiliations (*Internal Inquiry* ... 2008). Nevertheless, unlike Arar, they have been unsuccessful in obtaining either an apology or compensation, resulting in ongoing civil litigation with the Crown. Taken together, these cases underscore the transnational nature of intelligence sharing and investigation and larger international debates about jurisdictional evasion in the ethically troubling out-sourcing of torture to states with less than stellar human rights records. Again, the domestic and the international cannot be separated.

At the same time that the public was galvanized by the tale of wrongdoing regarding Arar, another detained Canadian continued to attract national and international attention: Omar Khadr, held at the American detention facility at Guantánamo Bay, Cuba, since his capture following a 2002 gunfight in Afghanistan. He was charged before a military commission, chiefly for allegedly having thrown a grenade resulting in the death of Sergeant Christopher Speer of the US Army. Khadr was fifteen years old at the time. He was brought to Afghanistan at the age of ten by his family and father, Ahmed Said Khadr, a charity fundraiser who later associated with al-Qaeda and was once released from detention in Pakistan in 1995 because of the personal intervention of Prime Minister Jean Chrétien during a "Team Canada" trade mission to South Asia. Indeed, whereas Arar would have been a highly sympathetic defendant in a potential lawsuit against the Canadian government, any public empathy that might have accrued to young Khadr was erased by his family's beliefs and alleged activities, a family later dubbed "Canada's first family of terrorism" by the media.[24] In fact, not until a number of outspoken opinion leaders took up Khadr's cause as a minor and child soldier, such as former Senator Roméo Dallaire, did the tenor of media and public scrutiny begin to shift, yet never with the same level of concern or compassion garnered by Arar.

Khadr's case remains controversial for a number of reasons. By 2009, Khadr was the only Western citizen still held at Guantánamo Bay. His case was much delayed given congressional retooling and approval of the process after the US Supreme Court's 2006 ruling in *Hamdan*. The issue of his age and status as a minor attracted international attention, that of Human Rights Watch, former US prosecutor for Sierra Leone's war crimes, David Crane, UN Special Representative for Children in Armed Conflict Radhika Coomaraswamy, and the United Kingdom's top five legal bar associations, which wrote a letter of protest to Prime Minister Stephen Harper in 2009. Khadr's military-appointed lawyer and chief counsel, Lieutenant Commander Bill Kuebler, was fired and then reinstated before the military commission hearing even began, and his Canadian lawyers Dennis Edney and Nathan Whitling had no official standing in any proceedings in a process still criticized for its lack of fairness. Reports circulated in the press regarding exculpatory evidence – Khadr was buried under a collapsed roof and could not possibly have thrown the grenade that killed Speer, or another person could have thrown the grenade – generating potential reasonable doubt. The Supreme Court of Canada ordered the disclosure of interviews revealing that federal authorities were complicit in his "enhanced interrogation" in Guantánamo Bay and therefore violated his Charter rights as well as Canada's obligations under international human rights law.[25] The courts were then challenged to rule on whether or not the government could be ordered judicially to seek Khadr's repatriation, but the Supreme Court overturned a Federal Court ruling, confirming that determinations of foreign policy are within the sole prerogative of the Crown.[26] Importantly, these decisions stressed both domestic and international legal violations, and the illegality of the Guantánamo Bay process, illustrating the potential extraterritorial reach of the Charter as well as domestic judicial efforts to enforce international legal instruments.

The strength of Khadr's case was never fully tested since Khadr pleaded guilty to murder, attempted murder in violation of the laws of war, conspiracy, providing material support for terrorism, and espionage in an eleventh-hour agreement among Khadr and Canadian and American authorities in October 2010. He was given an eight-year sentence, and after one additional year he could serve the remainder of his sentence in Canada. Nevertheless, the militarily selected jury effectively sentenced him to a symbolic forty-year sentence, the length of which is perhaps the greatest procedural condemnation of the entire process. Moreover, the Canadian government took an additional two years because of ministerial evaluation of psychiatric assessments of Khadr – attributed by his counsel and supporters as yet one more reason for delay – before he was finally returned to Canada in October 2012. Effectively, his repatriation had been stalled for an entire decade, and an October 2013 court ruling denied his legal challenge to inappropriate incarceration in a federal facility. Optics took precedence over ethics, human rights, concern over Charter violations, or the sovereign obligation to a Canadian citizen: every other state except Canada had petitioned the US government to bring home its citizens from Guantánamo Bay, including Australia and the United Kingdom. According to an anonymous US official, "your side balked [and said] no military jet with a Maple Leaf on its tail was taking Omar home" (cited in Koring 2012).

Politically, the handling of *Arar* and *Khadr* was slow, ineffective, and displayed a callous disregard for the rights of these Canadian citizens, regardless of the allegations against them. Each case had transnational and ethical implications. Unfortunately, their cases are part of a larger continuum that includes other well-publicized instances of Muslim Canadians running up against officials refusing to act until judicially compelled.[27]

Abousfian Abdelrazik was arrested and detained while visiting his mother in Sudan in 2003 and lived in limbo within the embassy in Khartoum from 2008 until 2009, when the Federal Court ruled that Canada was required to return him to Canada and that CSIS had been "complicit" in his detention in the first place.[28] In one respect, Abdelrazik's case is more damning: decision making was confined to one Canadian government department, so jurisdictional disputes or interdepartmental quarrels cannot be blamed for the inaction.

The arrest and trial of Momin Khawaja comprised the first full prosecution under the Anti-Terrorism Act. His arrest, linked to a London bomb plot, was the result of an investigation involving the RCMP and the London Metropolitan Police, dubbed Operation Crevice.[29] The case seemed both pathetic and deeply serious: Khawaja had travelled to Pakistan for "training" in 2003 that had involved little more than rudimentary small arms training that the judge likened more to a "'retreat' for like-minded jihadists for common bonding, reinforcing, and planning than ... a serious military combat training exercise."[30] In the basement of his parents' home in Orleans, Ontario, he was also developing a remote detonator for an improvised explosive device (IED) that he nicknamed the "hifidigimonster."

For security officials, the case illustrated the importance of transnational intelligence sharing, the simultaneity of producing intelligence and admissible evidence, and the risks of jeopardizing intelligence agreements and relationships should such information be released in open court, especially considering that Canada is a "net importer" of intelligence. For defence lawyers, widespread prohibition of disclosure potentially violated the principle of an open court and the ability of an accused to provide a full answer and defence. In Khawaja's case, the Federal Court balanced these two concerns, allowing the attorney general not to disclose hundreds of documents but still requiring that a summary be provided to his lawyers. Furthermore, an *amicus curiae* was appointed to protect the interests of the accused *in camera,* a role similar to the one envisaged by the special advocate amendments to the Immigration Refugee Protection Act after the *Charkaoui* decision. In the end, the trial judge found that Khawaja's actions did not meet the high *mens rea* test of having knowledge of a specific terrorist objective but accepted the prosecution's argument that Khawaja obviously knew that his device would be used to cause injury, death, and destruction. He was convicted of five terrorism offences and two explosives offences to an aggregate of ten and a half years in prison. Justice Douglas Rutherford took the opportunity in his judgment to stress Canada's tradition of multicultural tolerance and peaceful coexistence. Michael Byers summed it up best in a comment to the *Ottawa Citizen:*

> Instead of having secret prisons and courts making use of secret evidence, here we have a trial in open court where the perpetrator is sentenced to a minimum sentence of 10 years hard time ... It's a balanced, reasonable, yet

weighty outcome, one that shows our legal system, with all its checks and balances, can deal responsibly and effectively with terrorism. (Quoted in Chianello 2009)

The case of Khawaja demonstrated that terrorist trials can work – with due process and criminal law safeguards protected, sentences balanced, and confidentiality of sensitive intelligence maintained. However, in this case, the constitutionality of the general definition of "terrorist activity" was challenged, and the trial judge held that the motive requirement infringed on Charter guarantees of freedom of conscience, religion, thought, belief, opinion, and association, a lingering concern since the passage of the Anti-Terrorism Act. This argument was later rejected by the Court of Appeal and the Supreme Court because of the lack of a "causal connection" between the motive clause and a potential chill in religious and ideological expression. Meanwhile, Khawaja's sentence was increased to life imprisonment, indicating the willingness of the courts to take a tough line on terrorist activity more than a decade after 9/11.[31]

The largest and longest set of terrorist-related prosecutions since 9/11 has been the cases of the so-called Toronto 18. As a result of coordinated raids and the seizure of two tonnes of ammonium nitrate on 2–3 June 2006, ten men and five youths were arrested; two other suspects were already incarcerated, and a final suspect was arrested the following month. The details of the plot – as they unfolded in the media and a series of preliminary hearings and trials that stretched from 2007 to 2010, were fantastic, connecting two plans, either of which would have been devastating if even partially successful: the first to storm the Parliament Buildings in Ottawa and behead the prime minister if troops were not pulled out of Afghanistan; the second to detonate a series of truck bombs in downtown Toronto, including an attack on the Toronto Stock Exchange, the Front Street offices of CSIS, and the Dennison Armoury in North York. The net was cast widely in terms of initial arrests: charges were eventually stayed or dropped against seven of those arrested, including three youths. Of the remaining eleven, four were convicted at trial, and seven admitted guilt. The offence common to most of the defendants was participation in a terrorist group; others included the intention to cause an explosion, the importation of firearms, and training for terrorist purposes. Sentences ranged from two and a half years for the youngest offender, Nishanthan Yogakrishnan, to life imprisonment for plot masterminds Fahim Ahmad and Zakaria Amara. Amara's effort to appeal his life sentence was dismissed on 17 December 2010; the Ontario Court of Appeal also increased the sentences of Said Khalid and Saad Gaya, who both admitted guilt. Most sensational was the trial of Fahim Ahmad, Steven Chand, and Asad Ansari, with Ahmad switching his plea to guilty mid-trial and the establishment of a sweeping publication ban. Equally fascinating was the tale told to CBC's *The Fifth Estate* and later in court by paid CSIS and RCMP informant Mubin Shaikh, a self-described observant Muslim who defied all media stereotypes with his hip swagger and patterns of speech, addictions to both cocaine and Tim Hortons coffee, and an assault conviction. A former army cadet with valuable weapons and survival training, he worked undercover for two years, participating in "training camps." Shaikh was deeply critical of both US foreign policy and Canada's decision to send troops to Afghanistan yet equally opposed to the use of violence for political ends. Entrepreneur and informer Shaher Elsohemy was paid more than $4 million for his testimony and is now in a witness protection program. Feeding the now familiar narrative of alienation and radicalization, the group defies easy categorization, ranging in age from fifteen to forty-three and in experience from high school dropouts with marginal jobs to a computer programmer with a six-figure salary (Shepherd 2011). Overall, the case has spawned fierce debate within Muslim Canadian communities about the necessity of community self-policing amid persistent naysayers who suggest that the case was a setup designed to denigrate Muslims and justify the police and CSIS.[32]

The cases of Khawaja, the "Crevice 7" in the United Kingdom, and the Toronto 18 have become part of a larger scholarly debate on the nature and type of *jihadi* terrorism. Marc Sageman uses the Canadian cases as examples of "homegrown" terrorism in which "Western wannabes" such as Khawaja – not necessarily sophisticated or connected to al-Qaeda save for inspiration and ideology – are a greater global and domestic security risk than what Bruce Hoffman contends is the case with "Al Qaeda Central" (see Hoffman 2006; Hoffman and Sageman 2008; Sageman 2008). The argument is relevant to the allocation of resources: if Sageman is correct, then counterterrorism ought to privilege domestic law enforcement, with transnational involvement limited to intelligence sharing and joint investigation as required: that is, focused on the "home" game. If Hoffman's view prevails, then it makes more sense to focus on military-security resources abroad: that is, on the "away" game. In reality, it is impossible to separate the two approaches, if only because the home game continues to have an explicit transnational impact, which in turn enhances the complexity and number of players involved in coordinating a government response in the away game. Moreover, those involved in domestic plots have been strongly influenced by events abroad, seeing themselves as part of a global *jihadi* movement, notwithstanding the existence of any actual link to transnational groups such as al-Qaeda.

Canada in Afghanistan: The "Away" Game

While the Canadian government was creating new terrorism offences and detaining those suspected of terrorist-related activities with security certificates, and generating definitions in policy and law for security in a post-9/11 world, important decisions were being made about Canada's engagements abroad, specifically with respect to deploying the Canadian Forces. Meanwhile, domestic law "travelled" to the away game in ways that were not foreseen by the Canadian Forces and could hardly have been contemplated before 9/11.

Whether Canadians realized it or not, engagement in Afghanistan was certain given the Taliban government's support for al-Qaeda and the NATO decision to invoke Article 5 of the Washington Treaty on 12 September 2001, for the first time in the alliance's history. In so doing, all NATO states, including Canada, agreed that the 9/11 attacks were armed attacks against a NATO member, binding their cooperation individually and collectively, up to and including the use of force. Although this was well understood by men and women in uniform, Canadians often framed the combat mission in Kandahar from 2005 to 2011 as an effort to bolster relations with the United States following Canada's last-minute decisions not to support the American-led invasion of Iraq in 2003 and not to participate in the Ballistic Missile Defence program.[33] However, Canadian Special Forces from Joint Task Force 2 had already participated under American command in late 2001; this operation was followed in January 2002 by a separate deployment of the 3rd Battalion Princess Patricia's Canadian Light Infantry Battle Group to the southern Afghan province of Kandahar under operational control of a US Army brigade, a mission that lasted six months. In August 2003, Canada returned to Afghanistan as part of NATO's International Security Assistance Force, which had deployed under UN auspices to assist the newly recognized government of Hamid Karzai following the Bonn Accords. Canada's contribution of 1,900 soldiers was based in Kabul until 2005. Only then did Canada relocate its commitment to increasingly dangerous Kandahar, taking on its largest and longest combat role since the Korean War. Thus, what came to be known in the popular imagination as "the mission in Afghanistan" or "Canada's combat role" constituted a number of discrete but interrelated operations, all of which – save for the early Joint Task Force 2 deployment – were under the auspices of the United Nations but more directly under NATO command. This is not merely an issue of military semantics, for public opinion polls continued to demonstrate citizen preference for "peacekeeping" versus "combat" roles or, more to the point, those involving the United Nations rather than NATO. Notwithstanding popular mythology, the identity of Canadians as primarily peacekeepers was a partial fiction that represented only a slice of the full range of Canadian soldierly activities.[34]

Setting aside debates over Canada's historical role in peacekeeping, the classic blue beret experience – of multinational forces interposed between parties that allowed their presence to permit political solutions to be developed – was not relevant to Canada's involvement in Afghanistan, nor had it been for some time.[35] Those on the ground had already learned these lessons given previous deployments in Somalia, Bosnia, Rwanda, and elsewhere. Unfortunately, in a pre-9/11 world, these contributions were not seen as transformative or indicative of the changing nature of conflict, even though they attracted public attention because of ethical disregard for the rights of those whom Canadians were supposed to protect (as in Somalia) or because of the bloody intrastate conflicts with genocidal belligerents in which Canada's actions, along with those of its allies, were impaired by both numbers and limited rules of engagement imposed by the United Nations (as in Rwanda and Yugoslavia). Internally, the Canadian Forces was consumed with its own "decade of darkness" and resulting budget cuts.

Indeed, Canada's public and even scholarly contributions of the 1990s, partially because of the actions of Minister of Foreign Affairs Lloyd Axworthy as a "norm entrepreneur," shifted to developing a human security paradigm. Politics, ethics, and foreign policy merged successfully with Ottawa's effort to ban anti-personnel landmines and Canadian support for the International Criminal Court and the implementation of the Rome Statute. Unfortunately, even before 9/11, a deep disconnect developed between public middle-power longing for the perceived simplicity and "neutrality" of peacekeeping and the contemporary reality of the post-Cold War conflict, to which the Canadian Forces had front-row seats.[36] Two distinct narratives resulted, such that, when the "detainee crisis" first became front-page news, both the military and the public were blindsided by the responses of each other.

Prior to the 2005 deployment to Kandahar, Canadian policy consisted largely of handing those detained, who were suspected of being either al-Qaeda or Taliban, directly into the custody of the United States, on the rationale that they were the detaining authority under international humanitarian law. Canada did obtain assurances of humane treatment, but a 2002 above-the-fold photo in the *Globe and Mail* showing members of Joint Task Force 2 handing detainees over to Americans disrupted the national portrait of soldiers as peacekeepers and occurred just when the Bush administration was criticized domestically and internationally for its controversial determination that the Geneva Conventions did not apply to captured al-Qaeda or Taliban. Indeed, in the words of White House Counsel Alberto R. Gonzales, the Geneva Conventions had become "quaint," evoking rules by which new adversaries did not play (Gonzales 2002; see also Falk 2007). Furthermore, the volume and tenor of criticism increased as awareness grew regarding the interrogation of prisoners at Guantánamo Bay and the dramatic exposure of abuse at Abu Ghraib.

Historically, provisions of international humanitarian law relevant to detention in war are the 1949 Geneva Conventions and the 1977 Additional Protocols (AP1, AP2): Canada is a signatory to all three, with stated reservations regarding the protocols. Specifically, Article 4 of Geneva Convention III defines combatants as those who meet the criteria of being commanded by a person responsible for subordinates; wear a fixed distinctive sign; carry their weapons openly; and conduct operations lawfully.[37] However, the law presumes that one is either a combatant or a civilian, and the International Committee of the Red Cross, the guardian of Geneva law, has consistently refused to allow that the War on Terror has generated a new category of combatant – the enemy combatant or unprivileged belligerent. Nonetheless, a de facto category has emerged in the past decade: those who do not qualify as combatants and therefore have no legal right to wage war but do so regardless (see Dworkin 2005, 53–73; Newton 2005, 74–110). The United States has responded to this challenge through an imperfect process of status determination, indefinite detention, and most recently trial by military commission. All three have been fraught, particularly because of the controversial use of "enhanced interrogation" techniques that Bush administration lawyers sought to justify as anything but torture, which in turn have cast a long shadow over the veracity and admissibility of testimony in subsequent proceedings. Nevertheless, it is facile to suggest that an easy remedy is for states deploying forces abroad to recognize combatants as legitimate POWs, because to do so would confer an undeserved legitimacy, as if they act as regular armed forces, which they do not. Moreover, prosecution for unlawful violence would then be prohibited, and the unpunished protection of violent offenders operating in a theatre of war would undermine the original intent of Geneva law.

Two additional conventions affect the question of detention: the 1966 International Convention on Civil and Political Rights and the 1984 Convention against Torture and Other Cruel, Inhuman, and Degrading Treatment or Punishment (CAT). Both are considered as having *jus cogens* status, reinforcing legal obligation regardless of whether or not states are signatories. The International Convention on Civil and Political Rights also prohibits torture (Article 7) and arbitrary detention while guaranteeing the right to a fair trial within a reasonable time (Article 9). All persons deprived of liberty must be treated with humanity and respect for the dignity of the person (Article 10). The CAT is clear that under no exception can torture be used in a state of war, threat of war, internal political instability, or any public emergency – and the War on Terror seems to career across all four of these categories. Finally, the CAT prohibits deportation to jurisdictions known to practise torture. International humanitarian law allows for the detention of POWs and civilians if they take part in hostilities and are then given free and fair trials.

In 2005, Canada and Afghanistan agreed to a bilateral arrangement for the transfer of detainees to Afghan custody, under which the humane treatment provisions of Geneva Convention 3 would apply, detailed records would be kept, and International Committee of the Red Cross access would be provided. The agreement was criticized for a number of shortcomings: vague wording, no definition of facilities to be used or to which arm of the Afghan state transfer would occur, no provision of continued access to transferred detainees (as a similar Dutch agreement did), and potential transfer to a third party by the Afghan government. Moreover, the agreement was effectively a memorandum of understanding between two ministries of defence, not a bilateral arrangement between two states. After a series of articles in the *Globe and Mail* by Graeme Smith in 2007 that discussed how detainees were abused and tortured by Afghan security forces, a new agreement was negotiated, allowing for Canadian monitoring and requiring Afghan reporting of subsequent changes in status or location of detainees (Smith 2007a, b, c, d). Implicit in both agreements was an acceptance of captured Taliban as unprivileged belligerents, yet in the field the Canadian Forces is required to review each detainee's circumstances to determine status and continued detention. Both agreements were premised on Afghan institutional competence and respect for human rights, a naive assumption at best. Difficulties plagued detainee arrangements, such as a lack of differentiation between locals involved in petty crime and dedicated fighters. The requirement for Afghans to prosecute, in a state rife with corruption, presented the unsettling possibility that in practice the policy would be simply one of "catch and release." In the end, neither the security goal of keeping dedicated fighters off the battlefield nor Canada's obligation under international humanitarian law and human rights law to ensure humane treatment was perfectly met. Given that most contemporary conflict is intrastate, asymmetric, and involves irregular fighters, the legal status of such actors and what should be done with those captured and not killed will continue to plague future operations, whether or not they are construed as part of a larger War on Terror.

Against this legal backdrop and the complicated example of the mission in Afghanistan, Amnesty International Canada and the BC Civil Liberties Association sought to extend the territorial application of the Charter to non-Canadian detainees in the custody of the Canadian Forces. Although ultimately unsuccessful, this challenge was winding its way through the courts at the same time as Canadian officials, notably Richard Colvin in the Department of Foreign Affairs and International Trade, were presenting a disturbing picture of the treatment of detainees at the hands of Afghan authorities. The case was not without legal precedent: in *R. v. Hape*, a money-laundering case about a Canadian operating overseas, two Supreme Court dissents found that the Charter should apply extraterritorially where Canadian officials are complicit in violating the rights of a Canadian citizen.[38] The nexus was repeated in *Khadr I*, but this time the full court applied the Charter extraterritorially because Canadian actions also violated international human rights obligations, opening the potential for international law to be "read through" the Charter. However, in Afghanistan, the detainees were non-citizens. Canadian sympathy existed for Arar, diminished for Khadr, and barely registered when Afghans were effectively accused of torturing other Afghans. Still, the extent to which, and the circumstances under which, the Charter "travels" abroad should not be considered settled law, and ethical and security dilemmas remain unsolved.

Conclusion

In the post-9/11 world, Canada's "home game" cannot avoid the "away game" and vice versa. At home, responses to terrorism and security will continue to blur the conventional distinction between the "domestic" and the "international," sometimes with troubling ethical consequences. Terrorism law was enacted quickly in Canada and elsewhere – an unprecedented example of the international community responding with domestic laws built to UN specifications. Terrorist activity can arise entirely domestically, as was the case of the Toronto 18, yet only be understood in a global ideological context as an attempt to be part of an international conflict, or such activity might be part of a larger plot in another state, as in the case of Momin Khawaja. Both cases illustrate the transnational nature of domestic prosecution and the potential impacts on relationships with Canada's allies, particularly the United Kingdom and the United States. Canadian citizenship did not afford the protection that it should have to Maher Arar while travelling abroad, of deep concern given our multicultural and global society. The risk of human rights abuses abroad has been high, and both the Supreme Court in *Khadr II* and the O'Connor report on Arar have strongly rebuked the government for complicity in torture. Notice has repeatedly been taken of the violation of both the Charter and Canada's international legal obligations, surely intended as a salvo from the courts to the executive that the judiciary intends to regard both as binding and requiring enforcement. The government must recognize that failures at both the political level and the agency/department level occurred; interagency and transnational cooperation is part of the answer, but in the meantime it will be left to the courts and commissions of inquiry to determine fault and remedy.

Overseas, the detainee debacle demonstrates the extent to which Charter values, if not actual Charter protections, do travel abroad. Canadian foreign policy, in particular decisions about interventions involving the Canadian Forces, must consider not only questions of security – both traditional and human – but also the potential application of ethical norms inherent in prescribed Charter protections and more nebulous Charter values. The Canadian Forces is increasingly expected to square an impossible circle in meeting Canada's domestic and international legal obligations while fighting determined adversaries who operate illegally. Failure to do so quickly becomes front-page news, subject to court challenge and parliamentary wrangling back home. Regardless of the nature of future international operations, those serving abroad should have a solid understanding of Charter values as well as ethics and humanitarian law.

The merging of the home and away games also illustrates a process of legal and political verticalization in which events at home upload their consequences into the international arena, while Canada's actions abroad are downloaded into the national body politic. The longer post-Cold War theme of globalization, with the continual erosion of boundaries between domestic politics and international relations, comes into play, but the decade since 9/11 has put this trend into hyperdrive. The consequences – gross violations of human rights, including torture, the protection afforded Canadian citizens at home and abroad, the extraterritorial application of the Charter as matters of both law and policy – have never been more serious. Questions of balancing ethics with security cannot be ignored in either game, given broad arguments about the applicability of the Charter.

NOTES

1 His 20 September 2001 address to Congress was blunt and succinct: "The enemies of freedom committed an act of war against us."

2 By 2005, the second Bush administration was already backing away from this language, preferring to construe its efforts as the "global struggle against violent extremism" (see, in particular, Schmitt and Shankar 2005), but by this point the label – and the acronym GWOT – had stuck.

3 My understanding of the intersection of criminal and military approaches to counterterrorism owes much to Canadian Forces College students whom I had the privilege to supervise, including Ian Davis and J.P.S. McKenzie of the Canadian Forces and Debra Robinson of the Royal Canadian Mounted Police. I am indebted to J.P.S. McKenzie for his assessment of why existing Geneva law is ill suited to contemporary conflict. All three have completed excellent master's degree papers, available at http://www.cfc.forces.gc.ca/en/cfcpapers. Additional appreciation goes to Alex Neve and John Norris for amiably answering many questions, to James Cox, Shawn Osborne, Dan Livermore, Jules Bloch, Diane Bull, and two anonymous reviewers for commenting on earlier drafts, to Kent Roach for providing advice and sharing yet-to-be-published material, and to Rosalind Warner, the editor of this volume, for her professional guidance and support.

4 *Reference re Secession of Quebec,* [1998] 2 S.C.R. 217.

5 *R. v. Oakes,* [1986] 1 S.C.R. 103. *Oakes* also set out three criteria: a rational connection between the legislation and the legislative objective; a minimal impairment of the impugned right; and a proportionality test balancing the deleterious effects and benefits conferred by the Charter violation.

6 On the public debate on Bill C-36, see Daniels, Macklem, and Roach (2001); Roach (2003, 2011). This was an omnibus bill that not only created new offences but also amended a number of other existing laws, such as the Security of Information Act (the old Official Secrets Act), the Proceeds of Crime (Money Laundering) and Terrorist Financing Act, the Canada Evidence Act, and the National Defence Act.

7 The law used the United Kingdom's Terrorism Act, 2000 as a model; see Roach (2011, 238–308, 377).

8 *R. v. Stinchcombe,* [1991] 3 S.C.R. 326. Disclosure and secrecy issues can be challenged in the Federal Court, resulting in a complicated "two court" process in actual terrorist prosecutions.

9 *R. v. N.Y.,* [2008] CanLII 15908 (Ont. S.C.).

10 *Suresh v. Canada,* [2002] 1 S.C.R. 3 at paragraph 98. The court famously reuses the dissenting declaration of Justice Robert Jackson – "the Constitution is not a suicide pact" – from the 1949 *Terminiello* case in the United States, a free-speech case involving incitement.

11 *Application under s. 83.28 of the Criminal Code (Re)*, [2004] S.C.J. No. 40 [2004], 2
    S.C.R. 248 at 260–61.
12 Indeed, the title of Justice John C. Major's royal commission report is *Air India Flight
    182: A Canadian Tragedy* (2010). See also Rae (2006).
13 Inderjit Singh Reyat was convicted for ten years in 1991 for manslaughter in relation
    to the Narita airport bombing and later pled guilty to charges relating to the Flight
    182 bombing, receiving an additional five years; Ripudaman Singh Malik and Ajaib
    Singh Bagri were acquitted in 2005; see *R. v. Malik and Bagri*, [2005] B.C.S.C. 350.
    The alleged mastermind of the plot, Canadian citizen Talwinder Singh Parmar, was
    prosecuted in Canada but not in relation to the Air India bombings; despite the
    Canadian refusal to extradite him because of concerns for his safety, he was eventu-
    ally tortured and killed in India; see Roach (2011, 371–72).
14 The story first appeared in print in the *Boston Globe* on 13 September 2001, was later
    picked up by the *Washington Post*, the *New York Post*, and the *Christian Science
    Monitor*, and later yet was continually repeated, despite the decisive correction pro-
    vided by the 9/11 Commission and efforts by a number of ambassadors and foreign
    affairs officials. In a special episode of the television series *The West Wing* aired after
    9/11, terrorists cross the border from Ontario to Vermont (notwithstanding the geo-
    graphic inaccuracy). More seriously, the claim was repeated as late as 2009 by Sec-
    retary of Homeland Security Janet Napolitano on her first visit and reiterated soon
    after by Senator John McCain, prompting Canadian Ambassador Michael Wilson to
    issue a statement yet again reminding Americans that, as fully demonstrated by the
    9/11 Commission report, no 9/11 terrorists had come from Canada.
15 See *R. v. Martineau*, [1990] 2 S.C.R. 633; *R. v. Logan*, [1990] 2 S.C.R. 731; *R. v. Finta*,
    [1994] 1 S.C.R. 701.
16 *R. v. Malik*, [2005] B.C.J. No. 521 (S.C.) (QL).
17 *Charkaoui v. Canada (Citizenship and Immigration)*, [2007] 1 S.C.R. 350, 2007 SCC 9.
18 Amendments to IRPA now provide for "special advocates" – lawyers specially
    trained and appointed to protect the interests of subjects of security certificate hear-
    ings *in camera* – when information protected for reasons of national security is pre-
    sented and neither the subject nor his or her counsel can attend.
19 In particular, see *Almrei v. Canada*, [2009] F.C. 1263.
20 *Charkaoui v. Canada (Citizenship and Immigration)*, 2008 SCC 38, [2008] 2 S.C.R. 326.
21 *Harkat v. Canada*, [2010] F.C. 1241; *Harkat v.Canada*, [2012] F.C.A. 122.
22 *Canada (Citizenship and Immigration) v. Harkat* 2014 SCC 37.
23 However, Arar remains on the American no-fly list, and his civil action in the United
    States failed because of the invocation of the state secrets doctrine (Roach 2011, 362).
24 For a full discussion, see Shepherd (2008).
25 *Canada (Prime Minister) v. Khadr*, 2008 SCC 28, [2008] 2 S.C.R. 125 (*Khadr I*).
26 *Canada (Prime Minister) v. Khadr*, 2010 SCC 3, [2010] 1 S.C.R. 44 (*Khadr II*).
27 Some cases did not invoke national security yet did evoke a bureaucratic level of
    latent Islamophobia. During the hearings of the Reasonable Accommodation Com-
    mission headed by Gérard Bouchard and Charles Taylor, a number of cases of
    anti-hijab hysteria occurred in Quebec. Among others, eleven-year-old Azzy Man-
    sour was ejected from her soccer team for wearing a hijab, and Sondos Abdelatif was

fired from Montreal's Bordeaux Detention Centre for refusing to remove her head-scarf. Considerable documentation of these and other cases has been undertaken by the National Council of Canadian Muslims (NCMM), whose resources and publications can be accessed at http://www.nccm.ca. In 2004, the government of Canada created a Cross-Cultural Roundtable on National Security Issues to address potential antagonism between security law/policy and multiculturalism, but it has been largely silent.

28 Government lawyers argued that, because Abdelrazik was on the United Nation's 1,267 list, he could not be repatriated. See *Abdelrazik v. Canada*, [2009] F.C. 580.

29 The "Crevice 7" were convicted and sentenced to life imprisonment; they were also linked to those involved in the 7/7 bombings in London, raising serious questions about the allocation of intelligence resources in favour of Operation Crevice rather than the eventual subway bombers. Their UK trial included RCMP evidence: see *Khyam v. The Queen*, [2008] EWCA 1612 (C.A.).

30 *R. v. Khawaja*, [2008] O.J. No. 04-G30282 (S.C.J.) [Ruling re: Motion for Directed Verdicts of Acquittal] at 24.

31 *R. v. Khawaja*, [2010] O.N.C.A. 862; *R. v. Khawaja*, [2012] SCC 69, especially paragraphs 81 and 82.

32 See, for example, Bartlett, Birdwell, and King (2010), whose report, *The Edge of Violence: A Radical Approach to Extremism*, includes interviews and focus groups with young Muslims in Toronto and Montreal. On self-policing, see the many online and in-print media interviews with Tarek Fatah, author and founder of the Muslim Canadian Congress.

33 See, in particular, Stein and Lang (2007). For the perspective of one of the key players, see Hillier (2009).

34 Lewis Mackenzie has repeatedly argued that, even in the 1970s and 1980s, when Canada had about 1,500 soldiers deployed on various UN missions, there were 10,000 others deployed on the Central Front with NATO, armed with fighter jets and nuclear weapons. At the same time, Canada's navy was at sea as part of the North Atlantic Fleet. Mackenzie argues, along with historians J.L. Granatstein and Sean M. Maloney, that Canada's role in the Cold War was the number one foreign policy priority by far (see, e.g., Mackenzie 2006). The extent of Canada's engagement in peacekeeping missions is also often overestimated. The height of Canada's peacekeeping came during a time when there were fewer UN missions. The United Nations has run about fifty-four peacekeeping operations in its history – fourteen were before 1989 and forty since then, so 80 percent of UN peacekeeping operations occurred in 20 percent of that period (see, e.g., Valpy 2006). Thus, the explosion in the number of UN peacekeeping missions actually coincided with Canada's withdrawal as a major contributor to UN peacekeeping. Accordingly, between 1948 and 2003, there were only seven UN or non-UN missions to which Canada sent more than 1,000 troops (see, e.g., Ram 2004). However, the battle over numbers and percentages ignores the fact that peacekeeping was never a static concept, was very mission specific, and had changed dramatically in the post-Cold War world with the experiences in the Balkans – all before 9/11.

35 Zones of multiparty conflict and genocide in the former Yugoslavia or Rwanda in the 1990s were impossible. As hindsight shows, the result could only be ineffective at best or a humanitarian catastrophe at worst.

36 The debate within the military academy has been intense – within the pages of the *Canadian Military Journal,* for instance, over a two-year period from 2005 to 2007, the arguments for and against peacekeeping as a myth, a definitive aspect of Canadian identity, and its relevance in the post-9/11 security environment were hotly contested. In particular, see Anker (2005, 23–25); Dorn (2005–06, 105–06); Maloney (2007, 100–02); Wagner (2006–07, 45–54). For a well-documented polemic about the "harmful" effects of Canadian devotion to peacekeeping, see Granatstein (2007, especially 17–49). Although the debate has surfaced from time to time since 9/11 among political elites, I would argue that most Canadians have *not* engaged in it, nor do they understand the nature of the terminology involved. Polling on Afghanistan has been mixed – much depends on the nature of the question asked and the assumptions brought to bear on the answers given. See Ipsos Reid (2009); The Simons Foundation (2009).

37 Article 44 of AP1 confirms the combatant requirement to distinguish from a civilian population but allows for the retention of combatant privilege if arms are carried openly; perfidy in feigning civilian status to avoid detection or targeting is forbidden.

38 *R. v. Hape,* [2007] 2 S.C.R. 292.

References

Anker, Lane. 2005. "Peacekeeping and Public Opinion." *Canadian Military Journal* (Summer): 23–25.

Bartlett, Jamie, Jonathan Birdwell, and Michael King. 2010. *The Edge of Violence: A Radical Approach to Extremism.* London: Demos.

Bush, George W. 2001. "Address to a Joint Session of Congress and the American People." 20 September.

Canada. *Commission of Inquiry into the Activities of Canadian Officials in Relation to Maher Arar.* 2006. Ottawa: PWGSC.

Chianello, Joanne. 2009. "Canadian Legal System Works: Trial Shows More Aggressive Anti-Terror Laws Not Needed." *Ottawa Citizen,* 13 March.

Daniels, R., P. Macklem, and K. Roach, eds. 2001. *The Security of Freedom: Essays on Canada's Anti-Terrorism Bill.* Toronto: University of Toronto Press.

Dershowitz, Alan M. 2006. *Preemption: A Knife That Cuts Both Ways.* New York: W.W. Norton.

Dorn, Walter. 2005–06. "Peacekeeping Then, Now, and Always." *Canadian Military Journal* (Winter): 105–06.

Dworkin, Anthony. 2005. "Military Necessity and Due Process: The Place of Human Rights in the War on Terror." In *New Wars, New Laws? Applying the Laws of War in 21st Century Conflicts,* edited by David Wippman and Matthew Evangelista, 53–73. Ardsley, NY: Transnational Publishers.

Falk, Barbara J. 2007. "The Global War on Terror and the Detention Debate: The Applicability of Geneva Convention III." *Journal of International Law and International Relations* 3 (1): 31–60.

Gonzales, Alberto R. 2002. "Memorandum for the President." 25 January. In *The Torture Papers: The Road to Abu Ghraib*, edited by Karen J. Greenberg and Joshua L. Dratel, 118–21. Cambridge: Cambridge University Press.

Granatstein, J.L. 2007. *Whose War Is It? How Canada Can Survive the Post-9/11 World.* Toronto: HarperCollins.

Hillier, Rick. 2009. *A Soldier First: Bullets, Bureaucrats, and the Politics of War.* Toronto: HarperCollins.

Hoffman, Bruce. 2006. *Inside Terrorism.* New York: Columbia University Press.

Hoffman, Bruce, and Marc Sageman. 2008. "Does Osama Still Call the Shots?" *Foreign Affairs* (July–August): 163–68.

ICRC (International Committee of the Red Cross). 2004. "International Humanitarian Law and the Challenges of Contemporary Armed Conflicts." March. http://www.icrc.org/eng/assets/files/red-cross-crescent-movement/31st-international-conference/31-int-conference-ihl-challenges-report-11-5-1-2-en.pdf.

Internal Inquiry into the Actions of Canadian Officials in Relation to Abdullah Almalki, Ahmad Abou-Elmaati, and Muayyed Nureddin. 2008. Ottawa: PWGSC.

Ipsos Reid. 2009. *Views of the Canadian Forces.* Report submitted to the Department of National Defence, March.

Koring, Paul. 2012. "Omar Khadr's Return an "Unavoidable Evil." *Globe and Mail,* 1 October.

Mackenzie, Lewis. 2006. "Respect Needs More Than a Flag." *Globe and Mail,* 25 April.

Major, John C. 2010. *Air India Flight 182: A Canadian Tragedy.* Ottawa: PWGSC.

Maloney, Sean. 2007. "Why Keep the Myth Alive?" *Canadian Military Journal* (Spring): 100–02.

Mazigh, Monia. 2008. *Hope and Despair.* Toronto: McClelland and Stewart.

Newton, Michael. 2005. "Unlawful Belligerency after September 11: History Revisited and Law Revised." In *New Wars, New Laws? Applying the Laws of War in 21st Century Conflicts,* edited by David Wippman and Matthew Evangelista, 74–110. Ardsley, NY: Transnational Publishers.

Ram, Sunil. 2004. "Canada the Peacekeeper: A Myth that Should Die." *Globe and Mail,* 25 August.

Rae, Bob. 2006. *Lessons to Be Learned.* Ottawa: Public Safety.

Roach, Kent. 2003. *September 11: Consequences for Canada.* Montreal/Kingston: McGill-Queen's University Press.

Roach, Kent. 2005. "Canada's Response to Terrorism." In *Global Anti-Terrorism Law and Policy,* edited by Victor V. Ramraj, Michael Hor, and Kent Roach, 511–33. Cambridge: Cambridge University Press. http://dx.doi.org/10.1017/CBO9780511493874.023.

Roach, Kent. 2011. *The 9/11 Effect: Comparative Counter-Terrorism.* Cambridge: Cambridge University Press. http://dx.doi.org/10.1017/CBO9781139003537.

Sageman, Marc. 2008. *Leaderless Jihad: Terror Networks in the 21st Century.* Philadelphia: University of Pennsylvania Press.

Schmitt, Eric, and Thom Shanker. 2005. "U.S. Officials Retool Slogan for Terror War." *New York Times,* 26 July.

Shepherd, Michelle. 2008. *Guantanamo's Child: The Untold Story of Omar Khadr.* Toronto: John Wiley.

Shepherd, Michelle. 2011. *Decade of Fear: Reporting from Terrorism's Grey Zone.* Vancouver: Douglas and McIntyre.

The Simons Foundation. 2009. *Canada's World Poll.* January.

Smith, Graeme. 2007a. "From Canadian Custody into Cruel Hands." *Globe and Mail,* 23 April.

Smith, Graeme. 2007b. "Ottawa Stirs Storm of Confusion." *Globe and Mail,* 27 April.

Smith, Graeme. 2007c. "Top Solider Changes Tact, Expresses Doubt on Deal." *Globe and Mail,* 3 May.

Smith, Graeme. 2007d. "Watchdog: 'We Can't Monitor These People'" *Globe and Mail,* 24 April.

Stein, Janice Gross, and Eugene Lang. 2007. *The Unexpected War: Canada in Kandahar.* Toronto: Viking.

Valpy, Michael. 2006. "The Ballad of the Blue Beret." *Globe and Mail,* 11 November.

Wagner, Eric. 2006–07. "The Peaceable Kingdom? The National Myth of Canadian Peacekeeping and the Cold War." *Canadian Military Journal* (Winter): 45–54.

5

The Ethics of Mega-Event Security
When the World Comes to Visit

VERONICA KITCHEN

In 2010, Canada welcomed the world to two mega-events that garnered global attention: first the Vancouver Olympic Games in February and March and then the G8 and G20 Summits in Huntsville and Toronto in June. The Vancouver Olympics required the largest domestic security operation to date in Canada; the security operation at the G8/G20 was slightly larger in magnitude but sustained over a shorter period of time (BBC News 2010). Mega-events are important foreign policy events; they are designed to mirror an image of the host city (and country) and to attract investment and tourism for years after event visitors have left (Black 2007). States are therefore invested in making sure that a mega-event is successful, and part of the success is hosting an event that showcases the safety of the city from security threats (Coaffee and Rogers 2008). However, security operations at mega-events present states with a number of security dilemmas that challenge the ability of the state to maintain an ethical security policy.

The Vancouver Olympics were deemed by most reports to have been successful because there were no significant security incidents during the games. The G20, on the other hand, has been better remembered for the confrontations between police and protesters than for the summit communiqué. News reports, investigations, and inquiries confirm that police and other security officials violated the civil liberties of protesters, perhaps escalated violent behaviour in crowds, misled the public, and generally behaved in ways that challenge our views of appropriate behaviour for security officials. The contrast between the Olympics, deemed a successful security operation, and the controversial G20 nonetheless highlights some features that mega-events have in common that make balancing ethics and security particularly difficult. First, because mega-events are temporary, they are always exceptional in the sense that their security operations tend to operate under a different set of laws, norms, and rules than those that govern day-to-day public safety and security in democracies. There is a latent danger that these exceptional security measures, which might be morally undesirable for everyday life, will be integrated into normal politics. Second, mega-events are globally broadcast opportunities for cities to project particular views of themselves to the world. In the quest to look as safe as possible, the rights of citizens are sometimes secondary to the perceived security needs of dignitaries. Third, mega-events, and the accompanying protests, are a transnational phenomenon. Each mega-event occurs in the context of other mega-events, and security techniques are borrowed from one to the other. The pathological tendencies of security bureaucracies and the security dilemma can be magnified as they are duplicated across borders as well as time. The study of security at mega-events, therefore, can help us to understand how security and ethics intersect under some of the conditions of transnationalism and deterritorialization that characterize post-9/11 globalization.

Mega-Events as the Exception: "This Ain't Canada Right Now"

Mega-events such as the Olympics or the G20 happen regularly, but for any given country they are usually an extraordinary event.[1] They bring together internationally protected persons, members of delegations, journalists, protesters, and sometimes tourists into a constrained space for a constrained time. This can make mega-event spaces difficult to protect. Infrastructure might be temporary, and relationships might be formed between groups who do not normally work together, making command and control difficult (Decker et al. 2005, 66). Security officials must prepare for crimes and threats related to the mega-event (officials declared the biggest threat to security at both the Vancouver Olympics and the G20 to be criminal protest); low-probability, high-impact events such as terrorist attacks; and run-of-the-mill crimes (e.g., burglary and car theft) that go on in a city regardless of whether a special event is going on or not. For any given incident, security officials must make a quick decision about the danger that any particular person, package, or behaviour poses (Johnson 2008, 9). Mega-events are therefore almost always exceptional and operate, to some degree, outside normal politics.

The security operations at both the 2010 Olympics and the G20 were administered by Integrated Security Units explicitly created to secure each mega-event. Each unit was led by the RCMP in partnership with local police departments, the Canadian Forces, and other federal and provincial partners. At both events, the RCMP and police officers seconded from other units were responsible for securing access to, as well as the interiors of, official event sites (Olympic venues and the Toronto Convention Centre), and local police – the Vancouver Police Department and the Toronto Police Service – were responsible for security in the "urban domain": that is, in the streets of Vancouver and Toronto, where they were most likely to come in contact with protesters. Within the RCMP, responsibility for security planning belongs to Protective Policing Services, but the role of this unit is not well defined, and according to observers it is insufficiently resourced to act as an effective, permanent, centralized, planning, and management unit for the security of mega-events in Canada (Plecas et al. 2010, 47). This results in bureaucratic inefficiency, confusion, and potentially even security measures not justified by the level of threat (ibid., 13). The lack of a planning unit that can help with common tasks such as logistics, finances, intelligence, human resources, and other functions only adds to the ad hoc nature of the event. It means that more people are working outside their areas of expertise, and this increases the risk that unethical activities will occur.

In addition to the ad hoc nature of mega-event planning, mega-event security is governed by an ad hoc set of laws. There is no explicit law in Canada that covers mega-event security and regulates police authority. The question of police authority at mega-events was raised by two previous international mega-events hosted in Canada, both of which resulted in clashes between police and protesters: the 1997 Asia-Pacific Economic Forum in Vancouver and the 2001 Summit of the Americas in Quebec City (Radwanski 2010a). To fill the gap in legislation, the Canadian government amended the Foreign Missions and International Organizations Act to note that, at a multistate conference, the RCMP "may take appropriate measures, including controlling, limiting, or prohibiting access to any area to the extent ... and in a matter that is reasonable in the circumstance" (cited in ibid.). Without definitions of "appropriate" and "reasonable," this directive could be used to justify almost any police action. Other possible sources of law for governing police action at mega-events include the Federal Emergencies Act (not designed for such events) and the Criminal Code of Canada, the riot provisions of which also do not seem to apply (Pue and Diab 2010, 101). Wesley Pue and Robert Diab argue that the lack of legislation in Canada governing public order policing is a disservice both to police officers, who are forced to make up security guidelines as they go along, and to citizens, whose "rights are affected by police actions that cannot be measured against any publicly disclosed standard" (ibid., 89). Having a centralized planning unit helps to normalize a security event, and enacting a law, which can be challenged before the courts, at least leads to the ethical debates about the exceptional laws that we wish to endorse at mega-events. Establishing a planning unit was among the recommendations set forth in a review of Olympic security operations, and a similar recommendation was made in the Toronto Police Service's After-Action Review (Plecas et al. 2010, 47; Toronto Police Service 2011, 61).[2]

At the G20, police not only operated without a clear legal framework but also misled citizens about the special laws passed specifically for the summit. Toronto effectively became a deterritorialized space, outside Canadian law. This deterritorialization was best captured by the response given by a police officer to an individual who objected to a search of his bag. When the individual protested that this was Canada, and no one had the right to search his bag without consent, the officer replied, "this ain't Canada right now." Later in the exchange, when asked why he refused to consent to a search, the individual replied, "I just don't like to have my civil rights violated." To this the officer returned, "there is [sic] no civil rights here in this area" (cited in Baute 2011; toxicwaste26 2010). This was a clear instance of security protocol taking precedence over other rights. Toronto during the G20 was not part of Canada and therefore not subject to normal laws about search and seizure on the streets. Toronto had been deterritorialized into "G20-land," as observers in the video put it, a place where the security of visiting G20 delegates was more important than the civil rights of citizens. Although we might conclude that this trade-off is morally acceptable for the period of the mega-event, it is worthy of ethical reflection. The time for such reflection is not during the mega-event.

Didier Bigo (2006, 389) argues that one of the outcomes of modern security thinking is a prevailing view that security can only be ensured through the obsolescence not only of national borders for security but also of the divisions among war, defence, policing and public order, and international collaboration. The result, he says, is that security has been privileged over national sovereignty, particularly since the end of the Cold War. The debacle over the $5.5 million, six-kilometre-long security fence that stretched around the Convention Centre where the G20 was held nicely illustrates how this dynamic works both by emphasizing the exceptional nature of a mega-event and by privileging the security of certain groups over others. In the days prior to the G20, two activists were arrested under the Public Works Protection Act, which had not previously been mentioned as being among the laws providing for security at the G20. To justify the arrests, police cited a regulation, recently approved by the provincial cabinet (though not yet published in the *Ontario Gazette*), that gave them the authority to arrest anyone within five metres of the security fence who refused to show identification and consent to a search. Over the course of the G20, the Integrated Security Unit, Toronto's chief of police, and the Office of the Premier all mentioned the regulation, despite the facts that it did not exist and that the five-metre rule (which actually referred to a space inside, not outside, the fence) had been clarified to police before the G20 began (Radwanski 2010b). Although only two arrests were made, security officials seem to have used this regulation as a way of misleading people to behave in particular ways and comply with police preferences. A post-summit report into the implementation of the Public Works Protection Act concluded that the five-metre regulation was probably unconstitutional and legally invalid because the act was designed to protect infrastructure, not provide event security. Moreover, it was morally problematic because it gave police powers that were "unfamiliar in a free and democratic society," and its non-public nature meant that it was a "trap" for people who took reasonable steps to find out about police powers during the event (Marin 2010, 5).

The exceptional nature of mega-events can also distort the normal way of things by making citizens into outsiders. At the Olympics, visitors, spectators, and revellers were an integral part of the Olympic experience. For the most part, police embraced community policing tactics; they were highly visible but mingled with crowds and chatted with visitors.[3] Unlike at the G20, people had to enter the venues, the most protected zones, so they had to endure a (mostly cursory) bag check on the way in. However, there were instances in which the security of venues and athletes was clearly privileged over that of protesters. Martin French (2010) describes how known anti-Olympic activists were kept in a constant state of unease by police officers and intelligence officials who watched them and made it clear that they were watching them. At the G20, in contrast, anyone outside the security fence was considered a potential intruder. This was underscored by the spatial divide. For those inside the security fence, security was present but invisible (Rider 2010). Outside the fence, security was highly visible and all encompassing. The security of visiting dignitaries was clearly privileged over the freedom and security of residents, who had to carry special passes (Vu

2010), citizens, who were subjected to dubiously legal identity checks and even arrests (Yang 2010b), and protesters (and journalists and citizens), who were often detained under terrible conditions (Reinhart and Freeze 2010; Talbot 2010). These tactics produced security for those inside (mostly visitors) but generated insecurity for those outside (mostly citizens).

Mega-Events as Spectacular Events: Reassuring and Disturbing to Behold

Mega-events such as the Olympics and G20 are as much about selling a concept of the host city to the world as they are about the medals awarded or communiqués agreed (Black 2007). Demonstrating excellence at ensuring security is part of attracting mobile global capital and maintaining an impeccable global reputation as a safe city capable of responding to, and bouncing back from, threats to security (Coaffee and Rogers 2008). With protest a fact of life at mega-events, particularly international summit meetings, Martin (2011, 31) argues that part of this task of "showcasing security" is demonstrating an ability to deal with protesters.

The need to demonstrate the security of the city contributes to what Boyle and Haggerty (2009) call "spectacularization." Because it is impossible to predict low-probability threats such as terrorism, mega-events lead security officials to prepare for the worst possible threat rather than the most probable threat (ibid., 260). The need to prepare for all potential eventualities leads to ever-larger security operations. The spectacularization of security leads to a paradox: spectacular security must be at once visible, in order to demonstrate to people that security is being taken seriously, and invisible, so as not to intrude on the experiences of visitors or delegates (ibid., 265). This paradox manifests itself differently at different mega-events. At the Vancouver Olympics, the Integrated Security Unit launched high-profile exercises to practise for extremely low-probability events such as the discovery of a weapon of mass destruction ("Canada Stages WMD Drill Ahead of 2010 Olympics" 2009), but the unit head, Bud Mercer, also stressed that "I don't think Canada wants people leaving Canada after the Games remembering security, I think they want to leave remembering Canada beat the U.S. at hockey" (cited in Dembicki and Mackin 2009).

At the G20, the Integrated Security Unit held two information sessions for members of the public and the media. The first, in Toronto, epitomized the notion of spectacular security, featuring demonstrations of riot squad tactics, long-range acoustic devices (or sound cannons), and the K-9 unit. A journalist called it "reassuring and disturbing to behold" (Yang 2010a). The second, in Huntsville, "had a different feel" and was characterized by police chatting with children and joking by presenters (Nguyen 2010). In the days leading up to the summit, police also demonstrated or showcased other "less lethal" weapons such as water cannons (Wallace 2010a) and the ARWEN 37, a large, multishot, anti-riot weapon that shoots tear gas and plastic bullets that was originally designed for, but apparently never extensively deployed by, the British military because "it looked too menacing" (Seglins 2010). Furthermore, police were trained to deal with violence but not taught how to manage non-violent protest (McNeilly 2012). However, the responsibility for the escalation of a discourse of violence cannot lie exclusively with the police. At both the Olympics and the G20, as police accused protesters of violent intentions, protest leaders responded in kind by refusing to say that they would not use violence, usually arguing that "people will resist in ways that make sense to them" (quoted in Wallace 2010b; see also Wong 2010). When neither side can be confident of the other's intentions, escalation and therefore spectacularization are nearly inevitable.

There are many ethical dangers in spectacularization. The first danger stems both from the problem of spectacularization and from the problem of exceptionalism described above. According to sociologist David Murakami-Wood, security officials have a tendency to use mega-events as testing grounds for new security and surveillance tools (cited in CTV News 2010). In some cases, this includes the civilianization of military weapons (Murakami-Wood 2009). In many cases, police forces keep these tools after the mega-event, gradually incorporating them into normal policing practice. This "function creep" (CTV News 2010) can be ethically problematic because it equips police with classes of weapons and tools that they would not otherwise have and that citizens might think are beyond the requirements of day-to-day policing.[4] Indeed, this is what happened in Toronto after the G20, when the Toronto Police Service quietly, without public debate, decided to keep some of the equipment that it had acquired for the summit, notably the controversial long-range acoustic devices (Morrow 2011). At the Olympics, in contrast, almost all of the equipment was rented and returned, save for a set of mobile security cameras (Wallinger 2009).

The second danger is that spectacularity contributes to the creation of a mega-event security dilemma. Each host is compelled to present a security operation that matches the previous one in scale and technology. No one wants to host a mega-event during which a breach of security can be blamed on not having enough in the first place. The mega-event security dilemma works in two ways. First, just as in the interstate security dilemma, protesters and police are unsure of how each will behave. Decentralized tactics such as the "black bloc," in which protesters in black disguises commit violence and then remove their masks, blending back into the crowd, can be seen as a response to police attempts to limit or shape protests. Government attempts to help police space (e.g., by delineating protest zones, hosting summits in out-of-the-way places, or building fences) are responses to those decentralized tactics (Fernandez 2008, 92). Police might respond to protester desires to maintain anonymity by increasing surveillance, both before and during an event (ibid., 119). As we saw at the G20, protesters can turn this desire for anonymity back onto police by filming them and thus holding them publicly accountable for their actions. In Toronto, the case with the highest profile was that of Adam Nobody, assaulted by a group of officers who were not wearing appropriate identification. Video from citizens forced the Special Investigations Unit to reopen the case, after the unit initially said that it could not identify the officers involved (Friesen 2010; Woods 2011). The Toronto Police Service (2011, 58, 61) also acknowledged that its officers might have contributed to the escalation of protester behaviour by using riot police when they were not warranted and otherwise attempting to intimidate peaceful crowds.

Second, the securitization of more and more issues, including protest, does not necessarily generate more security. Rather, it tends to create *insecurity* (C.A.S.E. Collective 2006, 461). This process, too, can escalate tense situations. Securitization generates the need for more reassurance, which generates the need for stronger security measures, which in turn can contribute to further securitization. Although securitization can therefore be a tool for enhancing the image of the government, it must be careful that it does not cross the line of appearing incompetent (Huysmans 2006, 60). At the G20, the public perception was that police were slow to respond (Yang and McLean 2010), and there were even allegations that police had left police cars empty as "bait" (Cowen and Smith 2010, 31), though these allegations were denied by the Toronto Police Service (2011, 18). At both the Olympics and the G20, there was little distinction, in police discourse, between damage to property and violence against people, and all protesters began to be framed as violent (Dubinsky 2010; Nguyen 2010; Yang and McLean 2010). These tactics serve to frame police action in a particular way, psychologically priming the public to fear protest and turn to police for protection (Fernandez 2008, 159).

All of this contributes to the third ethical risk of spectacularization, the creation of a culture of fear, particularly when security officials begin to rely on the precautionary principle, taking drastic security measures against improbable but devastating threats (Goldsmith 2008, 145). Securitization, particularly the exceptional securitization at a mega-event, can create a culture of fear by drawing or reinforcing boundaries between social groups as a way of reinforcing political community (Huysmans 2006, 52). At the G20, for instance, there were reports that police targeted Quebecers, in particular, as potentially violent activists (CBC News 2010; Paperny 2010).

Like exceptionalism, spectacularization raises important questions about who is being secured at a mega-event. The decision to privilege the security of visiting dignitaries over that of ordinary citizens might be morally defensible but must be balanced with the rights of citizens. Instead of hosting the G20 in downtown Toronto, government could have followed the lead of several recent G8 summits and hosted the event at a more isolated location, where fewer citizens would have had their lives disrupted. However, this move in turn would have raised ethical questions about the right of protesters to be visible to visiting dignitaries, a recommendation that emerged (in the Canadian context) from the report on the protests at the Asia-Pacific Economic Cooperation conference at the University of British Columbia in 2007 (Canadian Civil Liberties Association 2010, 10). Spectacularization itself can be difficult to avert; even objects such as the security fence portray a particular message (Aradau 2010). Security officials could attempt to frame protests differently, but, because of the security dilemma described above, this too is hard to achieve.

Mega-Events as Transnational, Bureaucratic Events

Mega-events, by their nature, are temporary and often governed by temporary bureaucracies and imprecise regulations. However, there are particular features of even these temporary security bureaucracies that combine with the particular features of mega-events (deterritorialization and spectacularization) to create situations that are particularly problematic ethically. Critics of securitization theory, which argues that turning a security issue into an existential threat is the outcome of a discursive process, remind us that security threats can also be encoded in things, technologies, and routines (Aradau 2010; McDonald 2008). Moreover, just because something is not framed in political discourse as an existential threat does not mean that it is not a security issue with profound implications for society. Scholars of international political sociology in particular portray security as a technique of government rather than a discursive process. Security professionals are trained in particular ways and have particular interests.

The fact that mega-events are global events means that the referent group for rules and norms is not just the security bureaucracy of the host city or country but also the larger transnational community of security bureaucrats who have planned, managed, and policed mega-events. This community is explicitly transnational. Security officials tasked with planning a mega-event such as a summit or sporting event frequently send advance teams to other events to learn about tactics, and an elite cadre of planners often move from event to event, particularly at the Olympics (Boyle 2011). The media also help to transmit images and inculcate a sense of what is normal or expected for security at mega-events and counter-terrorism more generally (Goldsmith 2008, 144). Perhaps unsurprisingly, the security operations at the Olympics and the G20 received comparatively little foreign media coverage.[5] However, we do know that event teams from London and Seoul – host cities for the Olympics and G20 Summits following Canada's – watched closely (Curry 2010a, 2010b; Magnay 2010). South Korea purportedly tried to make its security less obtrusive by painting "beautiful artwork" onto the security walls (Curry 2010a). Thus, mega-events serve as a tool of foreign policy by transmitting expectations about security and ethics and by projecting an image of how a particular state manages the balance between ethics and security.

Among other things, techniques for policing mega-events have been transmitted among the advanced democracies. The literature on mega-event protest policing identifies a trend (in advanced democracies) away from the "negotiated management" model of protest policing, which dominates everyday protest policing and is characterized by communication with protest organizers before the event, some tolerance of community disruption, and limits on the use of force. Instead, mega-event policing relies on a harder style of policing based upon public order policing (Fernandez 2008; Martin 2011; Sheptycki 2005). Public order policing depends on prosecuting minor offences to maintain a semblance of order and discourage criminal activity. Protest policing at mega-events, established since the "Battle of Seattle" in 1999, tends to be characterized by the manipulation of laws, the shaping of discourse about protesters, and the control of urban space (Fernandez 2008; Martin 2011). In response to a perceived militant activism among anti-globalization protests, police developed techniques focusing on the use of overt and covert intelligence and surveillance prior to the event, the control of space, and the prosecution of minor events.[6] Unfortunately, many of the morally dubious techniques used by police officers at the G20 are well documented in the transnational mega-event protest policing community. Kettling (Allen

2010; Fernandez 2008, 130), the covering or removal of names and badge numbers (Morrow 2010), the use of paramilitary technology (CTV News 2010), and "friendly" visits to known activists (and their friends) (Dembicki 2009) are all characteristic of mega-event protest policing in Canada and abroad. This is true even as after-action reports acknowledge that they are counterproductive and should be used carefully (Her Majesty's Chief Inspector of Constabulary 2009, 53–54; Toronto Police Service 2011, 58) or as other parts of the security bureaucracy distance themselves from police believed to have behaved unethically.[7]

The fact that police services and other security agencies must be considered bureaucracies adds another layer of complexity to mega-events. Such events are not just transnational but also heavily bureaucratized. There is an extensive literature on the question of ethics and bureaucracy. Poor decision making at the planning stages is more likely to lead to morally questionable outcomes. The ideals of democracy (including substantive justice, liberty, and equality) often seem to be at odds with the ideals of bureaucracy (procedural justice, efficiency, standardization, and impartiality) (Denhardt and Catron 1989, 1093). Many scholars link the paucity of morals within bureaucracies to particular features of modern bureaucracy. Zygmunt Bauman (2000, 98–101) identifies two factors that can lead to immoral behaviour in bureaucracies. First, modern bureaucracies are characterized by a division of labour such that few people have a picture of the whole bureaucracy. This division leads to the substitution of technical for moral responsibility: individuals focus on the morality of their particular part of the whole bureaucracy rather than the morality of the outcomes of the entire bureaucratic process. These tendencies can be exacerbated at a mega-event governed by a temporary bureaucracy composed of bureaucrats who do not otherwise work together or who are working under unusual circumstances. For instance, before the G20, the various members of the Integrated Security Unit failed to project a cohesive message about how they would use security equipment (CTV News 2010). Tension between the RCMP and other police forces was often intimated but seldom discussed openly (Radwanski 2010c). To cite another example of bureaucracy affecting the ability to make good ethical decisions, the Toronto Police Service's After-Action Review reports "serious issues that directly affected operations" related to processing arrested individuals at the detention centre on Eastern Avenue in Toronto (2011, 45). This resulted from the fact that Court Services was divided into four sections in which the supervisor of each section had responsibility for organizing his or her zone. Few people had the big picture of what was going on in the facility, and procedures changed as shifts changed. The result was a prisoner management system shaped by competing visions of how the detention centre should work, and this competition resulted in delays in processing and releasing prisoners (ibid., 59).

Denhardt and Catron (1989, 1097) argue that one way to get around this problem is to focus on cultivating judgment among bureaucrats rather than expect them to follow rules, which cannot always be clearly specified independently of the situation that they are meant to address. They advocate a political approach to ethics that encourages focusing on results over procedures, responsibility over centralized authority, and responsiveness over standardization (ibid., 1099). This technique of putting responsibility into the hands of bureaucrats ought to work for policing mega-events, in which many of the bureaucrats involved (police officers and military officials) are well educated or at least well trained and should be capable of critical thinking. However, it assumes that, when security bureaucrats act (morally or immorally), they are doing so on the basis of reasoned decisions, taking the outcomes of their actions into account. This might not be the case (De Cremer et al. 2011, S2). Security bureaucrats, like other bureaucrats, are conditioned by how they have been trained, the social capital that they need to succeed, and other prevailing norms of their field. Security professionals make issues into threats not just by how they talk about them but also in the technology that they use and the routines that they enact (Huysmans 2006, 7–8). At the Vancouver Olympics, security professionals securitized protest by referring to it routinely in public meetings as a security threat (Sweeney 2009) and by monitoring protesters in public (Garr 2009). As previously discussed, at the G20, securitization was even more extreme. The security fence put up around the Convention Centre projected the clear message that violence was expected, as did the training received by front-line officers (McNeilly 2012). So did demonstrations, for the benefit of journalists and the broader public, of intimidating riot control technologies such as long-range acoustic devices and ARWEN. A firebombing at a bank in Ottawa a few days before the G20 was used as justification for the massive security operation. Minister of Industry Tony Clement was quoted as saying that, "early in the process, people were questioning why we needed so much security. Now, no one is questioning it" (Swainson 2010).

Conclusion

The policing of mega-events presents several connected ethical dilemmas. First is the dilemma of balancing the need to follow the rules with the need to allow a certain degree of latitude at the operational level. Ideally, a police officer should be allowed to use her or his judgment when faced with a situation in which the outcome is uncertain: that is, to be lenient when it is warranted or more cautious when instinct honed by experience demands it. On the other hand, too much latitude or a lack of rules and laws means that front-line security personnel have nothing to guide their behaviour; that citizens, visitors, and activists face an unpredictable environment during a mega-event; and that rules and laws cannot be challenged in a court of law before or after the event.

Second is the dilemma of balancing the rights and liberties of citizens and protesters with those of visitors, particularly dignitaries. By their nature, mega-events attract high-profile visitors, such as heads of state, who might have legitimate claims to additional security that warrant constricting the freedom of movement of citizens. Sequestering them at an isolated location, as has been attempted at some G7/G8 summits and trade negotiations, can ensure their security but mean that the ability of citizens to protest in places that are visible to dignitaries is limited.

Third is the dilemma of balancing security and publicity. Overpubliciz-ing or overdramatizing threats can cause fear and insecurity; conversely, a show of force sends an important signal to citizens, and to the world, that local security officials have security concerns well in hand. During a mega-event, the instinct of security officials is to keep operational details secret in part because doing so makes their job easier. However, as discussed above, citizens need to face a predictable legal environment and should therefore have some idea of how they can expect police officers to react to any given activity. Moreover, in a democracy, citizens should have as much information as possible (i.e., the definition of an operational secret or a matter of national security should be kept as narrow as possible) in order to determine the ethical limits of security policy. However, the cases of the Vancouver Olympics and Toronto G20 clearly show that too much public attention to security can be a bad thing, leading to spectacularization. Protesters and police alike contributed to escalations of rhetoric that ultimately contributed to the tense and confrontational atmosphere surrounding the G20 and increased the degree of spectacularization. Security officials need to avoid painting all protesters with the same brush and particularly lumping the threat from criminal or anarchist protest with the threat from terrorism. Protest leaders should balance an acknowledgment of a diversity of activist tactics with a willingness to distinguish between civil disobedience and wilful destruction of property.

The mega-event by definition is an exceptional event. Normal ways of operating are subverted, the stakes are high, and emotions can be intensified. For this reason, it is imperative that discussions on the ethics of security at mega-events occur before (and after) the events, when reasoned discussion is possible and prevailing wisdom can be challenged without the tendency to justify any policy in the name of security. But these dilemmas are not unique to mega-events. They pervade foreign policy decision making more generally. Thinking about how these dilemmas play out at mega-events can cue us to think about how they work in other contexts. Similarly, bureaucracy, transnationalism, and exceptionalism are common features of the post-9/11 foreign policy-making environment but interact at mega-events in ways that can make balancing security and ethics particularly difficult. If we can mitigate the effects of spectacularity and keep the interactions among security, bureaucracy, and exceptionalism to a minimum, then we might be able to balance ethical dilemmas better.

The security operation at the G8/G20 was complicated by the fact that the meeting was originally scheduled to be only a G8 meeting; the G20 Summit was added much later, leaving security officials with only a few months to prepare their security operation. After the Olympics, a group of independent evaluators concluded that developing a centralized bureaucracy would make security operations run more smoothly and be less ad hoc (Plecas et al. 2010, 47). The same benefit would follow revising Canada's laws governing mega-event security, which could then be debated in Parliament, and the courts, outside the context of any particular mega-event (Pue and Diab 2010). A planning and command structure for mega-events that allows only temporary deviations from established laws and regulations might help to reduce the temptation for ad hoc laws to be normalized into permanent ones, gradually eroding the rights of citizens or normalizing a security discourse that paints citizens as being against the state. Both of these measures would have the effect of normalizing mega-event security operations. This, according to Jef Huysmans (2006), is part of the key to ratcheting down escalation, which generates insecurity. Civil liberties and security are two sides of the same coin; each can be understood only in terms of the other. Regulating security is regulating freedom. Therefore, reducing the pressures of securitization is not just a matter of redressing the balance between civil liberties and security. Instead, security must be normalized by broadening the debate about the issue at hand, in this case protest. Rather than framing the right to protest as a threat to security, it should be presented as, for instance, a matter of social justice (ibid., 143). Despite the shocking scenes from Toronto (and the ones earlier in the decade in Quebec City), Canada so far has been comparatively lucky in its mega-events; most physical damage has been to property rather than people, and there have been no deaths. Maintaining security while ensuring the visibility of protesters and the safety of citizens at mega-events is politically charged and difficult, as this chapter has shown. Security operations therefore deserve to be analyzed on a metric of success more complicated than simply whether or not there was excessive police brutality or whether or not there were security breaches. The analysis of the Olympics and G20 shows that there are clear lessons to be learned. Although they might not avert violence at future mega-events, at least they prompt us to make ethically conscious choices rather than seat-of-the-pants decisions in the heat of the moment.

NOTES

1 There are a few exceptions to this rule, such as the pilgrimage to Mecca or the Superbowl, which happen annually in more or less the same place, but the focus of this chapter is on the more occasional events.

2 In the United States, for instance, the Secret Service's Major Events Division is always in charge of events that the president has designated "National Security Special Events."

3 Note that this style of policing might not prevent violence. Compare the relatively benign experience of the Olympics with the violence of Vancouver's Stanley Cup riots in June 2011, when police were criticized for having an insufficiently proactive response.

4 See, for instance, the concerns of the Canadian Civil Liberties Association (2010, 10) about the lack of a regulatory framework for the use of long-range acoustic devices.

5 But see Austen (2010).

6 On the development of protest policing in Canada, see De Lint and Hall (2009, 238–48).

7 For instance, an internal email reports that the Ontario Provincial Police and the RCMP refused to participate in a news conference with the TPS because they did not support the actions of the TPS during and after the G20, and they would have been "forced to contradict TPS in front of the media" (Radwanski 2010c).

References

Allen, Kate. 2010. "A Look Inside the G20 'Kettle' at Queen and Spadina." *Globe and Mail*, 8 November.http://www.theglobeandmail.com/news/national/toronto/a-look-inside-the-g20-kettle-at-queen-and-spadina/article1787949.

Aradau, Claudia. 2010. "Security that Matters: Critical Infrastructure and Objects of Protection." *Security Dialogue* 41 (5): 491–514. http://dx.doi.org/10.1177/0967010610382687.

Austen, Ian. 2010. "Concerns as Canada Balances Protests and Civil Liberties." *New York Times*, 11 February. http://www.nytimes.com/2010/02/11/sports/olympics/11protests.html?_r=0.

Bauman, Zygmunt. 2000. *Modernity and the Holocaust.* Ithaca, NY: Cornell University Press.

Baute, Nicole. 2011. "G20 Officer: 'This Ain't Canada Right Now.'" *Toronto Star,* 20 January. http://www.thestar.com/news/gta/g20/2011/01/20/g20_officer_this_aint_canada_right_now.html.

BBC News. 2010. "G8/G20 Summits Security Map." BBC News, 25 June. http://www.bbc.co.uk/news/10407733.

Bigo, Didier. 2006. "Internal and External Aspects of Security." *European Security* 15 (4): 385–404. http://dx.doi.org/10.1080/09662830701305831.

Black, David. 2007. "The Symbolic Politics of Sport Mega-Events: 2010 in Comparative Perspective." *Politikon: South African Journal of Political Studies* 34 (3): 261–76. http://dx.doi.org/10.1080/02589340801962536.

Boyle, Philip. 2011. "Knowledge Networks: Mega-Events and Security Expertise." In *Security Games: Surveillance and Control at Mega-Events,* edited by Colin J. Bennett and Kevin Haggerty, 169–84. New York: Routledge.

Boyle, Philip, and Kevin D. Haggerty. 2009. "Spectacular Security: Mega-Events and the Security Complex." *International Political Sociology* 3 (3): 257–74. http://dx.doi.org/10.1111/j.1749-5687.2009.00075.x.

"Canada Stages WMD Drill Ahead of 2010 Olympics." 2009. NTI: Global Security Newswire, 3 November. http://www.nti.org/gsn/article/canada-stages-wmd-drill-ahead-of-2010-olympics/.

Canadian Civil Liberties Association. 2010. "A Breach of the Peace." Canadian Civil Liberties Association. 29 June. http://ccla.org/2010/06/29/ccla-releases-a-preliminary-report-of-observations-during-the-g20-summit.

C.A.S.E. Collective. 2006. "Critical Approaches to Security in Europe: A Networked Manifesto." *Security Dialogue* 37 (4): 433–87.

CBC News. 2010. "G20 Officer Admitted Targeting Quebecers: Student." CBC News. July 4. http://www.cbc.ca/news/canada/toronto/g20-officer-admitted-targeting-quebecers-student-1.922302.

Coaffee, Jon, and Peter Rogers. 2008. "Reputational Risk and Resiliency: The Branding of Security in Place-Making." *Place Branding and Public Diplomacy* 4 (3): 205–17. http://dx.doi.org/10.1057/pb.2008.12.

Cowen, Deborah, and Neil Smith. 2010. "Martial Law in the Streets of Toronto." *G20 Security and State Violence* 3 (3): 29–49.

CTV News. 2010. "RCMP, Local Police Deliver Mixed Messages on Security." CTV News, 6 June. http://www.ctvnews.ca/rcmp-local-police-deliver-mixed-messages-on-security-1.519135.

Curry, Bill. 2010a. "A Summit with Seoul: Korea Learns from Toronto's G20 Mistakes." *Globe and Mail,* 17 October. http://www.theglobeandmail.com/news/politics/a-summit-with-seoul-korea-learns-from-torontos-g20-mistakes/article1761111.

Curry, Bill. 2010b. "Armed Officers Patrol South Korea for G20." *Globe and Mail,* 21 October. http://www.theglobeandmail.com/news/politics/ottawa-notebook/armed-officers-patrol-south-korea-for-g20/article1768174.

Decker, Scott H., Jack R. Greene, Vince Webb, Jeff Rojek, Jack McDevitt, Tim Bynum, Sean Varano, and Peter K. Manning. 2005. "Safety and Security at Special Events: The Case of the Salt Lake City Olympic Games." *Security Journal* 18 (4): 65–74. http://dx.doi.org/10.1057/palgrave.sj.8340212.

De Cremer, David, Rolf van Dick, Ann Tenbrunsel, Madan Pillutla, and J. Keith Mur-
nighan. 2011. "Understanding Ethical Behaviour and Decision Making in Management: A Behavioural Business Ethics Approach." *British Journal of Management*
22: S1–S4. http://dx.doi.org/10.1111/j.1467-8551.2010.00733.x.

De Lint, Willem, and Alan Hall. 2009. *Intelligent Control: Developments in Public
Order Policing in Canada.* Toronto: University of Toronto Press.

Dembicki, Geoff. 2009. "Police Question Friend of Olympics Critic Chris Shaw." *The
Tyee,* 5 October. http://thetyee.ca/News/2009/10/05/OlympicsShawQuestioning.

Dembicki, Geoff, and Bob Mackin. 2009. "Olympic Security Chief Likes to 'Be Out
Front." *The Tyee,* 21 October. http://thetyee.ca/News/2009/10/21/MercerSeries2.

Denhardt, Kathryn G., and Bayard L. Catron. 1989. "The Management of Ideals:
A Political Perspective on Ethics." *Public Administration Review* 49 (2): 187–93.
http://dx.doi.org/10.2307/977341.

Dubinsky, Zach. 2010. "In Wake of G20, Will Police Tactics Change?" CBC News. http://
www.cbc.ca/news/canada/in-wake-of-g20-will-police-tactics-change-1.865615.

Fernandez, Luis A. 2008. *Policing Dissent: Social Control and the Anti-Globalization
Movement.* New Brunswick, NJ: Rutgers University Press.

French, Martin. 2010. "Soft Security and Overt Surveillance." Paper presented at the
annual meeting of the Canadian Political Science Association, Montreal, 3 June.

Friesen, Joe. 2010. "How a Man Named Nobody Became the Battered Face of G20
Protests." *Globe and Mail,* 30 November. http://www.theglobeandmail.com/news/
national/toronto/how-a-man-named-nobody-became-the-battered-face-of-
g20-protests/article1818432.

Garr, Allen. 2009. "Beware the Terrorist with Hair Care Products." *Vancouver Courier,*
9 July. http://www.canada.com/story.html?id=1908fe54-22b5-4311-9988-462375c
5caed.

Goldsmith, Andrew. 2008. "The Governance of Terror: Precautionary Logic and
Counterterrorist Law Reform after September 11." *Law and Policy* 30 (2): 141–67.
http://dx.doi.org/10.1111/j.1467-9930.2008.00272.x.

Her Majesty's Chief Inspector of Constabulary. 2009. "Adapting to Protest." http://
www.hmic.gov.uk/publication/adapting-to-protest.

Huysmans, Jef. 2006. *The Politics of Insecurity: Fear, Migration, and Asylum in the
EU.* New York: Routledge.

Johnson, Chris W. 2008. "Using Evacuation Simulations for Contingency Planning to
Enhance the Security and Safety of the 2012 Olympic Venues." *Safety Science*
46 (2): 302–22. http://dx.doi.org/10.1016/j.ssci.2007.05.008.

McDonald, Matt. 2008. "Securitization and the Construction of Security."
European Journal of International Relations 14 (4): 563–87. http://dx.doi.
org/10.1177/1354066108097553.

Magnay, Jacquelin. 2010. "Winter Olympics 2010: London Keen to Learn Lessons from
Vancouver for Next Time." *Telegraph,* 12 February. http://www.telegraph.co.uk/
sport/othersports/winter-olympics/7215790/Winter-Olympics-2010-London-
keen-to-learn-lessons-from-Vancouver-for-next-time.html.

Marin, André. 2010. *Investigation into the Ministry of Community Safety and Cor-
rectional Services' Conduct in Relation to Ontario Regulation 233/10 under the
Public Works Protection Act: "Caught in the Act."* Ombudsman Report. http://
www.ombudsman.on.ca/Files/sitemedia/Documents/Investigations/SORT%20
Investigations/g20final1-en.pdf.

Martin, Greg. 2011. "Showcasing Security: The Politics of Policing Space at the 2007 Sydney APEC Meeting." *Policing and Society* 21 (1): 27–48. doi:http://dx.doi.org/10.1080/10439463.2010.540659.

McNeilly, Gerry. 2012. *Policing the Right to Protest: G20 Systemic Review Report.* Toronto: Office of the Independent Police Review Board. https://www.oiprd.on.ca/CMS/Publications/Reports.aspx.

Morrow, Adrian. 2010. "G20 Police Won't Face Criminal Charges." *Globe and Mail,* 25 November. http://www.theglobeandmail.com/news/national/toronto/g20-police-wont-face-criminal-charges/article1813764.

Morrow, Adrian. 2011. "Police Keep Range of Equipment Acquired for G20 Summit." *Globe and Mail,* 3 February). http://www.theglobeandmail.com/news/national/toronto/police-keep-range-of-equipment-acquired-for-g20-summit/article1893922.

Murakami-Wood, David. 2009. "Pittsburgh Police Use Sub-Lethal Weapons against Protestors." Notes from the Ubiquitous Surveillance Society. http://ubisurv.wordpress.com/2009/09/25/pittsburgh-police-use-sub-lethal-weapons-against-protestors.

Nguyen, Linda. 2010. "Security Officials Woo Huntsville Residents Ahead of G8 Summit." *Vancouver Sun,* 6 June.

Paperny, Anna. 2010. "G20 Charges Dropped over Lack of Warrant." *Globe and Mail,* 4 November. http://www.theglobeandmail.com/news/national/toronto/g20-charges-dropped-over-lack-of-warrant/article1786509.

Plecas, Darryl, Martha Dow, Jordan Diplock, and John Martin. 2010. *The Planning and Execution of Security for the 2010 Olympic Games: 38 Best Practices and Lessons Learned.* Abbotsford: Centre for Criminal Justice Research, University of the Fraser Valley. http://www.ufv.ca/Assets/CCJR/Reports+and+Publications/Olympic_Security.pdf.

Pue, W. Wesley, and Robert Diab. 2010. "The Gap in Canadian Police Powers: Canada Needs Public Order Policing Legislation." *Windsor Review of Legal and Social Issues* 28: 87–107.

Radwanski, Adam. 2010a. "When It Comes to Summit Security, Police Answer to No One." *Globe and Mail,* 22 June. http://www.theglobeandmail.com/news/world/g8-g20/opinion/when-it-comes-to-summit-security-police-answer-to-no-one/article1613960.

Radwanski, Adam. 2010b. "A Timeline on the G20 Five-Metre Rule that Didn't Exist." *Globe and Mail,* 1 July. http://www.theglobeandmail.com/news/politics/adam-radwanski/a-timeline-on-the-g20-five-metre-rule-that-didnt-exist/article1626001.

Radwanski, Adam. 2010c. "G20 Report Unflattering to Toronto Police Chief." *Globe and Mail,* 7 December. http://www.theglobeandmail.com/news/politics/adam-radwanski/g20-report-unflattering-to-toronto-police-chief/article1829120.

Reinhart, Anthony, and Colin Freeze. 2010. "Profiles of Four G20 Arrests." *Globe and Mail,* 27 July. http://www.theglobeandmail.com/news/world/g8-g20/news/profiles-of-four-g20arrests/article1620919/page2.

Rider, David. 2010. "G20 'Fake Lake' Makes Its Debut." *Toronto Star,* 23 July. http://www.thestar.com/news/gta/g20/2010/06/23/g20_fake_lake_makes_its_debut.html.

Seglins, Dave. 2010. "G20 Police Arsenal Includes Plastic Bullets." CBC News. http://www.cbc.ca/news/canada/g20-police-arsenal-includes-plastic-bullets-1.879188.

Sheptycki, James. 2005. "Policing Political Protest When Politics Go Global: Comparing Public Order Policing in Canada and Bolivia." *Policing and Society* 15 (3): 327–52. http://dx.doi.org/10.1080/10439460500168618.

Swainson, Gail. 2010. "Ottawa Firebombing Proves Security Need, Clement Says." *Toronto Star*, 21 May.

Sweeney, Steve. 2009. "2010 Olympics and Paralympics Security." Presentation at the City Council Meeting, Vancouver City Hall, 7 July.

Talbot, Michael. 2010. "Personal Story: How I Ended Up in a G20 Jail." *CityNews*, 29 June. http://www.citynews.ca/2010/06/29/personal-story-how-i-ended-up-in-a-g20-jail/.

Toronto Police Service. 2011. *Toronto Police Service After-Action Review*. http://www.torontopolice.on.ca/publications/files/reports/g20_after_action_review.pdf.

toxicwaste26. 2010. *G20 – Toronto – Incident with Cops – We Don't Live in Canada Anymore – Day 2*. 27 June. YouTube. http://www.youtube.com/watch?v=RjVtsuoPlzk&feature=youtube_gdata_player.

Vu, Liem. 2010. "Police Detail G20 Security Zone." *Globe and Mail*, 28 May. http://www.theglobeandmail.com/news/police-detail-g20-security-zone/article1584293.

Wallace, Kenyon. 2010a. "RCMP Adds Water Cannons to G8/G20 Security Arsenal." *National Post*, 21 June. http://news.nationalpost.com/2010/06/21/rcmp-adds-water-cannons-to-g8g20-security-arsenal.

Wallace, Kenyon. 2010b. "G8/G20 Protest Organizers Refuse to Condemn Violence." *National Post*, 22 June. http://news.nationalpost.com/2010/06/22/g8g20-protest-organizers-refuse-to-condemn-violence/.

Wallinger, Kevin. 2009. *Administrative Report (Memo to Standing Committee on City Services and Budgets Re: Emergency Management and Public Safety during the 2010 Olympic and Paralympic Winter Games – Acceptance of Funding for Temporary CCTV)*. City of Vancouver. http://vancouver.ca/ctyclerk/cclerk/20090326/documents/csbu7.pdf.

Wong, Jackie. 2010. "Olympic Critics Divided over Protest Violence, Vandalism." *Westender*, 24 February.

Woods, Michael. 2011. "SIU Closes Adam Nobody Investigation." *Toronto Star*, 18 July. http://www.thestar.com/news/gta/2011/07/18/siu_closes_adam_nobody_investigation.html.

Yang, Jennifer. 2010a. "A Glimpse behind the G20 Security Curtain." *Toronto Star*, 3 June. http://www.thestar.com/news/gta/g20/2010/06/03/a_glimpse_behind_the_g20_security_curtain.html.

Yang, Jennifer. 2010b. "G20 Law Gives Police Sweeping Powers to Arrest People." *Toronto Star*, 25 June. http://www.thestar.com/news/gta/g20/2010/06/25/g20_law_gives_police_sweeping_powers_to_arrest_people.html.

Yang, Jennifer, and Jesse McLean. 2010. "Anatomy of the G20: What Went Wrong; Reflections from Both Sides of the Fence – the People, the Police – on How a Gathering of World Leaders and Thousands of Peaceful Citizen Protesters Was Sidelined by a Small Band of Anarchists." *Toronto Star*, 21 August.

PART 3

FREEDOM FROM WANT: DEVELOPMENT, GENDER, AND ENVIRONMENT

What Does It Mean to Be a Country of Focus? Canada's Foreign Aid to Ethiopia

DAVID R. BLACK AND REBECCA TIESSEN

In the fall of 2009, twenty-five years after the massive Ethiopian famine of 1984–85, governments and non-governmental agencies alerted the world to widespread food insecurity in Ethiopia and an impending famine. Oxfam International captured the causes of poverty and food insecurity in Ethiopia in a report titled "Band Aids and Beyond: Tackling Disasters in Ethiopia 25 Years after the Famine." The report poignantly asked why famine is still prevalent today despite all that we have learned about food insecurity in previous decades. Band-Aid solutions and short-term food aid responses from donors do not address the food insecurity experienced in Ethiopia (Oxfam International 2009). The report concludes that longer-term solutions to prevent food shortages are essential. The need for such solutions was again apparent with the onset of regional food insecurity in Ethiopia, Somalia, and Kenya as a result of drought in 2011. Although the urgency of famine relief in war-torn Somalia gained the most media coverage, the realities of food insecurity in Ethiopia are ever present and were of great concern during this time of low rainfall. The food insecurity witnessed in Ethiopia, combined with large-scale international donations and development interventions, raises critical questions about the usefulness of foreign aid to Ethiopia and points to some telling trends in Canadian aid policy reflecting the ongoing erosion of humane internationalism as a policy influence. The nexus of security (in this case food security), ethics, human rights, and development offers an important lens on Canadian foreign policy decision making and programming efforts. Our research on Canada's, and specifically the Canadian International Development Agency's (CIDA), [1] impact in Ethiopia in terms of development assistance and food security raises important ethical questions about the success and impact of aid money. This chapter therefore probes Canada's presence in, and commitment to, aid and food security in Ethiopia in light of Canada's changing ethical and security image internationally.

Within the broader context of limited and ambiguous results from twenty-five years of development assistance, there is little information or analysis about the particular efforts of significant bilateral agencies such as CIDA, including its priorities and the impact of its efforts. The impact that CIDA has had can be measured in terms of outputs or outcomes as well as more encompassing ethical analyses of cosmopolitanism within Canadian foreign aid policy.

As an international development agency (and by extension the Canadian government), CIDA has historically projected an image reflecting a comprehensive view of foreign policy through commitments to UN conventions and international human rights principles (Irwin 2001) but also reflecting a larger view of ethics in foreign policy involving international norms and perceptions of what is right and fair in the world. Yet a clear shift in prevailing ethical norms in Canadian foreign policy can be observed over the past couple of decades (Black 2013a), a shift that has moved Canada away from a preoccupation with humane internationalism (and the related idea of human security) and toward an increasing emphasis on economic security for Canada and Canadians accompanied by a narrower and more instrumental view of development assistance. Rather than emphasizing the role of aid to Ethiopia as "acceptance of an obligation to alleviate global poverty, and to promote development in the [least developed countries]," Cranford Pratt's (1989, 16) classic definition of humane internationalism, Canada's aid policy regarding Ethiopia has been more narrowly preoccupied with rankings on the donor "league table" and "results" for Canadian taxpayers.

CIDA's and Canada's limited and ambiguous impact is especially striking since Ethiopia has been an important bilateral aid priority for Canada for much of the past twenty-five years. As CIDA attempted to bring a greater focus to its bilateral programming over the past decade, Ethiopia was designated as a country of concentration in 2002 and subsequently reconfirmed as one of twenty "countries of focus" in February 2009 and as one of twenty-five in June 2014. Similarly, food security became one of three CIDA-designated priorities in May 2009. In this chapter, we examine Canada's current priorities and how they have evolved over time in relation to Canada's historical tradition of humane internationalism. We also provide insights from aid workers in development agencies working in Ethiopia who have reflected on Canada's relationship with the country. CIDA's historical focus on, and financial commitment to, Ethiopia raise four broad sets of issues concerning what it means to be a country of concentration. First, to what extent does this status enable Canada to be a major player in, and influence on, the intra-donor and donor-recipient processes that have become such an integral feature of the international aid regime in the context of the aid effectiveness agenda institutionalized around the Paris Principles and the Accra Agenda for Action?[2] Second, what impact has its thematic focus on food security had in enabling Ethiopia to escape from the chronic recurrence of food emergencies, especially given the gender implications of food insecurity in the country? Third, how has Ethiopia's priority status affected the coherence of Canadian aid, particularly in terms of coordination between CIDA and its non-governmental "partners" in the country, on which the implementation of much of its work depends? And fourth, how have CIDA's activities in Ethiopia over time reflected the weakening of Canada's humane internationalist tradition? We address these questions in the context of international trends in aid effectiveness strategies: namely, the ethical implications of the fetishization of focus and the justifications offered for narrowing the scope of countries of concentration and policy priorities, with particular attention to the ethical repercussions of these trends.

We find that Canada's fetishization of focus, both bilaterally and thematically, has been greatly affected by shifting interests and rhetorical commitments over time, driven less by concerns over ethics and human security than by fiscal accountability and narrow understandings of efficiency and effectiveness. Moreover, the impact of these policies of focus has been significantly compromised by Canada's relatively modest presence "on the ground" in Ethiopia, its inconsistent and uncertain priorities, and its lack of delegated authority in the field – this despite being among the top five bilateral donors in the country. These findings have implications for Canada's participation in multi-donor aid effectiveness strategies and for its reputation as a promoter of human rights and equality. Thus, rather than leading "the world in ending ... the tragedy of ineffective aid" (Oda 2009), Canada's commitments to aid effectiveness, and to food security within it, ironically suggest that its principal ethical imperative in a country of focus such as Ethiopia is to ensure the sustainability of the image of good humanitarian donorship for the purpose of appealing to key

Canadian constituencies (Development Initiatives 2011) versus sustainable agricultural practices and disaster risk reduction strategies through programs designed to target human rights abuses and unequal access to resources. Likewise, the effect of Canada's approach has been to limit its impact in relation to either bilateral recipients or other donor "partners." Despite the dedicated efforts of officials and organizations in the field, the policy emphasis remains on rhetoric rather than action, on politics rather than security, and on efficiency of aid spending rather than rights for and moral obligations to those who are food insecure. These challenges raise obvious ethical concerns, particularly when food security is so intimately tied to the lives and well-being of people.

The Fetishization of Focus: Repercussions at Country and Sectoral Levels

In 2006, Danielle Goldfarb and Stephen Tapp, in a report for the C.D. Howe Institute, strongly criticized CIDA for its alleged ineffectiveness. Their report notes, among several key criticisms, that spending is too widely dispersed and that CIDA should move into line with other donors by concentrating on relatively few countries in a smaller number of thematic areas (Goldfarb and Tapp 2006, 2). The document expresses optimism on this front, noting that, "with renewed world attention on foreign aid and poverty reduction, and Prime Minister Harper's commitment to spend aid dollars more effectively, CIDA has a chance to take bold action to reform itself" (ibid., intro). The general thrust of this report has been reinforced by many other commentators, including the widely discussed Senate of Canada Standing Committee on Foreign Affairs and International Trade report *Overcoming Forty Years of Failure: A New Road Map for Sub-Saharan Africa* (2007). Brown (2008, 98) argues that although this report was "deeply flawed in its assumptions, methodology and argumentation," its wide-ranging critique struck a chord in official Ottawa. These commentaries and reports set the tone for the CIDA reforms that eventually followed. The logic behind focusing on a smaller number of countries of concentration is laid out in the C.D. Howe Institute report:

> A limited aid budget spread out over many countries, projects, and sectors likely will result in less effective aid because of increased administrative burdens for donors and recipients alike, as well as the possibility of project overlap. In addition, a limited field presence reduces donors' knowledge of local conditions and their ability to evaluate projects. It is unfortunate,

then, that CIDA has [historically] allocated aid so widely over the past few decades, with little focus on particular regions or themes. Canadian aid has been allocated mainly according to historical precedent and political considerations – aiding commonwealth and francophone countries in Africa and Asia, while simultaneously balancing broader responsibilities in the Americas ... – rather than an explicit set of aid effectiveness criteria. (Goldfarb and Tapp 2006, 8)

Current debates about aid effectiveness, in Canada and elsewhere, have thus placed considerable emphasis on the question of focus.[3] Lauchlan Munro, in his 2005 analysis aptly titled "Focus-Pocus," highlights that Canada's strategy of focusing on a smaller number of countries and fewer sectors is part of a global trend widely adopted by donor countries that have accepted the logic of increased concentration virtually without question. The ambiguity of focusing, however, is that aid continues to be shifted from one place to another. Only the parameters within which the shifting of aid takes place have changed. The result might be *reduced* (or at least oscillating) focus. For example, "Canada's decision to embrace the MDGs [Millennium Development Goals] helped lead CIDA to move back into agriculture, a sector where its support had been declining for a decade or so" (ibid., 429). In other words, the very process of deciding where and how to focus can introduce new uncertainties and inconsistencies, particularly if a new government takes office with a determination to place its own "stamp" on policy priorities.

The fetishization of focus creates a powerful impression that change is taking place. Increased aid effectiveness is the expected result of more focus. Yet there is no evidence to suggest that more focus will contribute to greater success. Indeed, Munro (2005, 444) argues that "too much focusing may cut down on synergies, and reduce the whole organization's ability to produce sufficient numbers of innovations through successful experimentation, and may expose the organization to catastrophe in the event that one of the organization's very few but large projects results in failure." The true test of aid effectiveness is the degree to which it reflects the management of good projects that meet the needs of those in the developing world. It is important, therefore, to assess the degree to which the process of focusing helps to meet this test. Only if it does so can aid be reasonably understood to enhance recipients' (human) security and reflect an ethical concern with ameliorating the plight of the poor.

Among the major changes in aid programming in recent years has been a policy shift to reduce the number of countries with which Canada formally partners in its development work, at least in a relatively intensive and sustained sense. The intention to concentrate efforts in a smaller number of countries became evident in 2002 when the government announced a focus on nine core partners, though it was never made clear how this intention would be realized. Later, in 2005, the Liberal government announced, in the context of its *International Policy Statement* (CIDA 2005), its intention to focus two-thirds of bilateral aid in twenty-five countries, though as Stairs (2005) pointed out, this had little impact in terms of any real concentration of resources in a smaller number of countries. Nevertheless, this shift did have significant consequences by enabling longer-term planning and greater concentration of bureaucratic resources in designated "partners." The Harper Conservatives' first effort in this direction was announced in February 2009. The government revealed, with negligible consultation, that it would focus the vast majority (80 percent) of its bilateral spending in twenty countries of concentration.[4] Several countries were dropped from the 2005 *International Policy Statement* list of twenty-five, including, in Africa, long-term bilateral recipients in Benin, Burkina Faso, Cameroon, Kenya, Malawi, Niger, Rwanda, and Zambia. Multilateral aid, "partnership" funds (through non-state actors), and humanitarian assistance continue to be dispensed in a somewhat larger number of countries, partly mitigating the impact of the shift. However, the list of "priority countries" was scaled back by 20 percent, while the percentage of resources to be concentrated in them was significantly increased.

In addition to a significant focusing of bilateral aid spending, the countries of concentration identified under the Conservative government suggested a "tilt" toward greater emphasis in Latin America and the Caribbean. Prior to this, in the prime minister's September 2007 address to the Council on Foreign Relations in New York City, expectations had been raised concerning a major change in the government's foreign aid policy, including a process of concentrating bilateral aid. The Canadian government's objective, it was later indicated, was to be among the five largest donors in each of its core countries (Black 2009). However, the evidence of real policy change flowing from the reduced emphasis on Africa and the increased commitment to Latin America and the Caribbean was slow to materialize, beyond the negotiation of bilateral free-trade agreements with Colombia and Peru and some increase in security cooperation (ibid.). Thus, as this protracted process continues to unfold, rhetoric must continue to be carefully evaluated against practice.

Along with the designation of a streamlined list of core countries of concentration, Bev Oda, then the minister of international cooperation, announced in a May 2009 speech to the Munk Centre at the University of Toronto that Canadian aid would focus on three thematic priorities: increasing food security, securing the future of children and youth, and stimulating sustainable economic growth. These priorities were to be accompanied by crosscutting themes of increasing environmental sustainability and promoting equality of women and men. These "new" priorities can be compared with the five thematic priorities outlined in the *International Policy Statement:* good governance, health (with a focus on HIV/AIDS), basic education, private sector development, and environmental sustainability, again with gender equality as a crosscutting theme (CIDA 2005, 11–22). The degree to which these shifts constitute real concentration and change of direction is a matter for ongoing empirical scrutiny and will take some time to become fully apparent. After all, there is a long history of shifting rhetorical priorities in Canadian aid policy, often with marginal but nevertheless disruptive policy repercussions (see Black and Tiessen 2007; Morrison 1998).

Although it is too soon to evaluate the effects of the Conservative government's 2009 plans for country and sectoral focus, now further complicated by the merger between CIDA and the Department of Foreign Affairs and International Trade (DFAIT) and a further revision to the list of countries of concentration in June 2014 (DFATD 2014), the more long-standing bilateral "partnership" with Ethiopia provides a useful basis upon which to assess the Conservatives' apparently more determined approach to providing greater focus in Canadian aid policies and programs.

Ethiopia as a Country of Concentration

Through the various revisions of the list of Canada's core bilateral partners over the past decade, Ethiopia has remained on the list of countries of concentration in part because of a long history of poverty and related hardships, including the seminal 1984–85 famine and recurrent challenges of food security and development. As shown in Table 1, it was among the top three bilateral recipients of Canadian aid in five of the eleven years between 2002 and 2012. The population of Ethiopia is about 85 million, making it relatively densely populated by African standards. Ethiopia ranks 174th out of 187 countries in the Human Development Index (UNDP 2010) and is one of the world's poorest nations, with 39 percent of the population living on less than US$1.25 per day (Government of Canada 2013).

TABLE 1

Canadian aid to Ethiopia and top three bilateral recipients (USD millions), 2002–12

Calendar year	Total Canadian ODA	Total bilateral ODA	Total ODA to Ethiopia	Top three bilateral ODA recipients
2002	2,004.16	1,500.71	6.88	(1) Cameroon – 80.29 (2) Afghanistan – 35.81 (3) Bangladesh – 30.87
2003	2,030.60	1,347.62	38.02	(1) Democratic Republic of the Congo – 74.49 (2) Afghanistan – 73.13 (3) Iraq – 47.86
2004	2,599.13	1,990.98	59.48	(1) Iraq – 71.99 (2) Ethiopia – 59.48 (3) Afghanistan – 56.24
2005	3,756.34	2,832.88	64.93	(1) Iraq – 385.53 (2) Indonesia – 95.89 (3) Afghanistan – 89.47
2006	3,683.16	2,533.94	62.48	(1) Cameroon – 206.88 (2) Afghanistan – 140.27 (3) Haiti – 97.45
2007	4,079.69	3,152.19	90.52	(1) Afghanistan – 354.39 (2) Haiti – 119.22 (3) Ethiopia – 90.52
2008	4,794.71	3,366.65	152.55	(1) Afghanistan – 207.86 (2) Ethiopia – 152.55 (3) Iraq – 152.00
2009	4,000.07	3,140.97	87.18	(1) Afghanistan – 232.58 (2) Haiti – 119.72 (3) Sudan – 105.04
2010	5,214.12	3,926.41	140.38	(1) Haiti – 458.87 (2) Afghanistan – 267.12 (3) Ethiopia – 140.38
2011	5,458.56	4,111.21	118.64	(1) Haiti – 242.04 (2) Afghanistan – 225.15 (3) Mozambique – 129.81
2012	5,650.26	4,052.69	123.37	(1) Haiti – 167.20 (2) Mozambique – 123.43 (3) VEthiopia – 123.37

Sources: Organization for Economic Cooperation and Development (2012a, 2012b).

The rationale for keeping Ethiopia on the list of core partners, according to CIDA officials, was that the country met the three core criteria established by the government: need for development assistance, ability to use aid effectively and for CIDA to engage with the recipient government in a meaningful way, and foreign policy considerations. Within the donor community as a whole, the Ethiopian government retains a reputation as having "a culture of discipline and performance" (Furtado and Smith 2009, 132), notwithstanding serious concerns regarding its record on human rights and political tolerance. Ethiopia is also regarded by major Western governments as a strategically important partner in a volatile neighbourhood, given its proximity to Somalia, Sudan, and the "Greater Horn" regional insecurity complex (Seymour 2010) – making it an important country in the context of concerns over regional stability and security. Finally, Ethiopia's capital, Addis Ababa, is a diplomatic hub for Africa, hosting the headquarters for both the African Union and the UN Economic Commission for Africa as well as numerous other international organizations. All of these considerations make it a strategically significant development "partner." It is therefore understandable that the Canadian government wants to maintain a significant presence in the country. Yet, when compared with other major donors, Canada benefits from a reputation as a relatively disinterested and humanitarian "player" (interviews, Addis Ababa, February 2010). Canada's long-standing donor relationship with Ethiopia is expected to continue as Canada strives to be among the top bilateral donors in the country in terms of volume. The DFATD's website claims that Canada is the third largest bilateral donor in Ethiopia and that Canada's programming will support initiatives for national poverty reduction as spelled out in Ethiopia's Plan for Accelerated Sustained Development to Eradicate Poverty (Government of Canada 2013).

In fact, the totals of bilateral aid provided in Table 1, though relatively substantial, understate the totals of aid to Ethiopia from all sources. In 2004–05, for example, Canada's official development assistance (ODA) to Ethiopia totalled $108.39 million (Government of Canada 2009). In 2007–08, the average gross ODA sent from Canada to Ethiopia was $122 million from all funding windows, ranking Canada seventh among the top ten donors and third among bilateral donors, following the United States at $592 million and the United Kingdom at $273 million (OECD 2010). In 2010, Canada was still among the top four donors, with aid levels roughly equivalent to those of Germany.

The Canadian government reports a very modest level of trade between Canada and Ethiopia, with a total of $22 million in 2007. Canadian exports to Ethiopia consist largely of cereal crops and machinery, while imports include mainly coffee and seeds. The value of Canada's exports to Ethiopia was approximately $15.4 million, while the value of imports totalled approximately $6.95 million (Government of Canada 2009). On the other hand, Ethiopia is increasingly attractive to Canadian-based companies, particularly in the mining sector and in consulting contracts for hydroelectricity. Business contracts are expected to expand after a number of recent agreements between the two countries, including a memorandum of understanding on tariff-free access for Ethiopian exports of textiles and apparel (2003) and a 2010 bilateral agreement to allow Ethiopian Airlines to fly to Canada twice weekly. In 2008, Canada also agreed to the sale of eight Bombardier Q400 turbo-prop aircraft (Tamene 2010). These new arrangements and agreements have paved the way for expanded commercial relations. At this stage, however, the links are far too limited to serve as a robust motivation for the maintenance of one of Canada's largest bilateral aid programs.

Canada's commitment to Ethiopian development has also involved a strong thematic focus on governance, including the monitoring of human rights and good governance in the country (Government of Canada 2009). This became a source of considerable sensitivity and controversy since the Ethiopian government has engaged in anti-democratic behaviour and been accused by Human Rights Watch, among others, of "politicizing" foreign aid for the purpose of regime consolidation (York 2010). For Canadian aid officials, an additional challenge of programming in the governance sector arose when this sector was officially dropped as a thematic priority by CIDA in May 2009. This challenge, and the resulting uncertainty, were partially resolved when it was determined, in February 2010, that governance programming could and should continue under the new thematic priority of "stimulating sustainable economic growth" (interviews, Addis Ababa, February 2010). Still, this subterfuge to sustain programming in what had been a major programmatic focus reflects some of the endemic policy ambiguities and challenges facing CIDA officials.

Despite its challenges, Ethiopia is also recognized for its substantial achievements between 2005 and 2010.

According to the measurement done between 2005 and 2010, Ethiopia's position comes at the top of the top movers of the development achievers ... [B]etween 2000 and 2010, Ethiopia's life expectancy at birth increased by almost 5 years, GNI per capita increased by 75 per cent, expected years of schooling increased by 4 years, while mean years of schooling remained the same. (UNDP 2010)

Some of the recent indicators of success include falling rates of poverty, high economic growth, and good harvests in the second half of the 2000s. The Government of Canada (2013) has noted that Ethiopia is on track to achieve six of the eight Millennium Development Goals.[5] The successes achieved in Ethiopia must be considered in light of a country prone to shocks, especially climate-related events such as drought, as seen once again in 2010–11. Therefore, the country presents a donors' dilemma: disturbing "governance" indicators and trends are combined with a relatively high degree of effectiveness in achieving social and economic development improvements.

Ethiopia's success over the past decade should be viewed in relation to a high level of donor engagement. The Organization for Economic Cooperation and Development (OECD 2014) has ranked Ethiopia at or near the top of ODA recipients in Africa, followed by countries such as Tanzania, Sudan, the Democratic Republic of the Congo, and Côte d'Ivoire. Until the aftershocks of the global financial crisis of 2008, net ODA to sub-Saharan Africa had also been growing steadily through the first decade of the new millennium and amounted to US$45.2 billion in 2009, an increase of more than 9 percent from US$40.9 billion in 2008 (ibid.). ODA is therefore a central factor in Ethiopia's development and growth. Ethiopia is one of the major recipients of foreign aid in the world and in 2006 was the seventh largest recipient of aid out of 169 aid recipient countries (Alemu 2009). Paradoxically, however, the country is relatively *less* aid dependent on a per capita basis than most African countries,[6] and the Ethiopian government has been relatively successful in asserting its policy and political independence and resisting aid conditionality (e.g., Borchgrevink 2008; Furtado and Smith 2009).

Ethiopia's economic development indicators must also take into account the increasing presence of China in the country. China's annual ODA flows to Africa have increased significantly in recent decades, from approximately US$310 million in 1989–92 to an estimated US$1.5–2 billion by the end of the first decade of the new millennium (Samy 2010, 81–82). China has also expanded its trade relations with Ethiopia, which China now views as its major economic and trading partner in Africa. Bilateral trade with China reached a total of US$1.376 billion in 2009, representing an increase of 12.4

percent from the previous year's total (*People's Daily Online* 2010). This trend, of course, is another major strategic incentive for Western governments to sustain a robust presence in the country.

Thus, Canada remains a key donor nation to Ethiopia and is now firmly committed to staying among the top donors to the country in the years to come. Among countries of concentration in Africa, Ethiopia is the one recipient that is not a member of either the Commonwealth or la Francophonie, making it a historical anomaly. Beyond the broader considerations noted above, Canada's continuing involvement can be seen in part as a historical legacy of massive Canadian response to the 1985 famine. Although the Canadian government clearly wants to remain a "player," broadly speaking, in one of the more important recipient countries in the international aid regime, a more concrete focus within Canada's foreign assistance to Ethiopia (both governmental and non-governmental) has always been the promotion of food security. CIDA's food security work in Ethiopia includes the provision of agricultural extension services, the rehabilitation of degraded watersheds and conservation measures, and agribusiness ventures to food-insecure areas (CIDA 2010). This food security emphasis is appropriate and welcome in a country that faces recurrent droughts and food shortages.

CIDA's ongoing commitment to food security/agriculture, one of three thematic priorities in the 2004–09 Ethiopia Country Development Program framework, was reinforced at the agency level by the May 2009 designation of food security as one of three overarching thematic priorities. The food security strategy is geared to responding to impacts of food crisis and climate change, focusing on food aid, nutrition, agriculture, and research (Oda 2009). At the country level, CIDA's funding commitments have also included assistance to small-holder farmers - namely, strengthening local organizations that support farmers, investing in supply systems for improved seed availability and livestock breeds, development of rural infrastructure, and water and soil conservation practices (CIDA 2011a).

According to CIDA, its development efforts have contributed to a high level of success in Ethiopia, particularly in improved economic growth, good harvests, and support for country-led programs geared to increasing food security and improving health and education services (CIDA 2011b). The 2010 Ethiopia Country Program Evaluation conducted under the auspices of CIDA's Evaluation Directorate also favourably assessed the agency's agriculture/food security programs for 2004–09 (CIDA 2010). In research conducted by Adenew for the Canadian Food Security Policy Group, however, he notes that CIDA's focus on agriculture has not been accompanied by adequate resources and that the "share of capital budget for the agricultural sector has been low and inconsistent" (Adenew 2006, 24). Adenew's critique raises key questions about the effectiveness of CIDA's aid programming as well as the appropriateness of resource allocations, in spite of Canada's ranking among the top five of all bilateral donors.

Given commitments to food security by Canada and other major donors to Ethiopia, the question of why famine persists in the country must be re-examined. Devereux (2009) attributes famines or food crises to a failure of response characterized by four key circumstances: lack of accurate and timely information; interventions that are inadequate and/or inappropriate; lack of political will by governments to protect vulnerable citizens; and late or non-response by donors. These factors, he argues, played roles in all three of the twenty-first-century global famines to date, including the famine in Ethiopia of 1999–2000. At first glance, the international donor funding to Ethiopia for famine prevention, preparedness, and relief appears to be significant, particularly compared with that for other African countries. As noted above, however, when evaluated on a per capita basis, Ethiopia receives among the smallest investments in development aid per citizen relative to other African countries (Kehler 2004). Per capita spending thus remains an important indicator to consider when evaluating the effectiveness of donor-funded food security initiatives. Other indicators of success hinge on the sustainability of food security programs (ibid.), gender-sensitive food security programs, effective CIDA-NGO relations, coherence of Canadian aid, and donor coordination. The impacts of donor contributions to food security in Ethiopia must also be understood in the context of the broader aid regime in which Canada vies to be a major player, notwithstanding relatively low per-capita aid spending.

CIDA and the Aid Regime in Ethiopia

Denis Stairs (2005) has argued with regard to the 2005 exercise in CIDA recipient focus that the impact of this exercise on the *actual* concentration of aid expenditures was negligible. The impact and sustainability of the more ambitious 2009 and 2014 targets remain to be seen. Despite these uncertainties, there are at least two related ways in which being designated a country of concentration should make a difference in aid policy and programming and hence in engagement with challenges of poverty alleviation and human security. The first is that this status is accompanied by relatively long-term planning horizons, buttressed by comparatively large and stable commitments of bilateral funding. The second is that these material commitments will be supported by comparatively large commitments of human resources, including significant field-level deployments of aid policy officers and in-country technical support units.[7] Taken together, these trends should result, in theory, in more contextualized and responsive programming and in greater ability to be a player in the collaborative field-level politics and processes of the aid regime. The importance of the latter has grown significantly because of the institutionalized emphasis on harmonization, alignment, and ownership and the trend toward collaborative program-based approaches among donors. This, surely, is the most substantial justification for the government's declared intention to be among the top five donors in designated countries of concentration – as a step toward the exercise of meaningful influence on both collective donor efforts and recipient country policies. To what extent have these expectations and aspirations been borne out in practice?

Interviews in Addis Ababa provided some evidence that CIDA personnel are well regarded by their donor peers and that they are active participants in the Donor Assistance Group that seeks to coordinate donor policies with each other and with the Ethiopian government, through program-based approaches and the various sector working groups that coordinate them.[8] In early 2010, for example, CIDA officers served as the vice-chair of the Governance Working Group and chair of the Regional Economic Development and Food Security Working Group. Nevertheless, their ability to engage fully with "harmonized" and "aligned" program initiatives was seriously compromised by the atmosphere of policy uncertainty and the preoccupation, bordering on obsession, with focus ("focus within focus," according to CIDA officials) within which they were working as a result of political dynamics emanating from Ottawa. These uncertainties have been compounded, in the medium term at least, by the repercussions of the merger of CIDA and the Department of Foreign Affairs and International Trade (DFAIT).

Collaborative and program-based approaches, whatever their advantages and disadvantages, require of donor agencies stable, long-term commitments of resources, priorities, and personnel, combined with a significant measure of flexibility to adapt to changing conditions and intra-donor and donor-recipient consultations. They also require an emphasis on "outcomes" versus "outputs," involving a willingness to subordinate discrete individual donor agency contributions to successful collaborative outcomes. The current Canadian government's particular emphasis on, and interpretation of, "managing for results" have made it extraordinarily difficult for Canadian aid officials to participate in, let alone lead, these "field-based" dynamics.

The protracted lack of clarity about program priorities has compounded these difficulties. CIDA's Ethiopia program was formally guided between 2004 and 2009 by the Country Development Program framework noted above; however, since the framework predated the election of the Harper Conservatives, and since the new government soon signaled that it would be rethinking aid policy, a cloud of uncertainty was cast over the utility of the framework. When it "expired" in 2009, there was no successor framework in place; in fact, by February 2010, it was reported that a new country strategy document had already been through thirty-two drafts without approval. Similarly, in terms of agency-wide thematic priorities, field-based personnel had to cope with a protracted vacuum as the Martin government's 2005 *International Policy Statement* was formally disavowed, but until May 2009 no new thematic priorities were articulated. Even when new priorities were announced, they were not accompanied by any strategy for implementation. The food security strategy document was not released until February 2010, while the sustainable economic growth strategy document was not released until October of that year.[9]

From May 2009 through February 2010, CIDA officials had to cope with another major source of uncertainty, for their erstwhile priority sector of governance was not among the Harper government's newly articulated priorities. Since the Ethiopia Country Development Program had developed important "niches" in this area, and accompanying expertise and relationships, this uncertainty raised important and difficult questions about the future of programming in this area. Program staff were finally informed that governance work could be carried forward under the rubric of sustainable economic growth, as an "enabler" or "soft infrastructure", providing a good illustration of the malleability of these ostensibly focused priorities. In the meantime, officials were required to give life to the government's new "signature" priority of maternal-child health, announced in January by the prime minister as a key priority for the Muskoka G8 Summit held six months later, in June 2010. As laudable as this priority is, it came as a policy bolt from the blue and, partly as a result, has been sharply criticized by policy makers and scholars alike (see Black 2013b; Carrier and Tiessen 2012).

Finally, though the Ethiopia program has been supported by a relatively robust field presence, and though the Canadian government has given lip service to providing more decentralized authority at the field level, the reality has been that aid policy making has become even *more* centralized under the Conservatives, with program and policy decisions being micro-managed within the minister's office to an unprecedented extent. As a result, it has not been possible to fulfill the theoretical advantages of more contextualized policy making in countries of concentration in any substantial or meaningful sense.

In sum, while being designated as a country of concentration suggests the *possibility* of a more active and extensive leadership role within the collaborative and coordinated aid policy-making processes articulated by the multilateral aid effectiveness agenda, in practice CIDA programming in the field was effectively prevented from achieving these possibilities because of the atmosphere of uncertainty, delay, and centralization within which officers were required to operate. That this appears not to have been a concern of their political masters in Ottawa suggests, at the least, indifference to the dynamics of the multilateral aid regime and a preoccupation with the domestic political "optics" of CIDA's "New Effective Approach to Canadian Aid" (Oda 2009). Perhaps this tendency of one of Ethiopia's larger bilateral donors led one non-governmental observer to conclude that

> aid is not effectively coordinated. It is fragmented and unpredictable. There are several donors that have several projects but only a small share of the aid market. Despite Ethiopia's early initiation of an in-country harmonization and alignment process, both at the sector and country levels, achievements have not been comprehensive. Most of the donors do talk positively about the agenda but are not able to walk the talk. Without political commitment at donor headquarters or incentive mechanisms to change the attitude and behaviour of donor staff, recipient countries are likely to be frustrated by the lack of meaningful progress. The other challenge is related to meeting the ideals and principles that underpin the Paris Declaration. (Interview with author, 2013)

The response provided by this NGO staff member in Ethiopia underscores the persistent gap between rhetoric and reality and the difficulty of translating Paris Declaration policy commitments into effective practices (see den Heyer 2012). Among the Paris Declaration goals of increased and more effective aid is a commitment to gender equality (paragraph 42) as part of the crosscutting issues heralded in the new approaches to aid delivery. The Paris Declaration is linked to the Millennium Development Goals, which also highlight gender equality and women's empowerment as central to the success of development programs.

Food Security and Gender Inequality in Ethiopia

Understanding the gendered impacts of food (in)security is essential to an analysis of the day-to-day challenges of implementing ethically compelling development programs such as sustainable agriculture in Ethiopia and addressing the human security challenges confronting Ethiopian women and girls in particular. However, widespread and socially sanctioned forms of gender inequality in Ethiopia impinge on the success of aid programming in the agricultural sector. Several key aspects of gender inequality throughout much of Ethiopia constrain women's ability to be effective agricultural producers: namely, a social division of labour that does not recognize women's agricultural contributions, women's limited access to land and technology because of gendered legal and social norms, and specific challenges faced by female-headed households.

Such households have a harder time than male-headed households in adapting to price fluctuations and sharp increases in food and fuel prices, which have been particularly prevalent over the past few years. The eroding purchasing power of female-headed households raises concerns regarding increased food insecurity and malnutrition among the women and children in these homes (Kumar and Quisumbing 2010). Improved food security in Ethiopia thus requires donor commitments to evaluating gender disparities in the agricultural sector and working with national government and local authorities to promote greater rights for women to access land, resources, and technology. Women's lack of access to labour-saving technology such as donkeys or oxen means that women have heavier burdens of work in the agricultural sector. If women are not seen by agricultural extension staff as legitimate farmers because of the socially defined agricultural roles that they play in crop production (hoeing fields rather than cultivating crops), then resources will not be directed to the most vulnerable individuals and households. Gender disparities in Ethiopian agricultural societies therefore have welfare consequences that correlate with nutrition and food security measures. Those welfare consequences include nutritional access but also broader health indicators.

Food shortages are endured by all community members. However, women often feel the impact first as the primary caregivers in Ethiopian households (Oxfam International 2009). The gendered implications of food security extend to adolescent girls. In a study of adolescents aged thirteen to seventeen from various areas of southwest Ethiopia, researchers found that, of the 2,084 adolescents surveyed, food-insecure girls were two times more likely than boys to report suffering from an illness. The risk of illness tripled when girls belonged to food-insecure households. Therefore, food insecurity combined with gender inequality is a predictor of an adolescent's self-reported health status. The greater risk associated with girls can be attributed, in part, to the social division of labour and cultural norms concerning who gets access to high-quality food and caloric intake. Girls who are required to assist their mothers in the labour-intensive work of firewood, fuel, and food collection are likely to require higher caloric intake for their health and well-being. Women who are pregnant and/or breast feeding also have nutritional requirements that often go unmet in a food crisis. Decisions about who eats first, most often, and the largest amounts are gendered decisions reflecting patriarchal values and societal norms that privilege men and boys within the family. Gender must therefore be regarded as an important variable in food security interventions (Belachew et al. 2010).

Historically, CIDA has made some efforts to ensure that gender issues are mainstreamed into food security programming. The agency's initiatives in this area began in the 1980s with the aim of addressing the root causes of food insecurity. More recently, attention to gender issues was reinforced through the agency's support of Ethiopia's Plan for Accelerated Sustained Development to Eradicate Poverty (2006–10; see also CIDA 2010, 32–33). Although this focus addresses the long-standing food insecurity problem, gender development and improvements to the status of women require greater and more concerted efforts, despite the agency's ongoing emphasis on gender (more recently recast as "equality between women and men") as a crosscutting theme.[10] Vercillo (2010) has argued that CIDA's development assistance for women in Ethiopia is unique because of the agency's attention to capacity-building and decision-making opportunities for women. One example of CIDA's work in Ethiopia is a child survival and maternal health program. The program is designed to ensure that mothers and children under five receive quality basic health services. Vercillo goes on to note, however, that this CIDA-funded program has failed to reach the poorest, most vulnerable women and those who are most affected by food insecurity. If the government of Canada is to fulfill its internationally agreed commitments, such as the Paris Declaration, the Millennium Development Goals, and other initiatives reflecting a more humane internationalist and ethically responsive foreign aid policy, then a renewed pledge to address gender inequality in programs such as food security is essential.

This example raises a number of issues. First, it demonstrates the potential value of carefully designed and sensitively implemented development interventions. Second, it demonstrates the importance of the interface/ coordination among governmental, non-governmental, and community-based organizations, a point to which we return in the next section. Third, however, as project evaluators have alluded to in other contexts (e.g., Partnership for Food Security), there are many challenges facing even the most promising interventions, of "graduation" from project assistance, of "scaling up" to reach larger numbers of people and diverse communities and regions, of inequities and resentments between communities included and excluded from development interventions, and so on. These challenges certainly justify the thematic emphasis now given to food security but will require a more consistent and, paradoxically, more flexible and contextualized approach to policy making in the area than has typically prevailed in the past. It remains to be seen whether Canadian aid policy makers can meet these requirements, given the challenges and constraints noted in the previous section. In the section that follows, we explore a particular dimension of these challenges: the relationship between CIDA/DFATD and NGOs operating in Ethiopia from the perspectives of both aid officials and NGO staff members who have worked with or are currently operating under CIDA/DFATD funding guidelines.

CIDA-NGO Relations
Canadian NGOs have a strong and long-standing presence in Ethiopia. Indeed, in 2006, with CIDA encouragement, some eighteen Canadian-linked NGOs formed an association, the Canadian Network of NGOs (CANGO), to concert their efforts. This can be seen as a reflection of the more extensive linkages and long-term concentration that designating a recipient as a country of concentration allows. Yet a key question associated with the multilateral aid effectiveness agenda is the degree to which the focus on harmonization among donor agencies and alignment between donor agencies and recipient governments will lead to greater marginalization of civil society organizations and NGOs and less sustained and effective collaborations between governmental and non-governmental actors. The evidence on this question from Ethiopia is ambiguous.[11] On the one hand, many of the tensions that frequently exist in the quasi-adversarial relationship between official and non-governmental development agencies in donor capitals seem to be attenuated in the field. Interpersonal relationships tend to be stronger and inter-institutional dynamics more cooperative. NGO representatives have appreciated CIDA officers' efforts to "make projects work" once they have been approved and are in motion. On the other hand,

the relationship between CIDA and NGOs/CBOs (community- based organizations) in Ethiopia has been considered by the NGO community to be unstable. Many organizations talked about CIDA funds going only to those organizations with proven track records, and many NGOs said that they did not think that it was worth seeking agency support for their efforts. The perceived low success rate, protracted and opaque approval process, and heavy burden of reporting mechanisms made CIDA funding unattractive to several organizations operating in Ethiopia. Other organizations commented on the lag between the time that money is committed and the receipt of funds. NGOs in Ethiopia noted that in some cases funds could take as long as forty-four months to be released. A time lag of one to two years between notice of funding and actual funding delivery is particularly difficult for organizations dealing with communities that are resource scarce and food insecure. Organizations also complained about lack of access to bilateral money, unlike other African countries where bilateral aid funds were more accessible. Some positive aspects of Canadian aid money were also noted, however, including Canada's relatively new (April 2008) policy decision to untie all food aid, followed by the September 2008 announcement that all aid would be untied by 2012–13.

In reflecting on Canada's involvement in Ethiopia, four organizations highlighted what they saw as the emphasis on investment over donor initiatives aimed at addressing the challenges of poor rural regions. Examples included the relative speed with which the Bombardier contract and Ethiopian Airlines landing rights agreement were negotiated versus the Benishangul Gumuz Project, a $20 million project involving a consortium of six NGOs plus CIDA, in collaboration with local, regional, and Ethiopian governments. One organization noted that planning for this project, focused on the priority theme of food security, was initiated in 2006 but that (when the field research for this paper was conducted in the early months of 2010) it had yet to start because of "CIDA's inefficiency." Incredibly, the project was finally launched five years after planning was initiated, in February 2011 (see the CANGO website).

Generally, the lack of consistent focus in Canadian development aid was noted. Some of the funds come in the form of multi-donor basket funds, while others are attached to the Ethiopian government's Productive Safety Nets program, a compromise initiative after the post-election violence of 2005, when donors backed away from the more unfettered General Budget Support but were not prepared to rupture their important aid relationship with the Ethiopian government.

Many of the organizations contacted in Ethiopia noted the limited Canadian presence there. Thus, while Canada now ranks among the top five bilateral donors in the country, its presence on the ground does not reflect this relative contribution. The lack of visibility was manifested in the small number of Canadians visiting projects and in the relatively few Canadians working "in country" in non-governmental organizations and at CIDA offices. This echoes the report of the C.D. Howe Institute, noted at the outset of this chapter, that was sharply critical of CIDA for basing 80 percent of its staff in Canada instead of in the field. Notwithstanding CIDA's *relatively* large field presence in Ethiopia compared with other Canadian aid missions, its presence stands in stark contrast to the large and impressive facilities and staffs of other major donors, including the United Kingdom and the United States.

Other organizational representatives noted the agency's slow response to humanitarian disasters. One NGO respondent noted that

> CIDA is one of the last to react *[laughs]* always, always. We have proposals for crisis, and I have multiple examples in Ethiopia. We had proposals for a crisis situation, you know, it was two months before approval, and by the time it was approved most of the other donors in Ethiopia had already released money, and projects were ongoing, and when ... we got the approval, when everybody had their team in the field already and everything was happening in terms of water, food, and security, and then we got [a] response from CIDA. That happened the last few times that there was a major crisis. The response was really, really late. I think that the most striking example of the opposite of that now is Haiti. I think the government has really reacted quite rapidly on this. I think there is a large constituency in Canada ... regarding Haiti, and that may be of influence in the country, but in the Horn of Africa certainly we have experienced a long delay for CIDA-approved humanitarian funding. (Interview by author, 2011)

Furthermore, the "new" focus on food security programs announced by then-minister Oda in 2009 was seen by some of the interviewees as a veiled reworking of older initiatives. As one informant noted, "Canada is providing similar programs wrapped up as Canada's 2009 food security strategy." Another noted that, "there's nothing especially new about Canada's commitments to food aid, agriculture, and research. Similar initiatives existed in the 1970s. More focus on women's involvement and local participation today, but the nature of development assistance remains the same: Canada's solutions to another country's problems." In a similar vein, a third informant asked, sarcastically, "if more of the same, can we expect it to work this time?"

NGOs with agricultural programs in Ethiopia have also been critical of the failure of CIDA to incorporate an emphasis on the challenges to food security brought about by climate change. Information is needed, first to gain a better understanding of how people are responding to climate change today, and then to help develop programs to support this process of adaptation in the future. Oxfam has summarized predictions regarding Ethiopia's food security challenges based upon evidence it has collected from climate scientists. One prediction supported by Oxfam's findings is that, "by 2034, the 50th anniversary of the 1984 Ethiopia famine, what are now droughts will become the norm, hitting the region three years out of every four" (Oxfam International 2009). Addressing climate shocks remains a core strategic imperative that must be addressed by donors and aid recipients alike. Yet a CIDA official candidly noted at a meeting in early 2010 that climate change and adaptation "fell off the [CIDA] radar" in the past ten years. This suggests the need for a far more sustained approach to this nexus of issues if long-term ethical and security challenges are to be adequately addressed.

A particularly sensitive issue is CIDA's continued focus on good governance in its programs – now apparently recast under the rubric of sustainable economic growth. Many organizations in Ethiopia considered CIDA to be an enabler of a repressive regime. As evidence, they noted CIDA's support of government-led industrialization of the urban core and the lack of effective domestic and international accountability in the aftermath of the 2010 election. The Ethiopian government has introduced new restrictions on Canadian and all other foreign NGOs, passing "chilling" legislation that outlawed human rights programming for any organization that receives less than 90 percent of its funding from Ethiopian sources. Yet CIDA and the Canadian government have done little to address these restrictions, underscoring their limited influence even in a country of concentration. Indeed, the findings from the case study of Ethiopia raise important questions about the experiences of other countries of concentration, the impacts of targeted programming in those countries, and the circumstances surrounding the commitments made to a select group of recipients. Additional research on other countries of concentration, as well as on those countries that have recently been dropped from the Canadian list of core partners, is needed and would bring comparative perspectives to the observations made concerning Canada's aid relationship to Ethiopia.

Conclusion

It would be inaccurate to suggest that Ethiopia's designation as a country of concentration has made no difference to Canadian aid policy and programming in this challenging but important African country. Budgets have been larger, time frames longer, and personnel in the field more plentiful as a result of this decision. Similarly, interaction with other donors and Canadian-linked NGOs has been more sustained and systematic.

On the whole, however, what is striking is how much the *potential* and *theoretical* impact of this privileged status has failed to materialize. As between CIDA and NGOs/CBOs in Ethiopia, for example, several ethical and practical problems stand in the way of promoting a strong and stable relationship with sustainable benefits for the security of Ethiopians. As NGO and CBO staff members in Ethiopia have highlighted, heavy reporting requirements, the low success rate of funding applications, long waits on funding decisions, slow responses to humanitarian disasters in the country, shifting priorities by the Canadian government, and the sense that Canada's interest in promoting development and security in Africa is waning all factor into perceptions "on the ground" concerning the unattractiveness of CIDA (now DFATD) funding. Other challenges noted by NGO and CBO staff members highlight the ethical issues in development assistance arising from a growing emphasis on investment over aid as well as previous challenges in the delivery of effective and responsive food security strategies. Among the problems identified with the Canadian government's past and present work in food security is the failure to mainstream environmental and gender issues. And, though some progress in CIDA's contributions to Ethiopia was noted by NGO/CBO staff, namely the untying of aid and increased knowledge of women's and girls' experiences with food insecurity, the challenges noted above overshadowed the gains.

Given the policy uncertainties, shifts, and centralized micro-management within which CIDA/DFATD personnel and their "in-country" non-governmental "partners" operate, they simply have been unable to engage in the systematic, sustained, and contextualized policy thinking and programming that a more focused aid program is supposed to facilitate. That this situation has been allowed to persist for so long strongly indicates the Canadian government's bedrock indifference to the field-level ramifications of its approach to "aid effectiveness" and the degree to which its own exercise in concentration is aimed principally at domestic Canadian audiences versus the putative beneficiaries of Canadian aid interventions in the context of a broadly based commitment to human security and rights. In short, being designated a country of concentration has mattered far less than it should. Insofar as aid has served as a principal manifestation of ethical objectives in Canadian external relations, and as a critical means of addressing insecurity (in this case specifically with regard to food), the findings of this chapter are sobering in relation to the central themes of this book.

In particular, despite Canada's commitments to international aid reform and development as reflected in its ongoing support for the Paris Declaration and the Millennium Development Goals, alongside its commitment to be consistently among the top five donor countries in Ethiopia, evidence of "cosmopolitan ethics" (Pratt 2001) in Canadian foreign aid policy and practice seems to be more remote than ever. As Cranford Pratt argued in 2001, ethical values have not had a sustained impact as determinants of Canadian aid policies and, despite the rising aid budgets of the 2000s (now succeeded by renewed cuts), continue to have a declining effect on Canadian development assistance priorities. Ethiopia is a case study of the decline of humane internationalism in Canadian foreign policy more generally (Black 2013a). If ethics, as Rosalind Irwin argued in 2001, are about "interpretation, choice and actions," then we might expect Canadians to demand that Canadian foreign policy and aid "meet both ethical standards and the challenges of new security issues" (274). The Canadian government's actions are not only scrutinized and experienced by Canadians, however. As we have demonstrated, the ethical ramifications of aid commitments are also evaluated in recipient countries such as Ethiopia, where Canada is measured against international and comparative ethical standards in the promotion of security and development. The obsession of the Canadian government with measurable "results for Canadian taxpayers" and "focus within focus," and its relative indifference to the developmental ramifications of these preoccupations for poor and food-insecure Ethiopians, reflect the degree to which ethical and human rights considerations have been marginalized in the policy process for this country of concentration.

NOTES

1 In the March 2013 federal budget, it was announced that CIDA would be merged with the Department of Foreign Affairs and International Trade to constitute an integrated Department of Foreign Affairs, Trade and Development (DFATD). At the time of writing, it is too soon to evaluate what impact this merger will have on long-established bilateral aid programs such as that in Ethiopia, though Ethiopia remains a major country of concentration. In this chapter, much of the analysis continues to focus on CIDA policies and sources.

2   For an excellent discussion of the aid effectiveness agenda and its incorporation into Canadian aid policy making, see Lalonde (2009).

3   This is in addition to, and theoretically complementary with, the characteristic Paris Declaration aid effectiveness "bundle" of harmonization (with other donors), alignment (with recipient priorities), and ownership (in principle by the recipient, but upon the basis of mutually agreed priorities).

4   The new list of priorities was Ethiopia, Ghana, Mali, Mozambique, Tanzania, Senegal, Sudan, Bolivia, the Caribbean region, Colombia, Haiti, Honduras, Peru, Afghanistan, Bangladesh, Indonesia, Pakistan, Vietnam, the West Bank/Gaza, and Ukraine.

5   On the Millennium Development Goals, see UNDP (2011).

6   Furtado and Smith (2009, 132) note, for example, that in 2004–05 Ethiopia received US$15 per capita in development assistance, compared with US$49 per capita for sub-Saharan Africa as a whole.

7   In Ethiopia, for example, as of early 2011, there were eight full-time CIDA officers "in country," including the program director, along with a support unit of ten locally engaged personnel attached to the Ethiopia Canada Cooperation Office (ECCO).

8   In February 2010, David Black conducted interviews with officials in CIDA and other bilateral aid agencies. He and Rebecca Tiessen also conducted interviews with representatives of non-governmental organizations and "think tanks" based in Ethiopia. Much of the analysis in this section is based upon information drawn from this research. The Ethiopia Country Program Evaluation (2010) also arrived at a positive assessment of CIDA officers' role among their donor peers.

9   Moreover, both are exceptionally spare (eight and seven pages respectively) and lack clear guidance for implementation. See the CIDA website at http://www.acdi-cida. gc.ca/acdi-cida/acdi-cida.nsf/eng/NIC-53131840-NB8.

10 CIDA, like all Canadian government departments, was required to (temporarily) change the language of "gender equality" to "equality between women and men" in all letters, speeches, and multilateral interventions as of 2011. Mid-level bureaucrats at CIDA and scholars alike argued that this significant shift in language was limiting in terms of how development programs were implemented, and it reflected a fundamental move away from internationally recognized discourse (Carrier and Tiessen 2013).

11 Research was carried out in Ethiopia in 2009 and 2010 and involved key informant interviews and email interviews with representatives from Canadian and Ethiopian government agencies and non-governmental agencies.

References

Adenew, Berhanu. 2006. "Effective Aid for Small Farmers in Sub-Saharan Africa: Southern Civil Society Perspectives; Ethiopia Case Study." Canadian Food Security Policy Group, Ottawa. http://www.ccic.ca/_files/en/working_groups/003_food_2007-01_small_farmers_research_report_ethiopia.pdf.

Alemu, Getnet. 2009. "A Case Study on Aid Effectiveness in Ethiopia: Analysis of the Health Sector Aid Architecture." Working Paper, 9 April, Wolfensohn Centre for Development. http://www.brookings.edu/research/papers/2009/04/ethiopia-aid-alemu.

Belachew, Tefera, Craig Hadley, Abebe Gebremariam, Kifle Wolde Michael, Yehenew Getachew, Carl Lachat, and Patrick Kolsteren. 2010. "Gender

Differences in Food-Insecurity and Morbidity among Adolescents in Southwest Ethiopia." *Pediatrics* 127 (2): 398–405.

Black, David. 2009. "Out of Africa? The Harper Government's New 'Tilt' in the Developing World." *Canadian Foreign Policy Journal* 15 (2): 41–56. http://dx.doi. org/10.1080/11926422.2009.9673486.

Black, David. 2013a. "The Harper Government, Africa Policy, and the Relative Decline of Humane Internationalism." In *Canada in the World: Internationalism in Canadian Foreign Policy*, edited by Heather Smith and Claire Turenne-Sjolander, 217–38. Don Mills, ON: Oxford University Press.

Black, David. 2013b. "The Muskoka Initiative and the Politics of Fence-Mending with Africa." In *Canada among Nations 2013: Canada-Africa Relations: Looking Back, Looking Ahead*, edited by R. Medhora and T. Samy, 239–52. Waterloo, ON: Centre for International Governance Innovation.

Black, David, and Rebecca Tiessen. 2007. "The Canadian International Development Agency: New Policies, Old Problems." *Canadian Journal of International Development Studies* 18 (2): 191–213.

Borchgrevink, Axel. 2008. "Limits to Donor Influence: Ethiopia, Aid, and Conditionality." *Forum for Development Studies* 35 (2): 195–220.

Brown, Stephen. 2008. "CIDA under the Gun." In *Canada among Nations 2007: What Room for Manoeuvre?*, edited by Jean Daudelin and Daniel Schwanen, 172–207. Montreal/Kingston: McGill-Queen's University Press.

Carrier, Krystel, and Rebecca Tiessen. 2013. "Women and Children First: Maternal Health and the Silencing of Gender in Canadian Foreign Policy." In *Canada in the World: Internationalism in Canadian Foreign Policy*, edited by Heather Smith and Claire Turenne-Sjolander, 183–200. Don Mills, ON: Oxford University Press.

CIDA (Canadian International Development Agency). 2005. *Canada's International Policy Statement: A Role of Pride and Influence in the World*. Ottawa: Government of Canada.

CIDA (Canadian International Development Agency). 2010. "Ethiopia Country Program Evaluation 2003–4 to 2008–9: Synthesis Report." Evaluation Directorate, Strategic Policy and Performance Branch, January.

CIDA (Canadian International Development Agency). 2011a. "Canada Announces Project to Enhance Agricultural Development in Ethiopia." 28 January. http:// www.acdi-cida.gc.ca/acdi-cida/ACDI-CIDA.nsf/En/NAD-128112120-M7D? OpenDocument.

CIDA (Canadian International Development Agency). 2011b. "Ethiopia." http:// www.acdi-cida.gc.ca/acdi-cida/ACDI-CIDA.nsf/Eng/JUD-124141017-QH6.

den Heyer, Molly. 2012. "Untangling Canadian Aid Policy: International Agreements, CIDA Policies, and Micro-Policy Negotiations in Tanzania." In *Struggling for Effectiveness: CIDA and Canadian Foreign Aid*, edited by Stephen Brown, 186–217. Montreal/Kingston: McGill-Queen's University Press.

Development Initiatives. 2011. "Canada." Global Humanitarian Assistance Country Profiles. http://www.globalhumanitarianassistance.org/countryprofile/canada.

Devereux, Stephen. 2009. "Why Does Famine Persist in Africa?" *Food Security* 1 (1): 25–35. http://dx.doi.org/10.1007/s12571-008-0005-8.

DFATD (Department of Foreign Affairs, Trade and Development). 2014. "Canada Updates List of Development Countries of Focus." News Release, 27 June. http://

www.international.gc.ca/media/dev/news-communiques/2014/06/27abg.
aspx?lang=eng.

Furtado, X., and W.J. Smith. 2009. "Ethiopia: Retaining Sovereignty in Aid Relations."
In *The Politics of Aid: African Strategies for Dealing with Donors*, edited by
L. Whitfield, 131–56. Oxford: Oxford University Press.

Goldfarb, Danielle, and Stephen Tapp. 2006. "How Canada Can Improve Its Development Aid? Lessons from Other Aid Agencies." *C.D. Howe Commentary* 232:
1–30. www.cdhowe.org.

Government of Canada. 2009. *Canada-Ethiopia Relations.* www.canadainternational.
gc.ca.

Government of Canada. 2013. *Ethiopia – Thematic Focus.* http://www.acdi-cida.
gc.ca/acdi-cida/ACDI-CIDA.nsf/eng/JUD-124141017-QH6.

Irwin, Rosalind. 2001. "Introduction: Linking Ethics and Security in Canadian Foreign Policy." In *Ethics and Security in Canadian Foreign Policy*, edited by Rosalind
Irwin, 3–17. Vancouver: UBC Press.

Kehler, Al. 2004. "When Will Ethiopia Stop Asking for Food Aid?" *Humanitarian
Exchange Magazine*, 27 July. http://www.odihpn.org/index.php?option=com_k2&
view=item&layout=item&id=2636.

Kumar, Neha, and Agnes R. Quisumbing. 2010. *Policy Reform towards Gender
Equality in Ethiopia: Little by Little the Egg Begins to Walk.* International Food
Policy Research Institute. http://www.ifpri.org/sites/default/files/publications/
ifpridp01226.pdf.

Lalonde, Jennifer. 2009. "Harmony and Discord: International Aid Harmonization
and Donor State Domestic Influence: The Case of Canada and the Canadian International Development Agency." PhD diss., Johns Hopkins University.

Munro, Lauchlan T. 2005. "Focus-Pocus? Thinking Critically about Whether
Aid Organizations Should Do Fewer Things in Fewer Countries." *Development
and Change* 36 (3): 425–47. http://dx.doi.org/10.1111/j.0012-155X.2005.
00418.x.

Morrison, David. 1998. *Aid and Ebb Tide: A History of CIDA and Canadian Development Assistance.* Waterloo, ON: Wilfrid Laurier University Press.

Oda, Beverley. 2009. "A New Effective Approach to Canadian Aid." Speaking notes
for the Honourable Beverley J. Oda, Minister of International Cooperation, at the
Munk Centre for International Studies, 20 May.

Organization for Economic Cooperation and Development (OECD). 2010. *Development Cooperation Report 2010.* OECD Development Assistance Committee.

Organization for Economic Cooperation and Development (OECD). 2012a. "Total
Flows by Donor (ODA+OOF+Private) [DAC1] – Canada." http://stats.oecd.org/
Index.aspx?QueryId=42230&lang=en#.

Organization for Economic Cooperation and Development (OECD). 2012b. "Aid
(ODA) Disbursements to Countries and Regions [DAC2s] – Canada." http://stats.
oecd.org/Index.aspx?QueryId=42233&lang=en

Organization for Economic Cooperation and Development (OECD). 2014.
"Statistics on Resource Flows to Developing Countries," Table 29, "Net Disbursements to Sub-Saharan Africa by Donor." OECD. http://www.oecd.org/dac/stats/
statisticsonresourceflowstodevelopingcountries.htm

Oxfam International. 2009. "Band Aids and Beyond: Tackling Disasters in Ethiopia
25 Years after the Famine." Oxfam Briefing Paper, 20 October.

People's Daily Online. 2010. "China Views Ethiopia as Major Economic, Trading Partner in Africa: Minister." *People's Daily Online,* 12 January. http://english. peopledaily.com.cn/90001/90776/90883/6865704.html.

Pratt, Cranford. 1989. "Humane Internationalism: Its Significance and Variants." In *Internationalism under Strain: The North-South Policies of Canada, the Netherlands, Norway, and Sweden,* edited by Cranford Pratt, 3–23. Toronto: University of Toronto Press.

Pratt, Cranford. 2001. "Moral Vision and Foreign Policy: The Case of Canadian Development Assistance." In *Ethics and Security in Canadian Foreign Policy,* edited by Rosalind Irwin, 59–77. Vancouver: UBC Press.

Samy, Yiagadeesen. 2010. "China's Aid Policies in Africa: Opportunities and Challenges." *Round Table: The Commonwealth Journal of International Affairs* 99 (406): 75–90.

Senate of Canada. Standing Committee on Foreign Affairs and International Trade. 2007. *Overcoming Forty Years of Failure: A New Road Map for Sub-Saharan Africa.* February.

Seymour, Lee. 2010. "The Greater Horn of Africa." In *The International Politics of Mass Atrocities: The Case of Darfur,* edited by D. Black and P. Williams, 49–69. New York: Routledge.

Stairs, Denis. 2005. *Confusing the Innocent with Numbers and Categories: The International Policy Statement and the Concentration of Development Assistance.* Calgary: Canadian Defence and Foreign Affairs Institute. http://www.cdfai.org/PDF/Confusing%20the%20Innocent.pdf.

Tamene, Binyam. 2010. "Canadian Council on Africa Sees Ethiopia's Potential." *Capital Magazine,* March. http://nazret.com/blog/index.php/2010/03/09/canadian_council_on_africa_sees_ethiopia.

United Nations Development Program (UNDP). 2010. *Human Development Index (HDI) – 2010 Rankings.* Human Development Reports, United Nations. http://geocommons.com/overlays/90284.

United Nations Development Program (UNDP). 2011. *Basic Facts about the Millennium Development Goals.* UNDP. http://www.undp.org/mdg/basics.shtml.

Vercillo, Siera. 2010. "The Ineffectiveness of CIDA's Ability to Impact Gender Equality." *Political Economy of Development,* July. Wordpress Blog. http://sieravercillo.wordpress.com/2010/07/09/the-ineffectiveness-of-cida%E2%80%99s-ability-to-impact-gender-equality.

York, Geoffrey. 2010. "Ethiopia 'Politicizing' Foreign Aid." *Globe and Mail,* 20 October.

7

Losing Gender Equality along the Way
The Failure to Mainstream Gender in Canada's Commitments to International Security and Development

REBECCA TIESSEN AND SARAH TUCKEY

Gender equality is an important lens through which to examine commitments to international ethics and security in Canadian foreign policy. A focus on gender equality involves more than understanding and addressing inequality between men and women: it focuses on masculinities and femininities and how gendered values and norms are shaped and sustained within institutions, organizations, cultures, and practices. Gender mainstreaming offers a potential strategy for ensuring that gender equality is addressed in all aspects of society, including the integration of gender equality into ethically grounded Canadian foreign policy efforts. In this chapter, we summarize the feminist contributions to security and development and the scholarly contributions that have paved the way for a transformative gender mainstreaming approach. We also highlight some of the challenges of gender mainstreaming when it is reduced to technical fixes and the instrumentalization of women for foreign policy purposes. The war in Afghanistan, for example, used women as instruments of foreign policy to create a buy-in within Canada for the continued war efforts in the region. As such, Canadian foreign policy makers and implementers have appropriated the category of women in an instrumental way and manipulated the discourse of gender mainstreaming – or the integration of gender into security objectives – to pursue and exploit broader strategic security goals. We draw many of our examples of the challenges of gender mainstreaming in security and development from experiences and evaluations of the Canadian International Development Agency

(CIDA), which merged, as of 2013, with the Department of Foreign Affairs and International Trade (DFAIT) to form the new Department for Foreign Affairs, Trade and Development (DFATD). (We refer to CIDA in the past tense in this chapter. Any references to CIDA refer to the analyses and evaluations carried out prior to the merger.) We conclude that there is potential for transformative gender mainstreaming that more fully integrates gender equality into international security programs, despite the weaknesses identified in practice to date. This chapter thus argues for a renewed commitment to gender equality within DFATD: one that puts transformational gender mainstreaming at the heart of its security and development programming.

Gender Mainstreaming

Gender mainstreaming involves the transformation of mainstream approaches to security and development, including organizations, policies, and practices, to incorporate a crosscutting gender perspective. The United Nations Economic and Social Council (ECOSOC 1997, 4) defines gender mainstreaming as "a strategy for making women's as well as men's concerns and experiences an integral dimension of the design, implementation, monitoring and evaluation of the policies and programmes in all political, economic and societal spheres so that women and men benefit equally and inequality is not perpetuated." Gender mainstreaming is a strategy arising out of the 1995 *Platform for Action* of the Fourth World Conference on Women in Beijing and builds upon the two major theoretical and practical approaches known as the women in development (WID) and gender and development (GAD) paradigms (Jaquette and Staudt 2006). Several important feminist contributions have therefore set the stage for gender mainstreaming approaches to security and development. The GAD approach, in particular, which emerged in the late 1980s, focused on transformational agenda setting and put women and development in the context of gendered power relations (ibid.). Recent efforts to mainstream gender into development programs require a consideration of men's and women's needs as well as their access to rights and powers so that men and women can benefit equally from development initiatives. To do so, we require a sound understanding of the nature of gender inequality and how it affects men and women. Gender mainstreaming and GAD emerged with the overarching goal of empowering both women and men and focused on questioning and, ultimately, transforming the inherent gender imbalances found within all facets of security and development concerns. The gender-focused approach to development calls for changing social gender relations and questioning the dominant development paradigms of the day (Mukhopadhyay, Steehouwer, and Wong 2006, 11) by addressing the ways in which gender is socially constructed and changes across places, cultures, and time (Karl 1995, 102). It is through this multifaceted focus that GAD takes on issues of power and inequality.

Jaquette and Staudt (2006, 18) highlight the theoretical beginnings of gender mainstreaming in how "GAD responded to the rise of postcolonial feminism and the impressive growth of Third World women's movements in the 1980s." Similarly, Rao and Kelleher (2005, 59) state that "gender mainstreaming is grounded in feminist theoretical frameworks, and its appeal to 'femocrats' and to gender activists [is] its promise of transformation." It has been a topic of much debate in development discourse since the Fourth World United Nations Conference on Women took place in Beijing in 1995, in which the document entitled *The Beijing Platform for Action* was created specifically to address and support the goal of mainstreaming gender equality (Mukhopadhyay 2003; Tiessen 2007). This platform "recognizes that governments enact legislation for the purpose of promoting equality between women and men" and "urges that gender analysis first be carried out and the effects of all programs and projects be examined for their potential impact on [them]" (Tiessen 2007, 13). Within the platform, "gender mainstreaming ... was identified as the most important mechanism to reach this ambitious goal" (Moser and Moser 2005, 11). A gender mainstreaming approach – through its promise of gender transformation (Parpart 2013) – has become part of the core lexicon in development and security studies. A transformative gender mainstreaming approach goes beyond the targeting of women as victims of poverty and insecurity to include them as active members in their communities as empowered individuals and as a method of changing institutions, programs, and policies. Gender mainstreaming can also be adopted to identify gendered institutions as well as the causes of gender inequality and barriers to women's active participation in societies (a rights-based approach to gender equality and security) in which rights and equality of opportunity are central.

Feminist contributions to international relations and security studies have played an important role in defining gender mainstreaming strategies. Feminist international relations scholars and critical security scholars have articulated the importance of integrating gender into security studies, and these feminist insights have shaped how we think about war, conflict, development, and gender. Ann Tickner and Laura Sjoberg (2011) provide a comprehensive analysis of the broad range of feminist thinking on security studies that has shaped international policy and practice, including gender mainstreaming. Canadian foreign policy scholars have also highlighted the significance of gender in Canada's international efforts (see Carrier and Tiessen 2012; Turenne Sjolander, Smith, and Steinstra 2003). The broad scope of feminist insights has shaped gender mainstreaming approaches while also challenging gender mainstreaming's shortcomings in an effort to keep the integration of gender equality central to security and development efforts. If or when it is conducted effectively, gender mainstreaming offers great potential as a tool for the realization of gender equality.

However, operationalizing gender mainstreaming and putting feminist thinking into practice comes with its own set of challenges. For example, gender mainstreaming continues to have limited success on a grand scale, for "most efforts are considered inconsistent," and many "policy commitments to gender mainstreaming frequently evaporate in planning and implementation processes" (Moser and Moser 2005, 15; see also Parpart 2013; Tiessen 2007). Indeed, one of the biggest obstacles facing gender mainstreaming is a reliance on technical solutions, creating an illusion that development agencies are taking gender equality seriously (Tiessen 2007). Furthermore, gender mainstreaming is critiqued for its "uncritical, technocratic discourses" (Parpart 2013, 2). In the section that follows, we examine some of the challenges of gender mainstreaming in Canada's commitments to security and development.

Canada's Experience with Gender Mainstreaming

According to the Department of Foreign Affairs, Trade and Development, the government of Canada is committed to gender mainstreaming through the adoption of the Federal Plan for Gender Equality enacted in 1995. At the heart of this plan arising from *The Beijing Platform for Action* is a commitment to "implement gender-based analysis throughout federal departments and agencies" (DFATD 2013). In addition, Canada has committed to integrating gender in contexts of insecurity and development. Along with many international commitments, Canada has signed UN Resolution 1325 and prepared a *National Action Plan on Women, Peace, and Security.* Although Canada was slow to introduce its National Action Plan relative to many other donor countries, the plan demonstrates a commitment to address inequality between men and women in conflict and peacebuilding efforts. Yet, as we argue in this chapter, these policy commitments have been usurped by a larger strategy involving the instrumentalization of women for security goals.

The instrumentalization of gender and development programming for security-related purposes can be witnessed in government commitments to address development-related challenges in fragile countries and conflict-affected communities (Blackwell 2012; Brown 2008; CIDA 2012b) and in superficial – yet highly strategic – attempts to address gender equality in the Canadian mission in Afghanistan, which has been justified partly as Canada's "crucial responsibility" to ensure "that the advances made by Afghan women over the last nine years are not lost" (Oda 2010). Canada promoted programs for women's equality in Afghanistan, including a commitment to human rights, girls' education, maternal health, and women's political participation. These programs were framed, however, in the context of liberating women as a core mission of the war in Afghanistan, first extolled by the United States in 2001 (Ferguson 2005). Scholarly writing on gender, security, and Canada's foreign aid contributions points to the instrumentalization of gender in the former CIDA's shift to security and development initiatives (Swiss 2010, 2012). For example, gender equality is being increasingly portrayed by the Canadian government as "'something' that is done by everything in the Canadian aid program," while security receives attention as a specific, targeted objective with reserved pools of funding, leaving gender to be merely a call to action rather than a visible, funded target itself (Swiss 2012, 152). In so doing, programs coded as gender focused treat women as objects and targets of Canadian foreign aid and security initiatives and fail to examine the underlying gendered institutions, norms, and practices that perpetuate gender inequality.

The marked lack of commitment to addressing gender equality in Canadian foreign policy highlights the ethical dilemma that Canada faces as it vies for international prominence among donor nations. Canada's commitment to gender equality is also linked to broader ethical challenges when viewed in the context of humane internationalism. First defined and expanded by Cranford Pratt (1989, 1990), humane internationalism is a framework that holds at its core "an acceptance of the principle that citizens of the industrial nations have moral obligations towards peoples and events beyond their borders; it implies a sensitivity to cosmopolitan values, such as the obligation to refrain from the use of force in the pursuit of national interests and the respect for human rights" (Stokke 1989, 10–11). However, as Black and Tiessen (this volume) argue, Canada's foreign policy approach to humane internationalism is waning, as are core values previously understood as distinctly Canadian values. Thus, Canadian foreign policy currently "has no discernible humane internationalist tradition in the terms elucidated by

Pratt" (Black 2013, 227). Evidence of the erosion of humane internationalism can also be found in the current Canadian government's weak (and
waning) commitment to gender equality. With the recent and pronounced
shift in Canadian foreign aid priorities from broader, humane internationalist development goals to a more narrow security focus that targets women
as instruments of foreign policy, and with the language of gender equality disappearing from official government communication, a commitment
to gender equality, we argue, has been lost along the way. Major critiques
from gender scholars and civil society organizations highlight that Canada's
efforts in gender mainstreaming, particularly in relation to security-related
development work, are empty, superficial, non-transformational, and even
erased or silenced in Canadian foreign policy (Brodie and Bakker 2008; Carrier and Tiessen 2012). Failure to incorporate a gender lens in Canadian foreign policy work begins with the removal of the language of gender: the shift
in language from gender equality to "equality between men and women" in
Canadian government documents, ministers' speeches, and official government materials (ibid.). This change in discourse away from gender equality
is problematic given Canada's recent programming focus on state fragility
and conflict, an arena increasingly recognized as deeply gendered. Indeed,
recent research suggests that ignoring gender can erode efforts to address
state fragility (Baranyi and Powell 2005). In addition, with the recent securitization of Canadian aid initiatives, civil society reviews have highlighted
that Canada remains unable to rework effectively the highly masculinist
and patriarchal status quo of the current security-oriented development
process.

Evidence of the instrumentalization of gender was found during a review
of CIDA's programs: there was a noticeable retreat within the organization
from gender equality work (Plewes and Kerr 2010). With an increased focus
on service delivery as well as former CIDA staff recommending to NGOs
that they remove the words *gender equality* from their proposals if they
wanted a chance to receive funding (Caplan 2010; Carrier and Tiessen 2012;
Plewes and Kerr 2010), CIDA was contributing to a shift away from fully
mainstreamed and transformational gender equality work. Within CIDA's
key sectors, for example, financial and human resource "investments in the
education and health sectors were deemed more likely to be GE [gender
equality]-designated than investments in other sectors," effectively preventing other key sectors from receiving a gender equality focus (WGWR 2009,
8). What is more, CIDA focused on "development results related to gender
equality rather than on processes, inputs and efforts" (Bazinet, Sequeira, and

Delahanty 2006, 105), a trend highlighted in CIDA's own review of its gender policy and frameworks (Bytown Consulting and C.A.C. International 2008, 9–10). Yet gender equality efforts experienced some of the biggest challenges through the increased securitization of CIDA-funded aid and the ethical obstacles attached to the highly masculine culture of security initiatives overall. While conflict and security remain major obstacles to gender equality, gender mainstreaming provides a definitively transformational opportunity for the government of Canada to fulfill its ethical obligations set forth in the Policy on Gender Equality created by CIDA (2010a). In this policy, CIDA (2010b, 2) outlined the growing ethical importance of recognizing that attention to gender equality is essential in fragile states. Indeed, with the release of an operational framework for CIDA's efforts with gender equality and peacebuilding (Woroniuk 1999), and its focus on effectively implementing gender equality initiatives in fragile states (CIDA 2012b), the organization made peace and security initiatives a major priority from the mid-1990s. Yet with this focus there was a marked marginalization of gender equality initiatives and limited efforts to mainstream gender into current security and development projects (Swiss 2010, 2012). According to Baranyi and Powell (2005), CIDA became fully committed in 2005 to contributing to whole-of-government responses in fragile states, nations that fit into CIDA's broad theme of supporting women and girls in the realization of their full human rights, as they are unwilling or unable to guarantee the provision of basic human security, health care, education, and livelihood to most of their citizens. However, within the emerging policy frameworks for this commitment, there was little consideration by CIDA of the gender dimensions found within fragile states or recognition of the constraints and opportunities for promoting gender equality within such highly unequal gendered nations (ibid.).

It is well documented within civil society and academic writing that "women and men are affected differently by various aspects of state fragility, including armed conflict and efforts to resolve it, large-scale human rights abuses, and political, economic and social marginalization" (Baranyi and Powell 2005, 6). This understanding is entrenched in the concept of militarism, defined by its overvaluing of military virtues, its glorification of war, its transference of military norms into civilian life, and its giving of inordinate powers or rewards to soldiers, which tends to entrench traditional masculine/patriarchal notions of authority and power (Gender and Peacebuilding Working Group 2007). Patriarchy is considered by many transformative feminist theorists to be "a principal cause both of the outbreak of violent societal conflicts and of the international community's frequent failures in providing long-term resolutions to those violent conflicts" (Enloe 2005, 281). In the case of the former CIDA and its efforts to mainstream gender equality initiatives alongside UN Security Council Resolution 1325 in Afghanistan, the Gender and Peacebuilding Working Group (2004a, 19) noted that "women's progress is tempered by deeply ingrained patriarchal values and traditions. Women restrict their participation in public life to avoid being targets of violence by armed factions and elements seeking to enforce the repressive edicts of the previous regime." Moreover, the GPWG (2007, 6) notes, "it has been demonstrated that women tend to be involved late in peace processes, only as observers or without sufficient preparation to articulate their needs and priorities." Women's absence from the masculinist nature of peace and security development processes represents one of the major reasons why CIDA was consistently unable to transform the mainstream of securitized development work. Such acts of omission entrench militarization and masculinization of peace and security development work.

As CIDA worked to frame its primary role as supporting the long-term Canadian national interest, integrating it more closely with the broader foreign policy process in Ottawa and increasing its credibility within other government departments (Black and Tiessen 2007), the co-optation of gender equality issues into this transition became more apparent. Indeed, Enloe (1991) notes that the gradual process of putting military needs in society above other needs requires the cooperation of a broad constituency, including women. The level of difficulty that CIDA faced in effectively mainstreaming its gender equality initiatives into this current development trajectory is elaborated by Parpart (2009, 61): "In many situations, particularly within conflict and post-conflict zones, and societies with widespread criminal activities, gender violence and deeply masculinist practices, the choice to publicly challenge male power is often extremely dangerous and even foolhardy." Thus, CIDA faced the added difficulty of working to mainstream a gender equality component into peace and security climates that have not only deeply entrenched patriarchal stances but also female populations who might inadvertently support and legitimize the masculinist status quo because they cannot or do not challenge it. This was exemplified in the lack of effective and transformative gender equality work conducted by CIDA. As noted by Baranyi and Powell (2005, 7), a North-South Institute critique of development donors, including CIDA, revealed that "major donors fail to systematically incorporate gender equality considerations into their emerging strategies on fragile states, despite having developed impressive gender equality processes and frameworks in other domains." Baranyi and Powell (2005, 8) go on to suggest that these weaknesses are potentially a result of the "good enough governance" or "realistic priorities" approach to engagement in fragile states advocated by the British Department for International Development and some UN agencies. In so doing, "this approach prioritizes building a state's capacity to deliver on basic obligations while avoiding socially and politically contentious issues that might compromise stabilization efforts" (ibid., 58). Because it is easier to revert to the "woman as victim" or "woman as mother" model of gender relations (ibid., 8), organizations such as the former CIDA effectively ignored women's legitimization of masculinist and patriarchal cultures within the development status quo and continued to carry out development work modelled on the national interest.

Civil society critiques of CIDA's focus on Canadian national interests in the securitization of development initiatives also demonstrated that CIDA often left many civil society partners confused and in the dark about the Canadian government's gender policy objectives, the use of peacebuilding frameworks and processes, and the reporting of gender equality outcomes. This was a significant barrier to the effective mainstreaming of gender equality initiatives.

Overall, CIDA's gender equality policy and action plan, gender and peacebuilding framework, programs, and practices remained largely non-transformational because of the propensity of the organization to fall back into WID terminology and easily integrated neoliberal goals that ultimately undermined the sustainability of its gender equality efforts. On its website, CIDA (2012a) equated the "equality of women and men" with "gender equality," a discursive blending that does not recognize the innate social, cultural, and structural inequalities that people of different gender, social status, age, and ability face on a daily basis. Moreover, when CIDA did highlight the special importance of gender equality within fragile states, it focused on the *integration* rather than the mainstreaming of gender equality into three thematic priorities: "increasing food security, securing the future of children and youth, and stimulating sustainable economic growth" (2010b, 1–2). As such, CIDA's gender action plan was a process of compartmentalized integration rather than widespread mainstreaming, emphasized explicitly in the policy as well. CIDA's practical solutions to these priorities included improving women's access to entrepreneurial training, financing, and small-holder farming; educating women on maternal, newborn, and child health;

and increasing education for both girls and boys to prepare them to be contributing members of their societies (ibid., 2). The solutions did not include the education of men on these issues, nor did they work to address the inherent gendered obstacles that women and girls face in attaining access to financial autonomy and education. These integrationist goals and initiatives effectively reinforced the fact that gender equality strategies repeat past mistakes and rely heavily on the WID logic of "add women and stir." Thus, as CIDA continued to integrate women into its gender equality initiatives rather than work toward ways to transform current development practices, it hindered its efforts to mainstream gender across the organization.

The failure to mainstream gender is noted several times in the former CIDA's commissioned review of its efforts to implement its gender policy, stating specifically that "too often in the case of investments that are not specifically focused on gender equality, actions to promote gender equality appear to be an 'add-on' to the design and planning that is not carried through, or not fully integrated into implementation" (Bytown Consulting and C.A.C. International 2008, 9). Moreover, the assessment highlighted that "many CIDA partners and even CIDA managers in the field still apply the 'practical needs and strategic interest' approach to gender equality and are not well aware of the 'three pillars' approach on access to rights, decision-making and development resources" for both women and marginalized men (Bytown Consulting and C.A.C International 2008, 9). Within the framework on gender equality and peacebuilding initiatives, CIDA articulated that, in many of its peace- and security-focused programs, attention was paid to increasing women's participation in project activities rather than considering the overall impact on gender inequalities and how to transform them (Woroniuk 1999, 5). Finally, in the civil society response by the GPWG regarding Canada's official report on its implementation efforts for UN Security Council Resolution 1325, it is apparent that "the report does not provide a strong sense that Canada's commitment to resolution 1325 has influenced the government's policy on peace and security issues, but rather gives the impression that consideration of these issues continues to be carried out in an ad hoc fashion, separate from any institution-wide strategy and weakly linked into broader institutional mandates" (GPWG 2004b, 3). These approaches are additive, integrationist, and above all easier to implement than projects and programs that attempt to transform the complicated security-oriented development climate. As such, these quick-fix solutions mean that organizations can develop simplistic and superficial solutions to complex problems through short-term deadlines and surface-level progress reports. Indeed, "NGOs have charged that CIDA's focus ... [was] on measuring progress and outputs, and meeting predetermined goals, rather than the development transformation that might entail increased participation of marginalized people and/or empowerment of these groups" (Black and Tiessen 2007, 206). For CIDA, the choice to implement these technical, short-term, superficial approaches resulted in the organization rarely addressing the political and attitudinal changes necessary for altering the status quo, an ethical obligation that Canada asserted to the international community that it would undertake.

Evidence of some of the potentially superficial programs can be found in the Gender Peacebuilding Working Group's review of Canada's gender-training initiatives within peace and security operations. The GPWG (2004, 5) argued that "there is a risk that [their] development allows Canada to feel that gender training is now taken care of, instead of viewing the training as a first step towards achieving meaningful changes in attitudes, practices and processes as they relate to gender and peacekeeping." These training initiatives appeared to harness the transformational GAD paradigm for gender equality, yet they were viewed by CIDA as solutions in and of themselves, leaving efforts at gender mainstreaming empty, superficial, and ineffectual. CIDA was not alone in this critique. At the practical level of application, critics have widely noted that "most development institutions have still to be constantly reminded of the need for gender analysis in their work" (Mukhopadhyay 2007, 135). Moreover, any institutional policy implemented under the GAD paradigm has yet to take a strong hold within development institutions themselves for a number of fundamental reasons. For instance, at the grassroots level, the tendency to fall back easily into an integrationist approach remains unaddressed. According to Karl (1995, 110), "women's participation in grassroots organizations is increasingly recognized as crucial to their empowerment and as a way for them to help shape development policies." Yet some feminist theorists find this reasoning problematic. Cornwall (2002, 207) notes that "no reason exists to assume that enabling women to have more of a voice in fora like development committees will necessarily make any contribution to transforming gender relations." This observation highlights a fundamental dilemma: when women are given the opportunity to raise their voices, they might articulate interests that affirm the culturally situated notions of ideal femaleness that outsiders often judge as oppressive. Moreover, Cornwall considers the possibility that women's voices might echo those that argue that women are incapable of making decisions and require male guidance to do so. Her assessment reinforces the importance of transformational thinking in gender mainstreaming to ensure that the superficial strategies employed to include and involve women translate into, and are accompanied by, much bigger and crosscutting solutions to address the sources of gender inequality.

In addition to being integrative and non-transformative, the former CIDA's gender equality initiatives were largely unsustainable in the long run, for a focus on their implementation often waned throughout the process from policy and program creation to implementation and completion. Moreover, by focusing on the initial stages of gender equality programming, CIDA failed to address adequately the deeply ingrained nature of gender inequality issues within its own work. This is perhaps the largest ethical dilemma that CIDA and Canada faced in trying to mainstream successfully a gender equality focus in their security-oriented development policies and programs. In its gender equality policy, CIDA (2010a, 7) described the use of gender analysis as a crosscutting tool throughout the organization as occurring in the early stages of implementation: "It is particularly useful in project design as it helps planners identify constraints and structure projects so that objectives can be met and measured." Kelleher and Stuart (2008, 11) noted in their study on the gender equality initiatives of the Canadian Council for International Cooperation (CCIC) members that CIDA's heightened interest in gender mainstreaming at the early stages of project and program implementation became a common complaint. Indeed, within CIDA's own analysis of its gender policy implementation efforts, it was highlighted that "gender equality is taken into account to some extent in the early stages of the project cycle ... but [that] attention to gender equality weakens throughout implementation" (Bytown Consulting and C.A.C. International 2008, 10). This "front-ending" of CIDA's interest in gender led some CCIC members to think that they could lessen their focus throughout the process as well, adding to the difficulty of effectively mainstreaming gender (Kelleher and Stuart 2008, 11). With respect to implementing gender equality initiatives in the application of peace and security development work, CIDA and Canada's response remained superficial. According to the GPWG (2004a, 4–5), gender training to deal with development issues in fragile states often amounts to no more than three days of unspecific cultural sensitivity and awareness training, often only on a case-by-case basis. These types of initiatives cannot hope to address the underlying gender inequality issues that remain so pervasive in cultures of conflict and post-conflict reconstruction. In the end, applying a management-style approach to gender equality initiatives, and focusing on performance, efficiency, and cost saving, might increase productivity and turnover of tangible gender equality programming but will not adequately address deeply ingrained gender issues or attend to the rights, interests, and needs of those receiving the aid (Hales 2007).

The Way Forward for a Transformative Gender Mainstreaming Strategy

Achieving transformative gender equality is challenging yet necessary to change the gendered institutions, practices, and policies that prevent the realization of equality between women and men of all genders and to address the ethical human rights commitments that Canada made to the international community. Civil society organizations and critics of the former CIDA have recommended a number of nuanced and critically assessed steps that consider the theoretical promise of the GAD approach at a practical, applicable level. Of these recommendations, four broad transformational themes stand out as ways to subvert the ethical dilemma that Canada faces. They are (1) calling for more transparency by the government of Canada to its stakeholders, partners, and the Canadian and international public; (2) suggesting more sustainable and practical solutions that allow DFATD to follow through on gender equality programming from planning to implementation; (3) addressing the issue that more men need to be involved in the process of gender equality implementation to allow for ownership of and support for the results across genders; and (4) addressing the need for stronger political backing from the Canadian government to highlight the importance of gender issues among the Canadian public and provide DFATD with a reliable source to whom it must be accountable.

Civil society documents called for increased transparency, clarity, and support for dialogue by CIDA and Canada in regard to how they approached and implemented gender equality initiatives, particularly in light of Canada's securitized foreign aid goals. Indeed, Mazurana et al. (2005, 22) noted that "new terminology and frameworks will assist us little unless we develop and refine the means to analyze the past and current states of disorder and how they are shaping the future." In regard to the peace and security climate of Canadian development aid, Baranyi and Powell (2005, 8) believed that the former international development wing of the Canadian government "could address the gender dimensions of state fragility more systematically. For instance the strategy could incorporate stronger language on the promotion of gender equality as a cross-cutting priority for CIDA and other government departments. It could also better link Canada's gender equality commitments through CEDAW [Convention on the Elimination of All Forms of Discrimination against Women] and UNCRC [UN Convention on the Rights of the Child] to broader international human rights commitments." Moreover, these documents highlighted the need for civil society organizations (CSOs) and NGOs to be equally as transparent and open to dialogue in the process of mainstreaming gender into the increasingly security-oriented development climate. The WGWR (2009, 9) noted that, "as development actors in their own right, CSOs must also recognize the need for accountability arising from their crucial, but diverse, roles in the development process as innovative agents of change and social transformation." The GPWG (2004a, 5) suggested that, in moving forward with gender training surrounding the Canadian implementation of UN Security Council Resolution 1325, "both government and civil society advocates of gender sensitive training need to define what it is that gender training can accomplish, what the skills are that peacekeepers should be equipped with, and what it is they will be able to do as a result of being made more gender aware." Through consistent, two-way dialogue, critical reflection on past and current peace and security development initiatives, and increased clarity and transparency within documents and frameworks outlining gender equality policies and processes, these civil society advocates believe that stronger mainstreaming of gender initiatives can occur within the newly formed DFATD.

Throughout their analyses, the CSOs and individual civil society representatives saw that CIDA's and Canada's focus on the mainstreaming of gender equality initiatives fizzled out and rarely reached definable conclusions or measurable results. Thus, many civil society members and groups recommended more practical, results-based solutions to the question of mainstreaming gender equality initiatives, citing their ability to be more understandable and therefore more sustainable in the long run. Bazinet, Sequeira, and Delahanty (2006, 106–7) believe that focusing on results will move DFATD closer to the true intention of mainstreaming originally envisioned at the Beijing conference. These critics believe that, by shifting its focus to results rather than processes, DFATD can prove gender mainstreaming to be more than an empty promise and contribute to real change (ibid., 107). Moreover, in the wake of Canada's new security-focused aid agenda, the GPWG (2004a, 10) notes that "providing clear and practical connections between day-to-day work and the content of the resolution would help people work towards effective implementation. It is helpful to support such a strategy with evidence that proves why it will make a difference if people support SCR 1325 as well as the ramifications of failing to take these issues into consideration." These suggestions reveal a belief among civil society representatives that practical solutions pull DFATD away from the theoretical ambiguities of the GAD approach and provide answers to the "how" of gender mainstreaming in development and not simply the "why."

Another common recommendation arising from civil society critiques was the suggestion that men be more critically and actively engaged in gender equality mainstreaming efforts, both within DFATD and among CSOs, NGOs, stakeholders, and recipients beyond the organization. It is imperative that organizations reassert the notion of gender as including both women and men in decision making and ownership of project creation and move past the superficial and patriarchal approach of "mainstreaming women." This recommendation comes with a heavy warning from the official evaluation of the former CIDA's implementation of its gender equality policy:

> Strategies to advance GE that do not address men's roles and responsibilities in gender relations neglect a critical factor in the sustainable reduction of gender inequalities. The potential for male resistance and "backlash" should be assessed as a risk factor, with appropriate mitigation strategies defined. The design and implementation of investments to "empower" [women] in economic, political or social spheres need to assure that men, too, are prepared to cope with changes in gender dynamics in the household, in the workplace, and in communities. (Bytown Consulting and C.A.C. International 2008, 19)

This recommendation is integral to ensuring that Canada's gender equality initiatives remain focused on effectively mainstreaming a gender perspective into the present securitized development atmosphere. Because the current development process involves a highly masculinized security agenda, the willing participation of men will ensure more consistent application of DFATD's gender policy, programs, and gender-sensitive peacebuilding efforts. Indeed, the GPWG (2004a, 10) encourages the education of boys and men regarding the implementation of UN Security Council Resolution 1325 within Canada's development process, recommending that "tools developed to support the implementation of SCR 1325 must seek to engage and educate boys and men about the importance of including women in peace processes as well as the role they themselves play in ensuring that the rights of women and girls affected by conflict are protected and upheld." By recommending the inclusion and consideration of men's gendered experiences in development, civil society provides a practical GAD perspective on how DFATD's gender equality initiatives can continue to uphold a gender mainstreaming focus.

Finally, several of the civil society critiques point to the importance of ensuring that strong political backing is present for gender equality issues, thus guaranteeing that DFATD is made accountable to an influential power for all its efforts to mainstream a gender equality perspective across its programming. As the official CIDA review of its gender equality implementation strategies elaborated, "commitment to greater gender equality on the part of the partner government – through appropriate national/sectoral policies, legislation and regulatory frameworks, and the administrative will to act, for example – is critical to redressing the systemic constraints and institutional inequalities that must change if sustained gains in gender equality are to be realized throughout the society" (Bytown Consulting and C.A.C. International 2008, 18). As well, according to the GPWG (2004a, 21), a lack of political will and broader awareness of gender issues overall is one of the primary obstacles to the effective mainstreaming of UN Security Council Resolution 1325 into the current development status quo. Thus, it is essential to develop a political commitment to gender mainstreaming, since a political discourse is better suited to raising awareness about what gender mainstreaming is meant to do. The political commitment needs to come from all levels, and "there needs to be more awareness of organizational politics and political strategy by gender equality advocates, and sharing of what works in what situations" (Kelleher and Stuart 2008, 2). Political dialogue and monitoring must come from both outside and within the organization, and a strategic focus on gender equality initiatives must be at the forefront of crosscutting political discussions. Moreover, some civil society reviews recommend bolstering political support for gender mainstreaming efforts within Canada and abroad through directives such as providing "support for women's participation in political processes and institutions of governance at all levels, through such initiatives as civic education programs, women's participation in party politics, capacity strengthening in policy development, and awareness raising on gender issues and capacity building programs involving female and male parliamentarians" (GPWG 2007, 8). The presence of appropriately gender-trained female political party members is thought by these civil society activists to add support to sympathetic political platforms, and increase the profile of gender equality initiatives with the public, allowing for greater mainstreaming to take place. This is the crux of Canada's ethical dilemma regarding mainstreaming gender within security-oriented development programs, policies, and practices. Moreover, "the argument that gender transformation should be left to politics ignores the daily struggles around gender, the everyday contestations over gendered assumptions and practices that are taking place in every corner of the world" (Parpart 2009, 63). To suggest that a greater political emphasis on gender mainstreaming – through a more politically open dialogue among government, DFATD, and civil society organizations – is the answer to transforming the masculinist development status quo remains ethically unjustifiable and ignores the fragile, complex, and multi-level nature of development organizations and the internal gendered politics with which they must deal daily (Parpart 2009).

Within the context of conflict and post-conflict situations, the GAD paradigm is still considered a valuable and relevant approach, for it is widely understood that "incorporating both genders and 'masculine' and 'feminine' characteristics into peace processes will at least make them more reflective of the societies with which they deal, thus allowing them a better chance to achieve a sustainable peace" (Hudson 2005, 793). The GAD approach has also revealed the importance of ensuring "that forms of insecurity experienced by men as a result of competing masculinities are also not lost from the analysis" (Barnes 2006, 17). Likewise, Jaquette and Staudt (2006) identify some arenas of power that must be taken into account in any revitalized effort to address women's practical and strategic interests. They suggest rethinking the current structures of bureaucracies, markets, states, civil societies, cultures, and families to account for the equality of women, since these elements are necessary for regaining momentum within the GAD approach. Although this suggestion sounds immensely difficult to implement, other scholars, advocates, and practitioners have called for a similar, grassroots attention to detail. Wendoh and Wallace (2005, 79) note that, "if a gender mainstreaming process is fully embedded within the communities, and takes time to start from there ... then it will be able to bring about change from within, rather than imposing it from outside." Moreover, if the GAD approach can introduce "new ideas and challenges in ways and at a pace that can stimulate and excite rather than threaten and demoralise" communities, then the approach will be all the more successful (ibid.). Of course, these solutions require considerable time frames and resources that Canada and DFATD have not conceptualized or tested in relation to the increasingly security-focused nature of development practice at all levels of policy and programming.

The question remains regarding where DFATD can go from here. Civil society organizations highlighted the real and troubling failures of gender mainstreaming to date and recommended a multitude of different directions for Canada's new security-oriented aid directives. In this chapter, we have highlighted other significant challenges of gender mainstreaming, including the instrumentalization of women for broader security purposes. Parpart (2009, 63) believes that a "developmental praxis that pays attention to feminist and masculinity studies' writings on masculinist power provides an entry point for understanding both the way power is gendered and the limits and possibilities for gender transformation. Moving beyond established development literature ... holds open the possibility that gender transformation can be understood and encouraged." Yet, as this study demonstrates, gender mainstreaming and the theoretical underpinnings of GAD highlight an unfinished process – one that has neither failed nor succeeded in the promotion of gender equality.

Conclusion

Gender equality is central to ethics and security in Canadian foreign policy, and gender mainstreaming is a potentially viable strategy for ensuring that gender equality is integrated into ethically grounded Canadian foreign policy security initiatives. However, as we have argued in this chapter, Canada has failed to do gender mainstreaming well. Rather, Canada has treated women as instruments for the promotion of a broader security agenda. The attention paid to the protection of women in Afghanistan offers an example in which women's needs and interests are reduced to simple solutions involving charity rather than careful mainstreaming of gender issues to ensure that the root causes of gender inequality are addressed. As such, CIDA's efforts to promote gender equality prior to its merging with DFAIT into DFATD were largely superficial, and the securitization of development funds increasingly resulted in women becoming the instruments of foreign policy rationalization. In this chapter, we have provided evidence of this instrumentalization of women in Canadian foreign policy. We have also summarized the potential for a transformative gender mainstreaming approach, keeping in mind the challenges and weaknesses of token gender mainstreaming strategies. Although there are many important critiques that need to be addressed, gender mainstreaming, particularly a transformative gender mainstreaming approach, carries much potential for ensuring that gender equality is integrated into security programs.

The civil society recommendations noted in this chapter arise out of the transformational GAD theoretical paradigm, in which current development practices are questioned and re-evaluated through an all-encompassing gender perspective. Yet, in practice, the GAD approach adopted by the Canadian government has demonstrated its obsession with technical fixes, frameworks, and measurements for highly nuanced processes that are qualitative and extremely hard to measure and codify. The failures that we have observed in current gender mainstreaming efforts include attention to popular and shifting terminology at the expense of real change. The potential for GAD and gender mainstreaming to transform the status quo remains given that they are ongoing processes that require maintenance, care, and constant innovation from development practitioners as well as theorists.

For some, a partnership with civil society organizations does not allow for gender mainstreaming to flourish, since these groups remain invested in the current processes of development for their livelihood. Indeed, according to Parpart (2009, 60), while "collaboration with gender sensitive organizations and building alliances with institutions, programmes and persons committed to gender equality and women's empowerment are important forces for change, transforming gender relations requires attention to how systemic blockages to gender equality and women's empowerment operate and maintain their grip on power." Yet, by looking at how practical aid constrains as well as provides useful development tools, transformative feminist critical reflection can reveal how everything within the development system has complex relationships with everything else and that creating systems of change requires strong values, good strategy, and persistence (Kelleher and Stuart 2008, 20). Thus, civil society partnership through GAD, and the process of gender mainstreaming, still holds value and remains relevant within Canada's gender equality initiatives; with the right focus, it "can become a venue for opening up new ways of thinking and performing gender, particularly in this time of global economic crisis and reactionary politics" (Parpart 2009, 65). The GPWG (2004a, 6) has harnessed this broadening characteristic of gender mainstreaming in its recommendations to Canada for implementing UN Security Council Resolution 1325 in its peace and conflict development initiatives, stating that "the development of new trainings should invoke broadening the concept of gender inequality to include the intersection of gender with class, race, ethnicity, age, culture, and religion both during conflict and in the reconstruction stages."

Civil society critiques of CIDA's and Canada's gender equality initiatives demonstrate the integrative and non-transformational nature of Canada's gender-related efforts. Furthermore, the Canadian government's interpretation of the GAD paradigm consistently resembled a non-transformative gender approach, especially when the language shifted from "gender equality" to "equality between women and men" under the Harper Conservatives between 2009 and 2013. The absence of a sound gender mainstreaming approach within CIDA's programs was evident from this analysis, particularly in the face of Canada's securitized development aid goals. Yet, by looking at GAD and gender mainstreaming as a process of limitless potential that can break down patriarchal and restrictive organizational and social structures, and by continuing to consider critically the perspectives and recommendations of civil society, DFATD and Canada can move beyond the non-transformational technical fixes and short-term goals of current initiatives and "pull away gender's reassuring public mask of comfortable blandness and reveal it for what it should be: a conceptual tool to make us see things at work that we would rather not see" (Enloe 2001, 113). To address fully the security needs and concerns in conflict and post-conflict communities, a gender analysis and gender mainstreaming strategies are crucial. Gender mainstreaming in security can assist all stakeholders in ensuring that men's and women's needs are understood and addressed. More importantly, a gender mainstreaming strategy for security-oriented development projects will reveal the underlying social and cultural norms of femininity and masculinity and how they are appropriated by policies, organizations, and institutions in ways that create and reinforce gender inequality.

In our analysis, we have noted the absence of a gender mainstreaming strategy within the former CIDA as highlighted by several civil society organizations and an internal evaluation of the organization. CIDA's long-standing commitment to gender equality provided a starting point for embracing gender mainstreaming strategies. However, CIDA's reputation as a key proponent of gender equality began to fade as Canada's commitment to gender equality receded. Indeed, the shift in development programming toward security-oriented endeavours within CIDA pointed to a further marginalization of gender equality programming. Needed now is a renewed commitment to mainstreaming gender into program priorities within DFATD. A renewed commitment to gender mainstreaming in development projects, particularly those in fragile countries and conflict-affected communities, requires a government-wide linking of security and gender and an understanding of the relationship between gender and humane internationalism, ethics, and security.

References

Baranyi, Stephen, and Kristiana Powell. 2005. *Bringing Gender Back into Cana-da's Engagement in Fragile States: Options for CIDA in a Whole-of-Government Approach.* Ottawa: North-South Institute.

Barnes, Karen. 2006. "Reform or More of the Same? Gender Mainstreaming and the Changing Nature of UN Peace Operations." Working Paper 41, York Space, Toronto. http://yorkspace.library.yorku.ca/xmlui/handle/10315/1322.

Bazinet, Lucie, Tamara Sequeira, and Julie Delahanty. 2006. "Promoting Institutional Change: CIDA's Framework for Assessing Gender Equality Results." *Develop-ment* 49 (1): 104–07. http://dx.doi.org/10.1057/palgrave.development.1100234.

Black, David. 2013. "The Harper Government, Africa Policy, and the Relative Decline of Humane Internationalism." In *Canada in the World: Internationalism in Cana-dian Foreign Policy,* edited by Heather A. Smith and Claire Turenne Sjolander, 217–38. Don Mills, ON: Oxford University Press.

Black, David, and Rebecca Tiessen. 2007. "The Canadian International Development Agency: New Policies, Old Problems." *Canadian Journal of Development Studies* 28 (2): 191–212.

Blackwell, Tom. 2012. "Canada's $1.5B Afghanistan Aid Effort 'Divorced from Reality,' According to Damning, Previously Unreleased Documents." *National Post,* 12 October. http://news.nationalpost.com/2012/10/12/canadas-1-5b-afghani-stan-aid-effort-divorced-from-reality-according-to-damning-previously-unreleased-documents/.

Brodie, Janine, and Isabelle Bakker. 2008. *Where Are the Women? Gender Equal-ity, Budgets, and Canadian Public Policy.* Ottawa: Canadian Centre for Policy Alternatives.

Brown, Stephen. 2008. "CIDA under the Gun." In *Canada among Nations: What Room for Manoeuvre?,* edited by Jean Daudelin and Daniel Schwanen, 91–107. Montreal/Kingston: McGill-Queen's University Press.

Bytown Consulting and C.A.C. International. 2008. *Evaluation of CIDA's Imple-mentation of Its Policy on Gender Equality: Executive Report.* Gatineau, QC: CIDA.

Caplan, Gerald. 2010. "The Harper Government, Women's Rights, and the Cost of Speaking Out." *Globe and Mail,* 4 June. http://www.theglobeandmail.com/news/politics/the-harper-government-womens-rights-and-the-cost-of-speaking-out/article1592858.

Carrier, Krystel, and Rebecca Tiessen. 2012. "Women and Children First: Mater-nal Health and the Silencing of Gender in Canadian Foreign Policy." In *Canada in the World: Internationalism in Canadian Foreign Policy,* edited by Heather A. Smith and Claire Turenne Sjolander, 183–99. Oxford: Oxford University Press.

CIDA. 2010a. *CIDA's Policy on Gender Equality.* Hull, QC: CIDA.

CIDA. 2010b. *CIDA's Gender Equality Action Plan.* Hull, QC: CIDA.

CIDA. 2012a. "Equality between Women and Men." http://www.acdi-cida.gc.ca/acdi-cida/ACDI-CIDA.nsf/eng/JUD-31192610-JXF.

CIDA. 2012b. "Canada Reaffirms Support for Afghanistan." http://www.acdi-cida.gc.ca/acdi-cida/ACDI-CIDA.nsf/eng/HEL-76212459-3P7.

Cornwall, Andrea. 2002. "Locating Citizen Participation." *IDS Bulletin* 33 (2): i–x. http://dx.doi.org/10.1111/j.1759-5436.2002.tb00016.x.

DFATD. 2013. "Mainstreaming of a Gender Perspective." http://www.international. gc.ca/rights-droits/women-femmes/mainstream-integration.aspx.

ECOSOC (Economic and Social Council of the United Nations). 1997. *Mainstreaming the Gender Perspective into All Policies and Programmes in the United Nations System* (esp. Chapter 4). New York: United Nations.

Enloe, Cynthia. 1991. "Does Khaki Become You?" *New Internationalist* 221. http:// newint.org/features/1991/07/05/khaki/.

Enloe, Cynthia. 2001. "Closing Remarks." *International Peacekeeping* 8 (2): 111–13. http://dx.doi.org/10.1080/13533310108413899.

Enloe, Cynthia. 2005. "What If Patriarchy Is 'the Big Picture'? An Afterword." In *Gender, Conflict, and Peacekeeping*, edited by Dyan Mazurana, Angela Raven-Roberts, and Jane Parpart, 280–85. New York: Rowman and Littlefield.

Ferguson, Michaele L. 2005. "'W' Stands for Women: Feminism and Security Rhetoric in the Post-9/11 Bush Administration." *Politics and Gender* 1 (1): 9–38.

GPWG (Gender and Peacebuilding Working Group). 2004a. *A Civil Society Perspective on Canada's Implementation of United Nations Security Council Resolution 1325 (2000) on Women, Peace, and Security.* Ottawa: CPCC.

GPWG (Gender and Peacebuilding Working Group). 2004b. *A Canadian Civil Society Response to the Official Government of Canada Report on the Implementation of United Nations Security Council Resolution 1325 (2000) on Women, Peace, and Security.* Ottawa: CPCC.

GPWG (Gender and Peacebuilding Working Group). 2007. *NGO Priorities for Canada's Action Plan on Implementation of United Nations Security Council Resolution 1325 on Women, Peace, and Security (CAPI).* Ottawa: CPCC.

Hales, Jennifer. 2007. "Rhetoric and Reality: World Bank and CIDA Gender Policies." *Convergence* 40 (1–2): 147–69.

Hudson, Natalie Florea. 2005. "En-Gendering UN Peacekeeping Operations." *International Journal (Toronto, Ont.)* 60 (3): 785–807. http://dx.doi. org/10.2307/40204063.

Jaquette, Jane S., and Kathleen Staudt. 2006. "Women, Gender, and Development." In *Women and Gender Equity in Development Theory and Practice: Institutions, Resources, and Mobilization,* edited by Jane S. Jaquette and Gale Summerfield, 17–53. Durham, NC: Duke University Press. http://dx.doi.org/10.1215/9780822387756-003.

Karl, Marilee. 1995. *Women and Empowerment: Participation and Decision Making.* London: Zed Books.

Kelleher, David, and Rieky Stuart. 2008. *Gender Equality, Promise to Practice: A Study of the Progress toward Gender Equality of CCIC Members.* Ottawa: CCIC.

Mazurana, Dyan, Angela Raven-Roberts, Jane Parpart, and Sue Lautze. 2005. "Introduction: Gender, Conflict, and Peacekeeping." In *Gender, Conflict, and Peacekeeping,* edited by Dyan Mazurana, Angela Raven-Roberts, and Jane Parpart, 1–27. New York: Rowman and Littlefield.

Moser, Caroline, and Annalise Moser. 2005. "Gender Mainstreaming since Beijing: A Review of Success and Limitations in International Institutions." *Gender and Development* 13 (2): 11–22. http://dx.doi.org/10.1080/135520705123 31332283.

Mukhopadhyay, Maitrayee. 2003. "Creating Citizens Who Demand Just Governance: Gender and Development in the Twenty-First Century." *Gender and Development* 11 (3): 45–56. http://dx.doi.org/10.1080/741954369.

Mukhopadhyay, Maitrayee. 2007. "Mainstreaming Gender or 'Streaming' Gender Away: Feminists Marooned in the Development Business." In *Feminisms in Development: Contradictions, Contestations, and Challenges,* edited by Andrea Cornwall, Elizabeth Harrison, and Ann Whitehead, 135–50. London: Zed Books.

Mukhopadhyay, Maitrayee, Gerard Steehouwer, and Franz Wong. 2006. *Politics of the Possible – Gender Mainstreaming and Organisational Change: Experiences from the Field.* Amsterdam: KIT Publishers.

Oda, Beverly. (2010). "Minister Oda Talking Points on Canada's New Role in Afghanistan." 20 June. http://www.afghanistan.gc.ca/canada-afghanistan/speeches-discours/2010/2010_11_16a.aspx?view=d.

Parpart, Jane. 2009. "Fine Words, Failed Policies: Gender Mainstreaming in an Insecure and Unequal World." In *Development in an Insecure and Gendered World: The Relevance of the Millennium,* edited by Jacqueline Leckie, 51–68. Surrey, UK: Ashgate.

Parpart, Jane. 2013. "Exploring the Transformative Potential of Gender Mainstreaming in International Development Institutions." *Journal of International Development* 26 (3): 303–408. http://dx.doi.org/10.1002/jid.2948.

Plewes, Betty, and Joanna Kerr. 2010. "Politicizing, Undermining Gender Equality." *Embassy Magazine,* 5 May. http://embassymag.ca/page/printpage/equality-05-05-2010.

Pratt, Cranford, ed. 1989. *Internationalism under Strain: The North-South Policies of Canada, the Netherlands, Norway, and Sweden.* Toronto: University of Toronto Press.

Pratt, Cranford, ed. 1990. *Middle Power Internationalism: The North-South Dimension.* Montreal/Kingston: McGill-Queen's University Press.

Rao, Aruna, and David Kelleher. 2005. "Is There Life after Gender Mainstreaming?" *Gender and Development* 13 (2): 57–69.

Stokke, Olav, ed. 1989. *Western Middle Powers and Global Poverty: The Determinants of the Aid Policies of Canada, Denmark, the Netherlands, Norway, and Sweden.* Uppsala, Sweden: Scandinavian Institute of African Studies.

Swiss, Liam. 2010. "Gender, Security, and Instrumentalism: Canada's Foreign Aid in Support of National Interest?" Paper presented at the CASID Annual Meetings, Concordia University, Montreal, 2 June.

Swiss, Liam. 2012. "Gender, Security, and Instrumentalism: Canada's Foreign Aid in Support of National Interest?" In *Struggling for Effectiveness: CIDA and Canadian Foreign Aid,* edited by Stephen Brown, 135–58. Montreal/Kingston: McGill-Queen's University Press.

Tickner, J.A., and L. Sjoberg, eds. 2011. *Feminism and International Relations: Conversations about the Past, Present, and Future.* London: Routledge.

Tiessen, Rebecca. 2007. *Everywhere/Nowhere: Gender Mainstreaming in Development Agencies.* Bloomfield, CT: Kumarian Press.

Turenne Sjolander, Claire, Heather A. Smith, and Deborah Stienstra, eds. 2003. *Feminist Perspectives on Canadian Foreign Policy.* Don Mills, ON: Oxford University Press.

Wendoh, Senorina, and Tina Wallace. 2005. "Re-Thinking Gender Mainstreaming in African NGOs and Communities." In *Mainstreaming Gender in Development: A*

Critical Review, edited by Fenella Porter and Caroline Sweetman, 70–79. Oxford: Oxfam GB. http://dx.doi.org/10.1080/13552070512331332288.

WGWR (Working Group on Women's Rights). 2009. *Strengthening Canada's International Leadership in the Promotion of Gender Equality: A Civil Society Response to the Evaluation of the Implementation of CIDA's 1999 Policy on Gender Equality.* Ottawa: WGWR.

Woroniuk, Beth. 1999. *Gender Equality and Peacebuilding: An Operational Framework.* Gatineau, QC: CIDA.

Spreading the Guilt
Canada and Climate Change Adaptation Funding

PETER STOETT

The impact of climate change is hardly shrouded in scientific mystery in this post-9/11 security context. It is happening, and Canadians are well aware of it. Since Canada assumed the chair of the Arctic Council in 2013, and as the Arctic ice continues to melt at an accelerating rate, the link between climate change and national security has never been stronger. Long-term security, however, must extend beyond the confines of national security, as several authors in this volume (see, e.g., Warner, Falk, and Kitchen) have asserted. It must be rooted in more global notions of distributive fairness and, to complicate matters further, intergenerational justice (see Stoett 2012). These concerns were painfully obvious as country representatives struggled to produce a coherent framework for climate governance in Doha in late 2012 and again in Warsaw in 2013. How to wed the concerns of global justice with the science and policy demands of climate change in a foreign policy of concern and action? For many, the answer is in making a solid contribution to the "opaque, underfunded, overly complex, and poorly coordinated" world of climate change adaptation funding (Oxfam International 2009, 11).

This international imperative emerges at a time when the Harper government, while withdrawing from the Kyoto Protocol of the United Nations Framework Convention on Climate Change, has embarked on its historic quest to establish Canada as an "energy superpower," set even to displace Saudi Arabia as the world's most prolific exporter of crude oil. This oil mercantilism has not gone unnoticed by those engaged in the pursuit of climate justice, especially in the southern hemisphere, where climate change adaptation is a matter of life and death to billions of people. Canada might receive the dinosaur award for its climate change mitigation policies, and it might be criticized for linking long-term economic security closely to environmentally deleterious natural resource development; however, its lack of coherent thinking about climate change adaptation is just as problematic, because the ability to pursue resilience to climate change is emerging as a key component of human security in every hemisphere. The ethics of security and foreign policy are intertwined with climate governance today. And, though there is healthy debate about the security implications of climate change, there is little question that associated variables, such as refugee movements, resource scarcity, extreme weather events, invasive alien species' expanded ranges, and the loss of life-sustaining biodiversity, are both national and human security concerns.

Foreign policy decisions related to adaptation will be especially complicated, since they evoke broader questions pertaining to the legitimacy and devilish details of development assistance and multilateral environmental commitments. Conceptualizing climate change adaptation strategies as security initiatives presents a further challenge to both the academic community and the policy community and can lead to the traps inherent in the securitization approaches criticized many years ago by Daniel Duedney and others. Worse, it can be argued that bilateral and multilateral funding in this area is designed primarily to dissipate the obvious fact that Canada remains a high-end carbon emitter with a recently deceased, though arguably revivable, affection for pursuing an active human security agenda in world affairs. I suggest not that funding for adaptation be lowered but that it should be matched with stronger domestic efforts to lower emissions and that we should maintain a critical eye on adaptation schemes that might play a bigger role in assuaging guilt than protecting vulnerable populations or advancing climate change resiliency.

I begin with a brief description of the climate change issue area and in particular the widely acknowledged, if still contestable in some areas, need for adaptation strategies both within Canada (and especially its northern and coastal communities) and abroad. I posit in a brief section that this is both an ethical and a security issue. Then I examine extant multilateral agreements and policies and policy directions under the present Harper government, which are tied inextricably to American political intransigence and/or stalemate on the issue, and offer some critical observations. Finally, I offer some suggestions regarding possible future directions, both immediate and long term, that policy makers and other Canadians can take if we are to avoid making the problem worse by trying to solve it through superficial or obfuscatory means.

Adaptation: Let's Talk about It (Finally)

My subtitle might seem curious, but the fact is that for decades (in the 1980s and early 1990s in particular) *adaptation* to climate change was a taboo subject from several angles, and – displaying in brilliant colours its tendency to take years to catch up with real-world events – academia was complicit in giving adaptation short shrift until recent years. Naturally, climate change deniers dismissed the need even to discuss adaptation. Worse, some environmentalists either likened serious discussions of adaptation strategies to acknowledging defeat by the forces causing climate change or to permitting the focus to shift away from the holy grail of mitigation (efforts to stop climate change altogether or at least slow it down considerably). However, a noticeable shift occurred toward the end of the 1990s with the negotiation of the Kyoto Protocol and subsequent agreements: it became apparent at so many levels that adaptation would be on any future agenda related to climate change that it became impossible not to give it attention. This was partially the result of real-word events, including extreme weather events that many would argue cannot be linked conclusively to climate change, and partially the result of bargaining table insistence that there is a price to pay for the West's historical emissions levels. Indeed, along with transgovernmental mechanisms to promote adaptation abroad, transnational calls for "climate justice" became common, often from an anti-capitalist perspective (Angus 2010).

Adaptation is now a central focus of international diplomatic discourse in several ways, including its presence in climate-related funding mechanisms.[1] First, the danger that this will displace serious mitigation strategies is exaggerated: where such strategies even exist, they have been hard-won policy changes that are unlikely to be dismantled easily, and where significant deregulation has occurred (e.g., under the Bush administration in the United States) this would have happened regardless of the extent to which adaptation was a real topic of concern. Second, many adaptation strategies and mitigation strategies blend together, to the point where it is difficult to distinguish them. Biofuel growth, for example, can be viewed as both a mitigation and an adaptation measure (overall, it might be neither, but that is another issue). Third, the simple reality is that climate change is already having a serious impact on many people's lives, and thus adaptation has begun. Yet we lack a solid means of ascertaining where public (or private) spending actually becomes spending as a result of the deleterious impact of climate change. This is an accounting nightmare. Nevertheless, adaptation strategies and costs are now the stuff of mainstream climate talks and negotiations as well as the clarion call of the more radical fringes of the discourse.

But where does this leave the next energy superpower, poised to gush 700,000 barrels of bitumen toward Texas every day and yet more to the growing industrial complexes of Asia? What can we say about the ethical and security implications of a world where climate change adaptation is becoming the norm as Canada seeks to increase exponentially its overall contribution to greenhouse gas emissions?

Adaptation: An Ethical and Security Issue[2]

Spurred by the climate change debate, in which an international dialogue is unavoidable, many authors are treating climate change ecopolitics as an aspect of environmental justice, from the local level to the global level (Athanasiou and Baer 2002; Boyle and Anderson 1998; Roberts and Parks 2007). This emerges in the context of a much broader, ongoing discourse on global environmental justice (Ehresman and Stevis 2011). Meanwhile, *adaptation* to climate change is emerging as the dominant human rights issue, since there are ample opportunities to ensure some measure of fairness as people strive to adapt to changes over which they have little or no control.

There are at least three obvious reasons why climate change is an ethical issue and why such a wide variety of literature is being produced on this topic. First, its effects were not caused in equal fashion; this is a classic case of differentiated responsibility. This is difficult to gauge in exact terms, but most of the fossil fuels that have been released throughout history originated from northern industrialization and transportation. The contemporary balance of responsibility is not dissimilar. The inequality here is startling. According to Roberts and Parks (2007, 146), "the average U.S. citizen dumps as much greenhouse gas into the atmosphere as nine Chinese ... eighty Bangladeshis ... and over five hundred citizens of Ethiopia, Chad, Zaire, Afghanistan, Mali, Cambodia, and Burundi." Of course, China, India, Brazil, Indonesia, and other large economies with significant industry, transportation, and/or forestry sectors have increased emissions in recent decades, though they still pale in terms of per capita emissions. There might well come the day when a rational analysis suggests that the BRIC countries (Brazil, Russia, India, and China) or others have actually overcome the deficit, but it is years away.

Second, and just as importantly if not more so, the deleterious impact of climate change will have a disproportionate effect on those who contributed the least to its cause. This is the fundamental claim made by those advocating climate justice and largely equating it with redistributive policies compensating the least advantaged, especially the African states. Indeed, the UN Convention to Combat Desertification has become a conduit for the argument that drought and land degradation related to climate change justify northern investment in sustainable development initiatives in the global South, particularly in Africa.[3] Much of this is based upon plausible conjecture. A recent report from the Climate Change, Agriculture and Food Security program estimates that "at least $7 billion per year in extra funding will be needed for irrigation investments, agricultural research and rural infrastructure" ("Act Now to Diversify Crops" 2011). Already the line between life and mass starvation is very thin, especially in the drought- and conflict-prone Horn of Africa; the Food and Agriculture Organization estimated in 2009 that a 70 percent rise in global food production will be necessary to feed the projected 9.1 billion Earthlings by 2050.

Of course, northern complicity in climate change can be taken to different extremes. Randal Hansen (2005) even refers to "ethnocide via climate change of Arctic Indigenous communities," for example. This mirrors other tendencies to overuse evocative terms such as "genocide," but one can certainly make the argument, as the Alliance of Small Island States has within the context of international legal measures, that there is at least wilful ignorance, at worst purposeful negligence, involved in the northern approach to global warming. Most philosophies of justice would accept the premise that guilt must involve self-conscious awareness of the accused; despite the work of climate change deniers and busy public relations firms, I do not think that northern industrialized states can claim to be unaware of the science and long-term implications of climate change, even if the latter remain largely unknown in the strictest definitive sense. Indeed, both the precautionary principle and the precedent of the Vienna Convention and Montreal Protocol on the ozone layer (which includes a multilateral fund to which Canada contributes $US 5 million a year and office space) suggest that the lack of certainty should not preclude present action, including redistributive financing commitments.[4]

Third, future generations will bear a disproportionate impact as well. The intergenerational aspect has been well covered by Edith Brown Weiss (1989) and others (Agius 2006; Vanderheiden 2007 111–42). But most of that literature, and some of the better contemporary work by Steve Vanderheiden

(2007) and others, deal with mitigation, not adaptation. The latter is perhaps even more important for future generations if we accept the premise that we should strive, as cosmopolitan citizens, to afford equal opportunities at life chances (Sen 1999). To deepen the hole in which future Africans and Asians begin their life journeys seems not only unjust but also, put bluntly, downright cruel. This is not to suggest that something as superficial as climate change adaptation funding through the Clean Development Mechanism (CDM) or Reducing Emissions from Deforestation and Degradation (REDD-plus) will equalize life opportunities. Debt relief, nutrition, education, women's rights – all are much more important pursuits. But, unfortunately, since we have failed to reduce the rate of greenhouse gas emissions, these programs are tempting gestures toward solving the intergenerational ethical dilemma.

It is less clear perhaps that climate change should be viewed as a security issue, unless one accepts a broad, maximalist definition of security (see Stoett 2000) or posits the argument that all foreign policy decisions that affect global ecological stability are security issues. If we are to view a security concern as emerging from a specific identifiable threat – for example, melting Arctic sea ice would be viewed as a threat only if we were aware of Russian designs to use this to military advantage and send a flotilla of newly agile arctic naval vessels our way – then we have less immediately compelling reasons. But broaden the scope even slightly and it becomes clear that we do face a security threat associated with the predicted and even observed impacts of climate change. At the least, they decrease our ability to respond to other military threats. More importantly, perhaps, the social disorder literature is mixed about whether climate change will result in the type of unrest that will ultimately affect northern and relatively isolated high-income countries such as Canada; however, it is not difficult to argue that refugee flows, economic dislocations, increased food prices, and other impacts will indeed lessen security for all (Homer-Dixon 1999). If we add a genuine concern for human rights to the mix, then diminished access to safe living environments for the poorest populations is certainly an agonizing condition.

Although some definitions of human security refer solely to protection from direct physical violence, a more nuanced perspective would include weather-related threats, whether or not they in turn induce physical violence and whether or not we go from there to accept the premises behind concerns with structural violence (see Stoett 2010b). Assuming that population movements, some sudden and perhaps linked to violent conflicts, will result from climate change, then adaptation strategies can be viewed as pre-ventive measures. Whether we are preventing pain among the affected or protecting ourselves from their presence and "managing the undesirables" (Agier 2011) in permanent refugee camps is another question. Increased ranges for diseases and invasive alien species are another direct threat to human security (see Stoett 2010a). Similarly, food production will become increasingly difficult as climate change advances without significant steps taken toward adaptation; to some extent, it can be argued, the history of agricultural development is about adaptation and technological innovation, but even slight yet rapid changes in climate can devastate agriculture. The Intergovernmental Panel on Climate Change (IPCC 2007, 275) is clear on this potential, especially with regard to small-holder and subsistence farm-ers, who will "experience the negative effects on yields of low-latitude crops, combined with a high vulnerability to extreme events. In the longer term, there will be additional negative impacts of other climate-related processes such as snow-pack decrease (especially in the Indo-Gangetic Plain), sea level rise, and spread in prevalence of human diseases affecting agricultural labour supply."[5] Converting cropland into biofuel production further limits adaptation strategies and prioritizes energy security over food security, a dubious hierarchization of needs.

Of course, energy security is directly related to climate change and does sneak onto most national security agendas. This is particularly relevant in the North American context, in which Canada in essence is the primary external source of energy security for the United States; the precipitous rise of shale oil and gas production has shifted this relationship somewhat, but war-weary Americans generally view Canada as a "secure" source of oil. Of course, we can easily dismiss this as a temporary form of security provision, a manifestation of a heavily interdependent relationship between two states that have yet to move past the carbon stage of development in convincing fashion. Canada's efforts to push oil and gas development in low-income states, through (now defunct) the Canadian International Development Agency and other programs, along with heavy Canadian private investment, fit into the broader pattern of a mercantile state itself born from heavy resource extraction. Yet, assuming that other countries take serious steps toward lowering their carbon emissions, dealing with a depressed oil market might become a climate change adaptation issue for fossil fuel exporters. I will leave the debate (is there a sustained debate?) over the wisdom of throwing so many collective eggs into the basket of further developing a long-term oil and gas export-led economy and its impact on future Canadians. Clearly, we are moving in that direction. Thus, the moral imperative to contribute to international climate change adaptation strategies becomes even stronger with each passing day. Or does it?

Adaptation: National and International Strategies

If we accept the widely held notion that Canada has acted as a laggard in international climate change negotiations, and we can do so regardless of how much we appreciate the wisdom of that position, then it follows that Canadian contributions to international adaptation measures, which can be made without the consent of the provinces, could be more reflective of a leadership role for Canada.[6] Given the constraints on the federal government to initiate pan-Canadian policies to reduce emissions significantly, we might ask whether adaptation measures and commitments are the next best thing. Although Ottawa has been reluctant to embrace fully the logic of funding the UN Framework Convention on Climate Change Adaptation Fund, it has touted the 2010–12 commitment of $1.2 billion as a serious contribution (note that this figure includes a previous contribution of $100 million to the World Bank's Pilot Program on Climate Resilience in 2008–09). According to the Progress Report on Canada's Fast-Track Financing, the government committed $974.64 million in delivered or "planned disbursements" from 2010 to 2012 (Canada 2012). However, nearly $300 million of this amount went to "concessionary financing" or relatively "cheap" loans; another $450 million went to private sector financing, in particular the Inter-American Development Bank's Canadian Climate Fund for the Private Sector. The contributions to grant financing, for clean energy, forestry and agriculture, and what is officially considered adaptation, are relatively small. A paltry $20 million has gone to the Least Developed Countries Fund[7] in support of urgent and priority adaptation needs of the poorest and most vulnerable countries in the world (by way of comparison, a 2006 study found $1.4 billion in extant Canadian subsidies for oil and gas alone).[8] Some funding has been funnelled through Canadian organizations (e.g., over $30 million has been invested in the International Development Research Centre). Problematically, some of these commitments are scored as contributions to overseas development assistance. Of course, in a cash-strapped, recessionary global economy, one might suggest that it is a good deal to kill two birds with one stone. However, if climate change adaptation policies detract from development assistance funding, then one could argue that they are harming rather than contributing to the improvement of life chances (this was the strong thrust of the Oxfam report cited above).

Meanwhile, the $100 million contributed to the World Bank's Pilot Program on Climate Resilience joined a pool of funds made available as concessionary loans, not grants, through the World Bank. Climate justice advocates suggest that loans are not an ethical response to the differentiated responsibility for carbon emissions. Even the close association with the World Bank, known for its conditional programs and lust for large-scale infrastructure investments, raises cautionary eyebrows. Wisely enough, the Least Developed Countries Fund, essentially the second-stage pilot project for global adaptation needs, will be administered through the Global Environment Facility, which has obtained some measure of autonomy from the World Bank over the past two decades.[9] It is understandable that donors to such funding want a say in how the funds are spent, not to mention accountability. However, the emphasis on Western, G8-driven gatekeeping gives rise to new claims that adaptation funding will become the next source of neoliberal conditionality, developed outside the context of the evolution of the United Nations Framework Convention on Climate Change. There are also concerns about the lack of wider consultation with receiving states in the process of establishing these funds (see Tan 2008). The Kyoto Protocol put adaptation up front: Articles 10 and 11 contain provisions to advance the implementation of the commitments of all parties found in Article 4.1 of the convention, on the same financial footing as provided by the convention. Article 12 of the protocol establishes the Clean Development Mechanism as a source of funding for adaptation and envisages the creation of an adaptation fund based upon proceeds from certified project activities, tentatively accepted at the Conference of the Parties in Cancun. Article 12.8 provides that.: "a share of the proceeds from certified project activities [will be] used to cover administrative expenses as well as to assist developing country Parties that are particularly vulnerable to the adverse effects of climate change to meet the costs of adaptation." But the CDM, itself controversial, has yet to pay off in this manner. And the more serious discussions on an adaptation fund have seemed to evolve largely outside the Kyoto framework, though Cancun brought them out again.[10]

Critics reach deeper, however. Indeed, a relatively new term has arisen in the critical literature: "carbon colonialism." This term emerges partially from critiques from the far left (Angus 2010), suggesting that the West's environmental governance platform is yet another thinly disguised mechanism to maintain imperial control and usurp the development agenda (Sachs 2002; more generally, Soederberg 2007), but it resonates as well in ecofeminist and southern nationalist circles of thought. The thrust of the argument is that the adaptation strategies that have been accepted and even proffered to some extent by Western corporations and governments have largely involved further expropriation and privatization of the commons. They often involve the forced resettlement of forest dwellers, for example. (Of course, this is an old complaint about international conservation efforts in general, which emerged from a historical narrative of colonialism in the first place; see Warner 2006). Worse, the programs are designed to attract and employ cheap labour in so-called green projects, many of which are of dubious environmental and labour standards quality. In short, the developed world is still using the South for its natural resources and cheap labour, but it is also using it to excuse its own profligate carbon output. According to Isaac Osuoka (2010, 168), "examinations of particular carbon offset projects within the context of the CDM (Bohm and Dabhi 2009) and the Reducing Emissions from Deforestation and Degradation program (REDD) ... have shown that in most cases emissions have increased, while corporations make extra profits by selling the offsets credits that are obtained by presenting claims of 'hypothetical' emissions reduction." Or, as an ecofeminist author argues, "environmental conservation led by neoliberal governments and large NGOs in the global North has become yet another instrument for the colonisation of Third World resources, in particular, women's work, and nature." She cites "the enclosure of rainforests as 'carbon sinks' or oxygen generators [and] the enclosure and commodification of women's labour which results from that move" (Isla 2009, 199).

Although they have obvious overlaps with adaptation strategies, the CDM and REDD-plus are viewed primarily as mitigation programs, designed to reduce emissions in the South. However, a more robust adaptation strategy could adopt a similar approach, essentially based upon rewarding northern financial contributions (by permitting continued polluting and avoiding the high political costs of strict emissions regimes at home) and promoting projects that Western economists and investment experts have deemed worthy. The CDM rewards southern governments for projects that reduce emissions that would have occurred in the absence of those projects, thus creating a perverse incentive to pursue high- emission development.[11] Furthermore, the conflation of adaptation and development, or even adaptation as the new form of development, opens more space for aggressive, state-assisted marketing by northern multinational corporations. As Philip McMichael (2010, 174) writes, commenting on a 2008 policy brief for the International Commission on Climate Change and Development, "adaptation (insurance schemes, crop rotations, irrigation systems, drought-resistant seeds, sea defences) reproduces conventional development practices," and such "climate proofing represents a new profit frontier, with agro-chemical and biotechnology firms like BASF, Monsanto, Bayer, Syngenta and Dupont filing over 500 patent documents on so-called 'climate ready' genes." This approach overlooks the resilient nature of local methods of adaptation, carrying forth the narrative of Western salvation from indigenous ignorance in the face of change. Even biofuel growth plantations, which displace cheap food from local markets, could be considered an acceptable adaptation/mitigation measure (see Holt-Gimenez and Shattuck 2010).

To paint all adaptation efforts with Western funding as imperialistic would be to engage in unfair caricature, of course, since there will be environmental impact assessments, and surely some "stakeholder participation" will be integrated into the process.[12] But the basic outline looks very familiar. The upshot: multilateral and bilateral adaptation funding is no panacea for climate change, must be watched closely lest it not only deviate from the spirit of international arrangements but actually worsen the human and ecological security of affected people, and should not be considered part of a convenient effort to top-off or slash the development assistance envelope.

The Cancun Adaptation Framework, adopted in 2010, calls for developed country parties to provide developing states, "taking into account the needs of those that are particularly vulnerable, with long-term, scaled-up, predictable, new and additional finance, technology, and capacity-building."[13] Of course, Canada's less than stellar record of Kyoto Protocol compliance and withdrawal does not lead one to expect the fulfillment of this promissory note in the annals of environmental diplomacy.[14] It certainly suggests, however, that current efforts are wide of the mark, especially if Canada is to take seriously its international commitments while making an increased contribution, both at home and abroad, to global warming. We should be having a discussion, at the national level, on which contributions Canada can and will make to adaptation funding in the future and how they can be secured regardless of economic downturns.

Adaptation: Realistic Responsibilities and Promises

It is impossible to overlook the obvious: the economic context is dire for large-scale foreign policy designs based upon humanitarian concerns. It is obvious that we need to strengthen multilateral efforts at disaster prevention and relief, disease surveillance and epidemiology, conflict prevention, poverty alleviation, and many other humanitarian demands, and none of these important issues should be sidelined by the current fears over global warming. Rather, they should be taken as part of a broader effort toward the limited redistribution of wealth and power to reflect a democratic world polity and to live up to the demands that enlightened self-interest makes on the privileged. "Global governance" will remain little more than a quickly tiring code phrase for imperial management (Soederberg 2007) if it does not involve a serious resource commitment from the wealthier states, and from wealthier individuals and corporations within states, in the pursuit of environmental justice. This need not entail the diminishment of the institution of sovereignty but a realignment of sovereign priorities.

Domestically, we can simply observe the absurdity of billions of public dollars being funnelled into what are, essentially, subsidized, large, final emitter industries, such as coal and oil, and, in some cases, the military industries (perhaps the most carbon-intensive producers/consumers on the planet). Although the practice of subsidizing carbon intensity has received widespread condemnation in Europe and elsewhere, it is still seen as a modernization project in much of the southern hemisphere, with or without authoritative state structures to maintain its hegemonic appeal. As Lester Brown (2006) suggests,

> at a time of mounting public concern about climate change driven by the burning of fossil fuels, the world fossil fuel industry is still being subsidized by taxpayers at more than $210 billion per year. Fossil fuel subsidies belong to another age, a time when development of the oil and coal industries was seen as a key to economic progress – not as a threat to our twenty-first century civilization. Once in place, subsidies lead to special interest lobbies that fight tooth and nail against eliminating them, even those that were not appropriate in the first place.[15]

Brown's figures are now outdated; the International Energy Agency estimates that global subsidies for fossil fuels reached $523 billion in 2011 (IEA 2012, 1). A G20 commitment to phase out subsidies made at the 2009 meeting in Pittsburgh has largely been ignored. If a large fraction of this subsidization were redirected toward the Cancun Adaptation Framework, then we would be on the right track toward making a constructive and historic contribution to increasing North-South trust and confidence, though this would simultaneously raise all the usual questions about how, and to whom, such resources can be directed without encouraging corruption and dependence. Faced by the enormity and potential severity of the climate change challenge, these seem to be procedural barriers that could be broken with intelligent and diligent implementation.

Yet there are reasonable limits to the responsibility system underpinning the Kyoto Protocol and Adaptation Fund. As Harris (2011, 116) suggests, it "may be too soon to demand that Brazil or India agree to binding limitations on their own emissions, but it may also be past time to demand that wealthy Brazilians and Indians do so." Surely the skyward increase in emissions in many southern states is a consequence of profligate economic growth shared by a new upper middle class, and they should be responsible members of society as well? Just as urban Canadians should help to pay for the deleterious impact of climate change on agricultural and northern lands, so too wealthy Beijing residents should help to pay for the displacement caused by increased flooding in a flood-prone country. It is rational to expect southern governments to tax their own wealthy citizens for such purposes. At any rate, to throw absurd amounts of valuable resources into adaptation is not the answer, no matter how unlikely such a policy response. Doing so would just exacerbate harmful dependencies, facilitate Western investment instead of domestic development, displace funding and political capital needed for future humanitarian purposes, and give the heavy polluters less cause to clean up their own acts at home.

Indeed, the main argument pertaining to international adaptation programs is that they permit a superficial sense of virtuous accomplishment by the heavy polluters.[16] They take the pressure off the more important task of reducing national emissions and even steal policy light from the adaptation needs in Canada itself, which will be significant. Every ecosystem will be hit in its own way, and there will be serious consequences across Canada, especially for lower-income communities. Although we should certainly increase our contributions to global adaptation funds, with a critical eye trained on their processes and outputs, approaching the politically difficult task of moving past the image of becoming a fossil fuel superpower is of equal importance. Part of the broader obligation related to climate change and its long-term impact will necessitate some measure of sacrifice by those living in relatively affluent societies.[17] But if this is easier said than done, it is perhaps even harder to force politicians to take professional risks, to avoid spreading the guilt and facing our collective obligations as leaders.

Conclusion

Climate change adaptation measures are subject to several valid criticisms at this stage, even as a new international norm concerning their legitimacy is slowly emerging. They can act as obfuscators, complicit in the presentation of an image of action by heavily polluting Western states, part of a slightly amended business-as-usual approach. They can be seen as back-door approaches to development assistance and as such critiqued for decreasing legitimate aid while increasing tied aid and even as part of a broader neocolonial project. Monitoring them, and the labour, environmental, and economic activity associated with their implementation, is a difficult task, not only because of state sovereignty but also because many of the Clean Development Mechanism projects occur in secluded forest areas and are subject to various accountancy and accountability issues. That said, it is vital that a global adaptation fund is maintained, given the historical and present discrepancies in contributions to the anthropomorphic cause of climate change, the emission of greenhouse gases. States such as Canada have an ethical obligation to contribute to such a fund in a meaningful manner but should also be aware of the various counterproductive pitfalls that might ensue.

The most compelling argument for effective climate change adaptation measures, if one need appeal to enlightened self-interest, is that it will conserve our fragile resiliency, our ability to respond to emergencies and maintain humanitarian options. The food crisis of 2008, as well as the tragic events in Somalia in the summer and fall of 2011, demonstrate that, if international food prices are out of control, we will have limited ability to respond to mass famine. Global food markets are not figments of our imaginations but determine prices that subsequently affect our ability to feed our own children. One might hope, of course, that a humanitarian heart still beats on Canadian soil and that we are not prepared to act solely from self-interest. But even if we are, it is time to act on this immediate security concern.

Adaptation strategies need not be overwhelmingly expensive or based upon carbon market activity. As the authors of a recent Canadian report suggest,

> expanding the tree canopy in urban centres, for example, helps to reduce the impact of an increasing number of hot days and heat waves. It also reduces the need for air conditioning, and so reduces greenhouse gas emissions from fossil-fueled electricity generation. Healthy trees also decrease the impact of intense rainfall, stormwater runoff and pollution – increasing sustainability for our communities. (Bizikova, Neale, and Burton 2008, 10)

Such initiatives can certainly be engineered without tremendous outlays of capital, biotechnology patents, or the complex and controversial world of carbon markets. The bigger challenges – agricultural production, fisheries conservation, biodiversity protection, population displacement – are already part of sustained activity within the scope of global environmental governance and human rights regimes, which in turn are being animated by climate change considerations. But we still need to reduce domestic emissions if we want to avoid accusations of blatant hypocrisy on the world stage and to examine seriously the prevailing wisdom that endless oil exports are a reasonable expectation when peak oil (the point where oil is simply too expensive to be economically justifiable) is within sight and when the tremendous costs of adaptation will soon become real priorities, not just scientific predictions. And we need to realize that any responsible discussion of security in the post-9/11, less-ice age must include serious considerations of global climate justice and adaptation needs at home and abroad.

Calls for climate justice will not go away just because an Adaptation Framework emerged from a recent COP of the UNFCCC. In effect, they carry forth the broader demand for international justice, defined succinctly by Paul Harris (1999) as "a fair and just sharing (or distribution) among countries of benefits, burdens and decision making authority associated with international relations, in this case within the context of international environmental issues" (see also Nardin 1989; Paterson 2001). Climate injustice could also help to usher in a revival of human security at the international level. Canada has hard choices to make; whether or not to contribute to the evolution of international environmental justice and human security should not be one of them.

NOTES

1 See Smit et al. (2000) for a discussion of the theme of adaptation. Smit was also one of the lead authors of the IPCC report on *Adaptation to Climate Change in the Context of Sustainable Development and Equity*, which can be found at http://www.ipcc. ch/ipccreports/tar/wg2/index.php?idp=641.
2 Parts of this section appear in Stoett (2012).
3 Harris (2011, 109) summarizes the IPCC: "Regional effects will vary, ranging from up to hundreds of millions of people exposed to water stress in Africa, increased flooding in the coastal and delta regions of Asia, significant loss of biodiversity in Australia, the retreat of glaciers in the mountains of Europe and water shortages in southern Europe, the loss of tropical forests and biodiversity in Latin America, water shortages and heat waves in North America, detrimental changes to natural ecosystems in polar regions, and inundations and storm surges in small islands."

4   See http://www.multilateralfund.org/71/English/1/7103.pdf.

5   Senior Worldwatch Institute researcher Brian Halweil (2005, 19) suggests that agriculture is "the industry that will struggle most to cope with more erratic weather, severe storms, and shifts in growing season lengths. While some optimists are predicting longer growing seasons and more abundant harvests as the climate warms, farmers are mostly reaping surprises."

6   This is an important distinction, often underplayed. The provinces, in effect, can scuttle federal commitments abroad, as the Chrétien government learned soon after pushing for ratification of the Kyoto Protocol. But they cannot directly hamper the federal government's decisions on foreign aid and financial contributions to multilateral environmental agreements. Thus, Ottawa cannot blame them for any paucity of action in this area.

7   The Least Developed Countries Fund is administered through the Global Environment Facility. Its primary role is to assist in the development of National Adaptation Programs of Action (NAPAs), which identify priority needs and strategies. The relevant website indicated that the fund stood at US$415 million and had approved projects in some forty-seven countries (mostly in Africa and among small island states) as of 1 October 2010. See http://www.thegef.org/gef/LDCF. On the other hand, Canada has made an incremental increase to the Global Environment Facility over the three years.

8   This study was conducted by the Sierra Legal Defense Fund, the Pembina Institute, Friends of the Earth Canada, and the late, great environmentalist and politician Charles Caccia; see http://www.pembina.org/media-release/1242.

9   The Global Environment Facility was formed in 1991 as a joint fund administered by the UNEP, UNDP, and World Bank. After the UNCED in Rio, it was restructured as an independent financial institution. Among many other responsibilities, it is the financial mechanism for the Convention on Biological Diversity, the Stockholm Convention on Persistent Organic Pollutants, the United Nations Convention to Combat Desertification, and the United Nations Framework Convention on Climate Change.

10 Of course, one can argue that, without American ratification of the Kyoto Protocol, discussions of long-term funding are inconclusive at best, especially in light of Europe's latest financial crisis.

11 "For example, if a government introduced tougher vehicle emission standards for public transport it could not then go on to apply for CDM credits for the sector, as emission standards would be seen as 'business-as-usual' rather than a project that had come about as a result of the CDM" (Jarman 2007, 53).

12 These concerns are fairly widespread and are, thankfully, becoming mainstream. For example, the Secretariat of the Convention on Biological Diversity recently released a report on the issue of how REDD-plus projects can avoid harm to biodiversity and indigenous peoples.

13 See Cancun Adaptation Framework, http://unfccc.int/adaptation/items/5852.php.

14 See the October 2011 Report of the Canadian Commissioner of the Environment and Sustainable Development on Kyoto Protocol compliance at http://www.oag-bvg.gc.ca/internet/English/parl_cesd_201110_e_35765.html.

15 Note that Brown's estimate for global subsidies is on the very low side. Adapted from Chapters 4 and 12 in Brown (2006).

16 I am aware that Canada's overall global contribution of greenhouse gases is small – unless, of course, it is measured on a per capita basis, in which case Canada competes with the United States and Australia for the title of heaviest polluter – but I think that it is justifiable to consider a self-proclaimed future fossil fuel–based energy superpower a heavy emitter.

17 See Maniates and Meyer (2010) for a set of fascinating essays on the topic of sacrifice.

References

"Act Now to Diversify Crops: Experts." 2011. *Gazette* [Montreal], 3 October

Agier, Michel. 2011. *Managing the Undesirables: Refugee Camps and Humanitarian Government.* Translated by David Fernbach. Cambridge: Polity.

Agius, E. 2006. "Environmental Ethics: Towards an Intergenerational Perspective." In *Environmental Ethics and International Policy,* edited by H. Have, 89–117. Paris: UNESCO.

Angus, Ian, ed. 2010. *The Global Fight for Climate Justice: Anticapitalist Responses to Global Warming and Environmental Destruction.* Black Point, NS: Fernwood.

Athanasiou, Tom, and Paul Baer. 2002. *Dead Heat: Global Justice and Global Warming.* New York: Seven Stories Books.

Bizikova, Livia, Tina Neale, and Ian Burton. 2008. *Canadian Communities' Guidebook for Adaptation to Climate Change: Including an Approach to Generate Mitigation Co-Benefits in the Context of Sustainable Development.* Vancouver: Environment Canada and University of British Columbia.

Bohm, Steffen, and Siddartha Dabhi, eds. 2009. *Upsetting the Offset: The Political Economy of Carbon Markets.* London: Mayfly Books.

Boyle, Allen, and Michael Anderson. 1998. *Human Rights Approaches to Environmental Protection.* London: Clarendon Press.

Brown, Lester R. 2006. *Plan B 2.0: Rescuing a Planet under Stress and a Civilization in Trouble.* New York: W.W. Norton and Company.

Canada. 2012. *Canada's Fast-Start Financing Progress Report.* http://unfccc.int/files/adaptation/application/pdf/fast_start_finance_progress_report_canada_-_final.pdf.

Ehresman, Timothy, and Dimitris Stevis. 2011. "International Environmental and Ecological Justice." In *Global Environmental Politics: Concepts, Theories, and Case Studies,* edited by Gabriela Kutting, 87–104. London: Routledge.

Halweil, Brian. 2005. "The Irony of Climate." *World Watch Magazine,* March–April. http://www.worldwatch.org/node/572.

Hansen, Randal. 2005. "The Future Is Now: Arcs of Globalization, Indigenous Communities, and Climate Change." Paper presented to the American Studies Association Annual Meeting, Washington, DC, November.

Harris, Paul. 1999. "What's Fair? International Justice from an Environmental Perspective." Paper presented to the International Studies Association Annual Meeting, Washington, DC, March.

Harris, Paul. 2011. "Climate Change." In *Global Environmental Politics: Concepts, Theories, and Case Studies*, edited by Gabriela Kutting, 107–18. London: Routledge.

Holt-Gimenez, Eric, and Annie Shattuck. 2010. "Agrofuels and Food Sovereignty: Another Agrarian Transition." In *Food Sovereignty: Reconnecting Food, Nature, and Community*, edited by Hannah Wittman, Annette Desmarais, and Nettie Wiebe, 76–90. Halifax: Fernwood.

Homer-Dixon, Thomas. 1999. *Environment, Scarcity, and Violence*. Princeton, NJ: Princeton University Press.

IEA (International Energy Agency). 2012. *World Energt Outlook 2012*. Paris: IEA.

IPCC (Intergovernmental Panel on Climate Change). 2007. *Fourth Assessment Report: Impacts, Adaptation, and Vulnerability: Contributions of Working Group II to the IPCC*. Cambridge: Cambridge University Press.

Isla, Ana. 2009. "Who Pays for the Kyoto Protocol? Selling Oxygen and Selling Sex in Costa Rica." In *Eco-Sufficiency and Global Justice: Women Write Political Ecology*, edited by Ariel Salleh, 199–217. London: Pluto.

Jarman, Melanie. 2007. *Climate Change*. London: Palgrave Macmillan.

Maniates, Michael, and John Meyer, eds. 2010. *The Environmental Politics of Sacrifice*. Cambridge, MA: MIT Press. http://dx.doi.org/10.7551/mitpress/9780262014366.001.0001.

McMichael, Philip. 2010. "Food Sovereignty in Movement: Addressing the Triple Crisis." In *Food Sovereignty: Reconnecting Food, Nature, and Community*, edited by Hannah Wittman, Annette Desmarais, and Nettie Wiebe, 168–85. Halifax: Fernwood.

Nardin, Terry. 1989. "Justice in the International Society of States." In *Poverty amidst Plenty: World Political Economy and Distributive Justice*, edited by Edward Weisband. Boulder, CO: Westview Press.

Osuoka, Isaac. 2010. "Operation Climate Change: Between Community Resource Control and Carbon Capitalism in the Niger Delta." In *Climate Change – Who's Carrying the Burden? The Chilly Climates of the Global Environmental Dilemma*, edited by A. Sandberg and T. Sandberg, 161–72. Ottawa: Canadian Centre for Policy Alternatives.

Oxfam International. 2009. "Beyond Aid: Ensuring Adaptation for Climate Change Works for the Poor." Oxfam Briefing Paper 132. http://www.oxfam.org/sites/www.oxfam.org/files/bp_132_beyond_aid_en_0.pdf.

Paterson, Matthew. 2001. *Understanding Global Environmental Politics: Domination, Accumulation, Resistance*. Basingstoke, UK: Macmillan. http://dx.doi.org/10.1057/9780230536777.

Paterson, Matthew. 2001. "International Justice and Global Warming." In *The Ethical Dimensions of Global Change*, edited by B. Holden, 181–201. New York: St. Martin's Press.

Roberts, J. Timmons, and Bradley Parks. 2007. *A Climate of Injustice: Global Inequality, North-South Politics, and Climate Policy*. Cambridge, MA: MIT Press.

Sachs, Wolfgang. 2002. "Ecology, Justice, and the End of Development." In *Environmental Justice: International Discourses in Political Economy, Energy, and Environmental Policy*, edited by J. Byrne, L. Glover, and C. Martinez, 19–36. New Brunswick, NJ: Transaction.

Sen, Amartya. 1999. *Development as Freedom.* New York: Oxford University Press.

Smit, Barry, Ian Burton, Richard J.T. Klein, and J. Wandel. 2000. "An Anatomy of Adaptation to Climate Change and Variability." *Climatic Change* 45 (1): 223–51. http://dx.doi.org/10.1023/A:1005661622966.

Soederberg, Susanne. 2007. *Global Governance in Question: Empire, Class, and the New Common Sense in Managing North-South Relations.* Toronto: Arbeiter Ring Publishing.

Stoett, Peter. 2000. *Human and Global Security: An Exploration of Terms.* Toronto: University of Toronto Press.

Stoett, Peter. 2010a. "Framing Bioinvasion: Biodiversity, Climate Change, Security, Trade, and Global Governance." *Global Governance* 16 (1): 103–20.

Stoett, Peter. 2010b. "What Are We Really Looking For? Eco-Violence and Environmental Justice." Paper presented to the conference Environmental Violence and Conflict: Implications for Global Security, Dalhousie University, Halifax, February.

Stoett, Peter. 2012. *Global Ecopolitics: Crisis, Governance, and Justice.* Toronto: University of Toronto Press.

Tan, Celin. 2008. "No Additionality, New Conditionality: A Critique of the World Bank's Climate Investment Funds." Third World Network Briefing Paper 2. www.foe.org/pdf/CIF_TWNanalysis.pdf.

Vanderheiden, Steve. 2007. *Atmospheric Justice: A Political Theory of Climate Change.* Oxford: Oxford University Press.

Warner, Rosalind. 2006. "The Place of History in IR and Ecology: Discourses of Environmentalism in the Colonial Era." In *International Ecopolitical Theory: Critical Approaches,* edited by Eric Laferrière and Peter J Stoett, 34–51. Vancouver: UBC Press.

Weiss, Edith Brown. 1989. *In Fairness to Future Generations: International Law, Common Patrimony, and Intergenerational Equity.* Dobbs Ferry, NY: Transnational.

PART 4

REGIONAL SECURITY: COUNTRIES AND AREAS

Ethics, Security, and Free-Trade Agreements
The Case of the Canada-Colombia Free Trade Agreement

JAMES ROCHLIN

The Canada-Colombia Free Trade Agreement (CCFTA), which came into effect 15 August 2011, entails a strong relationship among the themes of ethics, security, and political economy. The Harper government rushed to sign a free-trade agreement with Colombia despite strong reservations and protests by NGOs in both countries because of horrific levels of human rights abuses of Colombian trade unionists. Indeed, more than half of all assassinations of union members globally occurred in Colombia between 2006 and 2010.[1] And, though the number of assassinations has diminished over the past decade, for reasons discussed below, the game of fear persists through a steady number of credible death threats to unionists. Even the United States, the world's leading purveyor of neoliberalism, hesitated to conclude a free-trade agreement with Colombia because of the astonishing levels of human rights violations in the country. Thus, the case of the CCFTA represents an intersection of themes, including economic globalization, ethical concerns regarding human rights abuses, and a variety of security issues. Colombia is the site of the most intense internal warfare in the Americas, pitting the world's largest leftist guerrilla group, the Fuerzas Armadas Revolucionarias de Colombia (FARC), against right-wing paramilitary groups and the Colombian military, which, at various points over the past decade, has been the third largest recipient of US military assistance in the world (see Rochlin 2011b).

Relevant security issues for Canada are not limited to the human rights abuses of workers and ordinary Colombian citizens. Canadian businesses in the extractive sector pay considerable sums of money for protection by private military corporations, the Colombian military, and perhaps paramilitary forces, to stave off kidnappings, bombings, extortions, and the like. The central argument here is that the Human Rights Impact Assessments (HRIA) included in the CCFTA as a result of pronounced activism by social forces in Canada, the world's first such governmental HRIA included in a free-trade agreement, can have an important impact only if the civil societies in both countries give careful scrutiny to this important provision and insist on corrective measures if abuses are found.

I begin with a brief overview of various historical eras of Canada's foreign policy regarding Latin America and then shift to a consideration of the context of Colombian politics and labour's place within it. A brief discussion of the human rights provision of the North American Free Trade Agreement (NAFTA) is in order since this is the chief point of reference from which to consider the CCFTA amid a paucity of comparable cases. I then examine in detail Canada's free-trade agreement with Colombia, especially the labour HRIA contained in the agreement. A framework for an analytical study of the effectiveness of the HRIA is presented. Final thoughts are devoted to a conceptualization of the CCFTA and the path to an ethical foreign policy imbued with a respect for human rights.

The CCFTA in the Context of Canadian Policy Regarding Latin America

Canada's foreign policy with respect to Latin America has been shaped largely by shifting hegemonic structures. Until the Second World War, its policy regarding the region was viewed by the United States as a conduit for British interests. In fact, Canada lacked autonomy in the foreign policy realm until the fruition of the Statute of Westminster in 1931. Not yet secure in its role as the most powerful force in the Americas, Washington was suspicious of Canada's role in Latin America until the collapse of British hegemony in 1945. With the newly emerged heyday of US power in the Americas, Washington urged Canada to play a greater role in the region. But at this point Ottawa was hesitant, fearing, with good reason, that it would be drawn into Manichean conflicts framed by the harsh, binary world of early Cold War politics.

Prime Minister Trudeau's Third Option policy during the early 1970s was concocted when US hegemony was perceived to be in decline and led to greater Canadian involvement in the region. Canada perceived its role as a middle power that did not have to lean either right or left and that was simultaneously friendly to business interests and the promotion of greater social equity and human rights in the region. Insurgencies and anti-Americanism, from Ottawa's perspective, were rooted in highly inequitable divisions of wealth and political exclusion and not a result of Soviet/Cuban intervention. It was during this era that Canada joined the Organization of American States as a permanent observer, signalling the beginning of a greater commitment to the region.

The 1980s witnessed a major shift in inter-American affairs with the onset of the catastrophic Latin American debt crisis in 1982. The Reagan administration, through the US dominance of the International Monetary Fund, imposed on Latin America a radical economic and social restructuring deemed "neoliberalism" by critics. The ideological about-face to the right in Canada, through the election of Prime Minister Mulroney, spelled an ideological harmonization throughout the Americas. This served as the underpinning of the US-Canada Free Trade Agreement and in 1994 the initiation of NAFTA. Given this ideological convergence, Canada joined the Organization of American States as a full member in 1990.[2]

The Goldilocks scenario in the Americas, for both the United States and Canada, was bounded by the fall of the Soviet Union beginning in 1989 and the radical shift of the world order marked by 11 September 2001. Neoliberalism was largely unchallenged during that period, and socialism was deemed to be dead despite what was perceived to be its last gasps in Cuba. This was just as Ottawa hoped the Americas would be: a neighbourhood of ideational convergence where Canada could promote its business interests and where there was little about which to argue. The pivotal election of Hugo Chávez in 1998, and the emergence of the Argentine debt crisis at the beginning of the new millennium, which branded it as the first country ever to default on the International Monetary Fund, were not seen as harbingers of a dramatic shift in inter-American affairs that would be vividly reflected during the first decade of the twenty-first century.

It is important to note that, for all its faults, neoliberalism was accompanied by the strong development of democracy in many parts of Latin America beginning in the 1980s. Military governments that presided over mounting debt until 1982 were happy to return to the barracks and let civilian governments take the flak. Given the right-wing ideological convergence between 1982 and into the 1990s (the election of Chávez in 1998 was thought to be a fluke at the time), Washington promoted democratic structures since the election of a rightist candidate was virtually assured. This context also propelled Canada's support for democracy as Canada hosted the 2001 Summit of the Americas, at which it lobbied for the Inter-American Democratic Charter, signed later that year. To the surprise of both Washington and Ottawa, various leftist forces would dominate the decade not through insurgencies but through electoral victories. This included not only Chávez and the Kirchners in Argentina but also elected leftist governments in Brazil, Bolivia, Ecuador, Uruguay, Nicaragua, El Salvador, Honduras (until the US-supported coup in 2009), and Peru (the 2011 election of Humala), among others. Now the right-leaning governments of the United States and Canada seemed to be isolated from the general rebuke of neoliberalism throughout the Americas, with the exception of Mexico and especially Colombia. Prime Minister Harper praised Colombia's "long democratic tradition" during his visit there in 2007 that preceded the signing of the CCFTA in 2008. This was despite the country's deeply entrenched record of extreme violence and political exclusion.

The Context of Colombian Politics

Colombia's political history is characterized by extraordinary levels of violence, exaggerated political fragmentation, and one of the weakest states in Latin America.[3] It is the world's only country to host "violentology" as an academic discipline. Colombia faced almost non-stop civil wars between the Liberals and Conservatives in their vain attempts to achieve hegemony, a phenomenon that culminated in the War of 1,000 Days from 1899 to 1902, in which between 80,000 and 200,000 people lost their lives. With the country exhausted and depleted, the feud between Liberals and Conservatives did not percolate again until the 1940s, with the eruption of *La Violencia* during the period 1948–58. After that ordeal, in which an estimated 200,000 people lost their lives, a US-and-Spanish-sponsored peace accord was negotiated between the Liberals and Conservatives in Colombia that brought consociational government between 1958 and 1974. Through this agreement, the Liberals and Conservatives each had a stipulated four-year period in government in a revolving fashion over sixteen years. During this era, at the urging of Washington, the Liberals and Conservatives aligned to turn their attention to a new enemy, the insurgent left. This occurred against the backdrop of ripple effects throughout Latin America from the 1959 Cuban Revolution. Colombia remained one of the most violent countries in the world during the 1960s and 1970s, but the cast of belligerents had changed amid a Cold War context of left versus right.

The Fuerzas Armadas Revolucionarias de Colombia emerged as a peasant guerrilla group in 1964 and was nearly snuffed out by the early 1970s through Washington's Plan Laso, the largest US military operation in Latin America at the time. What was left of the FARC was pushed into the interior Amazonian region of the country during the 1970s, especially the departments of Guaviara, Caquetá, and Putumayo. As it turned out, these were precisely the regions that emerged as the bastions of coca growth and cocaine trafficking in the late 1970s and early 1980s, providing the guerrillas with an unanticipated windfall that rendered them among the most lucratively and independently financed insurgents in the Americas. Moreover, they did not need to rely on Soviet monetary and ideological support as Central American guerrillas had, and therefore they did not perish along with them in the 1980s as the USSR crashed and burned. Following an attempt at negotiated peace, the FARC was invited to field candidates and participate in Colombian elections during the late 1980s and early 1990s, which took the form of the newly created political party Union Patriótica. Tragically, some 3,000 to 4,000 Union Patriótica candidates were murdered by paramilitary forces with the apparent complicity of the Colombian government. Paramilitary forces were rooted in "self-dense" groups armed by the Colombian government in the 1960s to fight the FARC and then transformed as the armed forces allied with major Colombian drug traffickers in the 1980s and beyond. They have served as a strategic ally of the Colombian government to fight leftist insurgents.

By the early 1990s, given the failure of the Union Patriótica, the FARC saw no legitimate or secure space for democratic politics and engaged in all-out war with the Colombian government and paramilitary forces. That decade was a low point for Colombian politics as the country fell into a Clausewitzean orgy of violence amid a booming cocaine economy as well as a feeble and incompetent state. Although paramilitary forces had increased from an estimated 1,800 armed troops in 1990 to over 8,000 by 2000, the FARC was estimated to have about 20,000 troops at that time. The exact numbers of troops are uncertain and have been subject to political manipulation, but it is clear that the FARC reached the pinnacle of its power in 1998. During that year, the strategically inept government of President Pastrana ceded to the FARC a parcel of land about the size of Switzerland, where the insurgents consolidated their power and prepared to project forces elsewhere.

It was against this backdrop that the Clinton administration formulated Plan Colombia, a project of more than US$6 billion, of which at least 85 percent was composed of military assistance. Implemented in 2000, it catapulted Colombia to the third largest recipient of US military aid globally during various years of the first decade of the new millennium. Funding was initially aimed at vastly diminishing the power of the FARC, a task accomplished some ten years after its implementation. But the purpose of Plan Colombia transformed into the provision of armed security to the country's increasingly important extractive sector, host to a bounty of gold, carbon, petroleum, and the like. Furthermore, given the presence of leftist neighbours such as Chávista Venezuela and Correa's Ecuador, and the emerging global power of Brazil, Plan Colombia has been refocused to create a military, economic, and political bastion to project US interests in an increasingly hostile and well-armed South America. Peace negotiations between the FARC and the Colombian government that began in late 2012 have been accompanied by fierce combat between them, whereby the FARC has focused on the extractive sector as its main strategic target.

Labour and the Colombian Political Fabric

Labour in Colombia has been caught within the context of violence, warfare, and a weak state. Trade unionists were the target of a massacre during the 1928 banana strike, featured in Gabriel García Márquez's classic novel *One Hundred Years of Solitude*. Beginning in the 1920s, elements of labour were regarded by business and the state as aligned with subversive socialist forces. The union movement in Colombia was institutionalized in the 1930s and 1940s with the creation of major labour umbrella organizations such as the Confederación Sindical de Colombia. The country's labour movement reached its peak of power in the mid-1970s, when some 47 percent of finance workers and 46 percent of industrial workers were unionized. After national labour organizations collectively launched an unsuccessful strike in 1977, when almost no worker demands were met and many workers were dismissed from their jobs, the tide turned, and it has been on the decline ever since.

Colombian labour has been victimized by the aforementioned warfare involving the FARC, paramilitaries, and the Colombian state. Furthermore, as has been the case for trade unions globally, the Colombian labour movement withered under neoliberal politics that remain entrenched in the country. Many workers lost their jobs in the 1990s during this period of escalated violence. Foreign investment fell 70 percent between 1992 and 1999, and industrial production slid 17 percent in 1999 alone. Gini coefficients rose from an already horrific .55 in 1991 to .59 in 1999 – placing Colombia among the three most inequitable countries in Latin America.

Union membership declined from .0538 percent of the active workforce in 1994 to .0428 percent in 2002 (De Colombia 2002).

Between 1986 and August 2010, 2,842 Colombian trade unionists were assassinated, 4,826 were threatened with death, 1,696 were forcibly displaced, and 217 disappeared (Cuaderno de Derechos Humanos 2010, 46). Unions blame the paramilitary forces, acting with impunity from the government, as the chief perpetrator of these horrific levels of abuse, the worst in the world. The head of the country's intelligence agency, Jorge Noguera of the Departamento Administrativo de Seguridad, was arrested in 2007 and later convicted of conducting illegal intelligence activities against union members and providing the names and contact information of union leaders to paramilitary forces for the purpose of political assassination. Paramilitary forces grew from an estimated 8,000 in 2000 to some 20,000 by 2006.

There are flashes of relatively good news for trade unionists, though the overall context remains grave. Beginning in December 2002, the Colombian and US governments instituted plans to demobilize paramilitary forces and incorporate them into society, and 31,000 were demobilized in what appears to have been a shell game whereby some forces turned themselves in, only to re-emerge in other illegal armed groups. The *New York Times* of 4 July 2005 referred to the demobilization law as the "Impunity for Mass Murderers, Terrorists and Major Cocaine Traffickers Law." Those who demobilized needed to be on their best behaviour if they hoped to achieve what amounted to impunity for their horrific actions – about 70 percent of overall human rights abuses are believed to have been committed by paramilitaries. Remarkably, between 2005 and 2012, demobilized paramilitaries confessed to 25,757 individual homicides and 1,046 massacres, totalling 51,906 victims.[4]

Attempts by paramilitaries to reduce sentences through relatively better behaviour led to fewer abuses of trade unionists on an annual basis. For example, assassinations of trade unionists in Colombia declined from 193 in 2001 to 51 in 2010, to 28 in 2012, and to 26 in 2013. Yet labour unions suggest that abuses have simply transformed to achieve the same political effect. That is, rather than assassinating union members en masse, as was the case up to 2002, assassinations of key union leaders are calculated to yield a bigger political splash of fear. Moreover, death threats made to trade unionists – and more often their loved ones – have increased. So the politics of fear remain in place, though there are fewer carcasses. Beyond the motives of achieving impunity through what, in many cases, appears to be false demobilization, another major motive of this shift toward fewer assassinations has been a public relations attempt to win over a reluctant US Congress (mostly members of the Democratic Party) to approve a free-trade agreement with the United States.

The second item of positive news is that Colombian trade unionists realize that publicity from the attempt to pass the free-trade agreement with the United States has served to increase their security. It is only because of global surveillance by sympathetic social forces that abuses of labour have diminished, even if the game involving the politics of fear continues unabated. The abuse of unionists is the main reason why social forces in Canada urged the rejection of the CCFTA, and it was through their efforts that a labour HRIA was included. The Harper government would not have done so otherwise.

NAFTA in Comparison

A reference point for consideration of ethics and security in relation to the CCFTA is NAFTA. Although Mexico and Colombia are distinct cases, they share some broad themes, including insurgency, notable human rights abuses (including those associated with Canada's role in the extractive sector), and many issues associated with drug trafficking. In terms of security and ethics with regard to NAFTA, particularly noteworthy is that the nexus of ethics-security-foreign policy first drew great global attention not from the institutional arrangements associated with the trade agreement itself but from the surprise appearance of the Ejército Zapatista de Liberación Nacional on NAFTA's birthday. The Zapatistas – led by the charismatic and PhD-bearing Subcomandante Marcos – united indigenous causes, anti-neoliberalism, feminist themes, environmental issues, and more generally the plight of the marginalized. The Zapatistas cleverly used NAFTA as a vehicle to draw attention to their cause in a manner that stunned governments of member countries. This was a bottom-up, critical security approach by the world's first postmodern guerrillas, who ultimately relied on the Internet, not guns, to draw global political attention via personal computers around the planet. In the nearly two decades since their emergence, the Zapatistas have had a modest but clear effect for the marginalized social forces that they have represented (see Rochlin 2007, Chapters 5–8). The important point here in relation to the CCFTA is the potential for social forces to exploit the trade agreement in creative ways to draw attention to pressing ethical issues regarding human rights, the environment, and social justice.

A bottom-up, critical security approach from social forces is also relevant with regard to NAFTA's side accords. That is, the record suggests that the side accords themselves have been of dubious merit despite their superficial appeal. The labour side accord has impressive wording, including principles that surpass International Labor Organization standards of organizing and bargaining rights, the abolition of forced labour and child labour, and discrimination. NAFTA accords include themes associated with migrant worker protection, minimum wages and maximum hours, equal pay for equal work, and occupational health and safety. However, the accord requires a more inclusive and participatory framework for the workers whom the accord is designed to protect (see Delp et al. 2004, 40). Beyond that, a huge limitation is that the accord lacks an enforcement mechanism (see Lance Compa 2001), which means that pressure by social forces is key once problems are identified. Furthermore, civil society has the legal potential to change the side accord to incorporate an enforcement mechanism and to rescue it, in the words of one legal expert, from the "precipice of death and irrelevance" (Bieszczat 2008, 1401). Even an enforcement mechanism by itself is insufficient. Careful studies suggest that the environmental accord associated with NAFTA, which has an enforcement mechanism, is inadequately funded, lacks a financial mechanism for structural adjustment, and has faced strong resistance by the three governments to monitor environmental effects, let alone enforce them. Furthermore, the existing limited effects have been concentrated at the border with the United States and in urban centres (see Gallagher 2004; Mumme 2007; Rochlin 1997). Overall, such accords linked to free-trade agreements can incorporate respect for ethical elements associated with critical security such as human rights and environmental protections. But to have an important impact, they must come under the scrutiny and pressure of transnational civil society to convert words into reality.

Finally, with regard to NAFTA's relationship to security and ethics, it is important to emphasize the role of the extractive sector as the economic face of Canadian foreign policy in Latin America. Indeed, in 2009, 51.5 percent of Canadian mining assets abroad were located in Latin America, totalling about $45 billion.[5] But the bad apples in this sector should discourage Canadian travellers from wearing maple leaf insignias on their backpacks to distinguish themselves from Americans, since components of the extractive industry have given a black eye to the "boy scout" reputation that Canada had as recently as two decades ago. Anti-mining activists critical of Canadian mining corporations have been assassinated in highly publicized cases in Mexico, Guatemala, and El Salvador (see Keenan 2010). Furthermore, five activists were killed and thirty were injured in June 2011 in clashes with the Peruvian police amid protests against a proposed Canadian mine on the border with Bolivia, as reported by BBC News on 25 June 2011. The list of problems, regrettably, does not end there, and, as we will see, similar serious problems have appeared in Colombia. The point is that the extractive sector represents Canadian foreign policy's "Exhibit A" regarding the intersection of ethics, critical security, and political economy in Latin America, with the CCFTA representing a classic case study.

The CCFTA and Human Rights Impact Assessments

There are two principal reasons behind the Harper government's pursuit of a free-trade agreement with Colombia. First, in many ways, the Harper government has echoed US policy in the region to the point that Ottawa's foreign policy is virtually indistinguishable from Washington's foreign policy in Latin America (see Rochlin 2012). Such is the case in Colombia. Washington announced its intention of creating a free-trade agreement with Colombia in 2006, but this announcement was met with a haltingly loud outcry among some democratic congressional members and labour activists regarding the appalling state of human rights abuses of Colombian workers. While the United States was mired in domestic political opposition to the free-trade agreement, the Colombian president, Uribe, sought to establish free-trade agreements with other countries to demonstrate to the United States that it was missing an opportunity. In this context, a free-trade agreement with Canada was a good strategy, given the closeness between the United States and Canada. Talk of a free-trade agreement between Canada and Colombia emerged in 2007.

Second, beyond the ideological harmonization among the United States, Colombia, and Canada, and their shared embrace of neoliberalism, growing Canadian trade with and investment in Colombia underpinned the free-trade agreement. Canadian investment increased from about $740 million in 2007, for example, to $1.7 billion in 2011, while trade increased from about $1.3 billion in 2008 to $1.6 billion in 2011. Much of the increased investment is in Colombia's booming extractive sector – Canada's Pacific Rubiales, for example, produces daily about a quarter of Colombia's 1 million barrels of oil. Indeed, the extractive industry has become the face of Canada in many parts of Latin America.

Amid protracted negotiations in Canada regarding a free-trade agreement with Colombia, in March 2010 the Liberal Party of Canada boasted that the inclusion of the party's amendment to the CCFTA sets a "gold standard" for human rights reporting and renders the deal the first in the world that requires annual human rights impact assessments.[6] The Liberal amendment succeeded because of tireless pressure from a variety of well-informed NGOs in Canada, such as the Canadian Labour Congress and the Canadian Council for International Cooperation. Although there is no standard definition of HRIAs, functionally these assessments are designed to measure concrete human rights impacts associated with the free-trade agreement and to focus on the international legal obligations associated with the agreement and how they are implemented at the national level (see Harrison and Goller 2008, 5–7).

As with the NAFTA side accord on labour, the CCFTA's labour HRIA surpasses the International Labor Organization's 1998 Declaration on Fundamental Principles and Rights at Work – which includes the right to collective bargaining and the abolition of child labour, forced labour, and discrimination – to include protection of occupational health and safety, minimum wages and maximum hours, and migrant worker protection. The labour agreement stipulates that each country will develop a point of contact regarding complaints of violations of the terms noted above and that this point of contact will create guidelines for submission, acceptance, and review of complaints. If, through this process, either country determines that a complaint is valid, then there will be an attempt to resolve the matter through mutual ministerial consultations. This stage should be concluded six months after the submission of the complaint. If that process fails, then the country that launched the complaint can constitute a review panel, which can direct the country to impose a penalty of up to $15 million on the offending country. Furthermore, in mid-2011, Canada was in the process of implementing a $1.1 million program for labour technical assistance to Colombia, the dimensions of which remain unclear at the time of writing.

One can critically assess the HRIA associated with the CCFTA and its capacity to protect and promote human rights in Colombia. Given the paucity of HRIAs, the literature on this theme is scant (see Canadian Council for International Cooperation 2010; Harrison 2011, 162–87; Harrison and Goller 2008, 587–615). Human Rights Impact Assessments are a recent invention, and the one involving Colombia and Canada represents a pioneering effort. It is the first to implement governmental HRIAs and the first to implement annual governmental reports on human rights related to the free-trade agreement in both countries. Historically, the first declared HRIA was produced by the Thailand National Human Rights Commission in 2006, and it was designed to consider *potential and forward-looking* effects of a free-trade agreement with the United States that never reached fruition.

Once again, it did not measure actual human rights issues but imagined what some of them might be had the free-trade agreement come into effect. Another HRIA was sponsored by the Ecumenical Advocacy Alliance, which looked at *past impacts* of the right to food based upon trade liberalization in each country – it was not linked to a free-trade agreement and produced three studies (rather than the ongoing reports entailed in the Colombia-Canada case) (see Harrison 2009, 4–6). As observed above, NAFTA did not entail an HRIA.

HRIAs are essentially a work in progress. Indeed, the first HRIA associated with the Canada-Colombia free-trade agreement, released in May 2012, was rote. The Canadian government claimed that, "given the entry into force date of CCOFTA [Canada-Colombia Free Trade Agreement] on August 15, 2011, sufficient data is not available for an analysis of a full calendar year of activity in 2011" (Canada 2012, 3). The Colombian government did the same. There are many conceptual and methodological questions associated with HRIAs, and I will consider them in relation to the CCFTA. First, given that Colombia is the site of arguably the worst human rights abuses in South America, the focus should definitely be on human rights issues in Colombia rather than in Canada. An important point of departure is the construction of baseline data from which to measure whether or not the HRIA is improving the human rights situation in Colombia regarding workers. An important NGO in Colombia, the Escuela Nacional Sindical, is regarded by those sympathetic to labour as the most reliable source of information regarding abuses associated with trade unionists.[7] But its resources are limited, and it would be considerable work to document historical baseline data regarding reported human rights abuses by Canadian corporations operating in the country. Relevant information could also be provided by assorted unions in the country and by university researchers located where the extractive sector is concentrated, such as the department of Antioquia. Then there are the questions about the accuracy of any data available and whether the various parties involved would agree on their legitimacy. Beyond this, while information exists regarding unionized workers, the vast majority of employees in Colombia are not unionized, so considerable work would need to be done regarding any reported abuses on their behalf.

Second, who is to guard the guardians? Although it is highly commendable that the CCFTA stipulates the conduct of annual HRIAs by both countries that are available for public inspection, an important question arises about their thoroughness and accuracy. NGOs such as the CCIA, the Canadian Labour Congress, and the Escuela National Sindical will no doubt play the role of watchdog, but, as noted, their resources are limited. Related to this, there might be ideological polarization reflected in the HRIAs composed by the pro-business and neoliberal Canadian and Colombian governments, on the one hand, and the counterreports issued by anti-neoliberal NGOs, on the other. Polemics will do little to advance the cause of human rights for harrowed Colombian workers. It is precisely here that balanced academic investigations might be able to fill the gap by examining the accuracy of competing documents in a manner that gains the respect of all involved. I will consider what a framework for such a study might look like.

An academic study is doable since the HRIA is focused on one area, human rights for workers of Canadian corporations in Colombia, and these companies are concentrated in the extractive sector. That is, experts on the matter warn of HRIAs that are too broadly focused on human rights in general, but that would not be the problem in this case (Harrison 2009, 6). The study would need to be at least five to seven years to provide useful data and to win the trust of stakeholders such as the governments involved, relevant NGOs, and those who launch complaints. A key principle would be the celebration of balance in both data gathering and analysis. That is, though "objective" studies might be impossible, a balanced consideration of the perspectives apparent across the spectrum of stakeholders is achievable.

Some important methodological themes would need to be considered. Such a study would need to be interdisciplinary, involving, for example, specialists in development, human rights, security, and law. This kind of team would be capable of investigating the nexus of ethics, security, political economy, and foreign policy. More specifically, an academic study could begin by assisting NGOs through the provision of data aimed at constructing baseline data. That is, it could assess the accuracy of existing data offered by NGOs and attempt to fill gaps where data are not yet available. In terms of investigating and analyzing governmental HRIAs, both qualitative and quantitative analyses would be necessary (Berne Declaration 2010, 11). Regarding quantitative data, relevant statistics could be gathered on the number of complaints, the location of incidents, the number of persons involved, the type of industries in complaints, and so on. Furthermore, quantitative data would be helpful regarding the gender, race, and age of those issuing complaints and whether these workers were unionized or not (ibid., 12).

Qualitative data, including interviews from individuals and group meetings, would also be essential. These data would provide crucial nuances and contexts for empirical indicators and be helpful in determining whether the

HRIAs associated with the free-trade agreement were helpful or harmful, and to what extent, or whether they seemed to have little or no impact. Such data would need to be as inclusive as possible, affording those with something to say on the matter with a voice. Case studies would be particularly helpful; beyond the generalities of a larger study, specificities and important nuances could be detected that might be missed otherwise. Crucially, a methodology would need to be constructed that protected to the utmost the identities and safety of those who wished to participate in such a study. This is especially important given the violence and brutality of the Colombian context (Harrison 2009, 8).

Other elements would be important to this kind of study. First, causality would need to be probed. For example, if a complaint were lodged regarding human rights, could it be clearly established that the abuse was the direct fault of Canadian investment, or would other factors be involved (Harrison 2009, 14)? Second, beyond the identification of problems and abuses, such a study would need to focus on remedies to apparent problems – this is crucial for the realization of a more ethical foreign policy that stresses issues associated with critical security. Third, information would need to be disseminated in the broadest possible manner in an effort to improve the quality of HRIAs and to promote concrete results for the human rights of Colombian workers.

Conceptualizing the CCFTA and the Way Forward

There are at least three broad themes that require conceptualization vis-à-vis the CCFTA and the plight of labour in Colombia. First, one must address what can only be deemed the outrageous context of violence in the country both historically and currently. Second, beyond the broad theme of violence, what is the nature of the larger struggle in which labour finds itself a victim to the tune of thousands of assassinations over the past twenty-five years? Third, is there a feasible path leading out of this imbroglio?

Regarding Colombia's historical penchant for violence, the classic works of Hobbes and Clausewitz are particularly relevant. Hobbes's warning of what happens when there is no Leviathan, no strong state to monopolize the use of force, rings true in the Colombian case (1968, 189–201). Given the historical weakness of the Colombian state – characterized first by feuding for nearly 150 years between the rival Liberal and Conservative parties in their unsuccessful bids to gain hegemony and then by their war on the left for the past fifty years, a period when the state has been absent in nearly half the country's territory – it is not difficult to accept Hobbes's point. The lack of hegemony by any single actor, and the failure among actors to cede private interests for the greater good, are stark reminders of the weight of Hobbesian theory. The result has been a climate of fear and carnage for most of the people of the country.

Related to this is classic Clausewitzean theory. Within the Hobbesian dog-eat-dog world that fails to establish a Leviathan, the Clausewitzean doctrine that "the maximum use of force is in no way incompatible with the simultaneous use of the intellect" (Von Clausewitz 1986, 75) holds sway in Colombia. Force has been viewed in the country as the ultimate arbiter of conflict resolution. The Clausewitzean concept of maximum force was introduced during the early modern era, when combatants did not possess nuclear arms, biological weapons, and the like. Therefore, unlike in the nuclear age, it was perceived that there could indeed be a victor in warfare who would stand tall among the carnage and get his way after all. But in Colombia, no clear victor emerged, and the dark ball of political violence continues unabated.

The strength of texts such as those by Hobbes and Clausewitz is that they are a one-size-fits-all model that can be applied to various cases in which there is no monopoly on the use of force and violence rules the day. But there needs to be an explanation of the political struggle so that the prospect exists for conflict resolution. The Liberal and Conservative feud was characterized by rivals with little ideological difference whose frustrated attempts at hegemony over decades led to generational revenge as an important motor of warfare. Furthermore, in what is regarded as perhaps the greatest novel produced in Latin America and perhaps the best telling of political history in Colombia, one of García Márquez's characters observes, "what worries me ... is that out of so much hatred for the military, out of fighting them so much, you ended up as bad as they are. And no idea in life is worth that much baseness" (1970, 154).

During the 1960s, the Colombian imbroglio transformed such that warfare became a battle between the left and the right in the context of Fidel Castro's and Che Guevara's message to Latin America's underclass to struggle against pronounced economic inequity and social injustice. Historical materialism is highly relevant to appreciate the peculiarities of the recent Colombian context. In one of Latin America's three most inequitable countries (Mexico and Brazil have been competitors for this title, though Brazil has improved the lot of the poor since the election of Lula), class warfare in Colombia is painfully obvious. The country's gini coefficient has ranged between .57 and .59 over the past decade, indicating profound economic inequity. This is an important context for the case at hand, in which trade unionists have been the victims of murder and other abuses in their struggle to achieve better pay, healthier working conditions, and non-discrimination. Here we see a merger between Marxist class struggle and the world of fear and brutality explained by Clausewitz and Hobbes. Furthermore, the wider context of Latin America's general rebuke of neoliberalism since the election of Chávez in 1998 (which has been apparent in Bolivia, Brazil, Ecuador, Argentina, Uruguay, Nicaragua, and so on) must be viewed as a rejection of the inequity, social injustice, and class polarization associated with that model. Colombia stands as the major exception in South America, where transnational corporations can still operate under the highly inequitable neoliberal model with apparent protection by paramilitary forces. Class analysis is key to understanding important dimensions of the Colombian case and labour's place within it.

Critical security approaches and Kant's basic concept of enlightened self-interest (1991, 54–60) might point the way to conflict resolution in Colombia and the prospect of labour accords attached to the CCFTA to reach their potential. Critical security is a bottom-up approach that emphasizes the security of the majority population[8] and avoids the traditional focus on the national security of the state and the interests of powerful actors such as transnational corporations (TNCs). Respect for the human rights of workers in Colombia falls squarely within a critical security approach. Although it is crucial to appreciate the present nature of the conflict, it seems obvious that enlightened self-interest points the way out: that is, a strength of realism is its emphasis on self-interest as the motor of politics and economics. But it is possible to construct a scenario in which the interests of particular actors can converge in a way that benefits all. For my purposes here, if Canadian corporations investing in Colombia can see that the provision of community welfare projects, fair pay, and basic components of corporate responsibility not only benefits the communities in which they are working but also leads to greater security for the corporations themselves, then the path can lead to a win-win situation. TNCs in Colombia are the victims of extortion, kidnapping, bombing, and other acts of terrorism by leftist insurgents, and they must pay huge sums to private security firms, paramilitary forces, and the Colombian military for protection. But if TNCs are seen as a positive influence for the majority population among whom they are working, then there will be less community support for insurgents and a more secure and prosperous environment for all.

Finally, though some have rightfully feared the influence of TNCs and elements of the postmodern world of globalization, there is a bright side to this picture that must be celebrated and pursued. Transnational social movements, and solidarity among NGOs in various countries that focus on common issues, can help to balance negative consequences emanating from unabated interests of transnational capital. In the 1960s and 1970s, thinkers such as Poulantzas (1969) argued that the role of the state is to protect capital from itself. That is, capital seeks profits and quarterly results that will please investors. But those interests can prove to be myopic, and therefore the role of the state is to resist near-sighted interests of capital and implement social welfare policies and prudent economic redistribution to ward off social revolution, which would threaten capital to the extreme. In other words, the role of the state is to protect capital by taking a long-term view of things in a manner that would mutually benefit capital and society. The advent of neoliberalism changed all that whenthe state became the handmaiden of capital.

Left to their own devices, then, the Canadian and Colombian governments might opt to produce rote annual human rights assessments that promote the sole interests of capital. A hint of this direction was the Harper government's announcement in January 2013 that it was easing its ban on exports of assault weapons to Colombia, where, despite significant progress, high levels of violence persist. Canadian arms manufacturers can now sell fully automatic weapons with high-capacity magazines to Colombia.[9] Any claim that the government believed Colombia to be a secure country was debased a couple of days later when it announced that, by the end of 2013, it would start fingerprinting visa applicants from Colombia along with those from what Ottawa considered to be potentially dangerous places, such as Iran and the Palestinian Territories. These announcements suggest a myopic foreign policy that puts short-term profit in front of long-term stability and prosperity. A "for profit" foreign policy would perpetuate the insecure environment that persists in Colombia and acts against the interests of Canadian TNCs operating there.

Ironically, anti-neoliberal social movements might now play the role that Poulantzas (1969) assigned to the state during an era of national rather than transnational capital. In this postmodern era, transnational social forces can put the brakes on myopic policies of TNCs by turning floodlights on manifestations of the dark underbelly of globalization. In so doing, they can define the mutual interests, or enlightened self-interests, of both capital and social movements to create a more secure and prosperous environment for both.

Clear progress in this regard is already visible. An obvious example is the recent creation of Colombia's Ministry of Labour and the appointment of high-profile Rafael Pardo as its minister. This suggests that the push and publicity by civil society in Colombia, Canada, and globally are contributing to the development of institutional conflict resolution mechanisms in Colombia that can diminish the established pattern of extreme violence as the principal means of settling affairs. Vigilance by global civil society, a transnational panopticon from the bottom up, has also helped to reduce the number of violent attacks against unionists, though the politics of fear continue through other measures, such as death threats. There has also been increasingly sophisticated organization and networking by Colombian unions with their global counterparts.

Overall, Canadian foreign investment can make an important contribution in Colombia with regard to job creation, especially given the country's status as hosting the highest unemployment rate in South America. Investment can also foster a greater tax base to support social programs and the like. Social forces in Canada and Colombia can work together and act as the social conscience of the free-trade agreement and, more generally, Canada's relations with Colombia. They can offset the harsh consequences of a myopic for-profit foreign policy. Civil society, and especially NGOs, need to fortify their already growing network to publicize and then eliminate human rights abuses of workers in Colombia as a result of TNC investments, especially in the extractive sector, in which Canada dominates. Global eyes can promote justice, security, and a sense of ethics that would be lacking otherwise. That is the job ahead for social movements in Canada and Colombia regarding the CCFTA.

NOTES

1 For further statistics, see Bolle (2012); Rochlin (2011a).
2 For a historical discussion of Canada's relations with Latin America, see Rochlin (1993).
3 See, for example, Deas and Daza (1985); Orquist (1980); Safford and Palacios (2002).
4 See *El Colombiano,* 3 January 2012.
5 My calculations from data provided by Natural Resources Canada.
6 The announcement was posted on its website, www.liberal.ca, on 25 March 2010.
7 The website for this NGO is www.ens.org.co.
8 An excellent academic website is available from the University of Ottawa at http://criticalsecurity.ca/ .
9 As reported in the *Globe and Mail,* 2 January 2013.

References

Berne Declaration. 2010. *Canadian Council for International Co-Operation and Misereor, Human Rights Impact Assessment for Trade and Investment Agreements.* Report of the Expert Seminar, Geneva, 23–24 June.

Bieszczat, Frank. 2008. "Labor Provisions in Trade Agreements: From NAALC to Now." *Chicago-Kent Law Review* 83 (3): 1387–1408.

Bolle, M. 2012. *US-Colombia Free Trade Agreement.* Congressional Research Service Report for Congress, RL34759, January.

Canada. 2012. Department of Foreign Affairs and International TradeAgreement Concerning Annual Reports on Human Rights and Free Trade between Canada and the Republic of Colombia. 15 May.

Canadian Council for International Cooperation. 2010. *Human Rights Impact Assessments for Trade and Investment Agreements.* Report of the Expert Seminar, Geneva, 23–24 June.

Compa, Lance. 2001. "NAFTA's Labor Side Agreement and International Labor Solidarity." *Antipode* 33 (3): 451–67. http://dx.doi.org/10.1111/1467-8330.00193.

Cuaderno de Derechos Humanos. 2010. *Escuela Nacional Sindical* 22. http://www.ens.org.co/index.shtml.

Deas, Malcolm, and Fernando Gaitán Daza. 1985. *Dos ensayos especulativos sobre la violence en Colombia.* Bogotá: Tercer Mundo.

De Colombia, Gobierno. 2002. *Población económicamente activa y número de sindicalizados.* DANE pamplet.

Delp, Linda, Marisol Arriaga, Guadalupe Palma, Haydee Urita, and Abel Valenzuela. 2004. "NAFTA's Labor Side Agreement: Fading into Oblivion?" UCLA Center for Labor Research and Education. http://www.sscnet.ucla.edu/labor/publications/pdf/nafta.pdf.

Gallagher, Kevin. 2004. *Free Trade and the Environment: Mexico, NAFTA, and Beyond.* Stanford, CA: Stanford University Press.

Harrison, James. 2009. "Conducting a Human Rights Impact Assessment of the Canada-Colombia Free Trade Agreement: Key Issues." Background paper prepared for the CCIC Americas Policy Group.

Harrison, James. 2011. "Human Rights Measurement: Reflections on the Current Practice and Future Potential of Human Rights Impact Assessments." *Journal of Human Rights Practice* 3 (2): 162–87. http://dx.doi.org/10.1093/jhuman/hur011.

Harrison, James, and Alessa Goller. 2008. "Trade and Human Rights: What Does 'Impact Assessment' Have to Offer?" *Human Rights Law Review* 8 (4): 587–615. http://dx.doi.org/10.1093/hrlr/ngn026.

Hobbes, Thomas. 1968. "Of the First and Second Naturall Lawes, and of Contracts." Chapter 14 of *Leviathan,* 189–201. New York: Penguin.

Kant, Immanuel. 1991. "An Answer to the Question: What Is Enlightenment." In *Political Writings,* 54–60. Cambridge: Cambridge University Press.

Keenan, Karyn. 2010. "Canadian Mining: Still Unaccountable." *North American Congress on Latin America: Report on the Americas,* May–June: 29–42.

Márquez, Gabriel García. 1970. *One Hundred Years of Solitude.* New York: Harper and Row.

Mumme, Stephen. 2007. "Trade Integration, Neoliberal Reform, and Environmental Protection in Mexico." *Latin American Perspectives* 34 (3): 91–107. http://dx.doi.org/10.1177/0094582X07300590.

Orquist, Paul. 1980. *Violence, Conflict, and Politics in Colombia.* New York: Academic Press.

Poulantzas, Nicos. 1969. "The Problem of the Capitalist State." *New Left Review* 58: 67–78.

Rochlin, James. 1993. *Discovering the Americas.* Vancouver: UBC Press.

Rochlin, James. 1997. *Redefining Mexican Security.* Boulder, CO: Lynne Rienner.

Rochlin, James. 2007. *Social Forces and the Revolution in Military Affairs: The Cases of Colombia and Mexico.* New York: Palgrave Macmillan. http://dx.doi.org/10.1057/9780230609662.

Rochlin, James. 2011a. "Colombian Labor, Globalization, and a Ray of Hope." *Global Labor Journal* 2 (3): 180–207.

Rochlin, James. 2011b. "Plan Colombia and the Revolution in Military Affairs: The Demise of the FARC." *Review of International Studies* 37 (2): 715–40. http://dx.doi.org/10.1017/S0260210510000914.

Rochlin, James. 2012. "Canada and the Americas: There's Still Much to Discover." In *Canada Looks South,* edited by Peter McKenna, 3–26. Toronto: University of Toronto Press.

Safford, Frank, and Marco Palacios. 2002. *Colombia: Fragmented Land, Divided Society.* New York: Oxford University Press.

Von Clausewitz, Carl. 1986. *On War.* Edited by Michael Howard and Peter Paret. Princeton, NJ: Princeton University Press.

10

Canada's Moral Identity in Africa and Its Implications for Policy in the Twenty-First Century

EDWARD AKUFFO

Canada's relationship with African states originated partly from Canada's "double heritage" as a former colonial settlement of Britain and France, also the largest and most powerful colonial powers in Africa. In this regard, the "shared history" between Canada and former British and French colonies in Africa provided the opportunity for Canadian missionaries and teachers to work on the African continent in the nineteenth century. It follows that Canada's development work in Africa can be traced to the colonial period. However, formal relations between Canada and African states began in the post–Second World War era, when African states gained independence from the European colonialists. What is striking is that Canada has not departed from its traditional role of "helping" to develop Africa through the provision of aid. Contemporary Canadian diplomatic and foreign relations with African states are built upon the provision of development assistance and the supply of peacekeeping forces, especially under the banner of the United Nations. Instrumentally, the two pillars of Canada's foreign policy – development assistance and peacekeeping – are the vehicles for the pursuit of Canada's political, economic, and strategic interests in Africa. At the normative level, development assistance and peacekeeping as policy arenas have also helped to craft a moral image for Canada in Africa. Thus, Canada's moral identity is derived from how Africa is perceived as the poor and conflict-ridden "other."

In theory, Canada's moral identity helps to define the ethical boundaries for, opportunities of, and constraints on Canada's internationalism in Africa. The ethics of Canadian foreign policy in Africa derive from Canada's perception of Africa as poor and conflict ridden; in other words, Canada sees Africa as a continent that needs development assistance and peacekeeping to alleviate the plight of Africans. The objectives of Canada's policy are focused largely on the promotion of human rights, poverty reduction, democracy, good governance, and the rule of law. These foreign policy goals potentially position Canada as occupying a privileged position as a developed country that has a moral obligation to assist African countries to address their development and security challenges (Akuffo 2012). Nevertheless, knowledgeable observers of the Canada-Africa relationship would agree that Canada's foreign policy toward Africa has waxed and waned over time. David Black (2008, 2013) captures this succinctly when he argues that there are consistent inconsistencies in Canada's foreign policy regarding Africa. For instance, though human rights protection has been a central theme in Canadian policy since the 1980s, Canada has not applied its human rights criteria for development assistance evenly across the African continent. This has been evidenced by the discrepancies in Canada's anti-apartheid policies in South Africa (Canadian International Developoment Agency 1981; Howard 1988). The geographical focus of the Harper government's foreign policy on Afghanistan appears to follow the trajectory of post-9/11 politics focused on the "Global War on Terror" (Bell 2010; Jefferess 2009; Sjolander and Trevenen 2010). Together with a renewed interest in the Americas, this constitutes an important shift away from the priorities of the Chrétien government, which made Africa the centrepiece of Canada's international cooperation. Yet Canada's moral identity in Africa is not dependent only on how much aid Canada sends to African states or how effectively Canada implements its foreign policy objectives.

Canada's moral identity is a structural phenomenon deeply rooted in Canada's historical relationship with Africa as a non-colonizer. That is, Canada's moral identity runs deep into its historical relationship with the African continent. The amount of aid or shift in geographical focus of Canadian policy can only have minor or episodic impacts on Canada's influence in Africa. Indeed, Canada's moral identity was not "bought" with the provision of aid and peacekeeping to Africa but largely derived from how Canada compares historically with other actors in Africa. As a non-colonizing middle power, Canada's moral identity has been sustained by the twin pillars of development assistance and peacekeeping in Africa. Even though Canada has historical links with Britain and France, which have colonial baggage in Africa, Canadian governments have succeeded over the years in carving a moral status that sets Canada apart from colonialism. It is important to stress that Canada's moral image has an intersubjective understanding among Africans. Officials of Africa's regional organizations, think tanks, and NGOs see Canada as friendly and responsive to Africa's development and security challenges (Akuffo 2012).

Arguably, contemporary Canadian advocacy on behalf of African issues reached its peak at the 2002 G8 Summit in Kananaskis when Canada rallied the advanced industrialized countries to adopt the Africa Action Plan to implement the priorities of the "made-in-Africa policy," the New Partnership for Africa's Development (NEPAD). These, among other activities, have served Canada well in the past forty years by helping to build its moral image even as Canada and African countries foster closer cooperation to address pressing development and security challenges on the African continent and beyond.

Historically, African states have supported Canada's security role in the international arena. The only exception was in 2010 when the Conservative government of Prime Minister Stephen Harper failed to attract African votes in support of Canada's UN Security Council bid, which ultimately led to Canada's defeat by Portugal. African votes have proven crucial for Canada's six elections into the Security Council. The failure to garner African votes in 2010 was partly a result of Harper's shift of Canadian foreign policy focus toward the Americas and Afghanistan. I discuss the implications of this policy shift later in the chapter. For now, it is noteworthy that African states provided overwhelming support when Canada was last elected into the Security Council in 1999 under the Chrétien government. Canada's Security Council membership came at the back of Canada's leadership on the promotion of human security – the protection of people from political violence – in the 1990s. Canada's moral image provided an incentive as African states supported Canada's leadership in establishing key international institutions for human security, such as the responsibility to protect norm, the Ottawa treaty to ban landmines, the Kimberly Process Certification Scheme for rough diamonds, and the International Criminal Court. The importance of human security for African states cannot be overemphasized given the prevalence of violent conflict and endemic poverty in parts of the continent. For the Chrétien government, human security meant the protection of people from violent threats – freedom from fear. In this regard, the African continent provided an important political space for the Chrétien government's "human security–oriented" foreign policy. Human security was an important idea that helped to rationalize Canada's engagement in Africa and reinforced Canada's ethical behaviour on the continent.

Nevertheless, Canadian governments have not fully utilized Canada's moral advantage insofar as Canada's economic relations with African states are concerned. Since 2006, the Harper government has embarked on a "strategic withdrawal policy" in Africa, concentrating instead on building economic partnerships in Latin America and the Caribbean through the signing of free-trade agreements with states such as Colombia (see Rochlin, this volume) and Peru. As well, Harper has focused on post-conflict reconstruction in Afghanistan. His policy has attracted several criticisms. According to Chrétien, "we [Canada] have disappeared from Africa" (see MacCharles 2010). In fact, it was Chrétien who started the deepening of economic relations between Canada and Latin American and Caribbean states in the mid-1990s when Canada signed the first free-trade agreement with Chile on 5 December 1996 (see Canada, Foreign Affairs, Trade, and Development Canada 2012). Nevertheless, the Harper government has cut Canadian aid to poor African states such as Malawi and Rwanda and closed Canada's embassies in states such as Gabon, Guinea, and Malawi. Indeed, there is speculation that embassies in Cameroon, Tunisia, and Zambia will be closed shortly ("Move from Canada to Close Embassy in Cameroon" 2010). Why is Canada withdrawing from Africa at a time when states such as China, the European Union, and the United States have intensified their relations on the African continent? What are the ethical and security implications of the Harper government's attitude toward Africa? The following discussion tries to answer these important questions within the context of contemporary Canadian foreign policy. The next section further contextualizes Canada's moral image in Africa. That discussion is followed by a more detailed analysis of the significant changes taking place on the African continent and what these changes mean for Canadian foreign policy.

Constructing Africa: The Discourse of Poverty and Conflict and the Limits of Canadian Engagement

As noted earlier, Canadian foreign policy toward Africa is embedded in Canada's conception of Africa as poor and conflict ridden. In this light, Canada's peacekeeping policy and development assistance policy appear to be rooted in the idea of humane internationalism, "a vital tradition in Canadian political culture" (Black 2009, 49; Pratt 1994). According to Cranford Pratt (1990, 5), humane internationalism is "an acceptance that the citizens and governments of the industrialised world have ethical responsibilities towards those beyond their borders who are suffering severely and who live in abject poverty." This "self-accredited" ethical responsibility of the Canadian state informs the advocacy of the "counter-consensus" – Canadian civil society – that calls for more poverty-focused aid to African states. Nevertheless, the discourse of poverty in general and poverty-focused aid in particular, while it elucidates Canada's moral credentials, is anachronistic because it calls not for a change in policy approach but merely for a reframing of the objectives of the old policy instruments – development assistance and peacekeeping. As Black and Tiessen have pointed out in this volume, new themes of focus for Canadian aid represent a repackaging of old themes that do not contribute to poverty alleviation – defined broadly. Indeed, Canada's poverty-driven policy perpetuates the construction of Africa as poor and conflict ridden. In other words, these negative perceptions are "self-fulfilling prophecies." As a unidirectional view, the poverty-focused foreign policy does not recognize significant political, economic, and social changes on the African continent and the need for Canada to reimagine and recraft its foreign policy accordingly.

The debate in the literature on Africa's place in Canada's foreign policy is largely concentrated on the issue of development assistance and peacekeeping (see, e.g., Black 2005, 2009; Clark 1991; Dorn 2005; Freeman 1982; Howard 1988). Inevitably, the poverty-focused discourse of Canadian internationalism in Africa suggests that Canada should have a "permanent interest" in poverty alleviation and human rights promotion that underpins Canada's moral image and ethical behaviour in Africa. In fact, such arguments carry weight given the overwhelming evidence of poverty in parts of Africa; however, they also portray a tacit consensus among the Canadian government and civil society that the African continent is only good for aid. These perceptions of Africa are transcribed into Canada's security engagement. It is noteworthy that Canadians are generally opposed to the use of force in Africa, which explains why African officials see Canada as a non-belligerent power (Akuffo 2012). For instance, a Harris/Decima survey in February 2013 indicated that most Canadians were opposed to sending Canadian combat troops to fight Islamic insurgents in Mali, though over one-third of the respondents supported sending humanitarian aid to displaced civilians. Not surprisingly, the chairman of Harris/Decima, Allan Greg, argued that "the notion that Canadians are 'peacekeepers' and moral leaders – as opposed to a combat nation – seems to run very deep and clearly applies to the current conflict in Mali" (cited in "Most Canadians Against

Sending Combat Troops to Mali, Poll Suggests" 2013). This suggests that the ethical foundation of Canada's foreign policy in Africa is deeply embedded in the collective psyche of Canadians. Yet Canadian public perceptions of Africa also place limits on the foreign policy options of Canadian governments. This appears to pose a dilemma for Canadian governments.

The unidirectional perception of Africa as a place for development assistance and peacekeeping overlooks the transformative potential of Canada's moral image when it is wedded with a comprehensive policy that could foster mutual economic and political interests for Canada and African states. Given the potential for accusations of exploitation, it can be argued that it would not be unethical for Canada to pursue economic and geostrategic interests in Africa insofar as government policies and practices provide opportunities for the protection and promotion of human rights, the rule of law, and poverty alleviation. In fact, it would be analytically bankrupt to extol the virtues of Canada as a moral leader while overlooking the fact that security and economic interests are integral parts of Canada's internationalism in Africa. It is common knowledge that the Canadian government has used aid and Canada's multilateral affiliations in the World Trade Organization, the World Bank, and the International Monetary Fund to pursue political and economic interests in African states. For example, tied aid that promotes trade and other economic interests has long been an integral part of Canadian development assistance in Africa (Gendron 2000; Morrison 1998, 2000). Furthermore, the Standing Senate Committee on Foreign Affairs and International Trade report indicates that Canada's economic profile is rising in Africa. Canada does more business in sub-Saharan Africa than it does in each of the emerging markets of BRIC (Brazil, Russia, India, and China) (SSCFAIT 2007). Canada is labelled as a "mining superpower" in Africa even though Canadian mining companies have also been found culpable of human rights violations and poor environmental management in African states (Akuffo 2012). The total value of Canadian mining assets has grown from a mere US$233 million in 1989 to US$21 billion in 2010 (see Tougas 2008).

These developments suggest that "altruistic motives" are hardly the only reasons behind Canadian policy toward Africa. Perhaps what needs to be investigated further is how Canada's moral image assists the growth of Canada's economic role on the African continent and how Canada's morality can be systematically linked to the pursuit of economic and political interests. In short, keen observers of Canada-Africa relations should investigate how to *humanize* the growing economic role of Canada in Africa in the twenty-first century. Such an endeavour would contribute to sustaining Canada's moral identity and continue to set Canada apart from other powers that not only have negative images but also exploitative practices.

While not denying the development challenges in African states and the need for development assistance to supplement the efforts of African governments (see, e.g., Black and Tiessen's chapter in this volume), the continuous portrayal of Africa as poor and conflict ridden in Canadian public discourses distorts "the reality" of Canadian activities in Africa driven by economic and political interests. In many ways, dominant discourses of Canadian foreign policy on Africa appear to advocate a "rescue of the perishing" in Africa, even though in practice Canada has not lived up to this standard. The conservative focus on development assistance and peacekeeping has not only consigned Africa to a peripheral position on Canada's foreign policy agenda but also shifted attention away from creating a comprehensive and coherent policy that seeks to build "humane economies." This is the kind of economic development that upholds human rights and human security in African states. Indeed, the peripheral status of Africa on the Canadian foreign policy agenda is a structural deficiency that explains the flux in Canadian engagement on the African continent.

As noted earlier, the Chrétien government supported the New Partnership for Africa's Development (NEPAD) and established a five-year, $500 million Canada Fund for Africa to assist in the implementation of NEPAD's priorities, including peace and security, trade and investment, environmental protection, and information and communication technologies.[1] A significant feature of the Canadian Fund for Africa is that it was crafted in the framework of development assistance, with CIDA as the key implementation agency. At the normative level, the Canadian Fund for Africa helped to sustain Canada's moral image in Africa. At the practical level, however, apart from the tokenism of the fund when measured against the overwhelming challenges in Africa, the Canadian Fund for Africa had a short life span since the Harper government disbanded it when the program ended in 2008. Indeed, the status of NEPAD is not clear as far as Harper's policy is concerned. Moreover, Canadian resource contribution to Africa has waxed and waned over time. Canadian official development assistance that stood at 0.49 percent of GNP in 1991–92 was slashed to 0.34 percent in 1996–97 and further reduced to 0.25 percent in 2000 (Black 2009; North-South Institute 2003; Morrison 1998, 369; Tomlin, Hiller, and Hanson 2007). Canadian aid disbursement to Africa had some increases as Canada spent 16.5 percent and 37.0 percent of its total aid budget in 2001–02 and 2002–03, respectively, in Africa (see Tomlinson 2004). Under the government of Paul Martin, there was also a slight increase from $1.7 billion to $1.9 billion of aid disbursement to Africa in the 2005–06 and 2006–07 fiscal years (CIDA 2008, 42; 2009, 36). As well, fourteen out of twenty-five of CIDA's countries of focus in 2005 were in Africa.[2] The concentration as well as increase in aid to Africa was short lived under the Conservative government of Stephen Harper. Although the Harper government said in its February 2008 budget that it had achieved Martin's promise in Gleneagles to double aid to Africa by 2009 based upon the 2003–04 levels (Canada 2005; 2008, 16; 2010, 142), the February 2009 announcement of twenty "new" CIDA development partners shifted Canadian aid focus to the Americas and Afghanistan. Consequently, the number of Canada's development partners in Africa was reduced from fourteen to seven[3] under the "aid effectiveness agenda" of the Conservative government (see CBC 2009; CIDA 2010). The Harper government's 2010 budget put a cap on aid increases to Africa as the government turned its attention to accountability for Canadian aid expenditure on the African continent (see Canada 2010).

The flux in Canada's activism in Africa is also apparent in the area of peacekeeping. Canada's overall financial contribution to the UN peacekeeping budget has kept pace with the demands for peacekeeping, but there has been a substantial decline in Canadian troop contributions to UN peacekeeping operations in general and in Africa in particular since the early 1990s (Keating 2013, 162; Peacebuild 2009, 1–2). Canada's contribution of 1,942 troops to UN peacekeeping operations in seventeen African states since the 1990s stands in stark contrast to its contribution of 2,830 military personnel to a single mission in Afghanistan since 2001. Canada's contribution to UN peacekeeping operations in African states is shown in Table 2.

The declining contribution of Canadian troops to UN peacekeeping missions appears to be an important factor that has led Canada to rely on African Union intervention. In other words, Canada appears to have shifted the burden of troop contributions to African emergencies to African states. Notably, the Liberal and Conservative governments did not deploy Canadian Forces personnel to emergencies such as Darfur; rather, they provided some funding and training support to African peacekeepers of the African Union (Akuffo 2012; Black and Williams 2008; Nossal 2005). Similarly, the Harper government refused to deploy Canadian forces on the ground in support of France to fight Islamic insurgents in Mali in 2013. Nevertheless, Canada did deploy its Royal Canadian Air Force to enforce Security Council Resolution 1973, which allowed NATO to use airstrikes to protect civilians

TABLE 2

Canadian troop contributions to UN peacekeeping operations in Africa, 1960–2014

Name	Location	Dates	Canadian personnel
ONUC	Congo	1960–64	300 military
UNTAG	Namibia	1989–90	300 military + 100 police
UNAVEM II	Angola	1991–95	15 military
MINURSO	Western Sahara	1991-present	35 military (until 1994)
ONUMOZ	Mozambique	1992–94	4 military
UNOSOM I, II	Somalia	1992–95	759 military
UNOMUR	Uganda-Rwanda	1993–94	3 military
UNAMIR	Rwanda	1993–96	112 military
MINURCA	Central African Republic	1998–2000	80 military
UNAMSIL	Sierra Leone	1999–2005	5 military
MONUC	Democratic Republic of the Congo	1999–2010	12 military
UNMEE	Ethiopia and Eritrea	2000–03	450 military
UNMIL	Liberia	2003–13	4 military
UNOCI	Ivory Coast	2004-present	5 police
UNMIS(S)	Sudan/South Sudan	2005-present	28 military + 21 police
MONUSCO	Democratic Republic of the Congo	2010-present	9 military
UNIFSA	Sudan/South Sudan	2011-present	None
MINUSMA	Mali	2013-present	None

Sources: Canada, Department of National Defence (2008, 2013, 2014); Keating (2013); Peacebuild (2009); United Nations Association in Canada (2013).

in Libya in 2011. The nature and scope of violence in Libya and Mali, which involve terrorists and guerrilla groups, suggest that Canada should do more to sustain its peacekeeping tradition by supporting peace and security efforts in African states with relatively large Canadian troop deployments, as it did in the Congo, Namibia, Somalia, Rwanda, and Eritrea, as shown in Table 2. Although some of these peacekeeping operations encountered several challenges, especially the collapse of the Somalia state since 1992, and the genocide in Rwanda in 1994, the relatively high numbers of troop deployments demonstrated Canada's willingness to support international efforts to promote peace and security in Africa.

The overall picture, however, shows not only a significant rhetoric-resource gap in Canadian policy but also the extent to which Canadian public perceptions of Africa as poor and conflict ridden, and the discomfort of the Canadian public over the use of force in Africa, place structural limits on Canadian foreign policy. These are double paradoxes in the Canadian approach to Africa. On the one hand, there is the perception of Africa as poor and conflict ridden, yet there is a focus on pursuing economic and political interests; on the other, there is a moral identity that is not actively linked to the provision of resources. These paradoxes could be resolved when Canadian officials and the general public perform a more realistic appraisal of Canadian policy on Africa, taking into consideration the political, economic, and social changes taking place in Africa in the twenty-first century. In this light, it is important to reiterate that it is not unethical for Canada to pursue economic and geostrategic interests in Africa as long as government policies and practices provide opportunities for the protection and promotion of human rights, the rule of law, and poverty alleviation. Indeed, though development assistance and peacekeeping would remain significant in Canadian foreign policy, they would not be the only instruments of engagement in the "new" Africa.

A Changing Africa and the Need for a Comprehensive Canadian Policy

African issues have constantly featured on the international cooperation agendas of Canadian governments. Despite Canada's economic and political interests in Africa, there appears to be a consensus among the Canadian government and civil society groups that Africa is good for aid and peacekeeping because of the persistent poverty and violent conflicts in parts of the continent. This perception distorts the reality of Canada's role in Africa. In turn, it contributes to the perpetually peripheral status of the continent on Canada's geopolitical map. For instance, at a meeting with African diplomats in Ottawa on 20 January 2009, Minister of Foreign Affairs Lawrence Cannon said that the geographic priorities of the Harper government lie in Afghanistan, the Americas, and emerging markets (DFAIT 2009). This announcement marked a turning point in Canada's policy away from its earlier height with the launching of NEPAD and the repositioning of "Africa as a partner" of Canada.

Consistent with the prevailing narrative, it is not surprising that the policy focus of the Harper government raised concerns among politicians, civil society groups, academics, diplomats, and some government officials about Canada's long-term commitment to Africa's development (Akuffo 2012). These concerns focused on the moral obligation of Canada to continue to provide aid to African states. However, critics of Canadian foreign policy in Africa, and the Harper government's policy in particular, scarcely focused on how Canada can transform its strategic moral advantage into a comprehensive policy to reflect the current socio-political and strategic position of the African continent in the global economy. The growing importance of Africa in this economy was demonstrated partly by the launching of NEPAD and the renewed activism of states such as China, the European Union, and the United States on the continent.

The NEPAD initiative provided an important qualitative change in Canada's approach to Africa as the Liberal government tailored its response through the Canadian Fund for Africa to a wide range of areas, including agriculture, the environment, water, health, information and communication technologies, peace and security, and governance. Inasmuch as critics might be right in criticizing NEPAD because of its conformity to neoliberal ideology (e.g., see Taylor 2006), the wide range of issues that it covers is central to Africa's security and development. The Chrétien government, however, fell short of using the NEPAD framework as an opportunity to develop a morally responsible and comprehensive policy on Africa. That is, the government, though appearing to uphold Canada's moral obligation to Africa, failed to incorporate systematically more activist trade, investment, and security initiatives that would have real impact on and long-term support for Africa's development. The token five-year, $500 million Canadian Fund for Africa was woefully inadequate given the overwhelming development and security challenges in African states. Moreover, the Harper government retreated from NEPAD until January 2010, when Minister of Foreign Affairs Cannon attended a NEPAD Heads of State Implementation Committee meeting as part of the African Union Summit in Addis Ababa (DFAIT 2010).

As noted earlier, Canada's moral identity is a structural phenomenon built into Canada's historical relationship with Africa as a non-colonizer. It therefore makes sense that Canadian governments are "hooked" on maintaining a moral image in Africa by following in the tradition of peacekeeping in and providing development assistance to the continent. But troubling is that the Harper government, like previous governments, appears to be willing to sacrifice the development of a long-term and overarching policy toward Africa for short-term domestic and foreign policy interests. For instance, the Harper government, through its attendance at the NEPAD meeting in 2010, and through it endorsement of the January 2013 proposal to provide $13 million in humanitarian aid in addition to Canada's official development assistance to Mali (Payton 2013), wanted to appear sensitive to Canadian public opinion, which has criticized the government's withdrawal from Africa since it came to power.

Although Africa appears to have "regained" some importance for the Harper government in view of Harper's visits to states such as Uganda, Morocco, Senegal, and the Democratic Republic of the Congo, the government has given no indication of crafting an overarching, long-term policy on the continent (Akuffo 2013b). Visits by Governor General Michaälle Jean in 2006, and by Canadian government officials since 2012 (e.g., Minister of Trade Ed Fast led a trade mission to Ghana and Nigeria from 27 January to 1 February 2013) (DFAIT 2013a), do not represent a substantive shift in policy toward Africa. Canadian trade missions to Africa are nothing new. Indeed, they were a major policy activity of the Liberal government in the wake of NEPAD. In this light, the Conservative government's "re-engagement" with Africa is more of an attempt to please a Canadian public critical of Harper's development assistance policy toward the continent. Although the visits help to reinforce Canada's moral image, in themselves they do not constitute a sea change in Canada's role in Africa.

As noted above, Canada's attendance at the 2010 NEPAD meeting did little to attract Africa's vote for Canada's UN Security Council bid that year. It is hard to say whether this setback animated the Harper government's recent engagements in Africa as Canada seeks to reignite its moral leadership on the continent. The Conservative government's renewed interest in Africa, however, runs counter to the prevailing assumptions in the run-up to the Security Council vote. Lee Berthiaume (2010) argued that "experts acknowledge the potential link – and the unspoken concern – that once the [Security Council] campaign is over, Africa will again slide off the [Harper] government's radar." In view of the robustness of the moral identity structure, Canada's failure to attract African votes appears to be more a minor shift in African attitude toward Canada. African Union Chairperson and President of Benin Thomas Boni Yayi visited Ottawa in January 2013 to seek Canada's and NATO's assistance for the African forces fighting Islamic rebels and terrorists in Mali (BBC News 2013). It would therefore be an overstatement that Canada has lost its moral influence in Africa. Rather, from a critical standpoint, it appears that Canada's moral image is no longer enough to sustain Canada's influence in the "new" Africa if this image is not linked to more substantive efforts – in investment, trade, and security – to create jobs and promote human rights and the overall development of African states in the twenty-first century.

It is commendable that the Harper government is reviving Canada's engagement with Africa since the 2010 Security Council vote. For example, Harper's visit to Morocco in January 2011 sought to rejuvenate economic relations between the two countries, which have a two-way trade of about $500 million (CTV News 2011). Similar efforts to deepen economic relations were made by government officials who visited other African countries. Nevertheless, the persistent depiction of Africa as poor and conflict ridden might reduce the incentive to develop a long-term, comprehensive policy – a policy geared to developing humane economies that would secure human rights and human security and support the long-term interests of Canada and African states.

Africa has entered a new epoch in its security and development efforts that demands a fuller reassessment of the positions of the states and regional organizations on Canada's foreign policy map. This suggests that Canada should move past the treatment of Africa as a peripheral region to satisfy short-term national interests. To put it bluntly, it is in Canada's long-term interest to (re)commit more substantive resources to African states and regional organizations. As George MacLean (2006, 64) argues, "Canadian foreign policy has always been about self-interest. Any other basis for a foreign policy makes no sense." In this light, the changing geopolitical and economic environment in Africa requires that Canada rethink its long-term national interest even as it pays close attention to maintaining its moral identity on the continent.

Moral identity provides normative legitimacy to Canada's engagement in Africa. Nevertheless, the pursuit of a narrowly focused morality in the absence of a linkage to the emerging political and economic realities in African states is tantamount to a narrow conception of Canada's interests. Canada's foreign policy concentration on aid and peacekeeping, together with a weakening of diplomatic ties, would undermine Canada's institutional presence and influence in Africa. As mentioned above, Canada closed its high commission in Malawi just five years after it was opened (York 2009). Other Canadian embassies and consulates have been closed or downgraded, including those in Guinea, Gabon, and Cape Town (Berthiaume 2010). At the normative level, these actions might have minor impacts on Canada's historically produced moral identity, embedded in Canada's lack of a colonial past in Africa. At the institutional level, however, these actions limit Canada's scope of influence, vital for a long-term, comprehensive policy on Africa. To this end, there is a need for "new thinking" and a policy (re)focus that reconstructs Africa in a positive light to support the development of a long-term, comprehensive, and coherent Canadian foreign policy.

The African continent is changing after going through decades of economic and political reforms prescribed by international financial institutions such as the World Bank and the International Monetary Fund. Although the memories of colonialism linger, seventeen of the fifty-three African states celebrated fifty years of independence in 2010 (see Myjoyonline News 2010a). Moreover, even though political turmoil in places such as Zimbabwe and the 2010 *coup d'états* in Guinea and Niger (Reuters 2010; BBC News 2009) affected progress on democratic governance, a new generation of Africans is emerging and seems to be deeply concerned about political stability and economic security of African states and peoples. Countries such as Botswana, Ghana, Senegal, Tanzania, and Zambia have established stable democratic governments, the rule of law, and human rights. It is important to add that African economies recorded an annual growth rate of between 5 and 6 percent in the decade ending in 2008 even as the world economy was going through a financial crisis. Moreover, Africa's economic growth contributed to a decline in the annual rate of poverty reduction. Africa is reducing its poverty levels faster than the Indian subcontinent, which has a population similar to that of Africa (see Myjoyonline News 2010b).

The World Bank chief economist for the Africa region, Shanta Devarajan, has claimed that "Africa is on the brink of a take-off" (cited in Myjoyonline News 2010b). Similarly, Ngozi Okong-Iweala, the managing director of the World Bank Group, argued that

> people [including Canada] should look at us [Africa] as a pole of growth. Africa should not only be seen as a continent with cup in hand always looking for aid, but a continent where some of the countries are doing so well they can be seen as middle income countries. Africa has come of age and we do not just need aid. It is now an active member of the new multi-polar global economy. Old concepts of the Third World no longer apply in the new multi-polar global economy. (cited in ibid.)

Chris Alden (2007, 93) adds that "Africa, the erstwhile forgotten continent is once again the object of great power interest." Although Africa has often been constructed as poor and conflict ridden by various Canadian governments and civil society, global powers such as the United States and China, and powerful regional organizations such as the European Union, are forging closer ties with African states and regional organizations on a wide range of issues, including peace and security, democratic governance, human rights, trade, investment, energy, migration, and climate change. For instance, the African Union and the European Union instituted an annual Africa-EU Summit and signed an Africa-EU Strategic Partnership Agreement in December 2007 that defines the long-term policy orientations and interests of the two continents.[4] Furthermore, in spite of resistance from African countries, the United States has established an Africa Command (AFRICOM), a unified combat command for military operations to protect its foreign policy interests in Africa. AFRICOM also seeks to strengthen the defence capabilities of African states and regional organizations.[5] It is well known that China's quest for energy security has resulted in huge investments in Africa, especially in the oil sector. Moreover, China's trade with African states had a tremendous boost over the past decade. The *China Daily* reported in 2012 that Africa is likely to become China's largest trading partner in three to five years. This new trend in China-Africa relations should not be surprising; China has crafted an Africa policy and since 2000 been holding summits every three years with African leaders to deepen relations. China provided the entire funding of $200 million as a "gift" for the construction of an ultramodern office complex for the African Union (BBC News 2012). Indeed, China's incursion into Africa is having a snowball effect as African states are reorienting their foreign policies toward the East, even though Chinese investment practices are fraught with environmental degradation as well as human rights violations (Broadhead 2012). The weaknesses of China's investment practices on the one hand, and the belligerent or colonial image of states such as the United Kingdom, France, and the United States on the other, help to elucidate Canada's moral identity in Africa.

Conclusion

The strategic position of Africa in the global economy calls for a rethinking of Canada's approach to the continent. Indeed, Canada's investment and commercial profile is rising in Africa as Canada builds on its niche in the extractive sector. As noted above, Canada is touted as a mining superpower in Africa. To help secure the investments in mining and other sectors, Canada signed Foreign Investment Promotion and Protection Agreements

(FIPAs) – international treaties that aim to protect and promote foreign investment through legally binding rights and obligations – with middle-income African countries such as South Africa in 1995 (not yet implemented at the time of writing) and Egypt in 1996 (brought into force on 3 November 1997). A FIPA was extended to Madagascar, a lower-income country, in 2008 (DFAIT 2013b). Canada has concluded FIPAs with Benin, Cameroon, Madagascar, Mali, Senegal, and Tanzania. Moreover, negotiations are under way to conclude FIPAs with Burkina Faso, Côte D'Ivoire, Ghana, and Tunisia. It is expected that FIPAs will be extended to other African states. An important feature of FIPAs is that they have an environmental assessment component to ensure that Canadian investors adhere to strict environmental standards. According to the Canadian government, "FIPA encourages good governance ... [and] promotes sustainable development principles by ensuring that Governments will not lower health, safety or environmental measures in order to attract investment" (Canada. Foreign Affairs, Trade and Development Canada 2013).

The ethical standards underpinning FIPAs are impressive; however, Canada's FIPAs appear to protect the financial rights of Canadian investors more than the human rights of indigenous peoples. For instance, the Canada-South Africa FIPA, signed in 1995, has not been implemented because the disciplines of the agreement were at variance with the principles of the Black Economic Empowerment program of the South African government (see Akuffo 2013a). In this regard, Human Rights Impact Assessments (HRIAs), as argued by James Rochlin in this volume, could supplement the good intentions of Canada's FIPAs with African states. More importantly, a periodic HRIA would help to sustain Canada's moral identity in African states.

FIPAs comprise an important step toward deepening economic relations in Africa and shifting Canadian foreign policy away from its narrow focus on development assistance and peacekeeping, both of which have withered since the mid-1990s. Indeed, FIPAs sensitive to Africa's needs would go a long way toward improving the well-being of Africans even as Canada pursues its own national interests. In this light, the Canadian government should be more aggressive in expanding humane-oriented FIPAs sensitive to African conditions to other African states while deepening its relations in other areas, particularly the security sector, by channelling more resources to build a robust relationship with African regional organizations. As competition for influence in Africa keeps growing in the twenty-first century, Canadian foreign policy makers should restrategize their approach to the region by translating Canada's moral image into a genuine commitment of resources. They should build stronger partnerships covering a wider range of mutual interests – including energy, trade and investment, climate change, science and technology, democratic governance and human rights, and peace and security – that would improve the well-being of Africans.

The first step toward a comprehensive and coherent Canada-Africa policy would be the (re)construction of Africa in a positive light. Put differently, if the Canadian government, civil society groups, and the public were to reimagine Africa beyond the poor and conflict-ridden narrative, doing so would open the way for a stronger Canada-Africa relationship. Indeed, the value of any foreign policy narrative resides not only in the narrative itself but also in the pragmatic responses that the narrative can generate to address real problems. Thus, by translating its strategic moral identity into a comprehensive and coherent policy, Canada would sustain its moral leadership and have the edge over other competitors in Africa that are perceived as either undemocratic (China) or colonial and belligerent (France, the United Kingdom, and the United States). A morally crafted policy sensitive to African conditions will help Canada to make a genuine contribution to Africa's security and development while promoting Canada's own interests in the continent in the twenty-first century.

NOTES

1 For details of the projects supported by the Canadian Fund for Africa, see CIDA (2003, 2006).
2 The fourteen African countries were Benin, Burkina Faso, Cameroon, Ethiopia, Ghana, Kenya, Malawi, Mali, Mozambique, Niger, Rwanda, Senegal, Tanzania, and Zambia. For details, see CIDA (2005).
3 See Berthiaume (2009). The seven new development partners are Ethiopia, Ghana, Mali, Mozambique, Sudan, Senegal, and Tanzania.
4 For details of the AU-EU strategic partnership, see Council of the European Union (2007).
5 For more information on AFRICOM, see "About the Command," http://www.africom.mil/about-the-command.

References

Akuffo, Edward Ansah. 2012. *Canadian Foreign Policy in Africa: Regional Approaches to Peace, Security, and Development.* Aldershot, UK: Ashgate Publishing Company.
Akuffo, Edward Ansah. 2013a. "Beyond Apartheid: Moral Identity, FIPAs, and NEPAD in Canada-South Africa Relations." *Commonwealth and Comparative Politics* 51 (2): 173–88. http://dx.doi.org/10.1080/14662043.2013.774196.

Akuffo, Edward Ansah. 2013b. "A New Love for Africa." Canadian International Council. http://opencanada.org/features/the-think-tank/comments/a-new-love-for-africa/.

Alden, Chris. 2007. *China in Africa*. London: Zed Books.

BBC News. 2009. "Guinea Junta Pledges 2009 Polls." http://news.bbc.co.uk/2/hi/7811152.stm.

BBC News. 2012. "African Union Opens Chinese-Funded HQ in Ethiopia." http://www.bbc.co.uk/news/world-africa-16770932.

BBC News. 2013. "NATO Forces Needed in Mali, Says AU's Thomas Boni Yayi." http://www.bbc.co.uk/news/world-africa-20957063.

Bell, Colleen. 2010. "Fighting the War and Winning the Peace: Three Critiques of the War in Afghanistan." In *Canadian Foreign Policy in Critical Perspective*, edited by J. Marshall Beier and Lana Wylie, 58–71. Toronto: Oxford University Press.

Berthiaume, Lee. 2009. "CIDA Confirms Shift to Americas, Fewer Countries." *Embassy Magazine*, 25 February. http://www.embassymag.ca/page/view/cida_shift_americas-2-25-2009.

Berthiaume, Lee. 2010. "Is Security Council Bid Promoting Pseudo-Interest in Africa?" *Embassy Magazine*, 14 April. http://www.embassymag.ca/page/view/africa-04-14-2010.

Black, David. 2005. "From Kananaskis to Gleneagles: Assessing Canadian Leadership on Africa." *Behind the Headlines* 62 (3): 1–16.

Black, David. 2008. "Africa as a Serial Morality Tale in Canadian Foreign Policy." Paper presented to the annual meeting of ISA-Canada and the Canadian Political Science Association, Vancouver, June.

Black, David. 2009. "Out of Africa? The Harper Government's New 'Tilt' in the Developing World." *Canadian Foreign Policy Journal* 15 (2): 41–56. http://dx.doi.org/10.1080/11926422.2009.9673486.

Black, David. 2013. "Canada and Sub-Saharan Africa: Beyond Consistent Inconsitency?" Center for International Policy Studies. http://cips.uottawa.ca/canada-and-sub-saharan-africa-beyond-consistent-inconsistency/.

Black, David, and Paul Williams. 2008. "Darfur's Challenge to International Society." *Behind the Headlines* 65 (6): 1–23.

Broadhead, Ivan. 2012. "African Governments Criticized for Indifference towards Chinese Abuses." Voice of America. http://www.voanews.com/content/african_diaspora_criticizes_african_governments_indifference_towards_chinese_abuses/1447793.html.

Canada. 2005. *International Policy Statement: A Role of Pride and Influence in the World*. Gatineau, QC: CIDA.

Canada. 2008. *The Budget in Brief 2008: Responsible Leadership*. http://www.budget.gc.ca/2008/pdf/brief-bref-eng.pdf.

Canada. 2010. *Leading the Way on Jobs and Growth: Budget Report*. Jim Flaherty, 4 March. http://www.budget.gc.ca/2010/pdf/budget-planbudgetaire-eng.pdf.

Canada, Department of National Defence. 2008. *Details/Information for Canadian Forces*. http://www.cmp-cpm.forces.gc.ca/dhh-dhp/od-bdo/di-ri-eng.asp?IntlOpId=134&CdnOpId=156.

Canada. Department of National Defence. 2014. "Operation Crocodile." http://www.forces.gc.ca/en/operations-abroad-current/op-crocodile.page?.

Canada. Department of National Defence. 2013. "Operation Safari." http://www. forces.gc.ca/en/operations-abroad-past/op-safari.page?

Canada. Foreign Affairs, Trade, and Development Canada. 2012. *Canada-Chile Free Trade Agreement.* http://www.international.gc.ca/trade-agreements-accords-commerciaux/agr-acc/chile-chili/index.aspx?view=d.

Canada. Foreign Affairs, Trade, and Development Canada. 2013. "Canada's Foreign Investment Protection and Promotion Agreements (FIPAs)." http://www.inter-national.gc.ca/trade-agreements-accords-commerciaux/agr-acc/peru-perou/report-rapport.aspx.

Canadian International Development Agency (CIDA). 1981. *Canada's Development Assistance to Commonwealth Africa.* Ottawa: CIDA.

Canadian International Development Agency (CIDA). 2003. *Canada Fund for Africa: New Vision, New Partnership.* Ottawa: CIDA.

Canadian International Development Agency (CIDA). 2005. "CIDA Announces New Development Partners: Developing Countries Where Canada Can Make a Difference." News release, 19 April. http://news.gc.ca/.

Canadian International Development Agency (CIDA). 2006. *Canada Fund for Africa: Delivering Results.* Ottawa: CIDA.

Canadian International Development Agency (CIDA). 2008. *Statistical Report of Official Development Assistance.* Gatineau, QC: CIDA.

Canadian International Development Agency (CIDA). 2009. *Statistical Report of Official Development Assistance.* Gatineau, QC: CIDA.

Canadian International Development Agency (CIDA). 2010. "Haiti." 13 January. http://www.acdi-cida.gc.ca/acdi-cida/ACDI-CIDA.nsf/Eng/JUD-12912349-NLX.

North-South Institute.2003. *From Doha to Cancun: Development and the WTO.* Ottawa: North-South Institute.

CBC. 2009. "Canada's Military Mission in Afghanistan." 10 February. http://www. cbc.ca/news/canada/canada-s-military-mission-in-afghanistan-1.777386.

China Daily. 2012. "African Trade to Surpass EU, US." http://www.chinadaily.com. cn/china/2012-10/13/content_15814760.htm.

Clark, Andrew. 1991. *Mosaic or Patchwork? Canadian Policy towards Sub-Saharan Africa in the 1980s.* Ottawa: North-South Institute.

Council of the European Union. 2007. *The Africa-EU Strategic Partnership: A Joint Africa-EU Strategy.* http://www.consilium.europa.eu/uedocs/cms_data/docs/pressdata/en/er/97496.pdf.

CTV News. 2011. "Harper Avoids Local Politics on Moroccan Visit." http://www. ctvnews.ca/harper-avoids-local-politics-on-moroccan-visit-1.600452.

Department of Foreign Affairs and International Trade (DFAIT). 2009. "Notes for an Address by Honourable Lawrence Cannon, Minister of Foreign Affairs, to Heads of African Missions to Canada" http://www.international.gc.ca/media/aff/speechesdiscours/2009/386828.aspx?lang=en&view=d.

Department of Foreign Affairs and International Trade (DFAIT). 2010. "Minister Cannon Concludes Successful Discussions at African Union Summit." http:// www.international.gc.ca/media/aff/news-communiques/2010/51.aspx?lang=eng.

Department of Foreign Affairs and International Trade (DFAIT). 2013a. "Minister Fast Leads Trade Mission to Africa." http://www.international.gc.ca/media_commerce/comm/news-communiques/2013/01/27a.aspx?lang=eng&view=d.

Department of Foreign Affairs and International Trade (DFAIT). 2013b. "Canada's Foreign Investment Promotion and Protection Agreements (FIPAs)." http://www. international.gc.ca/trade-agreements-accords-commerciaux/agr-acc/fipa-apie/ index.aspx?view=d.

Dorn, Walter A. 2005. "Canadian Peacekeeping: Proud Tradition Strong Future?" *Canadian Foreign Policy* 12 (2): 7–32. http://dx.doi.org/10.1080/11926422.2005 .9673396.

Freeman, Linda. 1982. "CIDA, Wheat, and Rural Development in Tanzania." *Canadian Journal of African Studies* 16 (3): 479–504. http://dx.doi.org/10.2307/484556.

Gendron, Robin. 2000. "Education Aid for French Africa and Canada-Quebec Dispute over Foreign Policy in the 1960s." *International Journal (Toronto, Ont.)* 56 (1): 19–36. http://dx.doi.org/10.2307/40203529.

Howard, Rhoda E. 1988. "Black Africa and South Africa." In *Human Rights in Canadian Foreign Policy,* edited by Robert O. Mathews and Cranford. Montreal/ Kingston: McGill-Queen's University Press.

Jefferess, David. 2009. "Responsibility, Nostalgia, and the Mythology of Canada as a Peacekeeper." *University of Toronto Quarterly* 78 (2): 709–27. http://dx.doi. org/10.3138/utq.78.2.709.

Keating, Tom. 2013. *Canada and World Order: Multilateralist Tradition in Canadian Foreign Policy.* 3rd ed. Toronto: Oxford University Press.

MacCharles, Tonda. 2010. "Is Africa on Stephen Harper's Radar?" *Toronto Star,* 11 June. http://www.thestar.com/news/canada/2010/06/11/is_africa_on_stephen_harpers_radar.html.

MacLean, George. 2006. "Human Security in the National Interests? Canada, POGG, and the 'New' Multilateralism." In *A Decade of Human Security: Global Governance and New Multilateralisms,* edited by Sandra MacLean, David Black, and Timothy Shaw, 63–72. Hampshire, UK: Ashgate Publishing Company.

Morrison, David R. 1998. *Aid and Ebb Tide: A History of CIDA and Canadian Assistance.* Waterloo, ON: Wilfrid Laurier University Press.

Morrison, David R. 2000. "Canadian Aid: A Mixed Record and an Uncertain Future." In *Transforming Development: Foreign Aid for a Changing World,* edited by Jim Freedman, 15–36. Toronto: University of Toronto Press.

"Most Canadians Against Sending Combat Troops To Mali, Poll Suggests." 2013. *Ottawa Citizen,* 9 February. http://www.ottawacitizen.com/technology/Most+Canadians+against+sending+combat+troops+Mali+poll/7944331/story.html.

"Move from Canada to Close Embassy in Cameroon." 2010. *Cameroon Today,* November. http://news.cameroon-today.com/move-from-canada-to-close-embassy-in-cameroon/1517/.

Myjoyonline News. 2010a. "Gabby: Nkrumah Personified the Tragedy of 20th Century Africa." http://politics.myjoyonline.com/pages/news/201009/52707.php.

Myjoyonline News. 2010b. "World Bank Boss Upbeat about Africa." http://business. myjoyonline.com/pages/news/201004/45390.php.

Nossal, Kim R. 2005. "Ear Candy: Canadian Policy toward Humanitarian Intervention and Atrocity Crimes in Darfur." *International Journal (Toronto, Ont.)* 60 (4): 1017–32. http://dx.doi.org/10.2307/40204096.

Payton, Laura. 2013. "Canada to Provide $13M More Aid for Mali." CBC News, 29 January. http://www.cbc.ca/news/politics/canada-to-provide-13m-more-for-mali-aid-1.1321845.

Peacebuild. 2009. "Canada and UN Peacekeeping." http://www.peacebuild.ca/documents/CanadaUNPKOE.pdf.

Pratt, Cranford. 1990. "Middle Power Internationalism and Global Poverty." In *Middle Power Internationalism: The North-South Dimension*, edited by Cranford Pratt, 3–24. Montreal/Kingston: McGill-Queen's University Press.

Pratt, Cranford. 1994. "Humane Internationalism and Canadian Development Assistance Policies." In *Canadian International Development Assistance Policies*, edited by Cranford Pratt, 334–74. Montreal/Kingston: McGill-Queen's University Press.

Reuters. 2010. "Niger Coup Leader Silent on Election Timetable." 19 February. http://www.reuters.com/article/2010/02/19/us-niger-coup-idUSTRE61H4VB20100219.

SSCFAIT (Standing Senate Committee on Foreign Affairs and International Trade). 2007. *Overcoming 40 Years of Failure: A New Road Map for Sub-Saharan Africa*. Ottawa: Senate of Canada.

Sjolander, Claire T., and Kathryn Trevenen. 2010. "Constructing Canadian Foreign Policy; Myths of Good International Citizens, Protectors, and the War in Afghanistan." In *Canadian Foreign Policy in Critical Perspective*, edited by J. Marshall Beier and Lana Wylie, 44–57. Toronto: Oxford University Press.

Taylor, Ian. 2006. "When 'Good Economics' Does Not Make Good Sense." In *Beyond the "African Tragedy": Discourses on Development and the Global Economy*, edited by Malinda Smith, 85–104. Aldershot, UK: Ashgate Publishing Company.

Tomlin, Brian W., Norman Hiller, and Fen Osler Hampson. 2007. *Canada's International Policies: Agendas, Alternatives, and Politics*. Toronto: Oxford University Press.

Tomlinson, Brian. 2004. "A CCIC Briefing Note: Recent Trends in Canadian Aid to sub-Saharan Africa." http://www.ccic.ca/_files/en/working_groups/003_acf_2004-10_subsaharan_africa_aid_trends.pdf.

Tougas, Denis. 2008. "Canada in Africa: The Mining Superpower." *Pambazuka News: Pan-African Voices for Freedom and Justice*, 11 November, 407. http://www.pambazuka.org/en/category/features/52095.

United Nations Association in Canada. 2013 "The Canadian Contribution to United Nations Peacekeeping." National Defence and Canadian Forces. http://www.cmp-cpm.forces.gc.ca/dhh-dhp/od-bdo/di-ri-eng.asp?IntlOpId=134&CdnOpId=156.

York, Geoffrey. 2009. "Banned Aid." *Globe and Mail*, 29 May. http://www.theglobeandmail.com/globe-debate/munk-debates/banned-aid/article4261160/?page=all.

Conclusion
Moving Forward with Ethics and Security

ROSALIND WARNER

When leaders use terms such as "ethics" and "security," they activate key ideas that shape how decisions are made. Acting in the world means effecting ethical codes that have multiple origins and referents. The traditions of positive law, the framework of moral convictions, and the norms and rules enacted historically all play a part. At the beginning of the twenty-first century, events challenged Canadian decision makers to think clearly about the ethics of ensuring security. At the same time, rigorous and sustained analysis of the ethics-security balance has been relatively absent, a gap which this book seeks to address. Ethical analysis goes beyond a discussion of values by taking seriously the complexities of "real-world" decision making that necessarily imply trade-offs among incompatible choices. To protect national security while preserving human rights, actors must move between specific cases and general principles that guide decisions. Decision makers must frame their arguments in terms of coherent principles recognizable to their constituents, friends, and even enemies. The concrete and the abstract inform each other through analysis and action. Effective action means recognizing the ways in which ethics and security are connected and thinking through these implications using systematic methods.

In the introduction, we emphasized three main categories of engagement with ethics and security in Canada's international relations: the question of scope, the necessity of multilevel analysis, and the question of purpose and coherence. The contributors to this volume have examined key questions in their retrospective analyses: the meanings of ethics and security, the changes over the years since the 1990s, and the implications for Canada's place in the world and for policy decision making. The authors have analyzed these questions from different viewpoints and applied their own conceptions of ethics and security to explain the complexity of the world in ethical terms. In general, the authors have rejected a strictly oppositional view that would place ethics and security in distinct analytical compartments. Ethics and security exist in an often paradoxical and complex relationship, linked through thought and action. Although the authors have not agreed on a definition of either ethics or security, their findings address common themes and issues that point to the necessity of continuing inquiry. Action is always cloaked in a set of meanings that creates and interprets the world in a particular way and thus draws on ethical frames to either reproduce or challenge understandings. In general, the contributors have chosen to challenge rather than reproduce prevailing conceptions of ethics and security. In the process, they have shown that the twin notions of security and ethics are reference points for leveraging different imagined worlds.

Several trends animate a retrospective analysis. Although Canada remains engaged with the world, the nature of its internationalism has undergone important changes. To the extent that the language of human security allows a wider scope for ethical discussion, its muting means a narrowing of ethical debate. The War on Terror reinvigorated the idea of national security, but this framework does not fully encompass a twenty-first-century struggle involving global non-governmental actors and diffuse threats. The cases of Maher Arar and Omar Khadr tested the application of the ethical principles around national security without provoking a more profound reconsideration of the ethics-security nexus (see Kitchen 2013, 172–76). As indicated by the subject matter of this volume, narrowing and muting are found in a wide range of policy areas, including military and humanitarian action, anti-terrorism policies, development assistance, gender and food aid, climate policies, and trade. Edgar discusses the shrinking of humanitarian space, and Hendershot highlights this trend in the rise of the commercial military and security services industry. Black and Tiessen describe a trend toward focused aid policy. Tiessen and Tuckey analyze the implications of these trends for gender mainstreaming, while Stoett examines the ethical and security implications in climate adaptation. In terms of the scope for ethics in decision making, contributors (Edgar, Falk, Kitchen, Tiessen and Tuckey, most explicitly) have documented a trend toward securitization and militarization in Canada's international relations.

In their critiques of these trends, the authors have drawn attention to prevailing patterns of global power and Canada's role in it. As discussed in the introduction, these patterns remain in flux: state-based conceptions of national security are challenged by changes in humanitarian law and norms (Knight and Edgar), by the increasing speed and number of cross-border interactions (Falk and Kitchen), and by the changing nature and meanings of security priorities.

The overwhelming military presence of the United States and its continued engagement with world affairs are features of international relations that circumscribe the behaviour of smaller actors such as Canada. Should Canada align its priorities with those of key allies such as the United States, or should it strike out in new directions? Although necessity impinges on ethical calculations, decisions are never solely reactive or based only upon circumstantial imperatives. Attention to ethics permits an examination of the rationales for Canadian alignment. Indeed, one is struck by the instances when Canadian and American paths departed, as in the refusal of the Liberal government to participate in the Iraq War of 2003 and the Bush administration's Ballistic Missile Program. Under the Harper government, there have been significant tensions with US policy with respect to the Middle East and the environment (Pittaway 2013). These departures suggest that there is scope for Canada to act in ways that might seem contrary to the views of the superpower and raise questions about the goals and purposes of policies in light of these capabilities.

Toward what end will Canada's assertiveness be put? At the time of writing, the crisis of violence has reached a critical impasse in Syria, with the apparent use of chemical weapons against civilians (Associated Press 2013). Russia's provocative actions in Ukraine are testing NATO and proving resistant to economic and diplomatic pressures. The relatively light-handed responses to these activities are in contrast to the 1990s, when Canada was an active participant in the Kosovo War. Lloyd Axworthy, minister of foreign affairs at the time, defended Canada's support of the Kosovo action in terms of human security. Responses today are taking place with comparatively little discussion on the ethics of human rights, people-centred security, or the need for human dignity, despite the R2P report. The distancing of Canada's actions from its earlier active role in nurturing this "normative architecture" has left a void in the discussion. As Knight argues in this volume, "the fact that the norm is not being triggered by the crimes against humanity and war crimes in Syria today makes one question whether the R2P norm is now weakened to the point where it can be challenged by other norms" (52). In the absence of ethical dialogue, it is not hard to imagine that the lack of consensus internationally will result in more reactive and ad hoc patterns of decision making. Given these developments, it is even more vital to consider key questions of ethics and security. Will future actions be justified by international law? What roles will Canada's national interests and instrumental calculations play in determining engagements and judging outcomes? There are clear ethical questions about Canada's role in the world that call for analysis and public debate and consideration.

As discussed in the introduction, the underlying forces and patterns that impact decision making are central concerns of analysts of ethics. Critical international relations theorists analyze whether these forms reproduce or reinforce inequities in relations among groups. A sub-theme that emerges from these analyses is the persistent question of distributive ethics, a question that received considerable attention in *Ethics and Security in Canadian Foreign Policy* (Irwin 2001) and that continues to bedevil efforts to create ethically coherent security policies. Although distributive ethics are most apparent in development policies and gender mainstreaming efforts, they also impinge crucially on decision making regarding defence and humanitarianism. Efforts to protect populations from human rights violations or to ensure security from terrorism inevitably encounter the paradoxes of inequitable distribution, as described by several authors in this volume (see, in particular, the chapters by Hendershot, Stoett, and Rochlin). Even at the height of the discourse of human security in the 1990s, which at times worked hard to integrate economic concerns, the inequitable distribution of resources was a secondary consideration. With the rise in global attention to growing resource disparities both within and between societies, the need to address the ethics of redistribution will be increasingly pressing. Distributive justice considers issues not fully captured within the discourses of human or national security and provokes profound questions about the obligations of "fair sharing" in an interdependent world (see Penz 2001, 42, 46). In a world confronting global issues such as climate change, corruption, and deepening inequality, the fair distribution of costs and benefits among *people*, not just among states, will increasingly animate political action. How and why might calls for more equitable resource distribution and social equality impact Canada's international relations?

One of the most important themes of this volume is the continuing permeability of the state and the expanding transnational linkages that challenge the older notions of sovereignty that underpin international relations. In 1929, Frigyes Karinthy proposed that everyone is linked by six degrees of separation, referring to the idea that everyone is six steps away, on aver-age, from any other person on Earth. Recently, this idea was updated by the Facebook data team, who found that friends on Facebook are linked by only 4.74 degrees (or "hops") of separation (Backstrom 2011). At the time of writing, the Islamic State group was making effective use of social media to directly reach the public. Edward Snowden's revelations about the US National Security Agency's efforts to access and store large amounts of data had raised concerns around the world. And these events had prompted new considerations concerning privacy, abuse of public trust, legal restrictions on government activities, and the proper regulation of free and open chan-nels of communication among citizens. The shrinking of the world is mak-ing decision making more complex and demanding. The question remains: how will the ethical frames of decision makers, and their views on security, address the changing reality?

Younger Canadians are more aware of these linkages than younger Americans (Milner 2008). Canadians tend to be avid travellers and thus engage with international relations in personal ways. The chapters of this book have described and analyzed these linkages in ways that illuminate the implications of this awareness for ethical action. Kitchen and Falk remind us that security now is a transnational and deterritorialized concept. There are no discrete containers for the consideration of human rights, yet secu-rity techniques and agreements are designed to replicate the separation between domestic and international realms. The paradoxical clash of ethi-cal frames is most clearly demonstrated when police encounter protestors in the streets, when individuals are placed into legal grey zones, and when the "enemy among us" becomes instead the "enemy within us." These chap-ters focus attention on the individual and highlight that the treatment of the individual by the state apparatus is and should be the fulcrum of consider-ations of security.

In the 1990s, the idea of human security sought to shift the focus away from state security and toward individual security as the central goal of national policies. The idea of human security implied that it is in the indi-vidual that ethics finds its most vivid expression. Yet, as experience over the past decade demonstrated, individualism can also be instrumentalized and used to serve particular power and policy ends. If, for example, corporations are understood as proxies for individuals seeking human freedoms such as the right to free speech and the right to security, then individualism itself is not sufficient to invoke a cosmopolitan ethic in larger state policies. "Free-dom from want" in the human security paradigm imagined that individuals are the objects of action designed to secure economic freedom. However, there is little within the human security paradigm itself to prevent individualism from being applied in the service of the wealthy, who will argue in every instance that the principles of free commerce are the means to achieving freedom from want. In fact, some critical voices have argued that this was exactly the purpose of the "conditioning framework" of human security (Denholm-Crosby 2003). In its realization, the concept of freedom from want always struggled with the conflicting goals of self-serving or "other-regarding" actions. The bias of capitalist markets, at the least, is away from "ethical" action in this sense.

The authors of this volume demonstrate that economics and ethics remain close bedfellows but that the notion of security championed through Canadian economic policy remains self-serving and rooted in an instrumental focus on interests. The authors underline several dangers of this instrumentalized approach. Hendershot argues that such a focus detracts from, rather than contributes to, the goal of saving lives. As he states, "CMSCs occupy a troublingly close position to the structures and actors that uphold the inequitable distribution of global resources – for example, capital, space, food, and political influence" (96). As Rochlin argues in the case of Colombia, free trade and free commerce accompanied by neoliberal policies do not, in and of themselves, improve the provision of human rights, though such an improvement is possible. When given its fullest expression in foreign policy decisions, however, and subjected to the ongoing scrutiny of advocates for human rights protections, a human security focus can enable more democratic and accountable policies on human rights. Akuffo similarly points out that self-serving and narrowly based aid provision can obscure important features of economic relationships, such as the mutually beneficial alignments and interests through long-term economic development. Ignoring these relationships comes at the risk of lost economic opportunities. Stoett and Rochlin in particular suggest the term "enlightened self-interest" to activate the potential for a larger notion of ethically informed interests that can motivate cooperative and mutually beneficial behaviour.

In the case of development assistance and humanitarian intervention, motivations and outcomes are intimately tied together in the analysis of ethics. Whereas authorities can design anti-terrorism laws or military operations in Afghanistan with relatively unspoken strategic and tactical objectives, their ability to make aid policy in such a "quiet" way is far more circumscribed. Military security policy enjoys a privileged (and, as Tiessen and Tuckey point out, masculinized) position in foreign policy discussions.

Exemplified most strongly in the focus on defence, development, and diplomacy (the "three-Ds") in Afghanistan, the close association of security and development policy has blurred the line between humanitarian ethics and military security concerns (see also Edgar, this volume). The consequences of these trends are ethically complex. Prominent critics of securitization and militarization such as Samantha Nutt (2011) of War Child have become concerned that aid organizations and governments are compromising the norm of neutrality and therefore placing aid workers and security forces alike in greater danger in conflict zones. Another criticism is that military organizations are less well equipped to provide development assistance and that their activities are inherently less legitimate and thus less effective. As discussed in the introduction, there is a troubling silence about the ethics of Canada's growing military capabilities and apparent willingness to use force.

Earlier human security efforts such as the Ottawa Process leading to the Anti-Personnel Landmine Convention and the International Criminal Court involved close collaborations between governmental and nongovernmental groups. Although sometimes criticized as opportunistic, political cooperation between states and civil society actors to advance a common human security agenda contributed to ethical coherence based upon broad agreement on international goals. The trend toward the securitization of humanitarianism was accompanied in the past decade by a troubling absence of coherent ethical discourse. Humanitarian and development assistance efforts consequently have become less ethically coherent. Whether this trend will continue is unclear, but the underlying disjuncture that it represents has been well documented in this volume. Whether the issue is humanitarian intervention, environmental sustainability, or promotion of social justice and human rights, the retreat from ethics will likely constrain rather than expand the scope for Canada to make the kind of positive contribution to world order that characterized the past.

The past decade saw Canada's place in the world undergo profound changes, with implications for the scope of future action and effectiveness. Moving forward with ethics and security will likely require greater attention to key changes in the international system. Climate change and the opening of the Arctic passages pose unique ethical and security problems for Canada. Whether or not Canada will strongly pursue its sovereign claims to territorial waters and the resources of the Arctic, it will still have to contend with the environmental, human, and political responsibility of an expanded Arctic Ocean. Continuing financial instability in the global economy will also pose challenges to Canadians' prosperity and economic security, as will the tendency toward economic disruptions. In the past, multilateral institutions provided openings for Canada to contribute proactively to sustainability, economic growth, and peace. Indeed, Canada was instrumental in providing such openings and leading the charge to advance important and meaningful changes. Those opportunities and openings still exist. Canada can work to protect human rights, create a cooperative basis for environmental sustainability, and ensure the fair distribution of economic resources in the future. The potential is still strong to move forward toward truly non-self-serving and non-instrumental policies based upon a shared recognition of human needs and vulnerabilities. Addressing the challenges of a rapidly changing world means taking a long and deep view. It means considering who we are as Canadians and what we are willing to do in order to secure a future for our country, and for the world.

References

Associated Press. 2013. "NATO Chief 'Convinced' Syrian Regime Responsible for Chemical Attack, Calls for Strong Response." *National Post*, 2 September. http://news.nationalpost.com/2013/09/02/nato-chief-convinced-syrian-regime-responsible-for-chemical-attack-calls-for-strong-response/.

Backstrom, Lars. 2011. "Anatomy of Facebook." 21 November. https://www.facebook.com/notes/facebook-data-team/anatomy-of-facebook/10150388519243859.

Denholm-Crosby, Ann. 2003. "Myths of Canada's Human Security Pursuits: Tales of Tool Boxes, Toy Chests, and Tickle Trunks." In *Feminist Perspectives on Canadian Foreign Policy*, edited by Claire Turenne Sjolander, Heather A. Smith, and Deborah Stienstra, 90–107. Don Mills, ON: Oxford University Press.

Irwin, Rosalind. 2001. "Linking Ethics and Security in Canadian Foreign Policy." In *Ethics and Security in Canadian Foreign Policy*, edited by Rosalind Irwin, 3–13. Vancouver: UBC Press.

Kitchen, Veronica. 2013. "Where Is Internationalism? Canada-US Relations in the Context of the Global and the Local." In *Canada in the World: Internationalism in Canadian Foreign Policy*, edited by Heather A. Smith and Claire Turenne Sjolander, 164–82. Don Mills, ON: Oxford University Press.

Milner, Henry. 2008. "The Informed Political Participation of Young Canadians and Americans." Circle Working Paper Number 60. http://www.civicyouth.org/PopUps/WorkingPapers/WP60Milner.pdf.

Nutt, Samantha. 2011. *Damned Nations: Greed, Guns, Armies, and Aid.* Toronto: McClelland and Stewart.

Penz, Peter. 2001. "The Ethics of Development Assistance and Human Security: From Realism and Sovereigntism to Cosmopolitanism." In *Ethics and Security in Canadian Foreign Policy*, edited by Rosalind Irwin, 38–55. Vancouver: UBC Press.

Pittaway, Tina. 2013. "Politics Is the Biggest Obstacle on Canada-U.S. Energy Front." CBC News, 24 August. http://www.cbc.ca/news/canada/story/2013/08/24/pol-nanos-energy-policy-study.html?cmp=rss.

Questions for Discussion

Ethics and Security: New Issues and Contexts for Decision Making

Has security been redefined in the twenty-first century era? In what ways?

What is meant by "ethics'? How are values and ethics distinct?

What have been the changes (or lack thereof) in the ethics-security nexus in the last few years?

How are security and ethics linked? How should they be linked?

Does human security continue to have currency in the post-9/11 world?

Is human security a realistic goal in the twenty-first century?

Have globalization and interdependence provided more or less scope for ethical decision making?

To what ethical codes do decision makers refer when they make decisions?

Should states prioritize their own national interest, or should they adopt a wider scope for ethics?

In what ways has Canada been able to influence the course of international events?

How has Canada been hampered in its ability to influence the course of international events?

What role might Canadians play in achieving human security globally?

Part 1 Freedom from Fear: Humanitarianism and Military Security

What is a norm entrepreneur?

Does the responsibility to protect supersede state sovereignty in international law?

Are humanitarian protection and state sovereignty mutually exclusive ideas?

To what degree does international law now recognize humanitarian intervention?

Will Canada be able to repeat its past accomplishments and contribute substantively in the future to the development of international humanitarian law?

What barriers exist to the development of the responsibility-to-protect norm in international law?

Can Canadians ethically justify inaction in the face of atrocities?

Are economic sanctions an ethical alternative to military intervention in the face of atrocities?

How are prevention, reaction, and rebuilding connected?

What is the just cause criterion?

What is the last resort criterion?

Is there an unavoidable trade-off between security and ethics in approaches to foreign and defence policy?

Do we have a clear and commonly accepted understanding of security and its ethical content either in theory or in foreign and defence policy?

When evaluating security-related policies, is it more useful to consider right intentions or actual behaviour and outcomes (that is, intentions or consequences)?

Why have humanitarian aid workers – whether from international organizations, NGOs, or governments – increasingly become targets for violence by belligerents, when previously the neutrality of such workers generally provided them with a reasonable level of safety and security?

Given a worsening threat environment, do humanitarian aid workers now simply have to accept that they must become embedded in military forces or else make use of private security forces?

Is there an ideal balance of resource priorities between military and non-military activities in conflict management and post-conflict reconstruction? Where did NATO and Canadian resource priorities appear to lie?

Did NATO's use of civilian reconstruction programs (provincial reconstruction teams) as part of its military strategy render NGO humanitarian aid efforts more dangerous and less effective?

Did Canada have a coherent strategy and policy for humanitarian aid and civilian development programming in Afghanistan?

What are the benefits and drawbacks of contracting commercial military security companies (CMSCs) for humanitarian interventions?

Should Canada be more seriously considering the usage of CMSCs for humanitarian interventions?

Do CMSC operations violate the principles of humanitarianism?

Does the "need to save lives" mean that any and all options should be considered during a humanitarian crisis?

If Canada were to contract a CMSC to lead a humanitarian intervention, should that CMSC be a Canadian-based company?

Part 2: Security across Borders

How have Canadian courts, especially the Supreme Court of Canada, responded to security concerns and ethical dilemmas, such as the trade-off between increased security and Charter guarantees, since 9/11?

How have particular cases, such as those of Omar Khadr and Maher Arar, shaped the Canadian conversation regarding the reach of domestic and international authorities?

Why is it important to consider both domestic cases – in both law and policy – and international military deployments when contemplating contemporary security challenges and ethical dilemmas?

Are the ethical challenges worth the benefits of hosting a mega-event such as the Olympics? What about a non-sporting event such as a summit meeting?

Why are mega-events so difficult to secure?

Should the rights of some ever be constrained in order to provide security for others? Under what circumstances?

How does the drive to spectacular security create ethical difficulties for mega-events? Is it possible to hold (and receive benefits from) a mega-event without it becoming spectacularized?

What is the mega-event security dilemma?

Are the ethical difficulties of bureaucracies more or less exacerbated in a temporary security unit?

Part 3 Freedom from Want: Development, Gender, and Environment

What are the pros and cons of (1) greater focus in the selection of "countries of concentration" and (2) core themes in the delivery of bilateral foreign aid? On what basis should decisions regarding focus be taken?

What are Canada's core priorities in funding allocations? How do these priorities affect the nature of development programming?

What can we conclude about the results of Canadian bilateral aid to Ethiopia? Why is it so difficult to assess results and effectiveness?

What roles do bilateral agencies play in addressing short-term and long-term food security in drought-prone countries such as Ethiopia?

How is food insecurity a gendered issue?

What do you see as the major challenges of turning aid rhetoric into reality as it pertains to food security?

How might aid recipients and partners such as NGOs better influence aid programming?

What do you consider to be the most significant ethical problems standing in the way of food security in Ethiopia?

Do you agree that ethical considerations have weakened in Canadian bilateral aid programming? If so, why do you think this has happened?

How should bilateral aid donors such as Canada respond to developing-country recipients such as Ethiopia that combine relatively high levels of developmental effectiveness with political authoritarianism?

What would transformative gender mainstreaming look like in an international security-related program in a fragile state?

Do you think gender mainstreaming can be transformational? Why or why not?

Is it ethical to omit a gender equality perspective in international security programs? Why or why not?

When is gender equality important in the context of international security programs?

What methodological issues might arise when using a strategy such as gender mainstreaming in a security program?

What is limiting about the concept of equality between women and men, as expressed by the Canadian government? What gendered, cultural, racial, or social issues are missing from this conceptualization?

What does "transparency" mean? How can the Government of Canada be more transparent with the public regarding gender equality and ethical security programming abroad?

How can men provide a powerful voice to the strategy of gender mainstreaming?

What role do masculinities and femininities play in international security?

Why is climate change best viewed as an ethical issue?

Is the Canadian goal of becoming an energy superpower a reasonable one today?

What implications will climate change adaptation financing plans have on development assistance?

How is climate a security issue, from a national and human security viewpoint?

Part 4 Regional Security: Countries and Areas

What ethical responsibility do corporations and the Canadian government have regarding Canadian investment in volatile areas of the global South?

In what ways is it becoming easier or more difficult for civil society to influence the Canadian government on matters of ethical responsibility and foreign investment?

What ethical and other challenges do Canadian businesses face when investing in areas where violence and human rights abuses are entrenched? In what ways can the Canadian government and civil society help?

What do you understand "Canada's moral identity" to mean? How significant is the concept for understanding contemporary Canadian policy on the African continent?

Identify and discuss the key challenges that Canadian policy makers confront on the African continent.

Do you think African states should occupy a prominent position on Canada's foreign policy agenda? If yes, why? If no, why not?

What, in your view, should be the key factors to guide Canadian policy on the African continent in the twenty-first century?

Discuss the view that Canada needs a comprehensive policy toward Africa. What should be the key components of the strategy?

Conclusion: Moving Forward with Ethics and Security

What is the most appropriate balance between ethics and security in Canada's international relations?

What are the chief limitations on Canadian action over the middle-to-long-term future?

Given recent events, what factors should be foremost in the minds of Canadian government decision makers with regard to security?

To what extent do recent events suggest the need for more attention to cross-border security issues?

What opportunities and openings exist in Canada's international relations that might be pursued to advance ethical goals?

Which issues do you believe should be top priorities in Canada's international relations agenda?

What has this volume not addressed?

Suggested Readings

Ethics and Security: New Issues and Contexts for Decision Making

Bain, William W. 1999. "Against Crusading: The Ethic of Human Security and Canadian Foreign Policy." *Canadian Foreign Policy Journal* 6 (3): 85–98. http://dx.doi.org/10.1080/11926422.1999.9673187.

Beier, J. Marshall, and Lana Wylie, eds. 2010. *Canadian Foreign Policy in Critical Perspective*. Don Mills, ON: Oxford University Press.

Hawes, Michael K. 1984. *Principal Power, Middle Power, or Satellite? Competing Perspectives in the Study of Canadian Foreign Policy*. Toronto: Research Programme in Strategic Studies, York University.

Irwin, Rosalind, ed. 2001. *Ethics and Security in Canadian Foreign Policy*. Vancouver: UBC Press.

Keating, Tom. 2002. *Canada and World Order: The Multilateralist Tradition in Canadian Foreign Policy*. Don Mills, ON: Oxford University Press.

Michaud, N. 2011. "Values and Canadian Foreign Policy-Making: Inspiration or Hindrance?" In *Readings in Canadian Foreign Policy: Classic Debates and New Ideas*, ed. Duane Bratt and C.J. Kukucha, 433–51. Toronto: Oxford University Press.

Pratt, Cranford. 1989. *Internationalism under Strain: The North-South Policies of Canada, the Netherlands, Norway, and Sweden*. Toronto: University of Toronto Press.

Smith, Heather A., and Claire Turenne Sjolander, eds. 2014. *Canada in the World: Internationalism in Canadian Foreign Policy*. Don Mills, ON: Oxford University Press.

Part 1: Freedom from Fear – Humanitarianism and Military Security

Abrahamsen, R., and M.C. Williams. 2011. *Security beyond the State: Private Security in International Politics*. Cambridge: Cambridge University Press.

Avant, D. 2005. *The Market for Force: The Consequences of Privatizing Security*. Cambridge: Cambridge University Press. http://dx.doi.org/10.1017/CBO9780511490866.

Bellamy, Alex. 2009. *A Responsibility to Protect: The Global Effort to End Mass Atrocities*. Cambridge: Polity Press.

Benelli, Prisca, Antonio Donini, and Nora Niland. 2012. *Afghanistan: Humanitarianism in Uncertain Times*. Somerville, MA: Feinstein International Center. http://fic.tufts.edu/assets/Afghan-uncertain-times.pdf.

Campbell, D. 1998. "Why Fight? Humanitarianism, Principles, and Post-Structuralism." *Millennium* 27 (3): 497–521. http://dx.doi.org/10.1177/03058298980270031001.

International Commission on Intervention and State Sovereignty. 2001. *The Responsibility to Protect: Research, Bibliography, Background*. Ottawa: International Development Research Centre.

Keating, Tom, and W. Andy Knight, eds. 2004. *Building Sustainable Peace*. Tokyo/Edmonton: United Nations University Press/University of Alberta Press.

Knight, W. Andy. 2000. *A Changing United Nations: Multilateral Evolution and the Quest for Global Governance*. New York: Palgrave Macmillan. http://dx.doi.org/10.1057/9780333984420.

Maloney, Sean M. 2007. *Enduring the Freedom: A Rogue Historian in Afghanistan*. Washington, DC: Potomac Books.

Patterson, Kevin, and Jane Warren, eds. 2007. *Outside the Wire: The War in Afghanistan in the Words of Its Participants*. Toronto: Vintage Canada.

Rieff, David. 2003. *A Bed for the Night: Humanitarianism in Crisis*. New York: Simon and Schuster.

Rosén, F. 2008. "Commercial Security: Conditions of Growth." *Security Dialogue* 39 (1): 77–97. http://dx.doi.org/10.1177/0967010607086824.

Singer, P. 2003. *Corporate Warriors: The Rise of the Privatized Military Industry*. Ithaca, NY: Cornell University Press.

Spearin, C. 2004. "International Private Security Companies and Canadian Policy: Possibilities and Pitfalls on the Road to Regulation." *Canadian Foreign Policy* 11 (2): 1–15. http://dx.doi.org/10.1080/11926422.2004.9673363.

Spearin, C. 2011. "UN Peacekeeping and the International Private Military and Security Industry." *International Peacekeeping* 18 (2): 196–209. http://dx.doi.org/10.1080/13533312.2010.546099.

Turse, Nick, ed. 2010. *The Case for Withdrawal from Afghanistan*. London: Verso Books.

Windsor, Lee, David Charters, and Brent Wilson. 2008. *Kandahar Tour: The Turning Point in Canada's Afghan Mission*. Mississauga, ON: John Wiley and Sons.

Part 2: Security across Borders

Bennett, Colin J., and Kevin Haggerty. 2011. *Security Games: Surveillance and Control at Mega-Events*. New York: Routledge.

Bigo, Didier. 2006. "Internal and External Aspects of Security." *European Security* 15 (4): 385–404. http://dx.doi.org/10.1080/09662830701305831.

Boyle, Philip, and Kevin D. Haggerty. 2009. "Spectacular Security: Mega-Events and the Security Complex." *International Political Sociology* 3 (3): 257–74. http://dx.doi.org/10.1111/j.1749-5687.2009.00075.x.

Canada. 2006. *Commission of Inquiry into the Actions of Canadian Officials in Relation to Maher Arar*. Ottawa: Supply and Services.

Canada. 2010. Air India Flight 182: A Canadian Tragedy; Final Report of the Commission of Inquiry into the Investigation of the Bombing of Air India. http://epe.lac-bac.gc.ca/100/206/301/pco-bcp/commissions/air_india/2010-07-23/www.majorcomm.ca/en/reports/finalreport/default.htm.

Canada (Prime Minister) v. Khadr, 2008 SCC 28, [2008] 2 S.C.R. 125 (*Khadr I*).

Canada (Prime Minister) v. Khadr, 2010 SCC 3, [2010] 1 S.C.R. 44 (*Khadr II*).

Charkaoui v. Canada (Citizenship and Immigration), 2008 SCC 38, [2008] 2 S.C.R. 326.

Harkat v. Canada, [2010] F.C. 1241; *Harkat v. Canada*, [2012] F.C.A. 122.

Kitchen, Veronica, and Kim Rygiel. 2015. "Integrated Security Networks: Less Not More Accountability." In *Putting the State on Trial: The Policing of Protest during the G20 Summit*, ed. Margaret Beare, Nathalie Des Rosiers, and Abigail Deshman. Vancouver: UBC Press.

Monaghan, Jeffrey, and Kevin Walby. 2012. "'They Attacked the City': Security Intelligence, the Sociology of Protest Policing and the Anarchist Threat at the 2010 Toronto G20 Summit." *Current Sociology* 60 (5): 653–71. http://dx.doi.org/10.1177/0011392112448470.

Roach, Kent. 2011. *The 9/11 Effect: Comparative Counter-Terrorism*. Cambridge: Cambridge University Press. http://dx.doi.org/10.1017/CBO9781139003537.

Shepherd, Michelle. 2008. *Guantanamo's Child: The Untold Story of Omar Khadr*. Toronto: John Wiley.

Suresh v. Canada, [2002] 1 S.C.R. 3

Part 3: Freedom from Want – Development, Gender, and Environment

Adger, Neil, Jouni Paavola, Huq Saleemul, and M.J. Mace, eds. 2006. *Fairness in Adaptation to Climate Change*. Cambridge, MA: MIT Press.

Black, David. 2009. "Out of Africa? The Harper Government's New 'Tilt' in the Developing World." *Canadian Foreign Policy Journal* 15 (2): 41–56. http://dx.doi.org/10.1080/11926422.2009.9673486.

Black, David. Forthcoming. *Canada and Africa in the New Millennium: The Politics of Consistent Inconsistency*. Waterloo: Wilfrid Laurier University Press.

Black, David, and Rebecca Tiessen. 2007. "The Canadian International Development Agency: New Policies, Old Problems." *Canadian Journal of International Development Studies* 18 (2): 191–213.

Brown, Stephen, ed. 2012. *Struggling for Effectiveness: CIDA and Canadian Foreign Aid*. Montreal/Kingston: McGill-Queen's University Press.

Brown, Stephen, Molly den Heyer, and David R. Black, eds. Forthcoming. *Rethinking Canadian Aid*. Ottawa: University of Ottawa Press.

Ehresman, Timothy, and Dimitris Stevis. 2011. "International Environmental and Ecological Justice." In *Global Environmental Politics: Concepts, Theories, and Case Studies*, ed. Gabriela Kutting, 87–104. London: Routledge.

Enloe, Cynthia. 1990. *Bananas, Beaches and Bases: Making Feminist Sense of International Politics.* Berkeley: University of California Press.

Mazurana, Dyan, Angela Raven-Roberts, and Jane Parpart. 2005. *Gender, Conflict, and Peacekeeping.* New York: Rowman and Littlefield.

Moser, Caroline, and Annalise Moser. 2005. "Gender Mainstreaming since Beijing: A Review of Success and Limitations in International Institutions." *Gender and Development* 13 (2): 11–22. http://dx.doi.org/10.1080/13552070512331332283.

Parpart, Jane. 2009. "Fine Words, Failed Policies: Gender Mainstreaming in an Insecure and Unequal World." In *Development in an Insecure and Gendered World: The Relevance of the Millennium,* ed. Jacqueline Leckie, 51–68. Surrey, UK: Ashgate.

Parpart, Jane, and Marysia Zalewski. 2008. *Rethinking the Man Question: Sex, Gender and Violence in International Relations.* London: Zed Books.

Tickner, J.A., and L. Sjoberg, eds. 2011. *Feminism and International Relations: Conversations about the Past, Present, and Future.* London: Routledge.

Tiessen, Rebecca. 2007. *Everywhere/Nowhere: Gender Mainstreaming in Development Agencies.* Bloomfield, CT: Kumarian Press.

Turenne Sjolander, Claire, Heather A. Smith, and Deborah Stienstra, eds. 2003. *Feminist Perspectives on Canadian Foreign Policy.* Don Mills, ON: Oxford University Press.

Part 4: Regional Security – Countries and Areas

Akuffo, Edward A. 2012. *Canadian Foreign Policy in Africa: Regional Approaches to Peace, Security, and Development.* Aldershot: Ashgate.

Alden, Chris. 2007. *China in Africa.* London: Zed Books.

Black, David R. 2014. *Canada and Africa in the New Millennium: The Politics of Consistent Inconsistency.* Waterloo: Wilfrid Laurier University Press.

Canada. 2012. Department of Foreign Affairs and International Trade. *Agreement Concerning Annual Reports on Human Rights and Free Trade between Canada and the Republic of Colombia.* 15 May.

Medhora, Rohinton, and Yiagadeesen Samy. 2013. *Canada among Nations 2013: Canada-Africa Relations-Looking Back, Looking Ahead.* Waterloo: CIGI.

Pratt, Renate. 1997. *In Good Faith: Canadian Churches against Apartheid.* Waterloo: Wilfrid Laurier University Press.

Taylor, Ian, and Paul Williams. 2004. *Africa in International Politics: External Involvement on the Continent.* London: Routledge.

Conclusion: Moving Forward with Ethics and Security

Axworthy, Lloyd. 2004. *Navigating a New World.* Toronto: Knopf Canada.

Heinbecker, Paul. 2010. *Getting Back in the Game: A Foreign Policy Playbook for Canada.* Toronto: Key Porter Books.

Nossal, Kim Richard. 2013. "The Use – and Misuse – of R2P: The Case of Canada." In *Libya, the Responsibility to Protect and the Future of Humanitarian Intervention,* ed. Aidan Hehir and Robert Murray, 110–29. London: Palgrave Macmillan. http://dx.doi.org/10.1057/9781137273956.0010.

Nossal, Kim Richard, Stéphane Roussel, and Stéphane Paquin. 2011. *International Policy and Politics in Canada.* Toronto: Pearson.

Nutt, Samantha. 2011. *Damned Nations: Greed, Guns, Armies, and Aid.* Toronto: McClelland and Stewart.

Pratt, Cranford. 1989. "Humane Internationalism: Its Significance and Variants." In *Internationalism under Strain,* ed. Cranford Pratt, 3–23. Toronto: University of Toronto Press.

Pratt, Cranford. 1999. "Competing Rationales for Canadian Development Assistance: Reducing Global Poverty, Enhancing Canadian Prosperity and Security, or Advancing Global Human Security?" *International Journal (Toronto, Ont.)* 54 (2): 306–23. http://dx.doi.org/10.2307/40203379.

Contributors

Edward Akuffo is an assistant professor of international relations in the Department of Political Science at the University of the Fraser Valley, Abbotsford, British Columbia. He is the author of *Canadian Foreign Policy in Africa: Regional Approaches to Peace, Security, and Development* (2012).

David R. Black is a professor of political science and the Lester B. Pearson Professor of International Development Studies at Dalhousie University. His current research interests include Canada's role in sub-Saharan Africa (including human security, development assistance, multilateral diplomacy, and extractive industry investment) and the politics of sport mega-events.

Alistair Edgar is the executive director of the Academic Council on the UN System, co-director of the Laurier Centre for Military Strategic and Disarmament Studies, and associate professor of political science at Wilfrid Laurier University in Waterloo, Ontario. In addition to his work on sovereignty and humanitarian intervention, he has researched post-conflict peace and reconstruction programs and transitional justice and conflict-to-peace processes in Afghanistan, Cambodia, Uganda, and Kosovo.

Barbara J. Falk is an associate professor in the Department of Defence Studies at the Canadian Forces College, Royal Military College of Canada. She has written extensively on the persecution and the prosecution of dissent during the Cold War and on security and terrorism law and policy post-9/11.

Chris Hendershot is a doctoral candidate in political science at York University. His research focuses on the work that commercial military and security companies do for privatizing, militarizing, securing, and commercializing processes.

Veronica Kitchen is an associate professor of political science at the University of Waterloo and in the Balsillie School of International Affairs. She researches the global governance of domestic security, focusing on urban security and counterterrorism, security bureaucracies, the ethics of security, North American security governance, and mega-event security.

W. Andy Knight, a Barbadian by birth, is the director of the Institute of International Relations at the University of the West Indies, St. Augustine Campus, Trinidad and Tobago, and professor and former chair of the Department of Political Science at the University of Alberta. He is a Fellow of the Royal Society of Canada and the author of several books on multilateralism and the UN system.

James Rochlin is a professor of political science at the University of British Columbia. He has published widely on Latin American politics and critical security studies and explored new conceptions of security in Latin America, including those related to insurgenices, race and class, and the production of oil.

Peter Stoett is a professor in the Department of Political Science and director of the Loyola Sustainability Research Centre at Concordia University in Montreal, Quebec. His main areas of expertise include international relations and law, global environmental politics, and human rights. He was a 2012 Fulbright Scholar at the Woodrow Wilson International Center for Scholars, Washington, DC, and a 2013 Erasmus Mundas Fellow at the International Institute for Social Studies, The Hague. His latest book is *Global Ecopolitics: Crisis, Governance, and Justice* (2012).

Rebecca Tiessen is an associate professor in the School of International Development and Global Studies, University of Ottawa. Her research examines the role of Canada and Canadians in the world as well as gender and development. Her publications include *Everywhere/Nowhere: Gender Mainstreaming in Development Agencies* (2007) and a forthcoming book chapter in *Rethinking Canadian Aid*, edited by Stephen Brown, Molly Den Heyer, and David Black.

Sarah Tuckey is a doctoral candidate studying public administration in the School of Political Studies at the University of Ottawa. Her research explores Canadian foreign policy and gender equality in Afghanistan.

Rosalind Warner, a college professor of political science at Okanagan College, has researched and written about ethics, security, and Canadian foreign policy; the environment and trade; ecological modernization theory; disaster assistance and resilience; global environmental governance; and protected areas governance in North America. She is the editor of the volume *Ethics and Security in Canadian Foreign Policy* (UBC Press, 2001).

Index

Note: "(t)" after a page number indicates a table.

Printed and bound in Canada by Friesens

Set in Futura and Warnock by Apex CoVantage, LLC

Copy editor: Dallas Harrison